ANCIENT SCOTISH MELODIES

AMS PRESS INC.
NEW YORK

JOHNSON REPRINT CORP.
NEW YORK

ANCIENT SCOTISH MELODIES,

FROM

A MANUSCRIPT OF THE REIGN OF KING JAMES VI.

WITH

AN INTRODUCTORY ENQUIRY

ILLUSTRATIVE OF THE

HISTORY OF THE MUSIC OF SCOTLAND.

BY

WILLIAM DAUNEY, ESQ. F.S.A. SCOT.

EDINBURGH:
THE EDINBURGH PRINTING AND PUBLISHING COMPANY;
SMITH, ELDER, & CO., CORNHILL, LONDON.
M.DCCC.XXXVIII.

Reprinted with pcrmission from a volume in the George Peabody Branch, Enoch Pratt Free Library, Baltimore, Maryland, 1971

From the edition of Edinburgh, 1838

First AMS edition published 1971

Manufactured in the United States of America

International Standard Book Number:

Complete Set; 0-404-52700-0
Volume 59: 0-404-52769-8

Library of Congress Number: 76-144416

AMS PRESS INC.
NEW YORK, N.Y. 10003

JOHNSON REPRINT CORP.
NEW YORK, N.Y. 10003

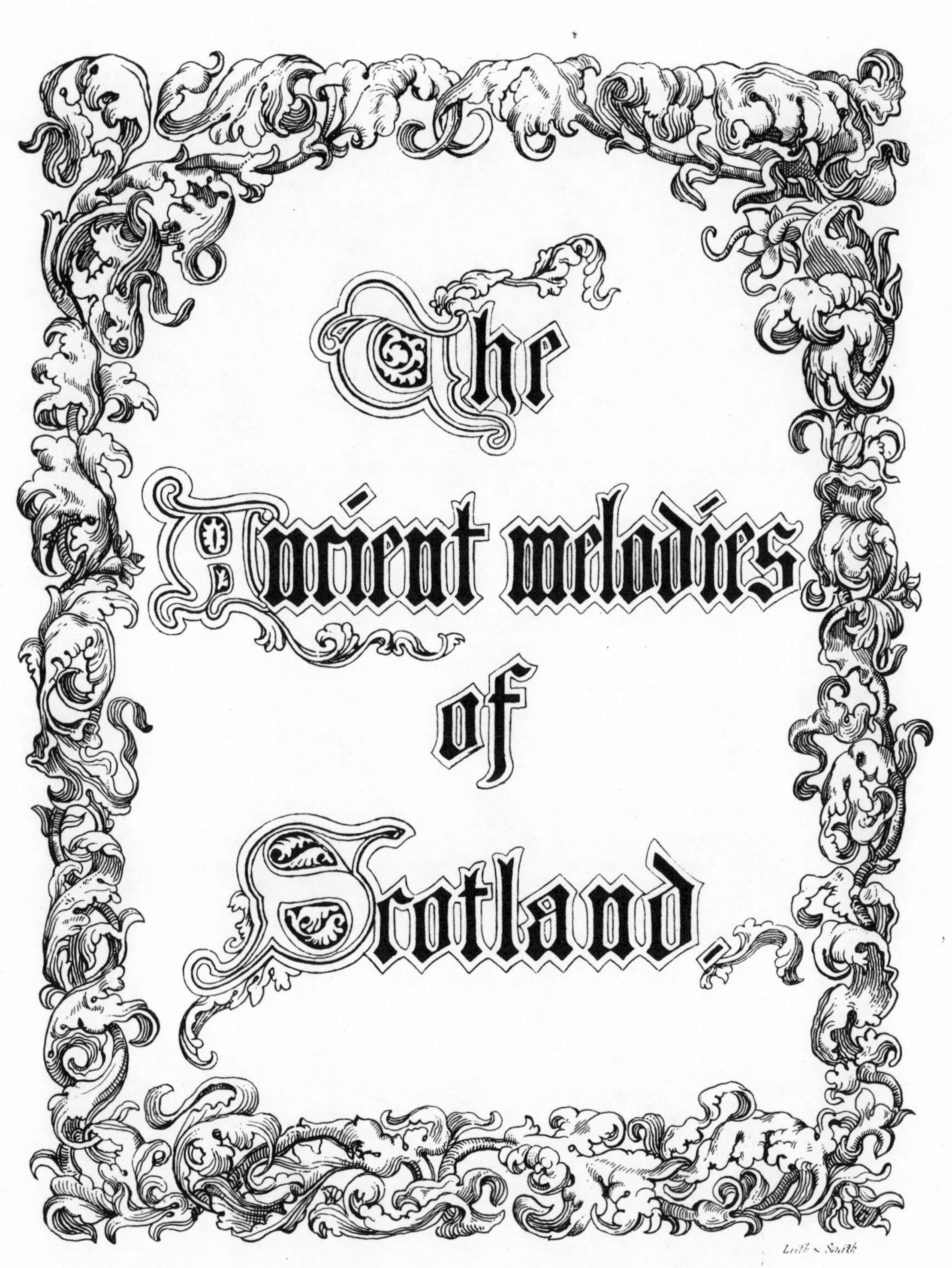

Leith & Smith

TO THE

PRESIDENTS AND MEMBERS

OF THE

Bannatyne and Maitland Clubs,

THIS WORK

(UNDERTAKEN THROUGH THEIR ENCOURAGEMENT)

IS MOST RESPECTFULLY

INSCRIBED.

CONTENTS.

PRELIMINARY DISSERTATION.

CONTENTS.

PAGE

I.—Ancient Scottish Lyrical Poetry.

II.—Ancient Scottish Musical Instruments, &c.

CONTENTS.

CONTENTS.

APPENDIX.

PRELIMINARY DISSERTATION.

While the translation into modern musical characters of this curious Manuscript is the work of a gentleman whose long experience, and well-known scientific and practical attainments, form a sufficient guarantee for the fidelity, the judgment, and the accuracy, with which that duty has been performed, a few words of explanation may be necessary on behalf of the Editor, by whom the preparation of the following Dissertation and Notes has been undertaken. Could he have formed any previous idea of the labour and research which it required, he would at once have deferred to some individual better qualified than himself to do it justice; and, had it not been that his deficiencies were, in some degree, supplied by the liberal assistance which he has been so fortunate as to receive from many who have distinguished themselves in the field of archæological research, and the free and unreserved access which he has been permitted to many interesting original documents, both printed and manuscript, he would scarcely have ventured to give publicity to the result of his labours; the more especially, as other avocations of a graver sort have greatly circumscribed the leisure which he has had it in his power to devote to the subject. At the same time, it is his belief, that had that leisure been extended to as many years as it has been months, the work could not fail to have been chargeable with errors and imperfections. Nor is it any affectation of modesty, on his part, to make this avowal—not only from the difficulty of obtaining authentic information in regard to topics where history and tradition are too frequently silent, or, what is worse, furnish *data* upon which no reliance can be placed, but because the complete illustration of these relics would have demanded a combination of acquirements which are rarely, if ever, united in one and the same individual. To accomplish that object satisfactorily, little less would have been requisite than the musical learning and critical skill of a Burney, the minute and accurate antiquarian knowledge of a Ritson, and that thorough acquaintance with the ancient manners and customs of Scotland, and particularly what may be termed the unwritten history of its inhabitants, with which the mind of Scott was so deeply imbued. The Skene Manuscript has indeed revealed itself at an unhappy moment. Had it been made known during the lifetime of these distinguished writers, the world would doubtless have been enabled to reap the full benefit of the discovery. There was even a period anterior to that of Scott and Ritson, when its appearance would have been hailed with greater enthusiasm, and would most probably have given occasion to greater discussion than is likely now to arise. Scotish music was a subject which much more frequently engaged the attention of the learned and the ingenious during the last century than at present; much was written upon its character, construction, and history, by Mr Tytler, the grandfather of our historian, Dr Beattie, Dr Gregory, Dr Campbell, Lord Kames, Dr Franklin, and others; and not a little is it to be regretted that the enquiries of these gentlemen into this branch of our national antiquities had not taken the same happy turn with those of their illustrious contemporary Lord Hailes. Had they been as diligent investigators of facts, and as cautious commentators upon them, as his Lordship, there can be little doubt that we should, ere now, have been in possession of information, touching this topic, infinitely more distinct and authentic than any thing that can be gathered from their writings. Neither is it likely that it would have been left to the present generation to have awakened from its slumbers a Manuscript, which, *per se*, and without comment, throws more light upon the history of Scotish melody, than all the disquisitions of those learned and accomplished men. It is now nearly sixty years since Mr Tytler's Dissertation on Scotish Music was published,[a] and, in the natural course of things, it may be presumed, that, at that time, more documents of the nature of the Skene Manuscript might have been elicited, had the attention of the public been sufficiently roused to the importance of these relics; yet, strange to say, although a great deal of historical research was bestowed by Mr Tytler on his Essay, which reflects the highest honour on his talents, as a scholar and a man of taste, he makes no allusion whatever, either to the existence or to the supposed non-existence of any ancient collections of Scotish music, nor does he say one word as to musical MSS., or even the oldest printed versions of the Scotish melodies; a circumstance the more unaccountable, as his Dissertation consists chiefly of an attempt to ascertain their individual antiquity by an analysis of their leading features, and the changes which have been wrought upon them in the course of time. In this way, the very line of investigation, which, if steadily followed out, would have conducted Mr Tytler's labours to a safe and satisfactory conclusion, was entirely overlooked.

If we except Mr Ritson, whose writings contain many general recommendations to that effect, there appears to have been only one individual in the last century, who, in turning his attention to this subject, felt the necessity of commencing by a well-founded and rational sys-

[a] It first appeared in 1779, in the appendix to Arnot's History of Edinburgh; and it is the more singular that the importance of these manuscripts should have entirely escaped Mr Tytler, as, in 1775, on the cover of the Scots Magazine, we find the following advertisement:—"This day is published, to be had at the shop of John Clark, engraver, first fore stair before the head of Forester's Wynd, the First Number of *Flores Musicæ*, or the Scots Musician, being a general collection of the most celebrated Scots tunes, reels, minuets, and marches, adapted for the violin, hautboy, or German flute, with a bass for the violincello or harpsichord, *collected from a variety of old MSS., wherein the errors that have crept into the former editions of the Scots tunes are traced*, and new variations added to many of them," &c. From the above announcement, we presume that this first number of the work was actually published, but what was its nature, or whether it ever reached a second number, the Editor has never heard, nor has he ever seen this Collection mentioned by any one who has written on this subject.

tem of analysis. This was Ramsay of Ochtertyre, who concludes a paper on Old Scotish Songs (published in Dr Anderson's periodical, The Bee, in 1791[a]) with the following judicious and sensible queries:—"What is the oldest book of Lowland vocal airs in Scots, either in public or private collections? What is the most ancient MS. or printed book in which the songs that carry intrinsic marks of antiquity are inserted?" And yet, at that time, so hopeless was the prospect of recovering any of our ancient melodies, that we find Mr Ritson, in a letter to our Scotish antiquary Mr George Paton, dated 19th May 1795, rejoicing, with no ordinary feeling of triumph, at the recovery of a solitary tune, which, however interesting from its frequent association with the songs and poems of the olden time, possesses little intrinsic excellence. "I have at last (says he) recovered the tune, to which 'The Banks of Helicon,' and 'The Cherry and the Slae,' were originally sung. Though lost in Scotland, and never perhaps known in England, it has been preserved in Wales by the name of 'Glyn Helicon.' Lord Hailes and Mr Tytler would have been glad of this discovery."[b] Well may the Editor in his turn exclaim, how would Mr Ritson and his *collaborateurs* have rejoiced in the recovery of so rich and varied a collection of ancient Scotish and English melodies as that which is now submitted to the public!

The Editor naturally felt that so valuable and interesting a production as this might almost be left to speak for itself; so that, when the alternative offered of giving immediate publicity to the collection, accompanied only with such observations and notes as might occur upon a brief though attentive examination of the subject, or of withholding, probably for years, a document essentially the property of the public, and which, as vindicating the antiquity, and perhaps it is not too much to say, elevating the character, of the justly celebrated melodies of Scotland, may be regarded as little short of a national boon,—he admits that he did not hesitate long as to the course which it would be most proper for him to pursue; and in adopting the former of these alternatives, and leaving it to the public to deduce for themselves the more remote and consequential

[a] Vol. ii. p. 209.

[b] Correspondence of G. Paton, p. 21.

results, which cannot fail to arise from a careful and deliberate analysis of the MS., he willingly resigns all higher ambition than that of rendering himself in some degree useful, by opening up the way, and excavating a few of the principal materials out of which others may be enabled, at a future period, to erect (it is to be hoped) a complete and well-digested history of Scotish Music.

The Collection of Ancient Music, now submitted to the public, is the property of the Faculty of Advocates at Edinburgh. It was bequeathed to that learned body, about twenty years ago, by the late Miss Elizabeth Skene, the last surviving member, in a direct line, of the family of Skene of Curriehill and Hallyards in Mid-Lothian, along with a charter-chest containing a variety of documents relating to that family, of which that lady had become the depository, as their representative, and great-great-grand-daughter of John Skene of Hallyards, who was the son of Sir John Skene, the author of the treatise '*De Verborum Significatione*,' and Clerk Register during great part of the reign of King James VI.[a]

When the MS. came into the possession of the Faculty, it consisted of seven detached portions or *fasciculi;* which, as they obviously belonged to the same set, were, by order of the Curators, bound up together so as to form one volume. Their contents in the order in which they stand are as follows:—

Part I.

1. Male Simme.
2. Doun in yon banke.
3. O sillie soul alace.
4. Long er onie old man.

[a] Memoir and Genealogy of the Skene Family, *penes* James Skene, Esq. of Rubislaw.

5. The Spanishe Ladie.
6. My dearest sueate is fardest fra me.
7. * * *
8. Hutchesoun's Galȝiard.
9. * * *
10. A French Volt.
11. Ladye Elizabeth's Maske.
12. Kette Bairdie.
13. Trumpeter's Currand.
14. Joy to the persone.
15. Comedians Maske.
16. Aderneis Lilt.
17. Sommersets Maske.
18. Johne Devisonns pint of wine.
19. Horreis Galȝiard.
20. Froggis Galȝiard.
21. I cannot liue and want thee.
22. I mett her in the medowe.
23. Prettie weil begann man.
24. Prince Henreis Maske.

Part II.

25. Lady, wilt thou love me.
26. The Lass o Glasgowe.
27. Shoe looks as shoe wold lett me.
28. Alace yat I came owr the moor and left my love behind me.
29. Bonnie Jean makis meikle of me.
30. My love shoe winns not her away.
31. Jennet drinks no water.

Part III.

32. A Frenche * * *
33. Scerdustis.
34. My Ladie Rothemayis Lilt.
35. Blew Breiks.
36. Aberdeins Currand.
37. Scullione.
38. My Ladie Laudians Lilt.
39. Lesleis Lilt.
40. The Keeking Glasse.
41. To dance about the Bailȝei's Dubb.
42. I left my love behind me.
43. Alace this night yat we suld sinder.
44. Pitt on your shirt on Monday.
45. Horreis Galȝiard.
46. I dowe not gunne cold.
47. My mistres blush is bonie.
48. * * *
49. A Saraband.
50. (Another copy of Trumpeters Currant.)

Part IV.

51. What if a day.
52. Floodis of Teares
53. Nightingale.
54. The Willow Tree.
55. Marie me marie me quoth the bonnie lass.
56. My Lord Hayis Currand.

57. Jean is best of onie.
58. What high offences hes my fair love taken.
59. Alman Nicholas.
60. Currand Royal, (Sir John Hope's Currand.)
61. Hunters Carrier.
62. Blew ribbenn at the bound rod.
63. I serue a worthie ladie.

PART V.

64. Canareis.
65. Pitt on your shirt on Monday.
66. Scerdustis.
67. Shoe mowpit it coming o'er the lie.
68. Adew Dundie.
69. Thrie Sheips Skinns.
70. Chrichton's gud nicht.
71. Alace I lie my alon I'm lik to die awld.
72. I loue for loue again.
73. Sincopas.
74. Almane Delorne.
75. Who learned you to dance and a towdle.
76. Remember me at eveninge.
77. Love is a labour in vaine.
78. I dare not vowe I love thee.
79. My Lord Dingwalls Currand.
80. Brangill of Poictu.
81. Pantalone.
82. Ane Alman Moreiss.
83. Scullione.
84. My Ladie Laudians Lilt.
85. Queins Currand.

Part VI.

86. Then wilt thou goe and leave me her.
87. I will not goe to my bed till I suld die.
88. The Flowres of the Forrest.
89. The Fourth Measur of the Buffins.
90. Shackle of Hay.
91. Com love lett us walk into the Springe.
92. Sa mirrie as we have bein.
93. Kilt thy coat Magge kilt thy coatti
94. Shipeherd saw thou not.
95. Peggie is ouer ye see with the souldier.
96. Ladye Rothemayis Lilt.
97. Omnia vincit amor.
98. I love my love for love again.
99. Ostend.
100. Sir John Moresons Currant.
101. Præludium.

Part VII.

102. Exercises.
103. Gilcreich's Lilt.
104. Blew Cappe.
105. Lady Cassilis Lilt.
106. Blew Breiks.
107. Port Ballangowne.
108. Johne Andersonne my Jo.
109. Good night and God be with yow.
110. A Sarabande.
111. Lik as the dum Solsequium.
112. Come sueat love lett sorrow cease.
113. Veze Setta.
114. A Sarabande.

The MS. is without date, and there is great difficulty in speaking as to the precise time when it was written. Indeed, upon this point we cannot venture upon a nearer approximation than twenty or thirty years. From the appearance of the paper, the handwriting, and the fact that some of the tunes are here and there repeated, with very little alteration, as regards the music, it is extremely probable, that they had been taken down at different times, during a period of about that duration. Farther than this, the most careful examination will only permit us to add, that one part of the MS. was written between the years 1615 and 1620, and that while none of it is likely to have been much more recent than the last mentioned era, some of the collection may have been formed as early as the commencement of the seventeenth century.

Among the tunes contained in Part I. there is one entitled "Prince Henrei's Maske." Prince Henry, the eldest son of James VI., was born in 1593, and died in 1612. He was created Prince of Wales in 1610, and upon this occasion the Masque here referred to was performed. It will be found in Ben Jonson's works,[a] under the title of "Oberon, or Prince Henry's Masque." Another of these tunes, "Sommerset's Maske," would bring down the date of this part of the MS. to 1615. Robert Carr, Viscount Rochester, the favourite of James VI., was created Earl of Somerset in 1613, and in 1614 was married to Lady Frances Howard, the divorced Countess of Essex. The Masque in question, the words of which were written by Dr Campion, and the music by John Cooper or Coperario, (as he preferred to style himself,) Lanière, and others, was performed at the Banqueting-room at Whitehall, on St Stephen's night, (Dec. 26, 1614.)[b]

Other circumstances of a like nature would indicate that this part of the volume had been written sometime between the years 1615 and 1620. "The Ladie Elizabeth's Maske" obviously refers to the daughter of James VI., who was married to the Prince Palatine of the Rhine, in

[a] Vol. v. p. 368, Edit. 1756.

[b] Hawkins' Hist. of Music, vol. iii. p. 372.

1613.[a] After her marriage she would most naturally have been designated the Princess Palatine; and as her husband was elected King of Bohemia, in 1619, if the tune had been inserted at any period subsequent to that, the name would most probably have been adapted to her new and more exalted title of "Queen of Bohemia."[b] Another tune, the "Queen's Currant," in Part V., must have referred to Anne of Denmark, the Queen of James VI., who died in 1619. In like manner, in the same Part, we have Lord Dingwall's Currant. This was Sir Richard Preston, who was created Lord Dingwall in 1609, and in 1622 we find him advanced to be Earl of Desmond. There seems, therefore, to be something like a series of contemporaneous historical evidence, tending to shew that great part of the collection had been written out about this time,—a conclusion which is, in some degree, corroborated by the consideration, that the ephemeral character of several of the tunes renders it very unlikely that they would have outlived the immediate and fleeting interest attached to the personages or events which they were intended to celebrate.

There is just one portion of the MS. which appears to be rather newer than the rest; this is Part IV. There is here a tune called "Sir John Hope's Currant." Now, if this related to Sir John Hope, the eldest son of Sir Thomas Hope of Craighall, Lord Advocate to James VI. and Charles I. (and the Editor is not aware of any previous Sir John Hope,) he was knighted and appointed a Lord of Session in 1632. It so happens, however, that there has been an obliteration in this place. The name first given to this tune in the MS. was "Currant Royal." This appears to have been deleted, and "Sir John Hope's Currant" afterwards interpolated, though evidently in the same hand. The superinduction, therefore, of Sir John Hope's name may have taken place a long while after the airs had been written out, so that, as an *ex post facto* operation, it cannot affect the strong presumptions above alluded to, which point to an

[a] This lady forms the branch by which her present Majesty is connected with the Stuarts.

[b] See in "Wit's Recreations," (reprint 1817, vol. ii. p. 26,) the sonnet by Sir Henry Wotton, addressed to "the *Queen of Bohemia*," beginning "You meaner beauties of the night."

earlier date; and, in any event, its effect will be limited to the contents of the *fasciculus* to which it belongs.

On the other hand, Part VI, which contains some of the most valuable of our national airs, is evidently the oldest of all. We draw this inference partly from the appearance of the paper, besides which, it looks as if it had been penned by a different and an older hand. The notes, in particular, are of a more antique form, which is also the case in Part V.; and there is an orthographical alteration in the word "Currant," which is elsewhere spelt "Currand." It should be added, that the alphabetical characters, though generally resembling those of the rest of the volume, are not precisely the same. The probability, therefore, is, that this part of the MS. was written *prior to* 1615, though how long prior to that period it is impossible to say.

Since this volume has attracted the attention of the antiquary, it has generally been considered to have been written by Sir John Skene himself,—an idea which, until its history came to be more minutely inquired into, derived some degree of support from the decided resemblance which the handwriting bore to that of Sir John. But although music was in these days an accomplishment infinitely more common (among gentlemen at least) than at present, there is no information on record, (and the Editor has perused several sufficiently circumstantial memoirs of Sir John Skene, in the hands of various individuals,) that he was either a proficient in, or a patron of, the art of music.[a] It would seem also, that his declining years had been greatly embittered in consequence of several unhappy family differences;[b] and the circumstance of his having lost his office of Clerk Register, without compensation, in a way, too, not a little provoking to a man of his shrewdness and sagacity.[c] Had it not been, therefore, for the general rumour, which

[a] Genealogical Account of the Family of Skene above mentioned; Memoir by Lord Auchinleck, prefixed to copy of "Regiam Majestatem," *penes* James Maconochie, Esq.; Messrs Haig and Brunton's Account of the Senators of the College of Justice.

[b] See Melros Papers, p. 128.

[c] The following are the particulars of this affair, as related by Spottiswoode, (History, p. 517.) "Sir John Skene had enjoyed the place (of Lord Register) a good many years, and being grown

has hitherto erroneously ascribed the authorship of this collection to this eminent lawyer, the Editor would have deemed even the above observations superfluous, especially as Sir John Skene's death took place on the 16th March 1617.[a]

The Clerk Register had a son John, who was admitted a Principal Clerk of Session in 1614,[b] and afterwards purchased the estate of Hallyards. This is the person who has already been alluded to, as the great-great-grandfather of the testatrix, by whom the papers of the family were bequeathed to the Faculty. The precise time of his birth is not known, and no nearer conjecture can be formed than what may arise from the circumstances that his father's marriage took place in 1574, and that he was his second son. John Skene died in 1644, and if the MS. had been written by any member of the Skene family, he was most likely to have been the person.[c] One thing rather favours this supposition. At the end of the 1st part, there are the words, "Finis quod Skine," written in a hand which bears a strong resemblance to some specimens of his writing, which are to be found among the Skene Papers, but the hand in which the music is written is different, and there is no reason to suppose that this

in age, and infirm, thinking to get his son provided to his office, had sent him to court with a dimission of the place, but with a charge not to use it unless he found the King willing to admit him; yet he, abused by some politick wits, made a resignation of the office, accepting an ordinary place among the Lords of Session. The office, upon his resignation, was presently disponed to the Advocate; which grieved the father beyond all measure. And the case, indeed, was pitiful, and much regrated by all honest men; for he had been a man much employed and honoured with divers legations, which he discharged with good credit, and now in age to be circumvented, in this sort, by the simplicity or folly of his son, it was held lamentable. The King being informed of the abuse by the old man's complaint, was very careful to satisfie him, and to have the son reconciled to his father, which, after some travel, was brought to pass: yet so exceeding was the old man's discontent, as within a few days he deceased." This, however, was not the case, as the transaction in question took place in 1612, and Sir John did not die till 1617.

[a] See Sir John Skene's testament, General Register House, recorded in the testamentary register of the commissariat of Edinburgh, 8th July 1617.

[b] For the information of our English readers, we may remark, that this is the same office which was held by the late Sir Walter Scott.

[c] This John Skene had a son John, who succeeded him in 1644; but this person was either unborn, or an infant, when, as above shewn, the greater part of the MS. was written.

John Skene was the writer of the MS. There can be little doubt, however, that it was his property, not only from the inscription above noticed, but several others in different parts of the book, which appear to be in his handwriting. We find also the name, "Magister Johannis Skine," in one place, and in another, "Magister Johannes Skeine, his book," inscribed upon the fly-leaves. As the family name was most commonly spelt "Skene," this deviation from the usual orthography might at first sight appear somewhat startling; but all who are accustomed to observe the singular want of uniformity which prevailed even in the spelling of family names, at that early period, will lay no stress whatever upon such a circumstance. Even among the Skene Papers we notice one deed where the name of Sir John Skene is spelt "Skeine," and another where the name is actually spelt in two different ways, "Skene" and "Skeine."

From these circumstances, there can be no doubt that this John Skene of Hallyards was the original owner of the MS., and most probably the person under whose auspices the collection was formed.

Although the authenticity of this document has never been called in question, and does not admit of the shadow of a suspicion, the Editor has felt it due to himself and the public, before saying any thing as to its merits, to enter into the above investigation of its history; at the same time, while he has here only adduced the general results of very minute and anxious inquiries, he feels that he has inflicted upon the reader details which, in the opinion of many, might perhaps have been spared. He trusts, however, it will be taken into view, that the peculiar nature of such a volume as the present rendered it a matter of more than ordinary importance that it should be known to have emanated from a source such as the one above described, rather than that it should have sprung from some unknown or obscure quarter. The grade in society to which Mr Skene belonged would at least have led to the selection of the best versions of the melodies, in point of style and character, which could be procured at the time when the collection was formed; and, making allowance for that want of careful revision which is to be looked for in a manuscript written entirely for private use, and the circumstance of the airs having been adapted, and, consequently, in many instances, altered in order to draw out to the resources of a particular instrument, the work bears internal evidence of its having been got up by a person of taste and judgment, exhibiting, occasionally, a simplicity, a beauty, and even a degree of elegance, which, from any thing we have seen of the productions of that age, we could scarcely have expected.

The next point to which the Editor would solicit the attention of the public is, how far this collection of Scotish airs precedes in date those that have hitherto appeared. And here it may occasion some surprise when it is asserted, *that it is at least one hundred years older than the earliest compilation of the kind which has ever issued from the press.* This was Thomson's *Orpheus Caledonius*, the first volume of which appeared in 1725, and the second in 1733.[a] In the former of these years, Allan Ramsay had published about seventy Scotish melodies with basses, as a sort of musical appendix to his " Tea Table Miscellany," which, in like manner, with respect to the poetry, formed the first complete collection of Scotish songs. It is not meant that our Scotish melodies had not, prior to this, found their way into other printed collections. In Tom D'Urfey's " Pills to purge Melancholy,"[b] originally published at the end of the seventeenth, and the beginning of the eighteenth centuries, and of which an

[a] Dr Burney (Hist. vol. iv. p. 647) says, " In February (1722) there was a benefit concert for Mr Thomson, the first editor of a collection of Scots tunes in England. To this collection, for which there was a very large subscription, may be ascribed the subsequent favour of these national melodies south of the Tweed. After this concert, at the desire of several persons of quality, was performed a Scottish song."

[b] Happily for the good taste, and, we may add, the morality of the present age, Tom D'Urfey and his Pills have long since sunk into oblivion. His verses, and those of his Grub Street friends, would now be considered little better than doggerel, while, in point of licentiousness, they have perhaps never been exceeded. They are of the school of Charles II., with whom D'Urfey seems to have been quite " Hail, fellow! well met," and it is not a little amusing to observe the self-complacency with which he announces one of his songs—" Advice to the City"—as " a famous song, set to a tune of Signor Opdar, so remarkable, that I had the honour to sing it with King Charles at Windsor, he holding one part of the paper with me." We may observe, *en passant*, that this perfectly accords with what is stated by Hawkins, (vol. iv. p. 359,) as to the musical proficiency of

enlarged edition appeared in 1719, there are some Scottish airs, and among these we recognise "Dainty Davie,"[a]—"The Lea Rig,"[b]—"My mother's aye glowrin o'er me,"[c]—"Over the hills and far away,"[d]—"Bonny Dundee,"[e] &c. Along with them, we have such precious *morçeaux* as

this monarch. "The king," says he, "understood music sufficiently to sing the tenor part of an easy song. He would sometimes sing with Mr Gostling, one of the gentlemen of his chapel, who was master of a fine voice, the Duke of York accompanying them on the guitar." Besides the patronage of "the Right Honourable the Lords and *Ladies*" who subscribed to his volumes of songs, D'Urfey seems to have been at all times a favourite with the reigning powers during an unusually lengthened career, having died, at an advanced age, in 1723. Addison says of him:—"Many an honest gentleman has got a reputation in his country by pretending to have been in company with Tom D'Urfey." And in D'Urfey's Preface to his Songs, he talks of having had the satisfaction of diverting Royalty "with his lyrical performances."—"And when" (says he) "I have performed some of my own things before their Majesties, King Charles II., King James, King William, Queen Mary, Queen Anne, and Prince George, I never went off without happy and commendable approbation." While the vicious tendency of D'Urfey's productions must be fully admitted, in forming a fair estimate of his character, something should be allowed to the force of bad example, the profligacy of the age, and, it may be added, the necessities of the man. That these were considerable, is apparent from a paper of Addison in the Guardian, No. 67, (28th May 1713,) preparatory to a public benefit obtained for him at the theatre, in which he says, "Tom observed to me, that after having written more odes than Horace, and about four times as many comedies as Terence, he was reduced to great difficulties by the importunities of a set of men who, of late years, had furnished him with the accommodations of life, and would not, as we say, be paid with a song." The whole of this article is exceedingly humorous, nor can we suppose that the chaste Addison would have espoused the cause of his "old friend and contemporary," as he familiarly calls him, with so much earnestness, had his character not possessed many redeeming points. Indeed, he represents him as being not only "a diverting companion, but a cheerful, honest, and good-natured man."

[a] Vol. i. p. 43. [b] Vol. i. p. 316. [c] Vol. ii. p. 110. [d] Vol. v. p. 316.

[e] We find also (vol. i. p. 294) the song "Deil tak the Wars;" but whether this very beautiful air is of Scotish or English extraction, it is difficult to say. It is mentioned by Leyden (Introduction to Complaynt of Scotland, p. 285) as appearing in a MS. of the end of the seventeenth century, under the title of "Foul tak the Wars," and we ourselves have seen it, *i. e.* the melody, under the same name, in a MS. volume about the same date, so that it had plainly, even at that early period, been adopted as a Scotish air, and it has ever since been generally regarded as such. On the other hand, it appears in "A Collection of the Choicest Songs and Dialogues composed by the most eminent Masters of the age," published by J. Walsh, London, where it is called, "Song in 'a Wife for any Man;' the words by Mr Thomas D'Urfey; *set to music by Mr Charles Powell;* sung by Mrs Cross." This might have been one of the Powells, the celebrated Welsh harp-players, of whom some notice will be found in Jones's Welsh Bards, pp. 50, 52; at the same time, we admit our inability to reconcile these discrepancies, and leave the question to the determination of others.

the following:—" A Scotch Song, by Mr Robert Brown"—" A Scotch Song, the words by Mr John Hallam, set to music by Mr John Cottrell"—" Bonny Scotch Lads that kens me weel, the words by Mr Peter Noble, set by Mr John Wilford," &c. These are, no doubt, ludicrous caricatures both of the Scotish music and phraseology, and are merely referred to in order to show that, about this time, the Scotish style of melody had begun to be very generally appreciated by the English public.

The celebrated Dr Blow, who flourished from 1648 to 1708, is mentioned by Dr Burney[a] as the first English composer who united the Scotish with the English style of melody, and of this, many illustrations will be found in his " Amphion Anglicus," published in 1700; so that its character, at this time, must have been very generally understood. Indeed, we find Dryden, in the following passage of his preface to his modernized version of Chaucer's Poems, also published in 1700, referring to it as a familiar topic of illustration:—" The verse of Chaucer, I confess, is not harmonious to us; but it is like the eloquence of one whom Tacitus commends—it was '*auribus istius temporis accomodata.*' They who lived with him, and some time after him, thought it musical; and it continues so even in our judgment, if compared with the numbers of Lydgate and Gower, his contemporaries;—there is the rude sweetness of a *Scotch tune* in it, which is natural and pleasing, though not perfect."

It was in the year 1680 when the Scotish air, " Katherine Ogie," was sung by Mr Abell, a gentleman of the Chapel-Royal, at his concert in Stationers' Hall. But, in reality, little is to be gleaned as to the publication and performance of these airs in England, before the appearance of D'Urfey's Miscellany. We believe that several of them were published in Playford's " Dancing Master," about the middle of the seventeenth century, but we have had no opportunity of examining that work. One Scotish air, however, we have seen in a collection entitled, " Catch that Catch can," published by John Hilton in 1652, and afterwards by Playford in his " Musical Companion" in 1667. This is the well-known tune, " Cold and raw the wind does blow, up in the morning early." It appears here in the shape of a catch, adapted to words which commence

[a] Hist. vol. iii. p. 453.

"I'se gae with thee, my Peggy," and the very same tune is introduced in the second part of Purcell's "Orpheus Britannicus," in the form of a bass to an ode in honour of Queen Mary, the consort of William III.; though how far this had proceeded from an intention on the part of this illustrious composer to do homage to our national melodies, may be judged of from the following statement of the circumstances which gave rise to its introduction into that work, and which we shall give in the words of Sir John Hawkins,[a] by whom the story is told:—"The Queen having a mind, one afternoon, to be entertained with music, sent to Mr Gostling, then one of the chapel, and afterwards Sub-dean of St Paul's, to Henry Purcell, and Mrs Arabella Hunt, who had a very fine voice, and an admirable hand on the lute, with a request to attend her. They obeyed her commands. Mr Gostling and Mrs Hunt sung several compositions of Purcell, who accompanied them on the harpsichord. At length, the Queen beginning to grow tired, asked Mrs Hunt if she could not sing the old Scotch ballad, 'Cold and raw.' Mrs Hunt answered, 'Yes;' and sung it to her lute. Purcell was all the while sitting at the harpsichord unemployed, and not a little nettled at the Queen's preference of a vulgar ballad to his music. But seeing her Majesty delighted with this tune, he determined that she should hear it upon another occasion. And, accordingly, in the next birth-day song, that for the year 1692, he composed an air to the words, 'May her bright example chace vice, in troops, out of the land,' the bass whereof is the tune to 'Cold and raw.'"

The predilection which Queen Mary, on this occasion, evinced for the music of her ancestors, seems to have been common to the illustrious race from which she was descended, and the anecdote reminds us of a story told somewhere or other, but where we cannot remember, which shews that her uncle, Charles II., possessed a heart capable of being warmed by similar associations. It relates to a Scotish laird who had been introduced to King Charles, with whom he had afterwards had many merry meetings, while in Scotland, enlivened by the song and the dance of his country. Having become unfortunate in his affairs, he is

[a] Hist. vol. iv. p. 6.

said to have found his way to London with the view of making an appeal to the royal favour, and for a long while to have been unable to obtain access, until one day, when he bethought himself of the expedient of slipping into the seat of the organist, at the conclusion of the service, in the Chapel Royal, and of arresting his Majesty's attention as he departed, with the homely and unexpected strain of "Brose and butter"—a tune which very naturally awakened the recollection of their former friendship, and in a few minutes brought about the recognition which it was so much his desire to effect.

The known taste and partialities of the Sovereign will at all times do much to influence those of the public, and it is not improbable that they may have had the effect of first introducing Scotish music to the favourable notice of the people of England. We were not aware, till lately, that young ladies, during the reign of Charles II., were taught to sing Scotish songs, as one of the fashionable accomplishments of the day; but we fear that the authority on which we make this statement will not warrant the supposition that the era of their popularity had at that time commenced. The following dialogue occurs in one of Shadwell's Plays, "The Scowrers," written about the year 1670. The *dramatis personæ* in the scene are two ladies, Clara and Eugenia, and Priscilla, a sort of privileged waiting-woman, with whom they are familiarly chatting over the manner in which they have been brought up:—

"PRISCILLA. ———— but you had music and dancing?

"EUGENIA. Yes;—an ignorant, illiterate, hopping puppy, that rides his dancing circuit thirty miles about, lights off his tired steed, draws his kit at a poor country creature, and gives her a hitch in her pace that she shall never recover.

"CLARA. And for music, an old hoarse singing man, riding ten miles from his cathedral to quaver out 'The glories of her birth and state;' or, it may be, *a Scotch song, more hideous and barbarous than an Irish cronan.*

"EUGENIA. And another music-master from the next town, to teach one to twinkle out *Lilliburlero* upon an old pair of virginals, that sound worse than a tinker's kettle that he cries his work upon."

In Scotland, we know of no more than one publication of secular music which appeared throughout the whole of the seventeenth century. This was a work entitled "Cantus, Songs, and Fancies, to several musicall parts, both apt for voices and viols; with a brief Introduction to Musick, as is taught by Thomas Davidson, in the Musick School of Aberdeen; together also with severall of the Choicest Italian Songs, and New English Ayres, all in three parts, (viz.) two trebles and a bass; most pleasant and delightfull for all humours." Of this book, editions appeared in 1662, 1666, and 1682, printed by John Forbes, in Aberdeen.

How the city of Aberdeen, or, as Forbes more appropriately (for our present purpose) styles it, "the ancient city of Bon Accord," should have distinguished itself above its compeers, and even the metropolis of Scotland, by giving birth to this unique musical production, it is not easy to explain; and we certainly can place no great reliance on the panegyrics bestowed by the publisher on this "famous place" in his dedication, in which, not satisfied with describing his patrons their "honourable wisdoms the Lord Provost, Bailies, and Town Council," as being "a harmonious heavenly consort of *as many musicians as magistrates*,"[a] he represents the city itself, as no less than "the sanctuary of the sciences, the manse of the muses, and nurserie of all arts," &c.; yea, (he adds,) "the fame of this city, for its admirable knowledge in this divine science, and many other fine enduements, hath almost overspread whole Europe; witness the great confluence of all sorts of persons from each part of the same, who of design have come (much like that of the Queen of Sheba) to hear the sweet chearful psalms, and heavenly melody of famous Bon Accord."[b] And yet, absurd as these bombastic encomiums are, they

[a] It appears to have been a common practice of the magistrates and citizens of Aberdeen, during the seventeenth century, to parade the streets, singing psalms, on all occasions of public rejoicing. In an act of council of 4th June 1630, for regulating "the solemnitie to be usit for the Queenis delyverie of a young sone," it is ordered that "all the youthes of the toune take thair muskattis, and accompany thair magistratis throw the streitis of the town, in singing psalmes and praising God." Council Register, vol. li. p. 542.

[b] We are so fortunate as to possess a description of this "heavenly melody" from another pen than that of Forbes. Mr Richard Franck, Philanthropus, in his "Northern Memoirs, calculated for the meridian of Scotland," originally published in 1658, and reprinted at Edinburgh, in

appear at least to have had this foundation, that the art was in reality cultivated with some degree of success in this place, one reason for which had, no doubt, been the comparative freedom from civil disunion which the inhabitants of this part of the kingdom enjoyed. The Editor has lately been shown a manuscript music-book of the reign of Charles II.,[a] which appears to have belonged to some member of the Keith-Marischal family, wherein, as the title bears, are "airs to three, four, and five parts, by M. Clandam, and other fyne pieces in French, Italian, and Spanish, composed by the best maisters of France; as also, other fine Scotish and Inglish aires, old and new, taught by Louis de France, now music-master of Aberdeen, having been the scholler of the famous musician, M. Lambert, being the King of France's cheife musician, for the method and manner to conduct the voyces." The book contains an excellent system of exercises in solmization, as taught by this Louis de France, who had no doubt been an able and eminent instructor, as he appears shortly afterwards to have been removed to what was probably a more lucrative employment at Edinburgh. In Mr Maidment's "Analecta Scotica,"[b] there will be found an application from him to the magistrates of Edinburgh as Governors of Heriot's Hospital, (dated 8th September 1684,) to "allow such of the boys as have ane disposition for the said art to come to the petitioner's school, that he may instruct them in the grounds of musick and the four parts of the psalmes." This seems to have been a gratuitous proposal of M. Louis, proceeding, as he expresses it, from a desire, not "to be idle or wanting in his dutie, whereby he can be serviceable to their honours and the good town," they having appointed him to profess and teach music within the city, with a yearly salary. It seems also, from an old account-book of the Faculty

1821, (p. 229,) speaking of the same music which he heard while at Aberdeen, observes—"Here you shall have such order and decorum of song devotion in the church, as you will admire to hear, though not regulated by a cantor or quirister, but only by an insipid parochial clerk, that never attempts further in the mathematics of musick, than to compleat the parishioners to sing a psalm in tune."

[a] *Penes* David Laing, Esquire.

[b] Vol. ii. p. 263.

of Advocates, that that learned body had at one time made him a *douceur*, and although a *quid pro quo* must in these cases be presumed, it is not easy to conjecture what the consideration was which had led to this act of liberality towards the musical professor, unless we are to suppose that it was intended as a public testimony of the estimation in which his talents and services were held; and that they had tended, not inconsiderably, towards the improvement of the public taste in music, may be presumed from the high character of his master, whose system he introduced into Scotland. Sir John Hawkins says of M. Lambert, who was born in 1610, and died at Paris in 1690,—"He had an exquisite hand on the lute, and sung to it with peculiar grace and elegance: his merit alone preferred him to the office of Master of the King's (Louis XIV.) Chamber-music, upon which he became so eminent, that persons of the highest rank became his pupils, and resorted to his house, in which he held a sort of musical academy. Lambert is reckoned the first who gave his countrymen a just notion of the graces of vocal music;" or rather, in the words of La Borde,[a] he was the first to give expression and elegance to the French style of singing, which, before his time, was little better than plain chant or *canto fermo*, which is precisely the sort of music to which the songs in Forbes's Cantus are adapted; and, if M. Lambert was the first person who in France appears to have successfully laboured to supersede that system by something approaching to the modern school of vocal melody, it is not likely that it had ever been imported into Scotland before the arrival of M. Louis, his pupil; so that, by securing the services of this gentleman, the city of Bon Accord would seem to have rendered even a more important service to the interests of music, than by the publication of their Cantus.

From about this era, we may perceive something like the dawn, we should rather say, the revival, of a taste for popular and national music in Scotland, to which the plays, balls, and other gaieties at Holyroodhouse, in 1682, during the short period when the Duke of York (afterwards James II.) and his Duchess held their court there,[b] no doubt gave

[a] Essai sur la Musique, vol. iii. p. 441.

[b] Archæologia Scotica, vol. i. p. 499.

a secret impulse ; not that any great progress could be expected, scarcely two years after the battle of Bothwell Bridge, in what was denounced by the puritanical spirit of the times, as part and parcel of the forbidden articles of our creed ;[a] but the seeds were probably at this time sown, which were destined in a succeeding age to spring up and ripen into maturity.

It may at first sight appear strange that this work, Forbes's *Cantus*, should not contain a single Scottish melody. In the edition of 1666, there are three pieces, not in the other impressions, and of these, two are sufficiently national in the subject, the one being " the Pleugh Song," in which all the " hynds" are summoned by name, and the various appurtenances of the plough are enumerated ; the other a Medley, consisting of scraps of old songs, to many of which, no doubt, favourite Scottish airs had once been attached. But even here, the music, instead of being of a national character, consists of a mere church chant, and the songs themselves, along with another commenc-

[a] Our readers may be amused with the following catalogue of " abominations," which we extract from the manifesto of four unfortunate Covenanters, who were seized in the neighbourhood of Edinburgh, and incarcerated in the Canongate Tolbooth. We should premise, however, that the body of the party were but slightly tinctured with the extreme fanaticism of the opinions which are here set forth. " We renounce the names of months, as January, February, March, April, May, June, July, August, September, October, November, December ; Sunday, Monday, Tuesday, Wednesday, Thursday, Friday, Saturday ; Martimas, Holydays, for there is none holy but the Sabbath day ; Lambas day, Whitsunday, Candlemas, Beltan, Cross stones, and Images, Fairs named by Saints, and all the remnants of Popery ; Yool or Christmas, Old Wives' Fables and By-words, as Palmsunday, Carlinesunday, the 29th of May, being dedicat by this generation to prophanity, Peacesunday, Halloweven, Hogmynae night, Valentin's even ; no marrying in the month they call May, the innumerable relicts of Popery, Atheism, and Sorcery, and New Year's day, and Handsell Monday, Dredgies and Likewakes : Valentein's Fair, Chappels and Chaplains ; likewise Sabbath days Feastings, Blythmeats, Banquetings, Revelling, *Pipings, Sportings, Dancings, Laughings, Singing profane and lustfull songs and ballads ;* Table-Lawings, Monklands, Frierlands, Blackfriar-lands, Kirk and Kirkyards, and Mercat Crosses, Fountstones, Images, Registers of Lands and Houses, Register Bonds, Discharges, and all their Law-works, Inhibitions, Hornings, Letters of Adjudications, Ships-passes, Prophanity, and all unchast thoughts, words, and actions, formality and indifferency, Story-books and Ballads, Romances and Pamphlets, Comedy-books, Cards and Dice, and all such like, we disown all of them, and burns them the 6th day of the week, being the 27th day of the 5th month, 1681, at the Cannongate Tolbuith Iron-house."

ing, " All Sones of Adam," are, with some reason, conjectured to have been a sort of Christmas carols, sung by peasants before the Reformation. But we should recollect, that the songs and melodies, of which we are in search, did not suit the austere sentiments and deportment of the Puritans, and were perhaps no great favourites with the aristocratic faction, so that, between the two, it is not to be wondered at, if Mr Forbes, in his courtierlike anxiety to render his work "most pleasant and delightful for all humours," had been induced to omit them.

The *Cantus*, however, is highly characteristic of the music then in vogue throughout Scotland, and which was publicly taught at the different music-schools.

Although the custom has been for many years in disuse, insomuch as scarcely to have left a vestige of its former existence, Music, both secular and sacred, unquestionably formed a branch of ordinary education in Scotland, upon the same footing as it now does in Germany and other parts of the Continent, not only during the sway of the Roman Catholic Church, but for many years after the Reformation. While, in England, the change of religion did not produce any great immediate alteration on the music of the church—in this country, there can be no doubt, that the annihilation of the great choral establishments, the exclusion of organs and other instruments from the service, and the severe simplicity of the style of psalmody introduced by the rigid disciples of Calvin and Knox, had a considerable effect in checking the progress of the art. This,—James, or rather, his advisers, saw with regret; and they, not improbably, thought, that there was some danger lest the same fierce and intolerant spirit, which, in destroying the images and idols of Popery, had, along with them, swept away many of the richest and most costly monuments of art, would shortly carry its indiscriminate zeal so far as to attack the whole system of Musical instruction, as one of the remaining symbols of Antichrist. Hence the following statute, passed on the 11th November 1579—" For instruction of the youth in the art of musik and singing, quhilk is almaist decayit, and sall schortly decay, without tymous remeid be providit, oure Soverane Lord, with avise of his thrie estatis of this present parliament, requeistis the provest, baillies, counsale, and communitie of the maist speciall burrowis of this realme, and of the patronis and provestis of the collegis, quhair sang scuilis are foundat, to erect and sett up ane sang scuill, with ane maister sufficient and able for instructioun of the yowth in the said science of musik, as they will ansuer to his hienes upoun the perrell of their fundationis, and in performing of his hienes requeist do unto his Majestie acceptable and gude plesure."

This Act must have had the effect not only of keeping up such music schools as had been previously established, but of causing the erection of others. We have documents before us, showing that in Aberdeen, Ayr, Cupar, Dunbar, Dundee, Elgin, Irvine, Lanark, St Andrews, &c., for many years after, and in some instances before, the passing of the act 1579, besides the teacher of the grammar school, an individual held the appointment of master of the music or song school. These consist of extracts from the accounts of the common good of certain Scottish burghs preserved in the General Register House,[b] relative to schools, and specifying the amount of salary paid to the different teachers. It would appear that the charge of the master of the music school was usually extended to the departments of reading, writing, and arithmetic;[c] and that the teachers were, originally at least, respectable members of the ecclesiastical body. Indeed, we find several instances of clergymen being advanced from this situation to wealthy benefices, and even bishoprics. Thus, William Hay, master of the music school at Old Aberdeen, in 1658, was

[a] Acta Parl. iii. 174. In the wording of this Act, which does not *command*, but simply *requests* the different functionaries therein specified to erect song-schools, &c., coupled with the sanction that they shall answer therefor, on the peril of their foundations, and followed up by the assurance that, "in performing of his hienes requeist, (they will) do unto his Majestie acceptable and gude plesure," there is something so anomalous and absurd, so exceedingly like the strange and not very consistent deportment of the sapient, half-witted Monarch, from whose counsels it sprung, that it is most likely that the statute had been dictated by himself, and if so, we may regard it as one of his earliest efforts at legislation. He always took a great interest in musical matters, and although he most probably thought with his preceptor, Buchanan, that it was neither becoming nor expedient for a king to possess much skill in that art, he appears about this time to have been ambitious of acquiring proficiency as a performer on the virginals. See *infra*, p. 111.

[b] See Appendix.

[c] See Extract Accounts above mentioned, and Orem's Description of Old Aberdeen, p. 211.

appointed minister of Perth, and subsequently Bishop of Murray; and about the middle of the sixteenth century, we find officiating in the same capacity in New Aberdeen, John Lesly, afterwards better known as Bishop of Ross, the historian, one of the most conspicuous agents of the Catholic cause during the reign of Queen Mary, and the associate and instigator of the Duke of Norfolk in the conspiracy against Queen Elizabeth, which, in 1572, cost that nobleman his life.[a]

Kennedy mentions,[b] that Mr Davidson, whose system of musical tuition is given in Forbes's Cantus, had teachers under him, and taught both vocal and instrumental music, particularly the virginal and the lute; and Orem, not only describes the music in Old Aberdeen as being taught by the same master, who gave instructions in reading, writing, and arithmetic, but under the same roof with these branches of education; its connexion with which may be still farther traced in the following entry in the Town Council Register of New Aberdeen, (vol. xlv. p. 858,) though the circumstance there recorded would seem to show that the system, at this period at least, was not very conducive to *harmony*:—"1612, 1 Dec.—On this day, the scholars of the grammar, sang, and writing schools, rose against their masters, seized the sang school, and held it by force of arms for three days." From a list of the ringleaders, it appears that they were for the most part the sons of the landed gentlemen and

[a] It is right, however, to mention, that we state this fact solely on the authority of Mr Kennedy, the author of the Annals of Aberdeen, and that it is very possible that the annalist may have drawn his inference from the mere *name* without farther evidence. If true, it is a circumstance in the life of this eminent person, which his biographers have hitherto omitted to notice. The following is a copy of the minute of appointment, as it appears in the town council register of Aberdeen, and from the date, it would seem that at this time he could not have been more than eighteen years of age. As he is styled "*Sir* John Lessly," it may be proper to state, for the information of those who are not versed in these matters, that this was a title formerly given to ecclesiastics, like the "Reverend" of modern times.—"1544, 18th September. The said day, the hale consale being convenit togidder, hes ordanit and elect Sir Jhon Lessly to be ane of the Prebendaris of the queir, and to haif the organis and Sang-schole for instructioun of the minds of gudis bairns, and keping of thame in gude ordour; and he to mak continual residence in the said queir. For the quhilk thai haif gifen him xx lib. yeirlie of fee, thankfullie payit to him yeirlie salary, as he remanis and makis gude service to the towne."

[b] Annals of Aberdeen, vol. ii. p. 135.

[c] History of Old Aberdeen, p. 191.

barons of Aberdeenshire. This music school in Aberdeen existed so lately as 1758, when the house was sold.[a]

By comparing what has been above stated with the subjoined notices from Dr Burney's Tour, published in 1773, our readers cannot fail to be struck with the perfect parallel which exists between the system here described, and that which prevailed in Germany at the period of his visit to that country, and which is there continued on the same footing to the present day. We may add, that while it has completely gone out of use with us, it has in the meantime extended itself to many other countries, especially to France and the United States.

"At Koningstein and Pirna there are schools for music . . . . . . At Pirna there is one for the children of officers, and one for those of the poorer sort, where they learn, as elsewhere, music, with reading and writing.[b]

"I crossed the whole kingdom of Bohemia from south to north; and being very assiduous in my inquiries how the common people learned music, I found out at length that not only in every large town, but in all villages where there is a reading and writing school, children of both sexes are taught music. At Teuchenbrod, Janich, Czaslau, Bömischbrod, and other places, I visited these schools; and at Czaslau, in particular, within a post of Colin, I caught them in the fact." (One would think, from this expression of the learned Doctor, that he had found them any thing but *well* employed.) "The organist and cantor, M. Johann Dulsick, and the first violin of the parish church, M. Martin Kruch, who are likewise the two schoolmasters, gave me all the satisfaction I re-

[a] Kennedy's Annals, vol. ii. p. 135. The following extract from an Aberdeen newspaper, the Journal, (August 23, 1748,) shews that music still continued at that time to be taught at the public schools throughout Scotland. "In justice to the merits of the teachers of the writing and music schools of this city, we have the pleasure to inform the publick, that last Thursday the Honourable Magistrates and Council paid them a visit, when the scholars in both performed their parts to the entire satisfaction of the visitors. But particularly the scholars in the musick school performed several parts of vocal and instrumental musick in presence of a polite and numerous auditory, and some persons of distinction, who were pleased to say, *they were the best performers of any they ever heard in a publick school in Scotland.*"

[b] Burney's Tour, vol. ii. p. 23.

quired. I went into the school, which was full of little children of both sexes, from six to ten or eleven years old, who were reading, writing, playing on violins, hautbois, bassoons, and other instruments. The organist had in a small room of his house four clavichords, with little boys practising on them all; his son, of nine years old, was a very good performer."[a]

Originally the clergy would naturally have been selected to officiate as masters of the music school, from their being the only persons qualified to give instructions in that science; afterwards the office fell into the hands of the schoolmaster;[b] and latterly, before its final extinction, it seems to have been united with the less literate functions of reader, precentor, and session-clerk.[c]

Forbes' Collection, therefore, is shaped precisely according to what might be expected from the source from which it emanated, and the prevailing taste of the day. If we find its contents somewhat heavy and monotonous, we must recollect that it is the production of a period when even the little dramatic music which was beginning to spring up in Italy and France, and which, however it might have startled the ears of our Presbyterian ancestors, would sound dull enough in these "most brisk and giddy paced times," was wholly unknown, and when our an-

[a] Burney's Tour, vol. ii. p. 4. For farther information on this point, see Mr Edward Taylor's "Airs on the Rhine," and Mr Planche's "Descent of the Danube."

[b] From the following extract from Lamont's Diary, (p. 20,) it would seem that this functionary was sometimes called upon for an exhibition of his vocal powers:—"1650, June 23.—The King's Maiestie (Charles the Second) came from Hollande to this kingdome. The 6 of July, leauing St Androis, he came to Cowper, where he gatt some desert to his foure-houres; the place where he satte doune to eate was the Tolboothe. The towne had apointed Mr Andro Andersone, scholemeaster ther for the tyme, to giue him a musicke songe or two whille he was at tabell."

[c] From the tale of the Prioress in Chaucer, it would appear, that in England, many hundred years ago, "to singen" was as much an established branch of the education of "small children" as "to rede;" and Hawkins, (vol. ii. p. 260,) speaking of the religious houses, says, that besides being schools of learning and education, "all the neighbours that desired it might have their children instructed in grammar and church music without any expense to them,"—a custom which was probably introduced soon after the establishment of the Gregorian chant, in the sixth century, when John the Arch-chantor and Abbot of St Martin's was sent from Rome to teach the monks of Weremouth the Service. Bedæ Ecclesiæ Historia, lib. iv. c. 18.

cient Scotish melodies, with their wild, varied, and original modulation, were but little relished. From beginning to end there is scarcely any composition which has the least pretension to life or gaiety, if we except Morley's still favourite glee, " Now is the month of Maying." The melodies, if melodies they can be called, are uniformly of a grave and sombre cast, and nothing can be less expressive, or, generally speaking, more at variance with the sentiment which they are intended to convey. Even where there is an attempt at sprightliness in the words, they are almost invariably set in the minor key, which, of course, hangs like a dead weight upon them, and makes most " tragical mirth." The verses are for the most part from the pens of our Scotish lyrical poets of the preceding century, especially Scott and Montgomery; and the music to which they are adapted consists in general of the productions of English composers. As the stock of melody was at that time extremely limited, it is not surprising to find several different sonnets adapted to the same tune. The air, " If floods of tears," which we have in the Skene MS., is here associated with two different sets of words; but the most interesting coincidence we observe is a sonnet of Montgomery, " Away, vain world, bewitcher of my heart," the air of which is that of

" Farewell, dear heart, since thou must needs be gone:
My eyes do show my life is almost done,"

with which all our readers are familiar, being the sonnet which Shakspeare puts into the mouths of Sir Toby Belch and the Clown, in the scene where their midnight orgies are interrupted by the unwelcome presence of Malvolio. In Montgomery's Poems,[a] the song, " Away, vain world," is mentioned as having been composed to the " toon" of " Sal I let her go," part of the burden of " Farewell, dear heart;" and if any doubt might at first have existed as to their identity, the fact is now satisfactorily established, the Editor having recently discovered the sonnet itself in a MS. of the year 1639, belonging to the Advocates' Library, set to the very tune which appears in Forbes' Cantus. Dr Percy has given the words of this song; but it has not

[a] Published in 1821, under the joint editorship of Dr Irving and David Laing, Esquire.

hitherto been known that the air to which it was sung was lurking unobserved in this curious volume.[a] We have the farther satisfaction of introducing a still older version of this air than that contained in Forbes or the above mentioned MS. in the Skene Collection, under a different name from any of the preceding—" O sillie soul alace."

Another feature of the *Cantus* must not be omitted. It contains a good many of the Godly and Spiritual Songs of the period. This was a style of composition introduced soon after the Reformation by certain of the clergy, in order, if possible, to unite religious edification with their musical recreations. Passages of scripture were paraphrased and set to music, but, as may be supposed, not in a way much calculated to uphold the dignity of the original, or to heighten the sublimity of the truths which they enforced. Of these some were adapted to the more fashionable compositions of the day, others to characteristic national melodies. A large collection of these appeared in the year 1590, and were reprinted by Andro Hart in 1621, under the title of " Ane compendious Booke of Godly and Spirituall Songs, collectit out of sundrie parts of the Scripture, with sundrie of other Ballates changed out of prophaine songes, for avoyding of sinne and harlotrie, with augmentation of sundrie gude and godly ballates not contained in the first edition."[b]

Some of the contents of this singular performance consist of songs of a sacred character, perfectly fit for church service; but the ballads changed out of profane songs, are either religious parodies of popular songs, or satirical invectives against the Catholic clergy, couched under that form. Wherever the great mass of a community require to be operated upon, ballads are a species of missives which have not unfrequently proved serviceable; and in the great contest between the

[a] Our National Anthem is said to make its appearance in Forbes' Cantus. This is not the case. " Remember, O thou man," (which will also be found in Ravenscroft's Melismata, among what he calls his country pastimes, under the name of " A Christmas Caroll,") bears a strong resemblance to it; but the coincidence is not such (especially as the former is in the major, and the other in the minor series) as to establish their identity, or even to warrant a charge of plagiarism against any of its reputed authors.

[b] Specimens of this work were published by Lord Hailes in 1764, and an entire reprint edited by Sir John Graham Dalyell in 1801.

Papal Clergy and the founders of the Reformed religion, they seem to have been made use of with considerable effect. It should be remembered that a feud had subsisted between the ballad-mongers and the Catholic clergy, even from very remote times. Mr Tytler[a] observes, "The clergy were the bitter enemies of the minstrels, whom they considered as satirical rivals or intruders, who carried off from the church the money which might have been devoted to more pious and worthy uses. They talk of them as profligate, low bred buffoons, who blow up their cheeks, and contort their persons, and play on horns, harps, trumpets, pipes, and moorish flutes, for the pleasure of their lords, and who, moreover, flatter them by songs and tales, and adulatory ballads, for which their masters are not ashamed to repay these ministers of the prince of darkness with large sums of gold and silver, and with rich embroidered robes." Neither did the party here assailed spare their ecclesiastical antagonists; and few as are the fragments which remain of their fleeting productions, (which is the less to be wondered at, as their enemies, the churchmen, were the only persons by whom any thing was committed to writing,) we see enough to convince us, that they rarely omitted an opportunity of exposing their hypocritical demeanour, their luxurious habits, and the corruption and profligacy of their lives. Our readers may take as an example, "The friar had on a coul of red," a distich of which is given in the medley at the end of Forbes' *Cantus*, (Edition 1666,) but which we shall not here repeat. We may, however, transfer to our pages, from the Compendium, the following satirical effusion, from which some idea may be formed of the general style of these compositions:—

With hunts up, with huntis up,[b]
It is now perfite day;
Jesus our King is gane in hunting;
Quha likes to speed they may.

[a] History of Scotland, vol. ii. p. 373.

[b] According to Puttenham, one Gray acquired the favour of Henry VIII., and afterwards that of the Duke of Somerset, for making "certain merry ballads," whereof one chiefly was "The hunte is up, the hunte is up." This, therefore, was an English song, though one of the many which were at that time popular in both countries. The tune is preserved in Lady Nevill's music book.—Burney, vol. iii. p. 115.

Ane cursit fox lay hid in rox
  This lang and mony ane day,
Devouring sheep, whilk he might creep;
  Nane might him shape away.

It did him gude to laip the blude
  Of ȝoung and tender lammis:
Nane could him mis, for all was his,
  The young anis with their dammes.

The hunter is Christ, that hunts in haist;
  The hunds are Peter and Paul;
The Paip is the fox; Rome is the rox,
  That rubbis us on the gall.

That cruel beist, he never ceist,
  By his usurpit power,
Under dispence, to get our pence,
  Our saullis to devoure.

Quha could devise sic merchandise
  As he had there to sell,
Unless it were proud Lucifer,
  The great master of hell?

He had to sell the Tantonie bell,
  And pardons therein was,
Remission of sins in auld sheep-skinis,
  Our sauls to bring from grace.

With buls of lead, white wax and reid,
  And uther whiles with green,
Closit in ane box, this usit the fox;
  Sic peltrie was never seene.

So numerous and so cutting had these and similar pasquinades become,—not to mention the more effective because more talented and ingenious productions of Sir David Lyndsay, which must always be classed among the leading, if not the most powerful, agents of the Reformation[a] in Scotland, that at a provincial council of the Roman Catholic clergy, held at Linlithgow, in 1549, it was thought necessary to enter a special denunciation against all who should be found in the possession of "*aliquos libros* RYTHMORUM SEU CANTILENARUM VULGARIUM *scandalosa ecclesiasticorum, aut quacunque hæresin in se continentia*;" and in 1551, an Act of Parliament[b] was passed, prohibiting the publication of "onie buikes, ballates, sanges, blasphemations, rimes or tragedies, either in Latin or in English," without royal licence obtained "fra our Soveraine Ladie and the Lord Governour." Nay, the Catholics were not satisfied with these denunciations and legal prohibitions; they appear at last to have found it expedient to resort to the *lex talionis* in self-defence. Some of their clergy are said to have been the authors of a satirical ballad, in very general circulation, against the Protestant faith, and the English for embracing it; and John Knox, in his History, (p. 36,) tells us that "ane Wilsoun, servant to the bischope of Dunkeld, quha (the said bischope) neither knew the New Testament nor the Auld, made a despyteful railing ballat against the preichours, and against the Governor, for the quhilk he narrowly eschapit hanging." Knox also mentions a "sang of triumphe" which the Catholic clergy composed, when Norman Leslie and his associates in the assassination of Cardinal Beatoun were taken from the castle of St Andrews, and consigned to the galleys:—

"Priestis, content you now,
Priestis, content you now;
For Normond and his companie
Hes filled the gallays fow."

The policy of the satirical ballads is sufficiently intelligible; that of

[a] See Sir John Graham Dalyell's Scotish Poems of the Sixteenth Century, vol. i. p. 30.
[b] Queen Mary, Par. 5, c. 27.

popularising, as it were, the doctrines of religion, by associating them with common secular songs and rustic and street tunes and dances, was an experiment of a much more doubtful character; and yet it was plainly entered upon under the honest and earnest conviction, that a greater service could not have been rendered to the cause of religion and morality. "In Princes' courts," says Hume of Logie, in the preface to his "Hymnes or Sacred Songs," (printed in 1599,) "in the houssis of great menn, and at the assembleis of yong gentlemen and yong dameselss, the chief pastime is to sing prophaine sonnets and vain ballattis of love, or to rehers some fabulos faites of Palmerine, Amadis, or uther such like reveries, and suche as either have the airte or vaine poeticke, of force they must shew themselves vane followeris of the dissolute ethnike poets, both in phraze and substaunce, or else they salbe had in no reputaunce. Alas! for pittie, is this the richte use of a Christianes talent?" Many of the songs were unquestionably of a licentious description; and it seemed to occur to these well-meaning zealots, that if they could only succeed in divorcing the innocent and artless tunes from their libertine associates, and in wedding them to verses of a divine character and import, the stream of pollution would gradually work itself clear, and the much lamented inundation of looseness and immorality be speedily dammed up. This idea, though it argued very little knowledge of human nature, was not altogether new. Thomas Sternhold, in the reign of Edward VI., tried something of the same kind, and with as little success. It is related of him, that being a "most zealous Protestant, and strict liver," the amorous and obscene songs used in the court of this Prince gave him such scandal, that he turned into English metre fifty-one of David's Psalms, and caused musical notes to be set to them, thinking thereby that the courtiers would sing them instead of their sonnets; but, says Wood, who mentions the circumstance, this they "did not, only some few excepted."[a] It must be allowed, however, that there was something much more reasonable in this project of Sternhold than in that of our Scottish Puritans, although they were both based upon the erroneous, impracticable, and we may add, un-

[a] Athenæ Oxoniensis, vol. i. p. 76.

scriptural principle, (which we see acted upon by fanatics in all ages,) that the exercises of devotion ought to be made to take the place of our amusements and recreations, and that the community, as a point of religious duty, ought to substitute divine songs for those of a secular nature. Still the former was not liable to the objection of irreverence, which applies so strongly to the other, and which, from the unhallowed allusions which it suggested—the indecency with which it jumbled together images the most sacred and profane—and the familiarity which it introduced in addressing the Deity—was calculated to do more real harm to the cause of religion, than the evil which it was intended to put down, and more than all the pious efforts of their authors could ever repair. The monstrous effect of the *seria mista jocis*, in matters of a religious nature, has seldom been so glaringly exemplified as in some of the "godly and spiritual songs," as they were strangely miscalled, to be found in this Compendium. "John, come kiss me now," as Mr Tytler well observes, "makes his appearance, stripped, indeed, of his profane dress, which had promoted "sin and harlotrie," but in exchange, so strangely equipped in his penitential habit, as to make a more ludicrous figure than his brother Jack in the "Tale of a Tub."

Johne, cum kis me now,
  Johne, cum kis me now;
Johne, cum kis me by and by,
  And make no more adow.

The Lord thy God I am,
  That John dois thee call;
John represents man,
  By grace celestiall.

My prophites call, my preachers cry,
  Johne, cum kis me now;
Johne, cum kis me by and by,
  And mak no more adow.

Till our gudeman, till our gudeman,
Keep faith and love till our gudeman :

For our gudeman in heaven does reign,
In glore, and blisse, without ending,
Where angels singes ever, Osan !
In laud and praise of our gudeman.

Adam our forefather that was,
Hes lost us all for his trespasse ;
Whais bruckle banes wee may sair ban,
That gart us lost our owne gudeman.

Quho is at my windo, who, who ?[a]
Goe from my windo, goe, goe.
Quha calles there, so like ane strangere ?
Goe from my windo, goe, goe.

Lord, I am here, ane wrached mortall,
That for thy mercie dois crie and call
Unto thee, my Lord celestiall ;
See who is at my windo, who ?

* * * * * *

O gracious Lord celestiall,
As thou art Lord and King eternal ;
Grant us grace that we may enter all,
And in at thy doore let me goe.

[a] The prototype of this song, "Goe from my window, goe," is one of the shreds and patches introduced by "Old Merry Thought," in Beaumont and Fletcher's "Knight of the Burning Pestle."

Qhuo is at my windo, quho?
Go from my windo, go;
Cry no more there, like ane stranger,
But in at my doore thou go!

Hay, now the day dallis,
Now Christ on us callis;
Now welth on our wallis
Appeiris anone:
Now the word of God rings,
Whilk is King of all Kings:
Now Christis flock sings,
The night is neere gone.

This was called *moralizing* popular ballads! It is alluded to by Shakspeare in the Winter's Tale,[a] where he speaks of a Puritan who sings psalms to hornpipes; and—what we could scarcely have looked for—it has been carried down so near our own times as till within these sixty or seventy years; a religious sect, denominated the Bereans, having signalized themselves by the production of a volume similar to that from which the above extracts are made, and of which the following are specimens:—

" Wat ye what I met yestreen
Lying in my bed, mama?
An angel bright," &c.

" Haud awa, bide awa,
Haud awa frae me, Deilie."

The only other Scotish volume of the same nature with the Compendium of Godly and Spiritual Songs, is one which appeared in 1683,

a Act iv. Scene

under the title of " The Saint's Recreation, Third Part, upon the Estate of Grace; containing, and methodically delineating, a Christian's progress, privileges, comforts, and duties, beginning at conversion; describing also the blessed Redeemer, Jesus, both absolutely and comparatively; and all these in spiritual hymns and songs suited to graue, sweet, melodious tunes: together with a plain paraphraze upon the margin, confirming all by Scriptures, explaining difficulties, and methodizing the songs. Compiled by Mr William Geddes, Minister of the Gospel, first at Wick in Caithness, and afterwards at Urquhart in Murray." This work is chiefly remarkable for the ingenious apology which the author offers for having presumed to blend the sacred with the profane. He says in his preface—" I cannot omit here to obviate an objection which may be raised by some inconsiderate persons, which is this: O! say they, we remember some of these ayres or tunes were sung heretofore with amorous sonnets, wherein were (may be) some bawdy-like or obscene-like expressions. To this I answer, first, That in this practice I have the precedent of some of the most pious, graue, and zealous divines in the kingdom, who to very good purpose have composed godly songs to the tunes of such old songs as these—' The bonny broom;' ' I'll never leave thee;' ' We'll all go pull the hadder,' (heather,) and such like, and yet without any challenge or disparagement. Secondly, It is alleged by some, and that not without some colour of reason, that many of our ayres or tunes are made by good angels, but the letters or lines of our songs by devils. We choose the part angelical, and leave the diabolical. Thirdly, It is as possible and probable that these vain profane men, who composed those amorous naughty sonnets, have surreptitiously borrowed those graue sweet tunes from former spiritual hymns and songs; and why may not we again challenge our own, plead for restitution, and bring back to the right owner; applying those graue ayres again to a divine and spiritual subject? Lastly, We find Paul, the great Apostle of the Gentiles, sanctified some sentences and verses of Greek poets, converting them into scriptural maxims, such as that—' *Cretenses omnes sunt mendaces*—the Cretans are always liars,' Tit. i. 12; and that in Acts xvii. 28, ' For in him we live, and move, and have our being,' &c.; and why may not we (finding the measures of a melodious tune or ayre indifferent in themselves) consecrate and apply them to a sacred poem?"[a] Mr Alexander Campbell remarks, in regard to the latter part of the above extract, that it contains the fanciful notion that our Scotish melodies had been originally sacred music, and that this idea was too ludicrous to merit serious refutation. Mr Ritson,[b] too, has observed, that the Scotish music owes nothing to the church-music of the cathedrals and abbeys before the Reformation; and these opinions, taken up upon such high grounds, have since passed current for something little short of authority upon the subject. It is somewhat dangerous, however, (as our readers will shortly see, when they look more particularly into the present collection,) for authors to denounce as absurd and groundless, opinions, merely because they happen to run counter to their own favourite theory. There are a few of the airs themselves, now that we have a clearer insight into them, which seem to tell a different tale; and we are rather inclined to think that the reverend gentleman, however slightly he might have been acquainted with the history of Scotish melody—in stating it not only as possible, but *probable*, that "the graue and sweet tunes" to which he refers had been derived from an ecclesiastical source, might have proceeded upon some credible and authentic tradition generally current at the time when he made the observation; but of this more hereafter.

As *Forbes*' book is the only publication of the seventeenth century to which we could have looked for the preservation of our native Scotish Melodies, we should have rejoiced even to have discovered a few of their "old familiar faces" peeping out from under the puritanical garb in which so many of the artificial productions of the "*Cantus*" are invested; but we have not been so fortunate, and we are forced to admit the utter absence of all printed evidence as to their nature and character, of an older date than that which has been above noticed.

In this dearth of all direct information, there are two collateral inquiries which ought not to be overlooked; the one relates to the lyrical associates of the tunes—the other to the musical instruments by which

[a] Introduction to History of Scotish Poetry, p. 364.

[b] Historical Essay on Scotish Song, p. 102.

they were performed and occasionally accompanied. To both of these subjects we shall now direct the attention of our readers, though not to a greater extent than we feel to be indispensable in the illustration of the particular topic which we are at present engaged in bringing under their notice.

I. ANCIENT SCOTISH LYRICAL POETRY.

It is obviously impossible to arrive at a just conception or appreciation of the character of the ancient vocal music of Scotland, without taking into view the songs and rhymes to which it was adapted, and of which it may be said to have formed a part. Music and poetry were much more intimately connected during the middle ages than they are at present; and whether the ancient melodies of Scotland were chiefly the invention of an order of men who, according to the imposing description of Percy, conjoined these two sister arts, and "sung verses to the harp of their own composing," who graced all scenes of festivity with the exercise of their talents, and were welcome guests in the halls of the great, and the humble cabins of the poor: or whether they might have emanated from a class of persons who, in the more sober language of Ritson, were little better than what he is pleased to call "mere instrumental performers, fiddlers, or such base-like musicians, who made it their business to wander up and down the country, chanting romances, singing songs and ballads to the harp, fiddle, &c.;" or whether they took their rise among shepherds tending their flocks, or maids milking their ewes, who actually felt the sentiments and affections of which they are so very expressive,—all must be agreed that a congeniality,—[a]a reciprocity, more or less perfect, must have (*originally*, at least, we will not say *always*) existed between the melody and the words, and that the genius of the one must have alternately inspired and awakened that of the other. The very rythm and measure of a verse, together with the sentiment, often seems to carry a certain intonation or air along with it, and Mr Allan Cun-

[a] See *Percy, Ritson, Beattie, Pinkerton*, passim.

ningham[a] has gone so far as to say, that when he was a boy, and committed to memory many ancient and modern songs, he never learned any of them without making himself master of some kind of melody which re-echoed the words, and that *most of the airs which the words suggested corresponded, in a great measure, with the proper tune,* the nature of the song, and its emphatic words, suggesting the general spirit and character of the air. Upon this somewhat remarkable declaration, we shall merely observe, that without meaning to call in question Mr Cunningham's veracity, and supposing it to be quite possible that a few casual coincidences of this nature might have occurred,—the slightest consideration of the almost endless variety of *musical* adaptations of which any given metrical arrangement of words is susceptible,[b] must at once lead to the rejection of all such ideas as hypothetical and unfounded. We need hardly say, therefore, that we do not participate in any such theory; we shall not even attempt to point out the affinities and resemblances which exist between the two; all we shall do will be to collect a few of the scattered notices which are here and there to be met with; and if they should serve to convey a tolerably correct idea of the favourite themes to which the ancient muse of Caledonia was wont to tune her lays, and the prevailing tone and character of her vocal compositions, it is all the information which we think can be expected, and, considering the few wrecks which the ravages of time have left, quite as much as the *data* before us are capable of supplying.

It is believed that until within the last three hundred years, our Scotish songs were but seldom committed to paper, and when left to the care of memory and tradition alone, they were perhaps not often destined to outlive their authors, or the events which they were intended to commemorate. In these cases, they probably evaporated in a few years,

[a] Cunningham's Songs of Scotland, vol. i. p. 26.

[b] Mersenne has calculated that the number of tunes or *Cantilenæ* which it is possible to extract from twenty-two notes (a compass of three diatonic octaves) is precisely 30553507534926l2960484. —Harmonicorum, Lib. vii. Prop. ix. It has also been computed, that to ring all the possible changes on twelve bells would occupy seventy-five years, ten months, one week, and three days. —Hawkins' Hist. vol. iv. p. 108.

without leaving any trace behind them, and in others, where they were reduced to writing, no care seems to have been taken of them. We need not wonder, therefore, when we set out in a pursuit of this nature, at the unsatisfactory and barren prospect that awaits us, and that, instead of apprehending the bodily substance of what we aim at, we feel ourselves, like beings wandering among the tombs, surrounded by the crumbled relics of former ages, with nothing to guide us to the objects of our search beyond a few casual inscriptions designative of the names by which they were known in their generation, and which now, that they have passed away, like epitaphs, serve merely to mark the period of their existence, or the spot where their ashes are laid.

The most ancient specimen of Scotish song, believed to be extant, is that which is given in Andrew Wyntoun's Rhyming Chronicle of Scotish History, written about the year 1420, where, speaking of the disastrous effects which resulted from the death of Alexander III., who was killed by a fall from his horse, in 1286, he says—

"This falyhyd fra he deyed suddanly,
This sang was made of him for thi.
Quhen Alysander, oure kynge, wes dede,
That Scotland led in luwe and le,
Away wes sons off ale and brede,
Off wyne and wax, gamyn and gle;
Owre gold wes changyd into lede;
Cryst, borne into vergyynyte,
Succour Scotland and remede
That stad is in perplexitie."

Another rhyme of the same period, and only a few years later, (1296,) is quoted by Mr Ritson from an old Harleian MS., and was made by the Scots at the siege of Berwick, the garrison and inhabitants of which, though ultimately overcome, and massacred by the victorious Edward, had at the commencement been successful. It runs as follows :—

"Wend Kyng Edewarde with his lange shankes,
To have gete Berwyke al our unthankes,
Gas pikes hym, and after gas dikes him."

We may next refer to the well known lines on the memorable battle of Bannockburn in 1314:—

"Maydens of Englande, sore may ye morne,
For your lemmans ye have lost at Bannockysborne,
With heve alowe.
What! weneth the King of England
So soon to have wone Scotlande?
Wyth rumbelowe."[a]

"This songe," says Fabian, by whom (as well as by Caxton, and also in a Harleian MS.) it is preserved, "was, after many daies, song in daunces in the carols of the maidens and mynstrelles of Scotland, to the reprofe and disdayne of Englyshemen, with dyvers others, whych I overpasse." Afterwards, in 1328, when Edward the Second's daughter Jane was given in marriage to David, the son of Robert the Bruce, and a treaty of peace entered into at York between the two nations, upon terms somewhat humiliating to the (at that time) crest-fallen martial spirit of England, we are informed by the same historian, Fabian, that the contempt of the Scots broke out in "diverse truffes, rounds, and songes, of the whiche one is specially remembred, as foloweth:—

[a] "*Heve a lowe rumbelow*" s said to be a sort of ancient chorus, but most commonly used by mariners. It is not unlike the modern "*yo-heave-o.*" On this account, in the old song on Bannockburn, it is supposed to carry with it an allusion to King Edward's having escaped in a small skiff from Dunbar; or, as the loyal Caxton discreetly insinuates, "forasmoche as he loved to gone by water." We should like much to know in what this "heve a lowe rumbelowe" originated. The "Hie down, down, derry down," is said to be a modern version of "Hai down, ir derry danno"—the burden of an old song of the Druids, signifying, "Come let us hasten to the oaken grove;" which was chanted by the bards and vades to call the people to their religious assemblies in the groves,—a curious proof how vestiges of ancient customs and manners are every now and then to be found lurking beneath conventional expressions, the most frivolous and apparently the most unmeaning. See Jones' Welsh Bards, p. 128.

"Long beirdis hartlis,
Paynted hoodes wytles,
Gay cottes graceless,
Maketh Englande thryfteless."

"Which ryme, as saieth Guydo, was made by the Scottes princypally for the deformyte of clothying that at those dayes was used by Englishemenne." We quote these lines, as they have been usually referred to in illustration of the Lyrical poetry of this remote age. We can scarcely conceive, however, that they had ever been intended for a *rounde* or *songe*. They are obviously much more of the nature of an epigram or *jeu d'esprit*, and that they were regarded as such, is apparent from the circumstance mentioned by Caxton, that they were inscribed on a placard, and fastened upon the church-doors of St Peter, towards Stangate.[a]

We find no traces of Scotish Song throughout the whole of the intervening period between the fragments above quoted and the Poems of James I., which we may suppose to have been written about the year 1430, and these only furnish us with the names of two compositions of this nature—"There fure ane man to the holt;" *i.e.* There went a man to the wood; and, "There shall be mirth at our meeting." The first is alluded to in the 6th Stanza of Peblis to the Play:—

"Ane ȝoung man stert into that steid
Als cant as ony colt;
Ane birken hat upon his heid,
With ane bow and ane bolt:
Said, mirrie madinis think nocht lang,
The wedder is fair and smolt;
He cleikit up ane hie ruf sang,

[a] The attaching of placards to church-doors is a practice which has descended to the present day. It was the principal method of publication at this time, and for many years afterwards. See Hume's History of the Reign of James I., where, after mentioning that on the union of the Crowns, in six weeks time his Majesty conferred the honour of knighthood on not fewer than 237 persons, he says, "*a pasquinade was affixed to St Paul's,* in which an art was promised to be taught, very necessary to assist frail memories in retaining the names of the new nobility."

Thair fure ane man to the holt,
Quod he,
Of Peblis to the Play."

The other in the 25th Stanza :—

" He fippillit lyk ane faderles fole,
And [said,] be still my sweit thing:
Be the haly rud of Peblis,
I may nocht rest for greting.
He quhissilit and he pypit bayth,
To mak hir blyth that meiting;
My hony hart, how sayis the sang,
Thair sall be mirth at our meeting,
ȝit,
Of Peblis to the Play."

Another tune is spoken of in the course of this piece, " The Schamon's Dance."

The ludicrous vernacular poem, called " *Cockelbie Sow,*" written rather before the middle of the fifteenth century, in the following passage contains several allusions to the ballads, songs, and dances, that were popular at that time :—

And his cousin Copyn Cull,
Foul of bellis ful ful,[a]
Led the dance and began,
Play us " *Joly Lemmane.*"[b]
Sum trottet " *Tras* and *Trenass,*"
Sum balterit " *The Bass;*"
Sum, " *Perdolly,*" sum, " *Trolly lolly,*"[c]

[a] " Full of bellis, ful ful," that is to say, all hung round with bells. In the Lord High Treasurer's accounts for 1513, we observe the following entry: " Item, to thirty dozen of bellis, for dansaris, delyverit to Thomas Boswell, iiij lb. 12s."

[b] " Jolly Lemmane," and " Tras and Trenas," must have been dances.

[c] " Perdolly," and " Trolly lolly," were probably the chorus or burden of popular songs. See Ritson's Ancient Songs, p. 92. " Trolly Lolly Lemman dou," in Complaynt of Scotland.

Sum, "*Cok craw thou* q^u *day*;"
"*Twysbank*[a] and *Terway*,"
Sum, "*Lincolne*," sum, "*Lindsay*,"[b]
Sum, "*Jolly Lemman dawis it not day*;"
Sum, "*Be yone woodsyd*" singis,
Sum, "*Lait lait in evinnyngis*;"
Sum, "*Joly Martene with a mok*,"
Sum, "*Lulalow lute cok*."[c]
Sum bakkit, sum bingit,
Sum crakkit, sum cringit;
Sum movit most mak revell,
Sum, "*Symon Sonis of Quhynfell*;"
Sum, "*Maister Peir de Cougate*,"
And uyir sum "*in Cousate*,"
At leser drest to dance.
Sum, "*Ourfute*," sum, "*Orliance*,"[d]
Sum, "*Rusty Bully with a bek*,
"*And every note in vyeris nek*."
Sum usit the dancis to dance
Of Cipres and Boheme:

[a] "Twysbank" Leyden considers to be the same with
"When Tayis bank wes blumyt brycht,"
in the Bannatyne MS. p. 229.

[b] It is probable that the names here given referred to productions popular in England. In Ritson's Ancient Songs, p. 30, there is "a song on his mistress, whom he admires as the fairest maid between *Lyncolne* and *Lyndseye*, Norhampton and Lounde, (*i. e.* London.) It is copied from a MS. of the reign of Edward II.

[c] Mentioned in Constable's Cantus.

[d] "Ouirfute and Orliance" are also mentioned in a poem in the Bannatyne MS. on "the laying of a Ghaist," which begins—
"Listis, Lordis, I sall you tell."
And similar to these, in all probability, are Platfute and Backfute, dances still known in some parts of the country. They take their names from the particular motion of the feet by which they are distinguished. In "Christ Kirk on the Green" Platfute is referred to.
"*Platfute* he bobbit up with bends."
Also in Sir David Lyndsay's "Complaynte of the Papingo," along with another, called *fute before*.
"To learn her language artificiall,
To play *platfute* and quhissel *fute before*."

Sum the faitis full yarne
Of Portugal and Naverne;
Sum counterfutit the gyis of Spayne,
Sum Italy, sum Almaine;
Sum noisit Napillis anone,
And uyir sum of Arragone;
Sum, "*The Cane of Tartary*,"
Sum, "*The Soldane of Surry*."[a]
Than all arrayit in a ring,
Dansit "*My deir derling*."[b]

No more vestiges of this branch of our literature are traceable till the commencement of the sixteenth century, when we turn to the poems of Douglas and Dunbar, for an addition to our catalogue of empty names. But amidst these shadows of the departed, we are happy to have it in our power to present our readers with something more substantial, which never before reached publicity. These are two metrical performances, at least so they may be termed, although one of them is a mere fragment, and it may occasion some surprise when we mention the place where they have been discovered, viz. the Minute-book of Burgh Sasines of the city of Aberdeen![c] To what they owe their insertion in this inauspicious volume, whether to the truant propensities of some incorrigible youth, whose poetical aspirations were not to be restrained by the dull routine of legal drudgery, or whether they had been entered, along with other public documents, for better preservation, (as it is technically called,) we know not; but certain it is, that they appear there "duly recorded" (1503–7) along with some verses by Dunbar.

[a] This must be intended for "Syria."

[b] Supposed to be the same with "My dayis darling," mentioned in Constable's Cantus.

[c] This and an unlooked-for discovery of music, which we shall afterwards have occasion to mention, may serve as examples of a truth well known to antiquaries, viz. that rarities of this description are often to be found where they are least of all to be expected. Sir John Graham Dalyell (Scotish Poems of the Sixteenth Century, p. 8) mentions a poem as having been found at the end of a manuscript of the Regiam Majestatem in the Advocates' Library, with two blank staves for music subjoined.

ADOWE DEIR HART OF ABERDENE.

"........... doue deir hart
.... off Abirdene
..... leman will depart me fro
..... will breke for duyl and wo
..... quair iver graven gren
Adowe deir hart of Aberdene.

I sall ger fasone weile a flane
And schut it fra my hart
The schaft sal be of soroweful mein
The hede of paines strang [smart ?]
Weile fedderit with the tyme has bene
Adoue deir hart of Aberdene.

..... hoivir passis ower the see
..... weile say fair leman myne
..... yon Inglis Kyng
..... or of the yong Dawphine
..... Mary Hewinis Quene
Adoue deir hart of Aberdene.

Send joy in their jurning
O sende my leman weile to me
Ye burche of Aberdene
... have hard say ande that with rycht
That thar may nane rest with resone
... Squiar, Clark nor Knycht
Or honorit M. A. Persone
Be this my exemple ye may weil sene
Adoue deir hart of Aberdene."

QUHY SO STRAT STRANG GO WE BY YOUE?

"Erle at the day doue,
Betuix the ald wark and the nowe,
I met ane wenkollet clede in ploue.
I said my fair and fresche of houe,
A bide lat nit our by youe,
Quhy so strat strang go we by youe?

Than scho wald nocht lene to me,
For luve the taile ende of hir E,
Bot saide away uncoucht man lat be,
And ye followe I wele fflee
Be gode man I defy youe.
Quhy so strat strang go wee by youe?

I saide my suet hart be the hicht,
Your dignitie may not decht nar decht,
Bot wile ye bide quhile it be neycht,
Under neicht ther bowes brecht,
Sum wncoucht spret wile spy youe.
Quhy so strat strang go we by youe?

Scho unbechot hir at the last,
And traistit that scho has traispast.
Sho saide suet hart ye ryve our fast.
It sennks me ye ar a gast.
. . . .
Quhy so strat strang go we by youe?"

These rude specimens of Scotish song may be justly accounted among the very dregs and "sweepings of Parnassus," but they are, nevertheless, curious, as illustrative of the language, the style and structure of this class of composition, and, in some degree, of the manners of the time. Mr Chalmers[a] observes, that the one half of the conversation of that age, both in England and Scotland, was made up by swearing; and if the reader will turn to certain contemporaneous productions in Ritson's Ancient Songs, pp. 98 and 101, he will observe the very same mode of address adopted on the part of the lady, and no inconsiderable resemblance in the general character of the phraseology.

From Gawin Douglas's Prologues to his translation of Virgil (1513) we only draw the following notices:—

12th Prologue.

" Some sang *ring-sangs, dancis,*[b] *ledis and roundis,*
With vocis schil, quhil all the dale resoundis;
Quhareto thay walk into thare karoling,
For amourus layis dois all the rochis ring;
Ane sang, '*The schip salis over the salt fame,*
Will bring thir merchandis and my lemane hame.'
Some other sings, '*I will be blyith and licht,*
My hert is lent apoun sae gudly wicht.' "

Do.

" —— our awin native bird, gentil dow,
Singand on hir kynde '*I came hidder to wow.*' "

[a] Works of Sir David Lyndsay, vol. i. p. 360.

[b] Leyden (Introduction to Complaynt, p. 130) says that " the ring dance, in which every aged shepherd leads his wife by the hand, and every young shepherd the maid whom he loves, was formerly a favourite in the south of Scotland, though it has now gone into desuetude." It was danced at the *kirn*, or feast of cutting down the grain, and with peculiar glee by the reapers, by whom the harvest was first dispatched, to the music of the Lowland bagpipe. They began with three loud shouts of triumph, thrice waving their hooks in the air, and they generally contrived that the dance should take place on an eminence, in the view of the reapers in the vicinity. Leyden adds, that " the dance is still retained by the Scottish Highlanders, who frequently dance the ring in the open fields, when they visit the south of Scotland, as reapers, during the autumnal months."

13th Prologue.

" Thareto thir birdis singis in thare schawis,
As menstralis playis ' *The joly day now dawis.*' "

The last mentioned tune, along with another, is alluded to by the Poet Dunbar, who flourished about thirty years after Douglas, in a satirical address to the merchants of Edinburgh.

" Your commone menstralis hes no tone,
But ' *Now the day dawis*,'[a] and ' Into Joun.' "

Although there are various musical allusions in Sir David Lyndsay's poetical writings, we only observe the name of one Scottish tune. This is in his " Complaynt," addressed to his royal patron, James V., in 1529, in which he recapitulates, in familiar terms, the services which he was wont to render him, in early life, when he acted in the capacity of his page and playfellow.

[a] " Hey the day now dawnes" is mentioned in the *Muses Threnodie*, a local poem, written at Perth in the reign of James VI., and Montgomery has a set of verses on the same theme, commencing—

" Hay! now the day dawis,
The jolie cok crawis."

In the Life and Death of the Piper of Kilbarchan, or the Epitaph of Habbie Simson, (Watson's *Scots Poems*, 1706,) there is the following line—

" Now who shall play, the day it dawes?"

from which, together with the citation from Dunbar, Mr Chambers (*Introduction to Scottish Songs*, p. 18) plausibly suggests, that the tune was probably the *Reveillée*, commonly played by the pipers or town's-minstrels throughout Scotland, to rouse the inhabitants to their daily labour; and this tune is believed to be the same with that to which " Scots wha hae wi' Wallace bled" is now sung. An absurd popular notion is attached to it, for which there is no foundation, viz. that it was Bruce's march at the battle of Bannockburn. All we can say is, that it is probably the same with the tune to which " The day dawes" was formerly sung, and this would appear, from the above notice, to have been a popular song, at least three hundred years ago; though, as we have not met with any written or printed copy of it earlier than those of the last century, even that opinion is liable to all the uncertainty of its being founded upon no better evidence than tradition, and the analogous structure and quantity of the verse.

"Than playit I twenty springs perqueir,
Quhilk was great pleasure for to heir,
Fra play thou let me never rest,
Bot '*Gynkertoun*'[a] thow luffit best."

It is in another production under a similar title, Wedderburn's "*Complaynt of Scotland*," originally published in 1548, that we find the most copious enumeration of the songs of that period. After having described his *Dramatis Personæ*, the shepherds and their wives, as having "tauld all thyr pleysand storeis," he tells us that they proceeded to sing "sueit melodius sangis of natural music of the antiquite," and among these,

"Pastance vitht gude companye[b]—The breir byndis me soir—Stil under the leyvis grene[c]—Cou thou me the raschis grene[d]—Allace I vyit ȝour tua far ene—Gode ȝou gude day vil boy—Lady help ȝour prisoneir[e]—King Villȝamis note[f]—The lang noune nou[g]—The cheapel walk—Fayththt

[a] A verse of this song, or rather an allusion to the tune, occurs in Constable's MS. *Cantus*—

"I would go twentie mile, I would go twentie mile,
I would go twentie mile, on my bairfoot;
Ginkertoune, Ginkertoune, till hear him, Ginkertoune
Play on a lute."

[b] A song beginning—

"Passetyme with good companye,
I love, and shall, unto I dye,"

is mentioned by Ritson, as being still extant, both words and music, in a MS. in his possession. It is supposed to have been written by Henry VIII., who, according to Hall, "was accustomed to amuse himself with playing at the *recorders*, flute, virginalls, and in setting of songes, or making of balattes."

[c] This song is in the *Maitland MS.* See Mr Laing's "Early Metrical Tales," p. 249.

[d] *i.e.* "Cull to me the rushes green," the burden of an old English song, of which Ritson (*Ancient Songs*, p. 54) has given both music and words.

[e] "Sen that I am a prisoneir"? Bannatyne MS., p. 215.

[f] Supposed, but improbably, to be the "Kingis Note" sung by Nicholas in Chaucer's *Miller's Tale:*

"And after that he song the Kingis Note,
Ful often blessed was his mery throte."

[g] "The lang noune Nou"—"Skald abellis Nou"—and "The Aberdenis Nou," are not easily explained; but the "Nou" was a common chorus in these days. See Ritson's *Ancient Songs*, pp. 64 and 270—"O Anthony, now, now, now."

is there none—Skald abellis nou—The Abirdenis nou—Brume brume on hil[a]—Allone I veip in grit distres—Trolee lolee lemmen dou[b]—Bille vil thou cum by a lute and belt thee in sanct Francis Cord[c]—The Frog cam to the myl dur[d]—The sang of Gilquhiskar[e]—Rycht sairlie musing in my mynde—God sen the Duc hed byddin in France, and de la Baute had nevyr cum hame[f]—Al musing of mervellis amys hef I gone[g]—Mastres fayr ye vil forfayr—O lusty maye vitht Flora Quene[h]—O myne hart hay this is my sang—The battle of the Hayrlau[i]—The huntis of Chevet[k]—Sal I go uitht you to rumbelo fayr—Greuit is my sorrou[l]—Turne the sweit Ville to me—My lufe is lyand seik, send hym joy, send hym joy—Fayr luf lent thou me thy mantil joy—The Perssee and the Mongumrye met, that day, that gentil day[m]—My luf is laid upon ane

[a] This is one of the songs mentioned in Lanehame's letter from Killingworth, 1575, as contained in a " bunch of ballets and songs, all ancient, fair wrapt up in parchment, and bound with a whip cord," which belonged to Captain Cox, the literary mason of Coventry.

[b] " Trolee Lolee," an old chorus.

[c] In Constable's *Cantus* the following lines are introduced into a Medley—

" Billie, will ye com by a lute,"
" And trick it with your pin trow low."

[d] Probably the same with " A most strange weddinge of the frogge and the mouse," a ballad mentioned by Warton, in his *History of English Poetry*, as licensed by the Stationers in 1580. Mr Kirkpatrick Sharpe has published a version of it (taken down from recitation) in his " *Ballad Book*," 1824. Many nursery rhymes on the same subject are still current. Pinkerton (*Select Ballads*, vol. ii. p. 33) says, that " The froggie came to the mill door," was sung on the Edinburgh Stage shortly prior to 1784. " The frog he would a wooing go" is still a favourite with children. The " Froggies Gagliard" in the *Skene MS.* is the oldest copy of the tune which exists; but it is to be regretted, that in this instance it has been so much altered and mutilated, in order to shew off the execution of the performer, that it is scarcely possible to reduce it to its original elements.

[e] Thought to be an historical ballad, but not extant.

[f] This was the Chevalier de la Beauté who was murdered by the Homes of Wedderburn in 1517, while Regent of the kingdom, in the absence of John Duke of Albany.

[g] A verse of this song occurs in Constable's *Cantus*.

[h] Printed by Chepman and Myllar in 1588, also with the music in Forbes's *Cantus*.

[i] A ballad still extant. See Mr Laing's " Early Metrical Tales."

[k] See Percy's *Reliques*, vol. i. p. 2.

[l] See Ritson's *Ancient Songs*, p. 93.

[m] Supposed to have been a Scotish copy of the common historical ballad of the Battle of Otterbourne.

knycht—Allace that samyn sueit face—In ane myrthtful morou—My hart is leinit on the land."

Seven of these ditties appear among the ballads changed out of profane songs in the Compendium of Godly Ballads, a work which supplies us with the first lines and general structure of a good many other popular songs, from which we may select the following, besides those which have already been cited :—

" Be blyth all Cristin men and sing."

" Richt sorely musing in my minde."

" For love of one I make my mone,
Right secretlie."[a]

" My loue murnis for me for me,
My loue that murnis for me,
I am not kinde, he's not in minde.
My loue that murnis for me."

" Tell me now, and in quhat wise,
How that I suld my lufe forga."

" O man rise up and be not sweir."

" Downe by yond river I ran."

" The wind blawis cauld furous and bauld,
This lang and mony a day."

" Hay trix trim goe trix, under the green-wood-tree."

" The wowing of Jock and Jenny,"—The ballat of Evil Wyffis, the ballat of Guid Fallowis, and several of the shorter pieces, which appear in the

[a] This is probably the original of " I love my love in secret."

Bannatyne MS. (1568,) may be considered as lyrical productions of this era, though most likely much older than the date of that collection. To these we may add the two songs, " Cummer goe ye before," and " The silly bit chicken," mentioned in the narrative of the congress of witches who met the Devil at North Berwick kirk.[a] We may farther recall to the recollection of our readers the favourite song of " Tak your auld cloak about ye," a stanza of which is put into the mouth of Iago, in Shakspeare's Othello,[b] and, " O Bothwell Bank thou blumest fair," of which the following anecdote is related in Verstegan's Restitution of decayed Intelligence, a work printed originally at Antwerp, in 1605. " So fell it out of late years, that an English gentleman travelling in Palestine, not far from Jerusalem, as he passed thorow a country town, he heard, by chance, a woman sitting at her door, dandling her child, to sing, *Bothwell bank thou blumest fayre:* the gentleman hereat exceedingly wondered, and forthwith in English saluted the woman, who joyfully answered him, and said, she was right glad there to see a gentleman of our isle, and told him that she was a Scottish woman, and came first from Scotland to Venice, and from Venice thither, where her fortune was to be the wife of an officer under the Turk, who being at that instant absent, and very soon to return, entreated the gentleman to stay there until his return; the which he did, and she, for country sake, to shew herself the more kind and bountiful unto him, told her husband at his home-coming, that the gentleman was her kinsman; whereupon her husband entertained him very friendly, and at his departure gave him divers things of good value."

We have now advanced to about the date of the Skene MS., but we are unwilling to close our extracts, where such scanty information is all that can be gleaned, without adding the series of fragments, however slight, which offer themselves in a curious medley, contained in a MS. Cantus, formerly the property of the late Archibald Constable of Edinburgh; because, although the date of that MS. is not older than 1670 or 1680, there are few of the songs to which they belonged likely to have been written in the course of that century, an age which, in Scotland,

[a] *Newes from Scotland,* 1591.

[b] This drama is said to have been written in 1611.

appears to have been the least fertile of any, in productions of this nature.

"The nock is out of Johne's bow."

. . . .

"First, when Robin, gude bow bare,
Wes never bairne so bold."

. . . .

"Sing soft-a, sing soft-a;
Of our pins
Ye know the gins,
Ye tirled on them full oft-a."

. . . .

"Methinks thy banks bloome best.'

. . . .

"Haill, gouke, how manie years."

. . .

"The mavis, on a tree she sat,
Singing with notes clear."

. . . .

"Joly Robin,
Goe to the greenwood, to thy lemman."

. . . .

"Titbore, tatbore, what corne maw ye?

. . . .

"Aiken brake at barnes door.
What horse in the towne
Shall I ride on?"

. . . .

"Come all your old malt to me,
Come all your old malt to me;
And ye sall have the draffe again,
Though all our dukes should die."

. . .

. . . .

"Thy love leggs sore bunden-a!"

. . . .

"The reill, the reill of Aves,
The joliest reill that ever wes."

. . . .

"Whaten a ȝeapin carle art thou!"

. . . .

"All of silver is my bow."

. . . .

"Johne Robison, Johne Robison,
That fair young man, Johne Robison."

. . . .

"Goe to the greenwood,
My good love, goe with me."

. . . .

"I biggit a bouir to my lemman,
In land is none so fair."

. . . .

"The humlock is the best-a seed,
That anie man may sow;
When bairnes greets after breid,
Give them a horne to blow."

. . . .

"The ring of the rash, of the gowan,
In the cool of the night came my lemman,
And yellow haire above her brow."

. . . .

"Silver wood an thow wer myne."

. . . .

"Come reike me the rowan tree."

. . . .

"Come row to me round about, bony dowie."

. . . .

"So sweetly sings the nightingale,
For love trulie, loly, lola."

. . . .

"All the moane that I make, says the gudeman,
Who's to have my wife, deid when I am,
Care for thy wynding-sheet, false lurdan,
For I shall gett ane uther, when thou art gone."

. . . .

"My gudame for ever and ay-a,
Was never widow so gay-a."

. . . .

"The beggar sett his daughter well."

. . .

"The fryare had on a coule of redd;
He spied a pretty wench kaming her head."

. . . .

"Be soft and sober, I you pray."

. . . .

"I and my cummer, my cummer and I,
Shall never part with our mouth so dry."

II. ANCIENT SCOTISH MUSICAL INSTRUMENTS.

As a great many musical instruments were anciently made use of in Scotland, especially in the Lowlands, much of the Scotish music must have been adapted to suit their particular genius, structure and compass. We feel it to be necessary, therefore, to enter shortly upon the consideration of their nature and history, as one of the most important elements in the present enquiry.

Giraldus Cambrensis, who wrote in the reign of Henry II. of England, and William the Lion of Scotland, (towards the end of the twelfth century,) in his Topographia Hiberniæ,[a] observes, that "the Irish use only two musical instruments, the harp and the tabour;—the Scots use

[a] Book III. c. ii. p. 739.

three, the harp, the tabour, and the bagpipe;—the Welsh also use three, the harp, the pipe, and the bagpipe." Whether, within the purely Celtic and Highland districts, the people at this time actually confined themselves to the use of the three instruments here specified—the harp, the tabour, and the bagpipe—we know not: Giraldus had never been in Scotland, and possessed no personal knowledge of the fact. But to the Scandinavian and Scoto-Saxon part of the nation we cannot conceive how this observation could be applied. The Norwegians, Danes, Saxons, and Normans, of whom it was composed, had each, in their several countries, cultivated many musical instruments; and these, along with their national music, they must of course be presumed to have carried into Scotland along with them. In the ornamental bas-relief still to be seen at Melrose Abbey, (founded by David I. in 1136,) there are representations of various instruments, among which are a flute with six holes, a bagpipe, a violin with four strings, and another of a form somewhat similar, supposed by Mr Barrington to have been a *crwth*.[a] Not that these remains, of themselves, would entitle us to conclude that such instruments prevailed in Scotland at that time, especially as the Abbey itself was the work of a Parisian architect, who was more likely to have borrowed the instruments of his own country for any purpose of mere ornament, than to have seized that opportunity of perpetuating those of a people so rude and uncivilized as the Scots then were. But the intercourse between this country and France, which afterwards became so frequent and intimate, had already commenced in the reign of William the Lion, while the importation and adoption of foreign manners and customs had begun a full century prior to that, under Malcolm Canmore,—there can be no ground of rational doubt, therefore, that at the time when Giraldus wrote, (1187,) most, if not all, of the instruments represented in the Gothic tracery of Melrose Abbey, and many others, were known and cultivated in Scotland—on the south of the Grampians at least.

Of these instruments, by far the most important, both in itself, and with a view to our present enquiry, was the harp. It is supposed, with

[a] Archæologia, vol. v. p. 3.

some appearance of truth, that it was known to the ancient Gauls and Britons,—that it was the instrument with which they accompanied the hymns which they addressed to their pagan deities,—with which, at their nuptials and funeral obsequies, their games and other public solemnities, they celebrated the praises of those who had signalized themselves by virtuous and heroic deeds,—and with which, at the head of armies prepared for battle, they at one time excited the ardour, and at another repressed the fury, of the combatants. But whether this was the identical instrument which has since been recognized under the appellation of harp, it is impossible to say. There is so much uncertainty in pronouncing any opinion as to the identity of the ancient lyres and *Cytharæ* with those of modern times, that Montfaucon, who examined six hundred of them, could not venture to affix particular names to any of them, or to ascertain their specific differences.[a] We cannot, therefore, be too cautious in points of this nature, but more especially in this instance, as our sole authority is Diodorus Siculus, who flourished in the time of Julius Cæsar and Augustus, and who says, "The Gauls have amongst them composers of melodies, whom they call Bards; these sing to *instruments like lyres*, songs of praise and satire."[b] Ammianus Marcellinus, a writer of the fourth century, also relates that "the Bards of the Celts celebrated the actions of illustrious men in heroic poems, which they sung to the sweet sounds of the lyre."[c] And yet, vague as is the expression "instruments like lyres," when, in conjunction with it, a few hundred years afterwards, we find the harp in the hands of their Celtic successors, the bards of Wales, Ireland, and Scotland, we see what we should conceive to be enough to satisfy any reasonable mind, that the harp, though probably of a ruder construction, and with fewer strings, was the instrument spoken of by Diodorus.

But holding that the harp was truly the instrument of the Druidical bards, we are not to assume that the Celtic race to which they belonged

[a] Antiq. Expl. tom. iii. lib. v. c. 3.

[b] *Ταῖς λυϱαις ὁμοιων*, lib. v. pag. 308. See also Vossius de Poem. Cantu et Viribus Rythmi, p. 18.

[c] L. XV. chap. ix.

were the original inventors of that instrument. If Mr Pinkerton's views are well founded, that Druidism had not existed long before the Christian era, and it certainly did not continue for many years after that period; and if the Celts, whom that writer admits to have been the aborigines of Britain, and of the greater part of Europe, were, as he represents, in a state of absolute barbarism, until the arrival amongst them of the Scythians or Goths, an event which he supposes to have taken place about three hundred years before the birth of our Saviour,—we should rather conclude that the Celts must have derived their knowledge of that instrument from them, to whom, according to Mr Pinkerton's theory, they were indebted for all the arts of civilized life. This is also the opinion of that writer,[a] who expressly says that the "harp was a Gothic instrument, first invented in Asia, and passing with the Goths to the extremities of Europe, and into the Celtic countries. The ancient Irish harp was small like the Gothic." Mr Gunn,[b] the author of a Dissertation on the Harp, intimates the same opinion, that it was of Asiatic extraction; and it is mentioned by Martianus Capella[c] as having been in use among the Gothic nations who overran Italy during the fifth century.

Whether the harp was known to the ancient Greeks and Romans, is a question which we shall not pretend to determine; probably it was,—but no exact delineation of it, that we are aware of, has ever been found on any of their coins, sculpture, or paintings, nor any description of it in their writings. Venantius Fortunatus, Bishop of Poictiers, who wrote in the sixth century, is the first author by whom the harp under its modern name is mentioned, and he pointedly distinguishes it from the Greek and Roman lyres, and assigns it to the Goths or *Barbari* in the following passage:—

Romanusque Lyrâ, plaudet tibi, *Barbarus Harpâ*,
Græcus Achilliaca, Crotta Britanna Canat.

Lib. vii. Carm. 8.

[a] Pinkerton's Enquiry, vol. i. p. 390.

[b] See Prospectus at the end of Mr Gunn's Historical Enquiry into the Performance on the Harp.

[c] See Du Cange, v. Harp.

It is supposed by Dr Ledwich,[a] that the *crotta*, or *crwth*, was the primitive national instrument of the ancient Britons, and that they and the Irish were first made acquainted with the harp by their conquerors, the Saxons and the Danes, whose Princes and Scalds were eminent performers upon it, and by whom it was highly esteemed and cultivated. But this opinion, which seems to have been mainly founded upon the passage which we have above cited from Venantius, is one, in which we feel it to be altogether impossible to concur. To suppose, as the learned antiquary does, (and he has not scrupled to express himself to that effect,) that the Celts either of Britain or of Ireland had allowed to be actually obtruded upon them, by their bitterest foes, a musical instrument which they have always cherished with a peculiarly warm feeling of patriotic regard, as one of the proudest symbols of their national independence, is an idea which can never be seriously entertained—and although we have no data to conclude as to the specific form of "the instruments like lyres," mentioned by Diodorus, and which Marcellinus, who follows after him, does not distinguish from lyres, we may at least be assured of this, that the *Crwth* (an instrument played with a bow, and supposed to be the parent of the fidicinal tribe) could not have been the instrument there referred to, bearing but a very slight resemblance to the lyre; while there is not a vestige, either in tradition or record, of any instrument possessed by the ancient inhabitants of Britain, which at all corresponds with that description, except the harp. This instrument, therefore, was either indigenous to the Celts,—or of Asiatic original, and communicated to them by the first Gothic colonists by whom they were visited, many years before the Christian era.

We should not have diverged into the regions of conjecture, so far as to make the above remarks as to a matter, in regard to which it must be admitted that we have no very authentic information to guide us; but it is by enquiries such as these, that the origin of the different nations of the ancient world is occasionally illustrated; and in that view, the early notices which exist of the harp are not the least important. It is to be hoped that much light will still be thrown upon this obscure subject.

[a] Antiquities of Ireland, p. 230.

Most of our readers are acquainted with the story of the Theban harp,—that ill-fated communication of the enlightened and enterprising Bruce of Abyssinian fame, to Dr Burney, which, from its extraordinary nature, was universally disbelieved, and drew down upon its author the unmerited *sobriquet* of the Theban *lyre*, (*liar*,) until very recently, when his memory has been rescued from this unmerited obloquy, by the researches of subsequent travellers. This was the delineation and description of a harp, from a painting contained in a sepulchre at the Egyptian Thebes. The instrument, as hastily drawn by Bruce, is represented with thirteen strings, and except that it wants the pillar or cross-bar, it is similar in construction to the harp with which we are familiar, while the general form and workmanship appear to have been superior in elegance to those of modern times. Mr Bruce remarked, that it overturned all the accounts of the earliest state of ancient music and instruments in Egypt; and in its form, ornaments, and compass, furnished an incontestable proof, that geometry, drawing, mechanics, and music, were at their greatest perfection when this harp was constructed. Dr Burney[a] observes—"The mind is wholly lost in the immense antiquity of the painting in which it is represented." And the subject was one which altogether would have excited much curious and useful speculation, had it not been that it was never broached, without being met with the answer, that it was a mere phantom of the traveller's imagination.[b] Now, however, that its authenticity has been established, we trust it will not be overlooked. To trace the harp, which so clearly appears to have been an instrument of the Scythians throughout their various migrations and progress, back to their first connection with Egypt, and the establishment of the first Scythic Empire—the very dawn of history itself—would form an investigation equally interesting and instructive.

We believe the Druidical hierarchy to have been but of very short duration. That it existed in Britain, there can be no doubt, as Cæsar himself[c] expressly says, that the Druids of Gaul derived their first instructions from those of Britain; but beyond that,—whether, as asserted by

[a] Vol. i. p. 225.

[b] See Walker's Irish Bards, Appendix, p. 114; Jones' Welsh Bards, p. 114.

[c] Cæsar, De Bell. Gall., lib. vi. c. 13.

Mr Pinkerton,[a] it was confined to Anglesey, the Isle of Man, and the Garonne, or the Southern bounds of Celtica in Gaul, and never found its way either into Ireland or Caledonia, is a question into which we shall not here enter. Divines—philosophers—legislators—physicians—poets—seers and musicians—the most extraordinary part of their history seems to have been the multiplicity of functions which their office embraced; and when the harp, as we have above noticed, fell from their hands into those of the bards, it would appear to have descended to an order of men little less distinguished for the variety of their attainments:

> " Musician, Herald, Bard, thrice may'st thou be renowned,
> And with three several wreaths immortally be crowned."

With such superhuman versatility as was here called into requisition, it is not surprising to learn, that the office should afterwards be subdivided and parcelled out into the separate vocations of poets, heralds, and musicians, and that these again should latterly subside into a series of different gradations, from the Invested Bard, down to the juggler, the crowder, and the tabourer. This branching out of the original profession of the bards, no doubt, foretells of the period of their decay,—and while in Wales the ruthless policy of Edward I., and the stern edicts of several of his successors, precipitated their downfall—in Ireland and Scotland the decline of the feudal system equally served to annihilate their independence, and to determine their fate.

We shall say nothing in detail as to the Cambro-British race of bards, some of whom, such as Aneurin and Llywarch-Hên, appear to have been warriors as well as poets and musicians, and to have borne a prominent part in their country's sanguinary struggles with the Saxons during the fifth and sixth centuries.[b] The accounts which have been

[a] Pinkerton's Enquiry, vol. i. p. 17.

[b] Amongst these was the celebrated Myrddin ap Morvyrn, or Merlin of Caledonia, a disciple of Taliesen, who was born about the beginning of the sixth century near Dunkeld in Scotland. Whether Aneurin, the author of the Gododin, was also a native of this country, we are not aware; but he lived under the patronage of one of the northern princes, Mynyddawg, of Edinburgh. Jones' Welsh Bards, pp. 16, 23.

handed down to us regarding these personages, and their own poetical remains, are so intermingled with the fabulous feats and *gestes* of their romantic contemporaries, Arthur and his Knights of the Round Table, equally famed in song, and celebrated for their skill on the harp, that they can scarcely be considered as falling within the pale of authentic history. "The poets," (says Hollingshed,[a]) "used for invention sake to faine such dreaming fables for exercise of their stiles and wits: afterwards, through error and lacke of knowledge, they haue been taken with the ignorant for verie true and most assured histories."

In like manner, Ireland may, for several centuries during the middle ages, have been (compared with many other nations) the seat of learning and civilization—we cannot vouch for the truth of what has never yet been satisfactorily established—but we believe that it must have been eminent for its proficiency in the art of music, far beyond either Wales or Scotland. The fact is certain, that about the year 1100, one of the Welsh princes (Gruffudd ab Cynan) invited to Wales a number of Irish bards to assist in framing a new code of musical regulations for his Cambrian subjects, and Caradoc their historian has acknowledged the obligation which his countrymen owed to Ireland on this occasion.[b] Giraldus Cambrensis, another of their compatriots, towards the end of the twelfth century, writes of the Irish, that they were incomparably better instructed in music than any other nation which he had seen,[c] and he had travelled over great part of Europe; although, he adds, that their attainments seemed to him to be confined entirely to their skill in instrumental music.[d] Another testimony of their excellence in this department is to be found in Galileo's[e] Dialogues on Ancient and Modern Music, first printed in 1582, (p. 143,) where, speaking of the harp as among

[a] Chron.

[b] Powell's History of Wales, pp. 115, 191.

[c] Topog. Hib. c. 11, p. 739. "Præ omni natione quam vidimus incomparabiliter est instructa."

[d] "In musicis *solum* instrumentis commendabilem invenio gentis istius diligentiam."—*Ibid.*

[e] This was the father of Galileo the famous astronomer. Even the great Lord Bacon, in his Sylva Sylvarum, pays the Irish the compliment of saying that "no harpe hath the sound so melting and so prolonged as the Irish harpe."

the instruments which were at that time in use in Italy, he says—" This very ancient instrument was brought to us from Ireland, as Dante has recorded, (this must have been about the year 1300,) where they are excellently made, and in great numbers, and the inhabitants of which island have practised on it for very many centuries; it being also the particular badge of the kingdom, and as such frequently painted and sculptured on their public edifices and coins."[a]

With these unexceptionable and thoroughly accredited proofs of their ancient superiority, the Irish, we think, ought to rest satisfied, and not to advance claims for which they can produce no proper authority. That the harp was known to the ancient Britons we have already seen; and yet the Irish historians[b] insist that they were the first to make the Welsh acquainted with the instrument; and in support of this notion, they found upon what may at once be seen to be a palpable, though no doubt an unintentional, misinterpretation, by Wynne,[c] of a passage in which Dr Powell, in his notes on Caradoc's history, speaks of the introduction into Wales of the Irish music and musicians by Prince Gruffudd, to which we have just now referred, and where, by confounding the expression "instrumental music" with "musical instruments," it has been made to appear as if Powell had asserted that the harp was upon that occasion imported into Wales from Ireland. They also say that the word " Telyn" (the Welsh name for harp) is derived from the Irish " Teadhloin," and has no radical etymon to which it can be traced in the Welsh; an argument at no time very conclusive, but least of all in the case of cognate tongues so nearly allied as those of Ireland and Wales.[d] Upon no better grounds than the above, the Welsh are likewise accused of having borrowed or stolen from the Irish their old favour-

[a] The figures on the Irish coins are said, by the best informed antiquaries, to have been triangles, not harps. Dr Ledwich says, that they were introduced simply to express the attachment of their monarchs to the Church, and its reciprocal support of them. It was Henry VIII. who first gave the Irish the Harp for their armorial bearing, to perpetuate, it is said, the celebrity of their performance on it in former times.

[b] Walker's Memoirs, pp. 70, 74.

[c] Wynne's History of Wales, (Edit. 1774,) p. 159.

[d] The Welsh, again, derive the word " *Telyn*" from a Cambro-British root " *Tél,*" signifying

ite instrument the *Crwth*;[a] and it is even said, that the Scots (we quote Mr Walker's own words) "are in all probability under the same obligation (to the Irish) as to the last mentioned instrument, *though not a trace of it can be found in any of their historians!*"—a remark conceived in so truly Hibernian a spirit, that it carries its own refutation along with it, and renders any farther comment superfluous.

That the Irish, however, introduced their national harp or *Clairseach* into this country, is more probable. Indeed, considering the extent of their early settlements in Argyleshire and Galloway, it is scarcely possible that it could have been otherwise. But there was a large portion of what is now comprehended within the territories of Scotland which was never occupied by the Scoto-Irish; and here it is equally probable that the early inhabitants possessed an instrument of this nature to which the Irish could lay no claim. Even the Picts were likely to have been acquainted with the harp,—and this, too, whatever theory we adopt in regard to their origin—whether we consider them to have been aboriginal Britons, or settlers of Gothic extraction. If the former, we have already seen that the harp was the favourite instrument of their bards, from whom it would no doubt have been transmitted to their descendants:—if the latter, (now the more generally received, and, as we are inclined to think, the sounder opinion,) they must have derived it from their Scalds, a race of men who appear to have stood in the same relation to the Scandinavians, as the Bards, to the British and other Celtic nations. The Laureate Bard among the latter is said to have been the eighth officer of the King's household—to have occasionally sat at his table, and to have been otherwise honourably distinguished. In the same way, we are told that the Scalds were ranked among the sovereign's chief officers, and always of his council;[b] and the functions which they performed seemed to have been precisely of the same nature with those of the Bards. They were the historians and genealogists, as well as the poets and musicians, of the Court

"stretched, or drawn tight;" and argue, that it must consequently have been coeval with the *first stringed instrument* with which their ancestors had ever been made acquainted.

[a] Walker's Irish Bards, p. 74.

[b] Pinkerton's Enquiry, vol. i. pp. 272, 273—389. Also Percy's Reliques, Introduction, pp. 20, 63.

—their verses, also, were sung with the accompaniment of the harp. It is reasonable, therefore, to suppose, that within the Pictish kingdom, and wherever Gothic population and influence extended, they, and not the Celts, were the introducers of that instrument. The learned Dr Percy, whose opinions on these matters have stood the test of time, as well as the pointless and misdirected shafts of Mr Ritson's ridicule, in speaking of the origin of the French and English Minstrels,[a] observes—" Though the Bards of the ancient Gauls and Britons might seem to have a claim of being considered as their more immediate predecessors and instructors, yet these, who were Celtic nations, were *ab origine*, so different a race of men from the others, who were all of Gothic origin, that I think one cannot in any degree argue from the manners of the one to those of the other; and the conquering Franks, Saxons, and Danes, were much less likely to take up any custom from their enemies the Gauls and Britons, whom they every where expelled, extirpated, or enslaved, than to have received and transmitted them from their own Teutonic ancestors in the North, among whom such customs were known to have prevailed from the earliest ages." All who are versed in the history of our literature are aware that the earliest Scotish, we may add, the earliest English, poetry which, it is well known, was first cultivated in the north of England,—furnishes strong hereditary proofs of its Scandinavian parentage;—nay, some authors have considered these northern nations to have been the originators of all European poetry whatever;[b] it might well be asked, therefore, to whom should we ascribe the first introduction of this instrument amongst us, but to those from whom the most ancient relics of our minstrelsy appear to have emanated?[c]

[a] Percy's Reliques, Introduction, p. 67.

[b] Ibid. p. 27.

[c] The most ancient Scotish representation of the harp is that which is delineated in the carved work of the monument near the church of Nieg in Ross-shire. An engraving of it will be found in " Cordiner's Remarkable Ruins." The figure of the harp is perfect, except that it wants the strings, probably from their having been effaced in the original. Mr Cordiner considered this monument to be nearly as old as the 11th century, and it is no slight confirmation of the foregoing views, to find it situated in a part of the country so essentially and indisputably Gothic in its origin, as the East Coast of Ross-shire. See also Ledwich's Antiquities of Ireland, p. 230.

In considering the origin of our musical instruments, and the circumstances which attended the formation of our national music, we must not only take into view the ancient Scandinavian part of our history, however obscure, and the extensive kingdom of the Picts, but the large and fertile tracts of country from an early period in the possession of a people, very slightly, if at all, differing from their Southern neighbours on the other side of the Tweed—and this, too, long before the junction of the Pictish and Scotish crowns in 843. It was in the fifth century that the Anglo-Saxons first of all made a descent upon Scotland, and in the course of the century following, they established the kingdom of Northumbria, which, besides the English provinces connected with it, embraced most of the Border district, Berwickshire, and the Lothians as far as the Firth of Forth; and this country did not fall under Scotish dominion until it was ceded to Malcolm II. at the beginning of the eleventh century. During this dark period of our annals, the inhabitants of this part of Scotland consisted of Anglo-Saxons, Danes, Normans, and Ottadini or ancient North-Britons, a colony of which last occupied Clydesdale, with Peeblesshire, Selkirkshire, and the upper parts of Roxburghshire, which were long maintained by them as a separate kingdom under the name of Strath-Clyde; besides which, independently of the Scoto-Irish part of the nation, the islands and several of the northern counties were in the possession of Scandinavians and Norwegians. A considerable number of Danes, also, the natural result of their occasional invasions between the ninth and eleventh centuries, had become intermingled with the inhabitants of the North-East Coast.

Such being the general description of the population, it is clear that—abstracting from the Celtic districts—there must, at this time, have been but a slight difference between the people of Scotland and the English nation. Before the great change which took place in the latter after the Norman conquest, it is believed that the language spoken by the Scoto-Saxons and the Anglo-Saxons was the same; and it would even appear, that there was no essential distinction between that spoken by them and the natives of Denmark and Norway.[a] The manners and customs

[a] See Paper by Dr Jamieson, Archæologia Scotica, vol. ii. p. 279.

of the Lowlands of Scotland, during these ages, could not, therefore, have been materially different from those of the Anglo-Saxons and Danes. And scanty and defective as are the early chronicles of that period, there is no feature connected with their character, which is more prominently brought forward, than their passionate attachment to the arts of poetry and music. To them the harp owes its modern name, (the Anglo-Saxon being **Hearpe**, and the Icelandic **Harpa**;[a]) and so invariably does that instrument appear to have been employed by them as an accompaniment for the voice, that in their translations from the Latin into Anglo-Saxon, it has been observed, that the word "*psalmus*" is sometimes rendered "harp-song," and "*cantare*," "to sing to the harp"—an accomplishment which must have been nearly universal, as it appears to have been customary to hand round a harp at their entertainments, when each of the guests was expected to perform by turns. This is well illustrated by the story of Cedmon, their earliest poet whose remains have come down to us, and who died in 680. Not being able to sing, it is said that when he was present on these occasions, and saw the harp on its way towards him, he generally contrived to effect his retreat, rather than expose his ignorance. As Cedmon was a Northumbrian, this may be taken as a proof of the cultivation of music in that part of our territories, which, as we have above described, was annexed to the Scotish crown in the eleventh century.[b] The high estimation, again, in which the character of the minstrel was held both by the Saxons and the Danes—the readiness with which he was at all times listened to—and his perfect freedom of access to the presence of persons of the highest distinction at all times, are amply testified in a variety of instances; but in none are they placed in a more conspicuous light than in the incidents known to every schoolboy, where Alfred, the King of the Saxons,—and at a subsequent period, Anlaff, the King of the Danes, availed themselves of their skill on the harp to personate minstrels, and in that character succeeded, it is said, in penetrating into the enemy's camp, and even in gaining admission into the royal

[a] Percy's Reliques, vol. i. Introduction, pp. 50, 51.

[b] See Bede's Ecclesiastical History, b. IV. c. xxiv. See also a Life of Cedmon, in Young's History of Whitby, vol. i. p. 182.

pavilion, where they acquired a perfect knowledge of the position and resources of the party with whom they were contending. The date of the first of these occurrences is 878—that of the latter 938; and they are both recorded by William of Malmesbury, who died in 1142; while that which relates to Anlaff is also mentioned by an historian of a somewhat earlier date,—Ingulphus, who was born in 1030, and died in 1091.[a] There is some reason, therefore, to believe that the narratives are well founded; and whether true or false, they may at least be presumed to contain faithful representations of the manners of the age.

There can be no doubt that, at this time, the Minstrels were a numerous body. Du Cange says, that the courts of Princes, during the middle ages, swarmed with them; and that the royal treasuries were frequently drained by the large sums which were lavished upon them. Indeed, this sort of extravagance seems to have continued to much later times. The Minstrels of the Anglo—we would add the Scoto—Saxons are said to have retained many of the honours of their predecessors, the ancient Bards and Scalds; but they were obviously persons, in point of station and acquirements, very inferior to the latter. This is evident from the fact, (if Dr Percy's statement be correct,) that the name of Scald comprised both poet and musician, and that the Danes had no separate and peculiar name for either of these professions taken singly; but among the Anglo-Saxons, although many of the minstrels "composed songs, and all of them could probably invent a few stanzas on occasion," the poet and the minstrel were early distinguished as separate persons. They also appear "to have accompanied their songs with mimicry and action, and to have practised such various means of diverting as were much admired in those rude times, and supplied the want of more refined entertainments."[b] The Troubadour or Provençal bards were doubtless of a higher grade; but the French minstrels are described by Mr Ritson in similar terms to the above,[c] "They sung either their own compositions, or the compositions of

[a] These anecdotes are related by other writers of good credit, besides the above; and among these, by Henry of Huntingdon, Speed, Sir Henry Spelman, and Milton.

[b] Percy's Reliques, Int. p. 1.

[c] Ritson's Essay on National Song, vol. i. p. 26.

others, to the harp, the vielle, viol, cymbal, and other instruments, danced to the tabour, played tricks of legerdemain and buffoonery; and, in short, accommodated themselves to every mode of inspiring festivity and mirth, so that they were everywhere welcome, and everywhere rewarded. The courts of France abounded with them; and during the reign of our Norman princes, they seem to have been no less numerous in England." Mr Ritson, however, was in error in denying, as he unscrupulously did, the existence of any class of men to whom the term "English minstrel" was applicable. Although the French minstrels largely intermingled with the latter, as long as the English monarchs retained any portion of their possessions in France, and with the Scotish minstrels to a much greater extent, in consequence of our long continued and intimate connexion with that country,—the profession was too lucrative, and too well patronized, not to be extensively practised at home. Mr Tytler[a] says, "there can be little doubt that in Scotland, as in France and England, the profession of a minstrel combined the arts of music and recitation, with a proficiency in the lower accomplishments of dancing and tumbling;" and that "in the reign of David I. at the Battle of the Standard, which was fought in 1138, minstrels, posture-makers, and female dancers, accompanied the army." Farther, he relates, that during the royal progresses through the kingdom, it was customary for minstrels and singers to receive the sovereign at his entrance into the different towns, and to accompany him when he took his departure. The country, he says, from a very early period, "maintained a privileged race of wandering minstrels, who eagerly seized on the prevailing superstitions and romantic legends, and wove them in rude but sometimes very expressive versification into their stories and ballads—who were welcome guests at the gate of every feudal castle, and fondly beloved by the great body of the people."

Mr Tytler also observes, that the harper was to be found amongst the officers who composed the personal state of the sovereign. This is strictly true.

[a] History of Scotland, vol. ii. p. 368, et seq.

Dr Percy[a] gives an extract from Domesday Book, showing that the *Joculator Regis*, or King's Minstrel, who he says was a regular and stated officer of the court of the Anglo-Saxon kings, had lands assigned to him for his maintenance. On turning to Robertson's Index of the Record of Charters, we find several royal grants in favour of harpers or *Citharistæ*. One in the reign of Robert II. to "Thomas Citharist of the forfalture of Gilloc de Camera—the lands of Gilloc within the burgh of Haddington." Another by David II. to "Patrick Citharist de Carrick, of lands in the county of Carrick." Another to "Ade Chichariste, (for Citharist,) of lands in Forfar." Another by David II. to "Nicholas Chicharist of the forfaultrie of Alexander Cruiks in Constabulario de Linlithgow." As several of these were forfeitures, they may be regarded as substantial proofs of the royal munificence to this class of persons.[b] Grants of lands in behalf of bards and minstrels were common also on the part of our feudal nobility. Jones, in his Welsh Bards, has instanced the lands of Tulli-barden, from which the Marquis of Tullibardine derives his title; and mentions that the Earl of Eglintoun had informed him that he had a portion of land near Eglintoun Castle, called the Harpersland, which used to be allotted by his ancestors to the bard of the family. Could this be the lands described in the Index of Charters as follows?—"A charter of the lands of Harperland, in the barony of Kyle, in favour of Sir John Foulerton, son and heir of Ade de Foulerton in Ayrshire, 5 March, 2nd year of the reign of Robert II." (1371.)[c]

From the Lord High Treasurer's accounts, extracts of which we have furnished in the Appendix, some idea may be formed of the band of instrumental performers kept by the Scotish sovereign for about fifty years, from the beginning of the 16th century.[d] Besides those in regular and

[a] Vol. i. Introduction, p. 64.

[b] It is right to state, however, that the word "Citharist," like "Harper," *may* here have been employed as a proper name, though originally used as designative of the profession, and although this is precisely the manner in which, as a musician, the individual would have been designed, see *infra*, p. 89. The particular sense in which it was here used we have no means of determining with certainty.

[c] Several of these allotments of land by Highland nobles and chieftains are specified by Mr Gunn in his Enquiry into the Performance of the Harp in the Highlands, pp. 45, et seq.

[d] An eminent antiquary has politely handed us two extracts from the Exchequer Rolls relative

stated attendance, musicians seem to have been collected, upon particular occasions, from the private establishments of the nobility, and all quarters whence they could be procured. In 1507, on the first day of the new year, payments were made to "divers menstrales, schawmeris, trumpets, taubroneris, fithelaris, lutaris, harparis, clarscharis, piparis,"—in all, to the number of sixty-nine persons; and among the performers, we see mention of Italians, French, English, Irish, as well as Scots. There is also a Moorish musician, called "The More taubroner." Another of these "taubroners," of whom there is a notice in the accounts for 1548, under the name of "Stewyn tabronar," was probably the person to whom the following anecdote in John Knox's History relates. We should premise that all "tabourers" went under the denomination of "minstrels," a word which, at this period, seems to have been used in the same sense with the generic term "musician," at the present day. "During the Queenis absence, the Papists of Edinburgh went down to the chapell to heir mess; and seeing thare was no punischment, they waxit more bold: some of thame, thinking thareby to pleise the Quene, upoun a certane Sunday, in February, [1565,] they maid an Even-song of thair awin, setting two priests on the one syde of the quire, and one or two on the uther syde, with *Sandy Stevin, menstrall,* (baptizing thair children and making marriages,) who, within eight dayes efter, was convinced of blasphemy, alledging, That he wald give no moir credit to the New Testament, then to a tale of Robin Hood, except it wer confirmed by the doctours of the church."

From the entries of ordinary fees and yearly pensions of 1538 and 1542, although we scarcely think that the enumeration here had included the whole,—there seem, about this time, to have been fifteen musicians more immediately connected with the Royal household—viz. five Italian

to "minstrels." One, dated 2d May 1398, is a payment entered as follows:—"Et duobus menstrallis de gratia auditorum ad præsens, xx^{s}.;" another, 3d July 1402, a similar payment to "Fulope menstrallo tempore Scaçcarii ex gratia auditorum ad præsens." As Balfour, in his Practics, p. 136, mentions, that the Auditors of Exchequer, and none others, were "judges competent in all actions and controversies anent allowances and accounts concerning the King's household," the above had most probably been sums awarded to these minstrels by the Auditors in their judicial capacity.

minstrels, four violists, two performers on the "swesch talburn,"[a] (probably the kettle-drums,) and four players on military trumpets or trumpets of war, as they are there called. The particular instruments, played by the Italians, are not mentioned; they were perhaps accomplished musicians, whose skill was not confined to any single instrument, and who were capable of taking a general direction of the whole. They formed a regular part of the establishment for many years, and in one of the entries,—that for 30th December 1515, their names are given as follows: "Vincent Auld, Juliane Younger, Juliane, Anthone, and Bestiane (*i.e.* Sebastian) Drummonth."[b]

Upon the decease of one of these Julians, about the year 1524, we observe that his place was filled up by one Henry Rudeman, whose appointment is entered in the Privy Seal Register[c] in the following terms:—"Preceptum litere Henrici Rudeman tubicinis, dando et assignando eidem, Henrico locum quondam Juliani Richert, Italiani tubicinis, et ordinando eundem Henricum adjungendum fore reliquis Italianis histrionibus et tubicinibus, et regi cum eisdem servire in loco quondam Juliani, durante tempore vite ipsius Henrici; pro quo servitio, dominus rex dat sibi durante vita sua, omnia feoda, stipendia, et devoria solita et consueta, etc. Apud Edinburghe x° Septembris anno etc. V^{c} xxiiii°." (1524.)

On the margin is written in an old hand, opposite to "tubicinis," *musician*, as if to indicate that "tubicen" was not here meant to imply "trumpeter," its primitive and more limited signification, but "min-

[a] "Ane thousand hagbuttis gar schute al at anis,
With *swesche-talburnis* and trumpettis awfullie."
Sir David Lyndsay's Testament of Squyer Meldrum.

Chalmers, in his edition of Lyndsay's Works, translates *swesche* "roar, or rather clatter." Jamieson, in his Dictionary, defines it, "a trumpet." Mr Pitcairn, however, in his Criminal Trials, vol. ii. p. 30, by a variety of entries from the Treasurer's books, has satisfactorily shown, that "swesch" means "drum," and nothing but "drum." One of these, in 1576, is a payment of sixpence for "tua stickis to the swasche."

[b] There seem to have been a similar set of Italians among the musicians of the household of Edward VI. They are called "the four brethren Venetians, viz. John, Antonye, Jasper, and Baptiste." Burney's Hist., vol. iii. p. 5.

[c] Vol. vii. p. 95.

strel." Another expression, in this document, it may be still more necessary to explain. This Henry Rudeman is conjoined with the Italian "Histriones;" from which it might be supposed that these gentlemen had figured in a dramatic capacity, but for this idea there is no foundation. "It is observable," says Dr Percy,[a] "that our old monkish historians seldom use the words *cantator*, *citharœdus*, *musicus*, or the like, to express a *minstrel* in Latin, but either *mimus* HISTRIO *joculator*, or some other word that implies gesture." In another place,[b] he says, "*Histrionia* in middle Latinity only signifies the minstrel art." There is also a charter to appoint a king of the minstrels, a copy of which will be found in Blount's Law Dictionary, *v.* King, where the French word "ministraulx" is expressed by the Latin "histriones."

The words "feoda, stipendia, et devoria," may be translated "fees, salaries, and dues," although, at first sight, it might appear as if the word "feoda" was meant to signify heritable property. But, although the musicians of the chapel royal, (founded by James III. and extended by James IV.) as members of an ecclesiastical institution, were amply provided in benefices, annualrents, and teinds, we are not aware of any public endowments which were ever granted in behalf of the secular musicians of the royal household. The charters above specified would seem to show that their services were sometimes repaid by grants of land from the sovereign, with whom, particularly with the Jameses, whose love of music was not one of the least remarkable features in their character, they had the best opportunities of ingratiating themselves. James III., in particular, was notoriously lavish in his attentions to minstrels and artists of every kind, and it may be to this that we are to ascribe an enactment by which certain escheats and fines are appointed to be given to the minstrels along with the heralds. This is contained in a statute which was passed during the reign of the last mentioned prince, in 1471.[c] It is one of the sumptuary laws of which there

[a] Percy's Reliques, vol. i. Introduction, p. 42; also pp. 70, 72.

[b] Ibid. p. 54.

[c] 1471, ch. 46.

are a good many in our Statute Book, and commences by deploring the great poverty of the realm, and the expense attending the importation of silks; it then appoints that "na man sall wear silkes, in time coming, in doublet, gowne, or cloakes, except *knichtes, minstrelles, and herauld*s, without that the wearer of the samin may spend ane hundred pundes woorth of landrent, under the paine of amerciament to the King of twentie pound, als oft as they are foundin wearand silkes, *and escheiting the samin, to be given to the herauld*s *and minstrelles*," &c.

Here, we have heralds and minstrels placed precisely on the same footing; but this is by no means unusual. If we look back to the early part of their history, we see one and the same person at one time officiating in both capacities. Taillefer, the Norman knight, at the battle of Hastings, is described as performing the part of Herald-Minstrel; and being permitted to commence the attack, it is said that he advanced, singing the song of Roland, and was among the first that were slain. Carpentier[a] says that the French *Hiraux* were actually minstrels, and sung metrical tales at festivals. They might have been selected for this double capacity, as among the Greeks,[b] on account of the strength and clearness of their voices,[c] which equally qualified them for animating the soldiers in battle, and for making proclamations at tournaments and public ceremonies. Though afterwards disjoined,—as long as the "pomp and circumstance" of the feudal system lasted, the herald and the minstrel were never far removed from each other. The former was the official bearer of all despatches and messages of truce: in the discharge of these duties, he was invariably accompanied by his minstrels; and the persons of both, in time of war, were held inviolate.[d] They were a necessary part of the retinue of the feudal baron; and Froissart, in describing a Christmas entertainment, given by the Comte de Foix, in the 14th century, furnishes us with a specimen of the munificent reception which occasionally awaited them. "There were many mynstralls, as well of hys

[a] Du Cange. Suppl. tom. ii. p. 750.

[b] Iliad, b. v.

[c] Burney's History, vol. ii. p. 275.

[d] Froissart, c. 140.

own as of straungers, and eche of them dyd their devoyre in their faculties. The same day the Erle of Foix gave to heraulds and minstrelles the sum of fyve hundred frankes, and gave to the Duke of Tourayn's mynstreles gownes of cloth of gold furred with ermyne, valued at two hundred frankes."[a]

According to the very correct and comprehensive description which Bishop Percy[b] has given of the minstrels, they were "protected and caressed" *only* "as long as the spirit of chivalry subsisted; because," during that period, "their songs tended to do honour to the ruling passion of the times, and to encourage and foment a martial spirit." Whatever, therefore, might have been their pristine status, its lustre had been considerably diminished long before the passing of the statute to which we have above referred, and the privilege there reserved to them of wearing silks in doublet, gown, and cloak, with the share allotted to them along with the heralds, in the fines thereby imposed, were probably the last compliments which the Legislature ever thought of bestowing upon them.[c] To judge from the Statute Book, it must be confessed, that their respectability from the first was not a little equivocal; and it is pretty clear, that they could never boast of being, what is technically termed, "favourites of the law;" on the contrary, the body to which they belonged was the object of many severe penal enactments. Much as they were encouraged and admired, there seems to have been always an idea on the part of the legislature, that the members of this profession might be more creditably and usefully employed in some other sphere;

[a] Froissart, B. iii. c. 31, English Translation, London, 1525.

[b] The work of Percy, the father of this department of our literature, still furnishes the best account which has hitherto been given of this order of men; and although Mr Ritson has written a great deal on the same subject, and with a degree of acrimony towards the Right Reverend author which, we believe, he afterwards regretted, we cannot perceive that he has either invalidated his statements, nor, with all his antiquarian research, has he succeeded in adding a single new fact of any importance.

[c] In proof of this, see another Act of the Scotish Parliament, 1581, c. 113, against "the excesse of coastlie cleithing," in which *minstrels are not excepted,* though there is a general reservation of the officers and servants of the King's household.

and the solicitude of some of our oldest laws upon this head is not a little amusing. We have an ancient ordinance of Eugenius which requires, that "all idle pepill, sic as juglaris, minstralles, bardis, and scaffaris, either pass out of the realm, or find some craft to win their living;" and another of Macbeth, which contains an injunction to the same effect, with the addition, that—"gif they refuse, they sal be drawin like horse in the pleugh or harrowis." No doubt, we disclaim the genuineness of these antiquated statutes; but unfortunately, there are some of a more recent date, and of an authenticity not to be questioned, which are not only conceived in the same spirit, but which even exceed them in point of severity. Honoured and revered during a barbarous age, it was the singular fate of this class of men, at a period when the world became more enlightened, and the arts which they professed better known and more highly cultivated, to be thrust into juxta-position with the very dregs and refuse of society, and stigmatized as rogues, vagabonds, and sturdy beggars. By 1449, c. 21, it is ordained, "Gif there be onie that makis them fuiles,[a] and ar bairdes, or uthers sik like rinnares about, and gif onie sik be fundin, that they be put in the king's waird, or in his irons[b] for their trespasses, als lang as they haue any gudes of their awin to liue upon—that their eares be nailed to the trone,[c] or till ane uther tree, and their eare cutted off, and banished the cuntrie—and gif thereafter they be funden againe, that they be hanged." Afterwards, by an Act of James VI., (1579, c. 75,) the persons above described are included in the description of "maisterful, strang, and idle beggars," and adjudged, upon conviction, to be "scourged and burnt throw the eare with an hote iron." Under the same statute are comprehended "all idle persons ganging about in any countrie of this realme, using subtil, craftie, and unlauchful playes, as juglarie, fast and lous, and sik uthers, &c.; and all minstrelles, sangsters, and taletellers,[d] not avowed in speciall service be some of the

[a] Jesters, or Gestours.

[b] Stocks, or Jougs.

[c] The Pillory.

[d] The different departments of "minstrelles, sangsters, and taletellers," enumerated in the above statute, are so distinctly described by a French author, in defining the "Gay Science," as to

Lords of Parliament, or great burrowes, or be the head burrowes and cities for their common minstrelles."

At the present day, there can only be one opinion as to the inhuman nature of such regulations. About a hundred years, however, after the passing of this statute, their severity, particularly the enactment of death for the second offence, seemed to afford much satisfaction to an arbitrary King's Advocate during an arbitrary period of our annals. We allude to the "bluidy M'Kenzie," the name by which Sir George M'Kenzie was commonly known to his contemporaries, and which he justly owed to the sanguinary persecutions that took place under his official direction. Instead of being repealed, these laws were ratified by Act 16th, 3d Session, 1st Parl. Charles II., upon which occasion, in his Observations on the Statutes, we find the following undisguised and characteristic expression of opinion:[a]—" In this Act, EXCELLENT OVERTURES are set down for punishment of vagabonds, &c., who by this Act are appointed to be burnt in the ear and scourged for the first offence, and to suffer death for the second: so far can the repeating of a crime heighten its punishment even in mean crimes. Analogical to this Act is the title in the *Digest de Fugitivis*, where likewise many *excellent overtures* are proposed." This reminds us of the story of the boys and the frogs. The poor bards and minstrels might well say, what was only *an excellent overture* to Sir George, was *death* to them!

At the same time, it must be acknowledged, that the gangs of vagabonds who for ages infested the country, required the most determined and rigorous coercive measures for their repression. Even so late as

leave little doubt that the Scottish school of minstrelsy was founded upon that of France. The only department that seems to have been awanting with us was that of the Troubadours; unless we are to hold that their places were in some degree supplied by our old romancers, such as "Thomas the Rhymer" and "Hucheon of the Awle Ryall. "Le corps de la Jonglerie etoit formé des *Trouveres* ou *Troubadours* qui composoient les chansons, et parmi lesquels il y avoit des *Improvisateurs* comme on en trouve en Italie: des *Chanteours* ou *Chanteres* qui executoient ou chanteoient ces compositions; des *Conteurs* qui faisoient en vers ou en prose les contes, les recits, les histoires: des *Jongleurs* ou *Menestrels* qui accompagnoient de leur instrumens." Pref. Anthologie Franc. 1765, 8vo. p. 17.

[a] M'Kenzie's Observations, p. 190.

1698, our Scotish patriot, Fletcher of Saltoun,[a] computes the number of these loose and disorderly characters throughout Scotland at not fewer than 100,000; and these were persons who, without being robbers by profession, wandered incessantly from place to place, extorting, by force and insult, food and alms wherever they went. Fletcher describes them as an unspeakable oppression to the country, especially to the poor tenantry; and yet, what were they but a class of society common to all the feudal nations,—the wretched offspring of a political system which provided for the interest of certain privileged orders, to the entire neglect of the great mass of the community, and reared up the pride and the personal aggrandisement of the one upon the misery and degradation of the other!

We shall only here attempt to glance at some of the circumstances which appear to us to have had the effect of bringing the bards and minstrels into the disreputable predicament which we have above noticed. Mr Ritson has merely looked at the predicament itself, proceeding upon which, he treats the whole body with the most sovereign contempt. It is not easy to conceive any thing more inconclusive or short-sighted than such a mode of reasoning. If these people were haughty, insolent, overbearing, and even formidable,[b]—if they had increased so as to become an intolerable multitude, and to require the intervention of the law for their coercion—it is plain that they could not have been the contemptible, the dishonoured, or the ill-remunerated class which he describes. The inference we would draw is directly the reverse. Their arrogance could only have been engendered by the attentions and adulation so prodigally lavished upon them; the extent of their numbers could only have been occasioned by the success of their professional exertions,—the honours, the wealth, the power, and the privileges which attended them.

[a] Second Discourse on the Affairs of Scotland, p. 145.

[b] Walker (Irish Bards, p. 53) says, that at one time (towards the end of the sixth century) the number of the bards in Ireland was equal to one third of the male population of the island, and that they had become so arrogant that they would demand the golden buckle and pin which fastened the royal robes upon the monarch's breast. In regard to the Welsh bards, it became necessary, by a law, to restrain them from asking for the prince's horse, hawk, or greyhound. Jones' Welsh Bards, p. 28.

The obvious occasion, therefore, of the passing of such statutes as those we have mentioned, both in England and in Scotland, was the favour with which these persons were received,—a favour so great, that vagrants of every description were at all times ready to assume the character of the minstrel as a passport to the hospitality and attention which the latter never failed to receive. Thus, an Act of Edward I.[a] (1315,) sets out with this preamble—" Forasmuch as .... many idle persons, *under colour of mynstrelsie,* and going in messages, and other faigned business, have ben, and yet be receaved in other men's houses to meate and drynke, and be not therwith contented yf they be not largely consydered with gyftes of the lordes of the houses." It then goes on to restrain more than three or four minstrels in one day from resorting (uninvited) to the houses of prelates, earls, and barons,—and that none come to the houses of " meaner men" unless desired. A letter of Edward IV.[b] (1489) also complains that a number of persons falsely assuming the privileges of minstrels, had, in that capacity, levied heavy pecuniary exactions in different parts of the kingdom. This was exactly the situation of matters in Scotland. The same liberties were here taken on the same pretext; so that, instead of being derogatory to the profession, the statutes which we have cited were plainly intended to put an end to such abuses, and thereby to protect from encroachment the privileges and respectability of the higher class of artists; for which reason the individuals denounced are merely minstrels, songsters, and taletellers, " not avowed in speciall service be some of the lords of parliament, or great burrowes, or be the head burrowes, for their common minstralles."

We believe, therefore, that it was more on account of the irregularities and abuses which we have endeavoured to point out, than the misconduct of the general body, that " unlicenced minstrels" (for the degradation seems to have extended no farther) fell under the ban of those penal enactments.[c] By a British statute, passed in the course of the

[a] Percy's Reliques, vol. i. Introduction, pp. 69, 70.

[b] Percy, ibid.

[c] See contemporary English statutes of Queen Elizabeth, st. 39, c. 4, § 2; st. 43, c. 16.

last century, strolling players are classed under the same odious denomination, and the old bards and minstrels have even the advantage of them, in being associated, under the Act of James VI., with a respectable literary class of culprits, viz. " all vagabound schollers of the Universities of St Andrewes, Glasgow, and Aberdene, not licenced by the Rector and Deane of Facultie of the Universitie to ask almes !"

It is not improbable, however, that these marks of public opprobrium had had a baneful effect on the character of the profession in both countries. Percy, their great advocate, seems to have considered the Acts which were passed in the reign of Queen Elizabeth as a death-blow to the art, and says, that, towards the end of the sixteenth century, they had lost all credit, and were sinking into contempt and neglect. It has been remarked, that Blind Harry the minstrel, the author of " The actes and deides of the illuster and vailȝeand Campion, Schir William Wallace," came nearer to the character of an ancient minstrel than any one in the age in which he lived. He chanted his heroic strains before the princes and nobles of the land, and is described by Major[a] as one " qui historiarum recitatione coram principibus, victum et vestitum, quo dignus erat, nactus est." The period during which he flourished (especially the reigns of James III. and IV.) was one which afforded all the encouragement to minstrels and artists which could be derived from royal munificence and example. In the Lord High Treasurer's accounts, during the early part of this last mentioned prince's reign, there are payments occasionally set down to " Blind Harry," who must at this time have been a very old man. Another entry, a few years afterwards, offers additional proof of James IV.'s partiality for this species of entertainment—" April 10th, 1496.—Item, to the tua fithelaris[b] that sang ' Gray Steil' to the king, ix^{s}."[c]

[a] Lib. iv. c. 15.

[b] M. Fauchet (De l'Origine de la Langue Francaise, p. 72) defines *jongleurs* ou *jugleurs*, c'est a dire *menestriers chantans avec la viole*.

[c] This " Gray Steil" was a highly popular romance. Mr Laing, in whose " Early Metrical Tales" it has been published, says, that it " would seem, along with the poems of Sir David

We find the bards alluded to, in no very respectful terms, in the "Cockelbie Sow," the "Houlate," (a production of the reign of James II.,) Dunbar's "Flyting," the works of Sir David Lyndsay, and other poems of the fifteenth and sixteenth centuries; and the last occasions in which they appear to have figured in their ancient capacity at the courts of our monarchs, were not nearer our own times than the reigns of Malcolm III. and Alexander III. At the coronation of each of these sovereigns, a bard or sennachie stepped forward and chanted a Gaelic poem containing a recital of the king's ancestors from the reign of Fergus I. After this, they were chiefly, if not altogether, confined to the establishments of our Celtic chiefs. Rhoderick Morison or Dall, a blind man, was perhaps the last of any note or respectability. He was bard and harper to the Laird of Macleod at Dunvegan Castle about the middle and towards the end of the seventeenth century,[a] and Mr Macdonald observes, that he was born a gentleman, and lived on that footing in the family. Mr Gunn says, that some of his compositions are still extant. After this, we hear of another of the name of Murdoch Macdonald, a pupil of this Rhoderick or Rory Dall, who was bard or harper in the family of Maclean of Coll, where he remained till 1734. The author whom we have last quoted rather thinks that there were no professional harpers bred in the Highlands, except in connexion with such establishments as these, and that if there were any, they had probably gone to the Lowlands to exercise their profession there. We have no doubt, that before the beginning of the last century there were many of these wandering bards and minstrels; and the

Lyndsay, and the histories of Robert the Bruce and of Sir William Wallace, to have formed the standard production of the vernacular literature of the country." It is noticed also by the same gentleman, that "in a curious manuscript volume formerly in the possession of Dr Burney, entitled, "An Playing Booke for the Lute—noted and collected" at Aberdeen by Robert Gordon, in the year 1627, is the air of "Gray Steel;" and there is a satirical poem on the Marquis of Argyle, printed in 1686, which is said "to be composed in Scotish rhyme," and "is appointed to be sung *according to the tune of 'Old Gray Steel.'*" See also Ellis' Metrical Romances, vol. iii. p. 308.

[a] Macdonald's Essay on the Highland Music, p. 11. Gunn's Enquiry, pp. 95, 97.

closing scene of their career is well depicted by Martine, (who is supposed to have been secretary to Archbishop Sharpe,) in his *Reliquiæ Divi Andreæ.*[a]—" The bards (says he) at length degenerated by degrees into common ballad makers; for they gave themselves up to the making of mystical rhymes, and to magic and necromancy. To our father's time and ours something remained, and still does, of this ancient order; and they are called by others and by themselves, Jockies, who go about begging, and use still to recite the sluggornes of most of the true ancient surnames of Scotland from old experience and observation. Some of them I have discoursed, and found to have reason and discretion. One of them told me that there were not now twelve of them in the whole of the isle; but he remembered the time when they abounded, so as, at one time, he was one of five that usuallie met at St Andrews."[b]

In the course of our examination of the musical instruments anciently in use in this country, we have been led into an apparent digression respecting the personal history of those for whose taste and genius it was reserved, to evolve their hidden harmonies, and to elicit from them those " sounds and sweet airs" in which our ancestors took delight,—we say *apparent*, because, in reality, the two subjects are necessarily and insepar-

[a] P. 3.

[b] In " Bishop Percy's Letters to George Paton" the antiquary, we observe the following memorandum of the latter, written about the year 1776:—" A set of beggars travelled up and down the south and western parts of Scotland, and were never denied alms by any one: they always carried alongst with them a horn, and were styled *Jocky* with the Horn, or Jocky who travels broad Scotland. The rhyme used by them to be enquired after." The rhyme was of some consequence; but we fear it has perished along with its reciters. Being perfectly free, therefore, to form all manner of conjectures, the answer which we would propound to Mr Paton's conundrum is, that these beings in " questionable shape," whose mysterious appearance seems to have so startled the imagination of the venerable gentleman, were no other than *the lastof the bards!* Their description completely corresponds with Martine's " Jockies who went about begging." *Jockie*, it may be observed, is most likely a corruption of " *Joculator*." They appear also to have been rhymers. The horn, though not so easily explained, is still another link of connexion with the olden time; and we can scarcely look upon the circumstance of their never being denied alms any where, in any other light than as the last lingering remnant of that hospitality which our ancestors never withheld from those whose exertions contributed so much to their enjoyment; and, as Percy says, " supplied the want of more refined entertainment."

ably connected with each other; and it would be as vain to attempt to furnish a complete account of the history of our music without reviewing that of our bards and minstrels, as it would be to trace the rise and progress of our poetry—our romances—our popular songs. It is very doubtful whether materials are extant sufficient to render such an object at all attainable; but if they were, we need hardly say, that they would demand a degree of analysis and research far beyond our present limits. We shall be satisfied, therefore, should the few hints which we have thrown out conduce, however slightly, to advance the main object of our inquiries.

As the harp was so favourite an instrument of the Scoto-Saxon minstrels during the middle ages, its use in Scotland could never have been confined to the Highlands, as Mr Ritson supposes,[a] although it certainly continued to subsist there for a much greater length of time than in the Lowland part of the country. In England, it was a common instrument in the time of Chaucer, that is to say, during the fourteenth century, and Mr Ritson says,[b] " it continued in use till after the reign of Queen Elizabeth, possibly till the civil wars, but was long held in the lowest estimation; since that time it has been entirely laid aside, or at least very rarely used as an English instrument." As to its having been held in the lowest estimation, we would caution our readers against too hastily adopting this notion. It might have been, as the learned author observes, " an ordinary retainer in taverns and such like places"—so is the violin, one of the most eminent of modern instruments. It was also frequently professed by the blind, because it offered perhaps the only means of support to persons who laboured under that misfortune; " blind harper," accordingly, might have become a term of ridicule—so is " blind fiddler" in the present day; nay, the harp might have been a less courtly or fashionable instrument than the lute or the virginals,—the secret of this, however, may have lain in the circumstance that a competent knowledge of the latter was more easily acquired by those who pos-

[a] Ritson's Ancient Songs, p. 41.

[b] Ibid.

sessed only a slight acquaintance with the art. An instrument so noble, so susceptible of expression, and variety of effect, as the harp, could never have sunk into the lowest estimation ; and at the very time to which Mr Ritson points, as the period of its degradation,—the fourteenth century,—we find a French poet, (Machau,)[a] in a poem entitled "Le Dict de la Harpe," praising it, as an instrument too good "to be profaned in taverns or places of debauchery;" (and) saying that "it should be used by knights, esquires, clerkes, persons of rank, and ladies with plump and beautiful hands; and that its courteous and gentle sounds should be heard only by the elegant and the good."

In Scotland, during the first part of the fifteenth century, if monarchical example could have contributed to render this instrument fashionable, something might have been expected from our James I., who, although he played upon many other instruments, is reported to have chiefly excelled on this. Fordun[b] says he touched it like another Orpheus; and Major[c] describes his performance on it as surpassing that of the most skilful Irish and Highland harpers of his day. In this remark, it is implied, that the latter were at this time the most successful cultivators of the harp, a fact of which we have no doubt; not so much from what we gather from Major, as from other historical testimonies; for the truth is, that this author is somewhat loose in his assertions on this head;[d] but greatly as these Highland harpers excelled their Lowland brethren, the harp might still have continued in use among the latter for nearly as long as it did on the other side of the Tweed.

Sir Walter Scott in his Border Minstrelsy[e] tells us that the ballad of the Lochmaben harper is "the most modern ballad in which the harp as a Border instrument of music is found to occur;" but not having any clue

[a] Burney's History of Music, vol. ii. p. 263.

[b] B. xvi. c. 28.

[c] B. vi. c. 14.

[d] As an example, he writes, "in former times, the harp, covered with leather, and strung with wire, was the favourite instrument, (in the Highlands;) but at present *it is quite lost*"—a statement which, at the time to which it refers—the beginning of the sixteenth century—we know to have been inconsistent with the fact.

[e] Vol. i. p. 70.

to the age of the ballad, we can gather nothing more from this statement than what may be collected from other productions of the same kind, such as "Thomas the Rhymer and the Queen of Elfland," and "Binnorie, or the Cruel Sister," viz. that the harp at one time was a common instrument in this part of the country; and many passages in our Lowland poetry might be cited to the same effect. Douglas, for example, in his "Palice of Honour," alludes to it.—

"In modulation hard I play and sing,
Taburdoun, pricksang discant, countering;
Cant organe figuration and gemmell,
On croud, lute, *harpe*, with monie gudlie spring."

The harp, also, figures among the instruments with which Queen Anne was greeted on her public entry into Edinburgh in 1590, celebrated by Burel.—

"Organs and regals thair did carpe,
With their gay golden glittring strings;
Thair wes the hautbois and the *harpe*,
Playing most sweit and pleasant springs."

We likewise see from the Lord High Treasurer's accounts,[a] that besides the occasional engagement of eminent harp performers from a distance,[b] harpers were constantly retained as part of the royal household.

Leyden[c] thought it probable that the Irish harp or *clarseach*, strung with wire, (and generally covered with leather,) rather than the Welsh harp strung with hair, (or gut,) was that with which the Scotish Lowlanders were acquainted. For this opinion no authority is given; and

[a] See Appendix.

[b] "July 11th, 1512, Item, to Odonelis Ireland man harpar, *quhilk past away with him at the king's command*, vii. lib." Lord High Treasurer's accounts.

[c] Introduction to Complaynt, p. 152.

we confess that the result of our own inquiries into this matter would tend to an opposite conclusion. There is an old MS. romance quoted by this author,[a] "Clariodus and Meliades," where, in enumerating the instruments of a concert, it is mentioned that

"Out of Irland there was ane *clersche*."

We should think, therefore, that the *clersche*, *clarseach* or *clarscha*, imported into this country by the Scoto-Irish ancestors of our Highland countrymen, had formed their proper national instrument; indeed, the word "clair-schochar" seems always to have been used to signify either an Irish or a Highland harper. Thus, in the treasurer's accounts for 3d January 1533-34, there is entered a payment as follows:—"Item, deliverit to the kingis grace, quhilk his hienes gaue to ane Ireland clairschochar, x lb." We observe, also, that there is a distinction sometimes drawn between the harpers and the clarschochars. In the above accounts for 14th April 1505, there is a payment to "Alexander harper, Pate harper clarscha, his son the Ersch clarscha, &c. ilk man, ix. s.—— iii. lb. xii. s.;" and in the enumeration of performers, on 1st January 1507, "clarscharis," as well as "harpers," are particularised. From these data we should infer, that the instrument chiefly employed in the Lowlands was the harp strung with horse hair or gut, and that the Irish and the Highlanders had been nearly the exclusive cultivators of the clarsach. It is clear, however, that both of these instruments were made use of by the latter. In "certeyne matters concerning the realme of Scotland," &c., "as they were anno Domini 1597," (London, 1603,) it is said—"They (meaning the Highlanders) delight much in musicke, but chiefly in harps and clairschoes of their own fashion. The strings of the clairschoes are made of brasse wire, and the strings of the harps of sinews, which strings they strike, either with their nayles growing long, or else with an instrument appointed for that use." We may observe in passing, that what we have here quoted is merely a new version by

[a] Introduction to Complaynt, p. 157.

this author of what Buchanan has stated on the same subject in his History of Scotland, Book I.

As to the ancient compass of the harp, Jones[a] would represent it as having possessed a scale of twenty-six diatonic notes, even as far back as the sixth century. This he deduces from certain Welsh melodies still extant, and which he says were played in the year 520, although upon this statement we can place no great reliance. Mr Gunn's observations on this head are worthy of more attention. This eminent professional gentleman, in the year 1805, at the request of the Highland Society of Scotland, examined two old Caledonian harps belonging to the family of Robertson of Lude, one of which had been presented by Queen Mary to a lady who had married into that family; and the other, an instrument of great antiquity,[b] quite as old, "if not older," than the celebrated harp of Brian Boiromh, the monarch of Ireland, who was slain in 1014,[c] and which is preserved in the Museum of the University of Dublin. The Caledonian harp is very similar to the latter, although its proportions are somewhat larger, being thirty-eight and a half inches in height, with thirty string holes, while the Irish harp is thirty-two inches high, and seems to have carried twenty-eight strings. In describing the Caledonian harp, Mr Gunn[d] mentions that the front arm is not perpendicular to the sounding board, but that its upper part, together with the top arm, is turned considerably towards the left, in order to leave a greater opening for the voice of the performer. This peculiarity, and a fact which is well known, viz. that the Caledonian, Irish, and Welsh harpers held their harps at the left side, and struck the upper strings with their left hand, render it probable that the accompaniment of the voice formed the chief province of the instrument. Mr Gunn[e] remarks, that there is no reason to suppose that the old harpers did not tune their harps to the diatonic scale, "as all the music still extant in Ireland and the Highlands (he might have

[a] Welsh Bards, p. 103.

[b] Gunn's Enquiry, p. 12.

[c] See Walker's Memoirs of the Irish Bards, p. 60.

[d] Gunn's Enquiry, p. 8.

[e] Ibid. p. 22.

added Wales) is reducible to that scale." O'Kane, the last Irish harper of any great eminence heard in Scotland, (about 1770,) tuned his harp on that system; and from Mr Bunting's account of the meeting of Irish harpers at Belfast, in 1792,[a] it appears that all the harpers who attended upon that occasion, though from parts of the country distant from each other, and taught by different masters, tuned their instruments upon the same principle. As the diatonic scale only gives two intervals of a semitone within the compass of each octave, some contrivance, of course, was necessary, in order to produce such accidental sharps and flats as might occasionally occur.[b] This was, first of all, effected by the performer running his hand up close to the comb, and dexterously stopping the note with the thumb, while he played it with the finger; and afterwards, by the invention of *double* and *triple* harps, by which the number of strings were multiplied, so as to embrace the whole series of the chromatic, as well as the diatonic system. But these improvements are not supposed to have been introduced earlier than the fourteenth or fifteenth century; and it was only about a hundred years ago that M. Simon of Brussels superseded their necessity by inventing the method, which has since been practised, of producing the half tones by pedals, and thus brought back the instrument to nearly its ancient simplicity of construction and number of strings.[c]

If we have dwelt at great length on the history of this instrument, it is because it formed the leading feature of the minstrelsy of the middle ages—not only diffusing its charms at the courts of princes, and in the houses of the nobility upon all festive occasions, but constituting a source of delightful and innocent recreation to all classes of the people, in the tranquillity of domestic life. Giraldus pictures such a scene, when speaking of the primitive manners of the Welsh, about the year 1188, and their hospitality to strangers, he tells us, that " those who ar-

a Bunting's " Ancient Irish Music." Introduction.

b Jones's Welsh Bards, p. 103, *et seq.*

c Burney's Present State of Music in Germany, Netherlands, and United Provinces, vol. i. p. 59.

rive at an early hour are entertained with the conversation of young women, and the music of the harp till evening; for here every family has its damsels, and harps provided for this very purpose. Every family too is here well skilled in the knowledge of that instrument."[a] And Major, in speaking of our Highlanders, says, that one of their amusements at their firesides consisted in the telling of tales, the wildest and most extravagant imaginable, and that the music of the harp was another. Giraldus describes the bishops, abbots, and "holy men" of his time, as so partial to this instrument, that they actually used to carry it about with them, and piously delight themselves with its strains.[b] We observe that he confines this remark to Ireland, the hierarchy of which had not at that time been completely brought under subjection to the see of Rome.[c] It was ordained by a canon of Edgar, the Saxon monarch, in 960, and there was passed a similar decreet of the Roman Council in 679, "that no priest be a common rhymer, or play on any musical instrument by himself, or with any other men, but be wise and reverend as became his order." These ordinances, however, even in England, had not been much attended to—not that we ever heard of the English (and far less of the Scotish) Catholic clergy having been classed among the number of "those who handled the harp;" but they must have paid but little regard to the former of these regulations, if Hawkins[d] is correct in considering them as, "for the most part, the authors and composers of those songs and ballads, with the tunes adapted to them, which were the ordinary amusement of the common people."

From the eleventh to the beginning of the fourteenth century, the troubadours and minstrels of France exercised the chief influence over the music as well as the literature of Europe. Dr Burney[e] says, that it was about the twelfth century when Provençal poetry, having arrived at

[a] Cambriæ Descriptio, c. x.

[b] "Cytharas circumferre et in eis modulando pie delectari consueverint."

[c] Dr Ledwich's Antiquities of Ireland, p. 240.

[d] Vol. ii. p. 88.

[e] Vol. ii. p. 233.

its greatest point of perfection, was begun to be sung to the sound of instruments; and that " at this period, violars, or performers on the vielle and viol; juglars, or flute-players; musars, or players on other instruments; and comics, or comedians, abounded all over Europe." This swarm of poet-musicians, who were formerly comprehended in France under the general title of *jongleurs*, travelled from province to province, singing their verses at the courts of kings, princes, and other great personages, who rewarded them with clothes, horses, arms, and money, which, though sometimes given unwillingly, served to augment the number of these strolling bards. If these minstrels had extended their excursions in the manner above described, a fact which we see no reason to doubt, they must have frequently visited Scotland, and disseminated, throughout that country, a knowledge both of their music and their musical instruments. During the reigns of Edgar, Alexander I., and David I., that is to say, from 1097 to 1153, particularly during the reign of the last mentioned monarch, who was considered by his subjects as almost a Frenchman, great efforts were used to engraft the more polished manners and customs of the Normans upon the rude parent-stock of the Scotish people; and from the reign of William the Lion, with whom, as we have previously had occasion to remark, our first direct national negotiation was opened with France—towards the end of the twelfth century—down to the reign of our unfortunate Queen Mary, the two countries continued the almost uninterrupted political friends and allies of each other. It is to the French, therefore, that we must ascribe the importation of most of the musical instruments with which our ancestors were acquainted.

The " viol" is described as having been so favourite an instrument with the minstrels of France, as to have disputed pre-eminence with the harp, to which it was frequently used as an accompaniment. Though, to all appearance, wholly unknown to the ancients, its existence in that country has been traced as far back as the eighth century.[a] It seems, during the earlier periods of its history, to have differed considerably in

[a] Burney, vol. ii. p. 264.

form from the modern violin, and to have had no fixed number of strings as at present; at least we see it in old delineations from the twelfth till the sixteenth century, represented with three, four, five, and even a greater number of strings.

It is important to remark, that in the *Fabliaux*, the instrument which is designated by the word "*vielle*," is that which has been above described, the "viol" or "violin," and not, as has been sometimes imagined, the more modern French *vielle*, or hurdy-gurdy—although, from an engraving of the latter, which we observe in La Borde,[a] taken from a MS. of the fourteenth century, it would also seem to be of some antiquity. The strings of this instrument, as most of our readers know, are kept in vibration by the friction of a wheel, which acts the part of a *plectrum* or bow. Hence it was called *rote* or *riote*, and, as such, we find it alluded to by English as well as French poets.[b] Gower, in his *Confessio Amantis*—

"——— Harpe, citole, and *riote*,
With many a tewne and many a note."

Chaucer also says of his mendicant friar—

"Wel coude he singe and plaien on the *rote*."

It is in this capacity, as the *Lyra Mendicorum*, that it still continues to figure at the present day, though seldom, if ever, in the hands of the natives of Britain. Perhaps this might have been its principal use in former times with us; although, from our closer habits of intimacy with our Gallic friends and allies, we should have expected it to have been more common in this country than in England. We certainly observe several tunes in the Skene MS. which, from their construction and compass, bear all the traces of their having been composed for this instru-

[a] Essai sur la Musique, vol. i. p. 305.

[b] Burney, vol. ii. p. 270.

ment; but it seems to have been very seldom noticed by any of our writers, and at the present moment, the only mention we recollect of it is in the following line of the Houlate, (1450,)

"The *rote* and the recordour, the ribus, the rift."

The notice which we selected from the treasurer's accounts of the payment in the reign of James IV. to the "tua fithelaris that sang 'Gray Steil' to the king," shows that our Scottish minstrels had imitated those of France by making use of the viol as an accompaniment to the voice. The instruments were most probably "rebecs" or violins, with three strings; at least La Borde says,[a] that these were most anciently in use, and that this was the description of violin alluded to by the French romancers and troubadours.[b] That these "rebecs" were very common in Scotland during the sixteenth century, would appear from the following passage in Brantome's "*Dames Illustres*," where he describes Queen Mary's reception by her Scottish subjects at Holyroodhouse on her arrival from France. Brantome accompanied her, and was no doubt an eye-witness of the scene.—"Estant logée en bas en l'Abbaye de l'Islebourg, vindrent sous la fenestre cinq ou six cents marauts de la ville, luy donner aubade de meschants violons et *petits rebecs, dont il n'y en a faute en ce pays là;* et se mirent à chanter pseaumes, tant mal chantez et si mal accordez, que rien plus. He! quelle musique et quel repos pour sa nuit." John Knox's description of these "*marauts*," or "raggamuffins," as Brantome styles them, is somewhat different. *He* calls them "a cumpanie of most honest men who," he says, "with instruments of musick, and with musicians, gave thair salutatiouns at hir chalmer windo. The melodie, (he adds,) as sche alledged, lyked hir weill, and sche willed the sam to be continewed sum nychts efter with grit diligence." We should rather think, however, that this must have been a considerable stretch of complaisance on the part of her majesty. Her taste had been fashioned in

[a] Essai sur la Musique, vol. i. p. 357.

[b] "A taberet, a luyte, and a *rebecc*," constituted the musical establishment of the Earl of Northumberland in the reign of Henry VIII.; and in the list of the household bands of Edward VI. and Elizabeth, provision is made for a "rebecke," one and two in number, distinct from the "vyalls," who were a more numerous body, consisting of eight performers.

the court of France, not after the Scotish, but the French and Italian models; and we have no reason to believe that our Scotish violars were at this time very distinguished either in point of musical skill or taste; although it is evident that the violin, or, to speak more correctly, the "viol," had been much cultivated in Scotland for many years prior to this.[a] Our readers will observe from the treasurer's accounts, that our sovereigns were seldom without "fithelaris" at their musical performances. On "Pasch Tiss-day," *i.e.* the Tuesday of Easter week, of the year 1505, we see five of them engaged. They are also included among the performers in 1507, on New-year's-day; and from the entries in 1538 and 1542, it would seem, that at least four players on the "veolis" were retained among the musicians of the royal household. Those who are curious in these matters, will also have the satisfaction of finding that the names of some of them are commemorated in the same record. In 1530 and 1533, "Cabroch the fidlar" appears to have taken the lead; and afterwards, in 1538, we find "Jakkis," *i.e.* "*Jacques* Collumbell," (whom, from his name, we take to have been a Frenchman,) singled out as the most distinguished of our artists in this department.[b]

On the night of the 20th February 1436, when our talented monarch, James I., fell by the ruthless hands of assassins, he is described in the contemporaneous narrative to have passed his tyme "yn redyng of romans, yn syngyng and pypynge, in harpyng, and yn other honest

[a] The "Violis" spoken of in the text were in several respects different from the modern violin. Their form was not precisely the same. They had six strings, which were tuned chiefly by fourths, and the finger board was fretted like that of the guitar. Burney says, that even so late as the year 1600, instruments of the violin kind were but little used in concert, or very ill played; and that Mersenne, in his "Harmonie Universelle," published in 1636, was the first writer on music who seemed to appreciate their excellence, and ventured to proclaim his opinion of their superiority over all other instruments. Violins, tenors and basses, are supposed to be of Italian origin, and never to have been known in this country until Charles II. introduced them into his band "instead of the viols, lute, and cornets, of which the court band used to consist." Burney, vol. iii. p. 174, 584. Hawkins, vol. iv. p. 116.

[b] In 1535, our great viol-maker seems to have been an Englishman, and from the price paid for his materials, as stated in the following entry, one would think that his wood must have been imported from abroad.—"Item, to the kingis grace to Richard Hume, Inglismanne, quhilk suld mak violis to the kingis grace, to by stuffe for the samin, xx lib."

solaces of grete pleasance and disport." This prince must have been an extraordinary proficient in music; and Bower, in his continuation of Fordun,[a] enumerates the following instruments upon which he could perform,—the tabour, the bagpipe, the psaltery, the organ, the flute, the harp, the trumpet, and the shepherd's reed;[b] in addition to which, Boethius mentions the lute—"He was richt crafty (says Bellenden his translator) in playing baith of the *lute* and harp," &c.

These instruments, along with others, are particularized in the Houlate, (1450,) in a stanza from which we have already made a citation.—

"All thus our ladye thai lofe, with lylting and lift,
Menstralis and musicians, mo than I mene may:
The *psaltry*,[c] the *citholis*,[d] the soft *atharift*,
The *croude*[e] and the *monycordis*, the *gythornis*[f] gay;
The *rote* and the *recordour*,[g] the *ribus*, the *rift*,
The *trump* and the *taburn*,[h] the *tympane*,[i] but tray;

[a] B. xvi. c. 28.

[b] The expressions in the original are, "in tympano et choro, in psalterio et organo, tibiâ et lyrâ, tubâ et fistulâ."

[c] The psaltery is frequently mentioned by Chaucer and the old French and English romancers. It was also an instrument known to the ancients; but so much difference of opinion prevails as to its antique form, that we shall not venture to say what *it* resembled. The modern instrument of that name was in the form of a flat unequal-sided figure, like a triangle, with the top cut off it. It had three rows of strings, and was played either with the fingers or with *plectra*. La Borde's Essai, vol. i. p. 303.

[d] Probably the "citole," or "cistole," a sort of "dulcimer," from "cistella," a little box.

[e] We need hardly observe, that the "crowde" was the viol or violin—the name, as well as the instrument, being obviously derived from the ancient British "crwth."

[f] Gythornis, *i.e.* "guitars." Chaucer generally spells this word "giternes," and "getrons." The "citterne," or "cistrum," a similar, but inferior instrument, is often confounded with the guitar. See Hawkins, vol. iv. p. 112.

[g] A species of flageolet, the tone of which was particularly soft and sweet. Milton speaks of—

"Flutes and *soft* recorders."

[h] The tabour, a small drum beaten with a drumstick, in which respect, and in its being covered with parchment at both ends, it differed from the *tambour de Basque*, with which it is often confounded.

[i] Tympane, *i.e.* the drum.

The *lilt-pype*[a] and the *lute*, the *cithill*[b] and *fift*,
The *dulsate* and the *dulsacordis*, the *schalm*[c] of affray;
The amyable *organis* usit full oft;
Clarions loud knellis,
Portatibis[d] and *bellis;*
Cymbaellonis in the cellis,
That soundis so soft."

The reader will find some of these instruments explained in the foot-notes; others, such as the "atharift," the "ribus," and the "rift," we admit our inability to define. But we must say a few words in regard to the "monycordis," a name liable to some ambiguity, and which has never hitherto been explained or illustrated.

There are various interesting notices relative to this instrument, some of which we shall shortly bring under the reader's attention. We may mention, in the meantime, that the following, which we lately obtained from the General Register House, is among the latest, while it is certainly not one of the least curious.

[a] "Lilt-pype" certainly did not signify "bagpipe," as Ritson supposes. It was, more probably, the shepherd's pipe, or other instrument on which were performed the tunes called "lilts." These, it will be observed, bear no resemblance whatever to bagpipe tunes; neither do they correspond with the description which Dr Jamieson, in his Dictionary, gives of the "lilt." Instead of being a "cheerful air," as defined by him, judging from the specimens which the Skene MS. has brought to light, the "lilt" would rather seem to have been an air of a plaintive character, and from the peculiar vein of melody which runs through such of them as we have seen, we should think that they must have sprung from the pastoral districts of the Lowlands of Scotland.

[b] The "cythill" may be here used as a quaint term to denote *cythara*, or harp: if not, we must suppose that all mention of the last instrument was here omitted—an idea of which Ritson has availed himself to argue that the harp was not in general use in the Lowlands at this time.

[c] Schalms and clarions are fully explained *infra*, p. 114, 115, 116.

[d] Portatibus, *i.e.* portativi, or regals, were a kind of diminutive portable organ, formerly much used in public processions. Hawkins speaks of it as being not uncommon in Germany even in his day.—The regal was borne through the streets on a man's shoulders; when the procession stopped, it was set down upon a stool; the performer then stepped forward—played upon it; and the man that carried it blew the bellows. Hawkins, vol. ii. p. 449.

Extract from the Testament of Edward Henrysoun, " Maifter of the Sang Scole of Edinburgh, and Prebendare of St Gelis Queir, quha deceist 15 Aug. 1579. [Recorded 6 Nov. 1579]."

" Item, thair wes awin to the said umquhile Edward Henrysoun, be the gude toun of Edinburgh, for bigging of the Sang Scole, xlj lib.

" Item, I leif to my sone, James Henrysoun, my gown, my coitt, my bumbasie dowblet, and the bodie of poldavie, my kist, my bybill, ANE PAIR OF MONYCORDIS, my hat, thre of the best sarkis, ane pair of round scheittis, foure serviottis," &c.

The cause of the ambiguity of this word " monycordis" is, that it is sometimes spelt, as in the above extract, and at other times " monochord,"—modes of orthography which suggest very different ideas,—the last being descriptive of an instrument of one string, and the other of—the very reverse—a " polychord," or instrument of many strings. What renders it the more necessary that we should here enter into some explanation is, that, although the " monochord," or " monycordis," appears to have been much employed during the fifteenth and sixteenth centuries, we have no where seen any attempt to define its nature ; and we believe that for these many years no very definite ideas have been attached to its name.

There are no fewer than three instruments to which the name of " monochord" has been applied. The first and oldest is the harmonic Canon of Pythagoras, which was latterly much used by the Greeks. It consisted literally of a single string; and the instrument or frame to which it was attached was marked off by sections and subdivisions, corresponding with the intervals of the scale. There were three bridges, two stationary, one of which stood at each end ; the other, which was placed between the two, was moveable, and, by being applied to the different divisions of the scale, showed the relation which the sounds bore to the length of the string, and, in this way, familiarised the student with the series of intervals which it embraced. This instrument was not employed in the performance of music. But there was a one-stringed instrument called a "monochord," or "unichord," used for that purpose, not by the ancients, but by the moderns of the sixteenth and seventeenth centuries, of which Mersenne and other authors have given a description.[a] Another appellation by which it was known was the Marine Trumpet, though the reason why it was so called does not very distinctly appear; unless, as is supposed by some, it had been invented by a person of the name of Marini. It seems to have been about five feet long, of a pyramidal shape, fitted up with a finger board and bridge, and played upon like a double-bass, with a bow, except that the performer, as is sometimes done in the execution of concertos on the last mentioned instrument at the present day, confined himself to the extracting of the *harmonic* sounds; by which means, effects were produced similar to the notes of the trumpet.[b] We mention this strange instrument, because it bears the same name with that under consideration. As for the thing itself, there is no evidence, and no probability, that it was ever used in Scotland, or that it ever became much known in France or in any other country.

The "monicordis," or "monochord," used by our ancestors, was certainly not an instrument of a single string; but, on the contrary, one of the class of instruments most remarkable for the multiplicity of their strings. It seems to have been the same with the "clavichord," or "clarichord," and as such to have been one of the precursors of the spinet, the virginals, the harpsichord, and the piano-forte of modern times.

Michael Prætorius, who lived in the latter part of the sixteenth and beginning of the seventeenth centuries, in the second volume of his work, "Syntagma Musicum," &c., under the head of "Organographia," p. 60, expressly says, that "the clavicord was invented and disposed *after the model of the monochord.*" This *may* be correct; but we find the former designation, "clavichord," used at a very remote period. Mr

[a] Mersennus de Instr. Harm., lib. i. prop. 37, 38. See also La Borde's Essai, vol. i. p. 279.

[b] See a Paper on the Trumpet and Trumpet-Marine, by the Hon. Francis Roberts, in the Philosophical Transactions for 1692. See also Hawkins' Hist. of Music, vol. iv. p. 121.

Strutt, in his "Manners and Customs of the English,"[a] makes the following extract from an old MS. book of instructions for music, as old as the reign of Henry IV.

"Who pleythe on the harp, he should pley trew;
Who syngythe a song, let his voyce be tunable;
Who wrestythe the *clavycorde*, mystunyng eschew;
Who blowthe a trompet, let hys wynd be mesurabyle;
For instruments in themself be firm and stable,
And of trowthe, would trouthe to every man's song,
Tune them then trewly, for in them is no wrong."

Unless, therefore, Mr Strutt has been in some mistake as to the age of this MS., the "clavycorde" must have been in existence some time between the years 1399 and 1413; and, if so, as our James I. was educated at the court of Henry IV., it is rather extraordinary that the "clavycorde" or the "monocord" should not have been one of the many instruments upon which he performed. A century posterior, it seems to have been a favourite with his descendant, James IV. On the 10th April 1497, in his treasurer's accounts, we read of a payment of 9s. to "John Hert, for bering *a pare of* MONICORDIS *of the kings* fra Aberdene to Strivelin." On the 15th October 1504, there is a payment of 18s. "that samyn nycht in Dunnottir to the chield playit on the *monocordis* be the kingis command;" and in the circumstantial account which John Young, Somerset herald, gives of James IV.'s nuptials, he is described as having entertained his royal bride, first of all by his performance on the "clarychordes," and afterwards on the lute.[b] From these and other notices, we should think it probable, that at this time "clavichord" and "monochord" had been used synonymously.

[a] Vol. iii. p. 116.

[b] Leland's Collectanea, vol. iv. pp. 284, 285. We are surprised to find a writer so well informed as Mr Gunn representing the word "clarychordes," in the passage to which we have above referred, as probably a typographical error, or alteration of "clarsho," (Enquiry, p. 72.) It is possible, however, that the word "clarichord," the etymology of which is not so evident, may have arisen from error or indistinctness in the spelling of the word "clavichord."

Julius Cæsar Scaliger, who died in 1558, in the first Book of his "Pöetices," chapter 48, says, that the original of the "Monochord" was the *simmicum*, an instrument of thirty-five strings, supposed to have been invented by *Simmicus*, (the ancient Greek musician;) and in the same passage, which, as it does not appear to have been noticed by Burney, Hawkins, Martini, or any of our common authorities, we here subjoin, the connexion between this instrument and the "clavicymbalum," "harpsichord," and "spinet," is distinctly traced. "Fuit et simi[a] commentum illud, quod ab eo simicum appellatum, quinque et triginta constabat chordis, à quibus eorum origo, quos nunc *monochordos* vulgus vocat. In quibus, ordine digesta, plectra subsilientia reddunt sonos. Additæ dein plectris corvinarum pennarum cuspides ex æreis filis expressiorem eliciunt harmoniam, me puero, clavicymbalum et harpichordum, nunc ab illis mucronibus, spinetam nominant."

It is to be observed, that Du Cange, in his Glossary, confounds the "monochord" with the "manichordion"—an instrument of more recent invention, and very little different in construction from the harpsichord.[b] Farther, he describes both of them as being instruments of "one string;" and Carpentier, although, in his Supplement, he notices the former error, seems to have no idea of the distinction between the monochord of the ancients, and that of the fifteenth century.

From what has been already observed, it is obvious that "monycordis" was a corruption of "monochord." It is certainly very extraordinary that the latter term (like *lucus a non lucendo)* should come to signify something so very opposite from what is implied in the word itself, but there can be no doubt of the fact. The idea of Scaliger that the *simmicum*, a species of lyre, was the prototype of these keyed instruments, may probably have had no other foundation than the circumstance of its having been furnished with a greater number of strings than any other instrument of antiquity; we should rather look for the history of this and

[a] This word seems to be a mistake for "simmici."

[b] Mersennus, de Instr. Harm. lib. i. prop. 42.

our other keyed instruments, in that of the instrument to which the name of "monochord" was formerly applied.

It may perhaps be doubted whether the instrument of this name, the study of which was recommended by Guido in the eleventh century,[a] as the best method of teaching beginners their musical intervals, and which probably remained in use for many years after his time, was the identical Pythagorean monochord which we have described. We find it impossible to procure any distinct information upon this point. If it were the same, Dr Burney[b] thinks that "it probably" had "a neck, and was fretted; as bridges like those on a common monochord could not without much practice have been moved quickly enough" to answer the purposes of the teacher. Whether this may not have gradually led to the introduction of a "polychord," is a question well worthy of the consideration of the musical antiquary. For ourselves, we are by no means satisfied that it did; for, admitting that the inconvenience alluded to had been the occasion of furnishing this instrument with a neck and frets, and that it may have extended to a "polychord," there would still have been a wide step between this and the mechanical adjustments of a keyed instrument; nor does it appear very obvious that the one would have suggested the other. Notwithstanding the fact, therefore, which is certainly a very remarkable one, that the most ancient form of construction of these keyed instruments went under the name of "monochords;" the commonly received notion appears to us to be still the most plausible, that they originated simply in the idea of subjecting the harp, or some such instrument, to the sort of mechanical process by which they are regulated.[c]

There is just one circumstance which we would suggest as explanatory of the reason why these "polychord" instruments were called

[a] Hawkins, vol. i. p. 449.

[b] Vol. ii. p. 78, note.

[c] "As the harp came from the *cithara*, so the harpsichord had its origin from the harp, being nothing more than a horizontal harp, as every one who examines its figure with that idea must see." Burney's Hist. vol. iii. p. 173.

"monochords." From being an instrument employed to represent the scale, and the succession of intervals used in music, the name of "monochord" naturally came to signify the scale or system of sounds itself. We see it expressly used in this sense in the following passage of Joannes de Muris' Tractatus de Musica, written in 1323:—"Guido monachus qui compositor erat gammatis *qui monochordum dicitur*, vocas, lineis et spaciis dividebat." We observe that Dr Burney, in his history,[a] applies this word in the very same way; and La Borde[b] says, after describing the monochord, "ce qu'on appele systeme, est *la monochorde divisé;* et comme il est possible de le diviser de plusieurs manieres, c'est ce qui fait la multiplicité des systêmes." It is unnecessary to go farther. What could be more natural than that an instrument, the strings and keys of which were arranged according to the series of intervals into which the gamut or monochord was divided, should be called a "monochord?"[c] Indeed, we rather think, with reference to the passage which we have above cited from "Prætorius," where he observes that "the clavichord was invented and disposed after the model of the monochord," that *this* must have been his real meaning, and not that the clavichord which, from all that we have had occasion to observe, appears to have been the same instrument with the monochord, ever since the invention of the former, had been constructed after the pattern of another and a different *instrument* under the name of the latter.

We trust that we need no farther apology for dwelling at some length on the history of the "monochord," than its importance as the parent of that instrument, which, in modern times, is not only the delight of every fashionable circle, but extends its influence throughout many of the humbler grades of society; and this, too, not in our country alone, but over

[a] Vol. ii. p. 86.

[b] Vol. i. p. 244.

[c] This sort of metonymy is very common in the history of our language, and in music more particularly. The dance or tune "hornpipe" is so called from the instrument upon which it was played. "Jigg" is another example, being a sprightly tune well adapted to the violin. It received its name from "geig," the German name of that instrument.

the whole face of the civilized globe. We should add the fact, that it has somehow or other been mistaken, or overlooked, by all the musical historians to whose works we have had it in our power to obtain access. We shall endeavour, however, to make amends for our prolixity in this instance, by touching more briefly on what farther remains of this subject;—and we have the less hesitation in so doing, as we have reason to believe, that by the time these pages meet the eye of the public, our deficiencies will be much more than supplied from the pen of a distinguished antiquary, to whom his country is largely indebted for the accuracy, the usefulness, and the extent of his historical researches. The brief Tract which Sir John Graham Dalyell proposes to devote to the illustration of the ancient musical instruments of Scotland, will, we understand, be accompanied with engraved delineations of most of them;—not only a valuable addition to the interest of every work of this nature, but one which is perhaps indispensable to their proper elucidation, as no written description can furnish more than a vague and imperfect idea of their form and construction.

There is one description of keyed instrument, of great antiquity, not embraced within the class to which we have alluded, and in regard to which we have hitherto said nothing;—this is the organ. This instrument, (by which we mean the pneumatic organ, not the *hydraulicon* of the ancients,) as it was known in Italy in the seventh,—in France in the eighth,—and in England (during the time of St Swithin and St Dunstan) in the tenth century, was probably introduced into Scotland 150 or 200 years after the last mentioned era; at least, it is not easy to imagine that a monarch like David I., who did so much towards the erection of churches and monasteries, should have omitted to furnish some of the former with what must have been, at the time, accounted the most important adjunct to the solemn magnificence of the Catholic ritual.

So far as we are aware, the earliest mention of the organ in any of our historians is by Fordun, who, upon the occasion of the removal of the body of Queen Margaret from the outer church at Dunfermline for re-interment beside the high altar, in 1250, describes the procession of priests and abbots, by whom the ceremony was conducted, as accompanied by the sounds of the organ, as well as the chanting of the choir.[a] And we may suppose, that from about that time,—Scotland, which is described by Dempster as, (under the able superintendence of Simon Taylor, a Dominican monk,) in 1230, emulating the splendour of Rome herself in the excellence of her ecclesiastical music,—which, from the constant intercourse of her clergy with those of the Continent, must have always kept pace with the improvements of the age, and which unquestionably adopted the same style of sacred music with that which prevailed in Italy, France, and England,—was not likely to have been much behind the last mentioned country, in this particular department. Mr P. F. Tytler, to whose observations we refer our readers,[b] has pointed out the error into which his relative, Mr Tytler, the author of the Dissertation on Scotish Music, fell, in representing James I. (of Scotland) as the first introducer of the organ into this country; when all that he actually did, was to introduce organs of an improved construction. Our principal churches and abbeys had most probably been furnished with them more or less from about the era to which we have above referred. The Chapel-Royal at Stirling, founded by James III., to all appearance upon the model of that of Edward IV., was a very complete and richly endowed ecclesiastical establishment for the cultivation of church music; and several entries of sums, laid out by our sovereigns in the upholding of the organs at Stirling and Edinburgh, are to be found in the Treasurer's Books, of which our readers will find some specimens in the extracts printed in the Appendix.[c] There is also a very curious inventory of the "Buikis" of the "Quher" of the Colleges of St Andrews, as old as the middle of the fifteenth century, with a copy of which we at one time intended to have furnished our readers, together with other information of a like nature, of which a great deal may still be recovered from our char-

[a] Fordun, a Goodall, vol. ii. p. 83.

[b] History of Scotland, vol. ii. p. 374.

[c] Mr P. F. Tytler, in his History, vol. ii. p. 378, has remarked, that the churchmen were "the great masters in the necessary and ornamental arts; not only the historians and the poets, but the painters, the sculptors, the *mechanics*, and even the jewellers, goldsmiths, and lapidaries of the times." Thus, one of the entries above alluded to, on 12 Jan. 1507, is as follows:—"Item, To the *chanoun of Halyrudhous that mendit the organis* in Strivelin and Edinburgh, vij lb."

tularies, and other ancient documents. But we have forborne to do so, or to enter into any investigation of this subject,—partly from the accumulation of materials which we have been enabled to collect for our more immediate purpose—the illustration of the Skene MS., and with it the secular music of Scotland; and partly, because the effect of that information (although it would no doubt constitute an accession to our stock of Scotish history) would be little more than to show that, for the ages preceding the Reformation,—in our monastic institutions, our cathedrals, and our collegiate and parochial churches, the same regulations prevailed as to the chants, offices, and service of the church, as in other Catholic countries.

The accounts of the Lords Treasurers are a never failing source of interesting and authentic information with respect to the private lives of our sovereigns, and from the very unreserved nature of the explanations with which they are generally accompanied, they exhibit their habits, occupations, and amusements, in all their variety. Besides other entries to the same effect, in 1533, we observe the following: —" Oct. 19.—Item, For ane dozen luyt stringis send to the kingis grace in Glasgow, vi[s]. Nov. 2.—Item, For iiij dosane luyt stringis send to the kingis grace in Falkland, xxiiij[s]." Thus it appears that the lute was the favourite instrument of James V. It was also that of his daughter, Queen Mary.—" Elle avoit (says Brantome) la voix tres douce et tres bonne; car elle chantoit tres bien, accordant sa voix avec *le luth*, qu'elle touchoit bien solidement de cette belle main blanche et de ces beaux doigts si bien façonnés, qui ne devoient à ceux de l'Aurore." Besides the lute, Mary, as Sir James Melville told Queen Elizabeth at the celebrated interview when his courtesy was so severely put to the test, " occasionally recreated herself with playing on the virginals;"[a] upon which, the latter also, as Sir James relates, played " excellently well;" and if, as Dr Burney[b] remarks, " her majesty was ever able to

[a] Sir James Melville's Memoirs, pp. 50, 51.

[b] Vol. iii. p. 15.

execute any of the pieces that are preserved in her virginal book," which is still extant, " she must have been a very great player, as some of these pieces . . . . . are so difficult, that it would be hardly possible to find a master in Europe who would undertake to play one of them, at the end of a month's practice."

At a time when music, instrumental as well as vocal, was taught at the public schools as an ordinary branch of education,—when to sing one's part at sight, and to play on some instrument, was a common accomplishment in every one, and considered almost indispensable in persons of high rank, we need not wonder at the number of crowned heads who excelled in music, and that we should scarcely be able to find any, called to that high station, who were not more or less possessed of these qualifications. In the history of the House of Stuart, we scarcely know a single instance to the contrary. With the exception, perhaps, of James II., (of Scotland,) whose time and attention were entirely absorbed in the art military, the monarchs of this family were all either promoters or cultivators of music; nor have the passion and taste which prompted them to patronise, and enabled them to excel in, that accomplishment, abated in the latest of their successors; and during the brief duration, hitherto, of a reign which we fondly hope may continue among the longest in history, no member of that august family has ever done more to honour the efforts of artists, or, by her own genius and example, to exalt and adorn the art, than the talented and amiable Personage who now fills the throne of these realms.

No doubt, Dr Burney[a] has hazarded the assertion in regard to one of her Majesty's illustrious predecessors, James I., (of England,) that it did not appear that " either from nature or education he was enabled to receive any pleasure from music." But, allowing that his natural capacity did not qualify him to acquire distinction in any branch of the fine arts, (although specimens of his " vein" still extant, not to mention his " Cauteles" for the guidance of professors, sufficiently evince his fondness for poetry,) we doubt very much whether he was incapable, either

[a] Vol. iii. p. 323.

by nature or education, of receiving pleasure from music; and from any facts which have come within the range of our observation, we think that in this respect Dr Burney has taken a very erroneous, and, we are constrained to add, what appears to us to be, a very prejudiced, view of his character. Even Sir John Hawkins[a] bears testimony to the same effect, that "he did not understand or love music;" but, with great deference to both of these learned authors, whose opinions, accompanied as they generally are by extensive research, are entitled to respectful consideration, we hold these statements to be neither well founded in themselves, nor very gracious (if they are to be considered as expressive of the sentiments of the musical profession) towards the memory of one who appears, from the first, to have been both a sincere and an active patron of the art; and if the mind of Burney had not, in this matter, from some cause or other which we cannot explain, been unfavourably biassed, the very circumstances which he himself had occasion to record would have at once brought him to an opposite conclusion. It is remarkable that the Doctor follows out the very same sentence, in which he gives utterance to the observations we have cited, in the following words—" *However*, early in his reign, the gentlemen of his chapel, assisted by the influence and solicitation of several powerful noblemen who pleaded their cause, severally obtained an increase of ten pounds to their annual stipend." In the preceding paragraph, we are told, that Elizabeth, though extremely fond of splendour and show, was so parsimonious in rewarding talent, "that she suffered these gentlemen of her chapel, till the time of her death, to solicit *in vain*" for this augmentation of salary; . . . . and that the celebrated Dr Bull, and Dowland, the friend of Shakspeare, had been actually obliged to quit the kingdom in search of better patronage elsewhere!

After this we see this very Dr Bull, who is described by Burney (whether correctly or not we shall not here stop to enquire) as having been obliged to find employment abroad, retained in the establishment

[a] Hist. vol. iii. p. 321.

of Prince Henry, the son of James I., along with some of the first musicians of the age.[a] In a subsequent part of his work, the author, in a paragraph in which he says something about his own "historical integrity,"—a profession which does not appear to have *always* accorded with his practice,—observes—"It may perhaps be necessary for me to mention, that James I., UPON WHAT BENEFICIAL PRINCIPLE IT IS NOW DIFFICULT TO DISCOVER, *incorporated the musicians of the city of London into a company,*" with all the privileges of such, &c. The "*historical integrity*" of the Doctor's views, in this particular instance, is farther exemplified in another passage,[b] where, in speaking of "the periods of our own history, in which music has been the most favoured by royalty," while Queen Elizabeth, Charles I., and Charles II., are respectively lauded for their exertions, all mention of the reign of James I. is purposely avoided;—so that, in spite of his liberality, his absolute zeal in the promotion of this branch of the fine arts, and the solid and substantial benefits which he conferred upon its professors, his name has been handed down to posterity as that of one who, having no "music in his soul," was the adversary, rather than the friend, of their interests!

Under these circumstances, had it not been that the facts which Dr Burney himself has brought under the attention of his readers, seemed to furnish a sufficient refutation of his aspersions, we should have felt it right to say a few words, in order to rescue the memory of an inconsistent, but well-meaning monarch, from the unhappy predicament in which these musical historians have left it. We may recall to recollection that it was in his reign, and (although he was only in his 14th year) not improbably at his suggestion, that the institution of music-schools in the principal cities throughout Scotland became part of the law of the land. It may be added, that Dr Burney was in a complete mistake as to the musical part of his education. In the treasurer's accounts for 1580, there is the following article of charge:—"September, Item, be the kingis

[a] Burney's History, vol. iii. p. 326.

[b] Vol. iii. p. 483.

majesteis precept, to his servitour James Lawder ij[c] merkis, as for the dew price of *twa pair of virginellis* coft be the said James in London, *be his hienes directioun and command, and deliverit to his maiestie*, &c. ij[c]. li." King James was at this time in his fifteenth year.

We observe another entry a few years after this; but whether we should quote it as an additional illustration of King James' munificence to English professors, we know not. We are not informed as to the extent of their services on this occasion, and therefore can form no estimate of the comparative rate of their remuneration; but we subjoin the extract, as it may possibly amuse our readers, from the very circumstantial manner in which the mode of payment is set forth.—"March 1596, Item, be his majesties speciall directioun, *out of his awin mouth*, to *four Inglis violaris in Haliruidhous*, 32 lib."

Dr Burney informs us,[a] that, during the sixteenth and seventeenth centuries, the lute was the favourite chamber instrument of every nation in Europe; and that about the end of the former of these eras, James and Charles Hedington, two natives of Scotland, were eminent performers upon it, and much in favour at the court of *Henri Quatre*. There seem to have been a great many varieties of the lute species,—the theorbo, the arch-lute, the guitar, the *cystrum* or citterne, the pandora,[b] the mandora, and others of different names, at least, if not of different kinds; but into their specific distinctions it is not our intention, in this place, to enter. They are fully described by Mersenne[c] and other authors, with all the advantage of delineations, without which it would be quite needless to attempt any explanation of their peculiar forms, and the details of their construction.

It may be mentioned, however, that the mandora, mandour, or lesser lute of four strings, was the instrument to which the airs in the Skene MS. are adapted; and the lute tablature, or notation in which they are

[a] Burney's Hist. vol. iii. p. 274.

[b] "Two Pandores" are mentioned among the instruments provided for the musicians of the Chapel-Royal at Holyroodhouse in 1633. See information touching the Chapel-Royal in the Appendix.

[c] De Instr. Harmonicis, lib. 1.

written, is the same with that in which the numerous collections of French court airs, which were printed about the beginning of the seventeenth century, were noted by the composers of that period.[a] We are also informed that, at this time, "the lute and the virginals were the only instruments for which any tolerable music was expressly composed."

Another kind of "chamber music," common in these days, was of a very opposite description, and gives us a far less favourable idea of the good taste of the people of the sixteenth century. From the accounts in Hall's and Hollinshed's Chronicles, we learn that, in 1530, Cardinal Wolsey, at a masque at his palace, Whitehall, entertained his patron, Henry VIII., with "a concert of drums and fifes." But this (says Dr Burney[b]) "was soft music compared with that of his heroic daughter, Elizabeth, who, according to Henxner,[c] used to be regaled during dinner with twelve trumpets and two kettle-drums, which, together with fifes, cornets, and side-drums, made the hall ring for half an hour together."

At this time, the dinner hour seems to have been reckoned the most propitious moment for entertaining the company with music; of which, if necessary, many more instances might be given, in some of which vocal as well as instrumental music was introduced.[d] In these points, and in many others, our Scotish monarchs and nobles took their cue from the courts of England and France, and as parallel examples to the above, we may cite the following entries from the treasurer's books:—"Dec. 1596.—Item, to the violaris, taburris, and sueschearis at the prince's baptisme, conforme to the Lordis of Chekkaris warrand, xxx[li]. Item, conforme to the Lordis Ordinance, for sueschearis, and ane pephe-rare that playit at Barganei's mariage, x[li]."

Another entry in these books gives us an opportunity of comparing the instruments used upon such occasions, and the performers in ordinary attendance on the royal family of Scotland, during the reign of James V., with those of the court of France at the same period.

[a] Burney's Hist. vol. iii. p. 582. Ibid. p. 143.

[b] Vol. iii. p. 143.

[c] Itinerarium, p. 53.

[d] See Burney's Hist. vol. iii. pp. 6, 7.

The nuptials of this prince with Magdalen, eldest daughter of Francis I., were celebrated at Paris on 1st January 1537, with a degree of splendour, which, says Pitscottie, who gives a very graphic description of the proceedings, "was never seen in France since the time of Charles the Main." The festivities seem to have lasted for the better part of five months. In the month of May, a fleet left Scotland for France, in order to bring James and his Queen to their kingdom, and the whole party arrived on the 28th of that month, along with a magnificent convoy, consisting of about fifty vessels, the greater part of which the French king sent to accompany them; or, in the words of the last mentioned historian, "to squyer the King of Scotland and his Queen through the sea." Relative to this occasion, we observe, among others, the following entries in the interesting record to which we have so often referred.—"1537.—In primis, to iiij. trumpetouris, iiij. tabernaris, and iij. quhislaris, quhilkis passit in the schippis to France, the vij. day of May, xxxiij. elnis, reid, birge, satyne, and yallow, equaly to be thame dowblatis, xvj. li. xij. s̃. vj. d.

"Item, gevin to the King of Francis trumpettis for thair new ȝeir giftis, - - - - . . . . . crounis.
"Item, gevin to his howboyis, - - xxij. . .
"Item, gevin to his siflers, - - - - vj. . .
"Item, gevin to the cornatis, - - xvj. . .
"Item, gevin to the Quene of Navernis howboyis, - x. . .
"Item, gevin to the Quene of Scotland's tabirnar, xij. . ."

As this formed part of the expenditure of the year 1537, the New-year's gifts, above mentioned, must have been presented to those French musicians, either on the occasion of the marriage, when the King of Scotland and his nobles were in Paris, or, it is possible that they might have formed part of the escort, and received the money upon their arrival in this country, where it is likely that they had remained, along with many others of their countrymen,[a] until after Queen Magdalen's decease,

[a] See extracts from Lord High Treasurer's accounts, in Pitcairn's Criminal Trials, Appendix, p. 292.

which unhappily took place only forty days after she had reached Scotland.

Among the instruments of the French band, we should think that the hautboys and cornets must, about this time, have been regarded as novelties in Scotland. We notice, in 1550, a payment to "certane *Franchemen* that playit on the cornettis;" and it is probable that, at this period, they and the natives of Italy were the principal performers on that instrument. The "cornet" was a sort of horn, but made of wood, and perforated like a flute for the modulation of the sound; and we are told by Mersenne,[a] that, though naturally very loud and powerful, its tones, in the hands of a master, were capable of being graduated, so as to produce effects the sweetest and softest imaginable. Anton Francisco Doni, in his *Dialoghe della Musica*, published in 1544, speaks of it, or rather of the performance of certain celebrated cornetists, in the most rapturous terms. "Il divino Antonio da cornetto perfettissimo——e M. Battista dal Fondaro con il suo cornetto ancora; che lo suona miracolosamente."[b] Dr Burney remarks, that the cornet has been supplanted in the favour of the public by the hautboy. The former, no doubt, is no longer in use; but the latter is an instrument of a totally different structure and quality, being straight, and blown through a reed, while the cornet was curvular, with an open mouth-piece like a trumpet or French horn. It seems rather to have been the *schawme*, *shalmele*, or *chalumeau*, to which the hautboy succeeded. Sir John Hawkins, in his analysis of Luscinius' work, describing the *schawme*, along with another instrument, called the *bombardt*, expressly says, "the second of the two instruments, above delineated, is the *schalmey*, so called from *calamus*, a reed, which is a part of it, the other, called *bombardt*, is the bass to the former; these instruments have been improved by the French into the hautboy and bassoon." The "schawmes" and the "bombardt" are frequently mentioned by our older historians and poets, though the nature of them, in modern times, seems to have been very ill understood.

[a] De Inst. Harm. lib. ii. prop. 15.

[b] Burney's Hist. vol. iii. p. 174.

"In such accorde, and such a sowne,
Of *bombarde* and of clariowne;
With cornemuse and *shalmele*,
That it was halfe a mannes hele,
So glad a noyse for to here."[a]

"On crowd, lute, harpe, with monie gudlie spring,
Schalmes, clariouns, portativis, hard I ring."[b]

"With rote, ribible, and clokarde,
With pypes, organ, and *bumbard*."[c]

"Trumpettis and *schalmis* with a schout,
Played or the rink began."[d]

In quoting some of these passages, Dr Leyden[e] commits the error of confounding the "schawme" with the cornet or crum horn of the Germans. He says, "the stock horn, in the strict sense, is the *cornet* or *crum* horn of the Germans, the SHALMEY, or *chalumeau*, used with the trumpet at tilts and tournaments." This learned writer may possibly have been induced to form this opinion from a casual expression of Sir John Hawkins,[f] where, in speaking of the *crum* horn, or crooked horn of the Germans, he says, that "it signifies a cornet *or small shawm*;" and to add to the confusion, Luscinius has given some representations of an *artificial* form of crum horn, constructed with the addition of a reed —an instrument which, in consequence, might, without impropriety, be termed a "shawm." But taking the cornet (or crum horn) represented by Mersenne, our best authority, as the genuine instrument of that name,

[a] Gower.
[b] Douglas.
[c] An old Metrical Romance, entitled "The Squire of Low Degree."
[d] Evergreen, vol. ii. p. 177.
[e] Introduction to Complaynt, p. 155.
[f] Hist. vol. ii. p. 452.

the reed forms no part of its construction, and without that, it could never be denominated a "shawm." The very derivation of the word from *chalumeau*, and that again from the Latin *calamus*, leaves no room for question upon that point.

The "cornet," then, may be regarded as an instrument of a different generic character, from any with which we are acquainted, at the present day. The "shawm" appears to have been a rude and warlike species of hautboy, and the "bombardt" of the same general construction with the "shawm," but larger, and of a much deeper quality of tone.[a]

The "trumpet" and the "clarion" would seem to have stood in the same relation towards each other as the two last mentioned instruments. La Borde[b] describes the clarion as "an instrument of the trumpet kind, used in former times, of which the tube was narrower, and the sound more acute, so that the trumpet formed the bass of the clarion." It is supposed to have been of Moorish origin, and was one of the principal military instruments during the feudal ages. Sir David Lyndsay makes the following heraldic allusion to it, as such, in his "Testament of Squyer Meldrum."

"Amang that band, my baner sal be borne
Of silver schene, thrie otteris into sabill:
With tabroun, trumpet, CLARIOUN, and horne,
For men of armes very convenabill."

The "siflers," or "sifleurs," whom we see mentioned among the French musicians, correspond with the Scotish "quhislaris," or "whistlers," and as the whistle is the popular appellation in Scotland for every species of flute, fife, or flageolet, these "sifleurs," or whistlers, may be considered as synonymous with flute-players. It is most likely that their instrument was the flute *à-bec*, or beaked flute, blown from the end, and held perpendicularly, and not transversely, like the *flauto-traversiere*,

[a] There were six different sizes of these "bombardes," all of them reed instruments. The largest was about ten feet in length—a deep and powerful bass instrument.

[b] Essai, vol. i. p. 249.

German, or Helvetian flute, now in use;—and yet, although the latter carries the name of these nations along with it, the probability is, that it only owes to them its modern introduction, as the statue of the piping faun, and other antiques, have placed the fact beyond doubt, that the ancient Greeks and Romans were acquainted with it. Even in Germany, early in the sixteenth century, we doubt very much whether it had come into general use. Luscinius's *Musurgia*, a German work, published at Stuttgard in 1536, only gives one specimen of a flute of this kind; and this, too, differs in some respects from the modern German flute, being much slenderer, and having fewer holes. In a paper on the fashionable amusements in Edinburgh during the seventeenth century,[a] Mr Tytler has stated, that "the flute *à-bec* was the only flute used at that time, (that is to say, in 1695.) The German, or traverse, of modern invention, was not then known in Britain. I have heard, that Sir Gilbert Elliot, afterwards Lord Justice Clerk, who had been taught the German flute in France, and was a fine performer, first introduced that instrument into Scotland about the year 1725." In this statement, Mr Tytler has gone a great deal too far. In Strutt's "Manners and Customs of the English,"[b] there is a curious representation of a masque in the time of James I. of England; where, among a party of six musicians, the only wind instrument is a *German flute*. Farther, we have reason to believe, that this instrument was played in Scotland by the common minstrels of the city of Aberdeen, at least, if not of other royal burghs, so long ago as the year 1574. This fact we gather from the Town Council Register of that city, a record to which we have previously had occasion to refer, and which, both for its antiquity and its copiousness, is one of the most valuable we possess. On the 24th November 1574—"The said day, the haill counsale being warnit to this day, ordanit Johnne Cowpar to pas everie day in the morning at four houris, and everie nycht at eight houris at ewyne, throu all the rewis of the toune, playand upon the ALMANY QUHISSEL, with ane servante with him

[a] Archæol. Scotica, p. 509.

[b] Vol. iii. plate xi.

playand upon the taborine, quhairby the craftismen, their servandis, and all utheris laborious folkis, being warnit and excitat, may pas to their labouris in dew and convenient tyme."[a]

"Almany whistle" in Scotish is synonymous with "German flute;" but from its having been here accompanied with the tabour or tambourine, it is more likely that the term was intended to denote the smaller instrument of that species—the *minor fistula Helvetica*,[b] or fife, which is usually associated with instruments of a pulsatile nature, assimilating better with the latter, and being less liable to be overpowered by them than the common flute.

With the ancient inhabitants of Scotland, whether Picts or Celts, Saxons or Scandinavians, we believe that the horn was perhaps the oldest military instrument.—"In battle (says Pinkerton,[c] speaking of the Scandinavian nations) the horn was chiefly used down to the fourteenth century." Many delineations of this instrument are to be found among Strutt's Illustrations of the Ancient Anglo-Saxon Manners and Customs, and many of the horns themselves are still extant. They generally united the purposes of a drinking cup with those of an instrument for the emission of sound. With our Scotish troops, in former times,[d] it was customary for every man in the host to carry a horn "slung round his neck, in the manner of hunters," the blasts of which, together with the furious yells with which they were accompanied, not only served to drown the cries of the wounded and dying, but sometimes struck terror into the enemy.[e] That the Scots were more than

[a] See Analecta Scotica.

[b] Mersenne de Instr. Harm. lib. ii. prop. 6.

[c] Enquiry, vol. i. p. 390.

[d] Froissart's Chronicles, vol. iv. ch. 7.

[e] Such, also, were their use and effects among the Gauls, as described by Polybius, in the account which he gives of the battle between them and the Romans, on the coast of Tyrrhenia, or Tuscany. B. ii. c. 2. (We quote from Hampton's Translation, p. 185, Edin. 1766.)—"The Romans were elated with no small joy when they saw that they had thus inclosed the enemy as in a snare;—but, on the other hand, the appearance of the Gallic forces, and the unusual noise with which they advanced to action, struck them with great amazement; *for, besides their horns and*

usually expert at these practices, we have the testimony of Froissart in several of his descriptions. One occasion of their employing these horns was within their encampments at night; as the same historian tells us, in detailing the particulars of Edward III.'s first expedition against the Scots[a]—" They made immense fires, and about midnight, such a blasting and noise with their horns, that it seemed as if all the devils from hell had been there." This was a night in August 1337; and the following evening it appears that the performance was repeated. Barbour, in his " Bruce," alludes to the same custom:—

" For me to morne her, all the day
Sall mak as mery as we may:
And mak us boun agayn the nycht,
And than ger mak our fyrs lycht;
And blaw our hornys, and mak far,
As all the warld our awne war."[b]

To any one accustomed to consider the bagpipe, the inspiring effects of which upon our Scotish troops is well known, as our leading national instrument, it must appear strange, that in the very circumstantial accounts which have come down to us of the many sanguinary conflicts in which our ancestors were engaged, there should be no allusion to its spirit-stirring sounds,—and, so far as we have observed, no mention even of its name, in the early part of our history. Although its use unquestionably prevailed in the Lowlands, we see no *proof* of its ever having been assumed by the inhabitants of that part of the realm, as a warlike

trumpets, the number of which was almost infinite, the whole army broke out together into such loud and continued cries, that the neighbouring places every where resounded, and seemed to join their voices with the shouts and clamour of the instruments and soldiers."

[a] Froissart's Chronicles, b. i. c. 18.

[b] A similar custom seems to have prevailed among the Jews. " Blow the trumpet in Tekoah, and set up a sign of fire in Beth-haccerem, for evil appeareth out of the north." Jeremiah, ch. vi. verse 1.

instrument; and in so far as regards the Highland portion of the population, the earliest notice which we can remember of it in that character is in the narrative of the Battle of Balrinnes,[a] in 1594, in which many of the Highland clans were engaged, and where it is spoken of, as "the principal military instrument of the Scotish mountaineers." We should have thought, that the bagpipe must have been in requisition at the Battle of Harlaw, in 1411; but in the ballad, in which the details are very minutely commemorated, it is not mentioned, although "trumpets" and "drums" are particularised. This is the more extraordinary, as a "pibroch," called "The Battle of Harlaw," appears, from Drummond's "Polemo-Middinia," to have been popular in Scotland during the early part of the seventeenth century;[b] and the probability after all is, that the tune, like the ballad was coeval with the event; although it must be confessed, that the absence of all mention of an instrument, which in modern times has had such an effect in inciting the valour of the native Highlander, would lead us to infer, either that it had not been used on that occasion, or that its martial character had not at that time been fully established.[c]

[a] Dalyell's Scotish Poems of the Sixteenth Century, vol. i. p. 151.

[b] The following are the lines in which it is alluded to:—

> "Interea ante alios dux Piper Laius heros,
> Precedens magnamque gerens cum burdine pypam,
> Incipit *Harlaii* cunctis sonare *battellum*."

Through the medium of one of Mr Blaikie's MSS., precisely contemporaneous with Drummond's poem, this tune, hitherto supposed to be lost, has been recovered, and is now presented to the public in the Appendix of this work.

[c] We mean among our Gaelic countrymen. The bagpipe is said to have been a martial instrument of the *Irish* kerns or infantry, as far back as the reign of Edward III., and to have continued as such down to the sixteenth century. In the sixth century, we find it mentioned by Procopius, (lib. ii. c. 22,) as the instrument of war of the Roman infantry, while the trumpet was that of the cavalry; and Pinkerton (Enquiry, vol. i. p. 391) observes, that from this circumstance, commenced its warlike use in Britain and the other countries subject to the Romans. It may be so; but we cannot say that we have seen any evidence of its having been employed in that manner so near the time of the Romans as to countenance that supposition.

Dr Leyden has gone even farther than this, and maintained that there is no direct evidence that the bagpipe was known to the Highlanders at a very early period. But although its adoption as an instrument of war may have been an event of more recent occurrence, as almost every nation in Europe appears, from the earliest ages, to have been acquainted with it, we have no doubt, that, long prior to this, it contributed to their amusement in their hours of relaxation. Dr Solander told Mr Pennant,[a] that in the oldest northern songs in the Hebrides, the bagpipe was mentioned under the name of the *soeck-pipe;* and we have already seen, that Giraldus Cambrensis, towards the end of the twelfth century, speaks of it as one of the instruments in use both in Scotland and in Wales. His words are as follows :—" Hibernia quidem duobus tantum utitur et delectatur instrumentis—cythara scilicet et tympano: Scotia tribus, cythara, tympano, et *choro:* Gwallia vero cythara, tibiis et *choro.*"[b]

It will be remembered, that the same word "chorus" is used by Bower, in his enumeration of the musical accomplishments of James I., (of Scotland,) and in rendering that word by *bagpipe,* we are quite aware that we have entered upon debateable ground. Mr P. F. Tytler, in his History,[c] has faltered as to its meaning, and substituted for it (as he himself admits, somewhat rashly) the word " cornu." That he should have hesitated as to the proper signification of the word " chorus," is not to be wondered at. Pinkerton did not comprehend it; Leyden, Ritson, and Jones, misinterpreted it; and the Reverend Mr Macdonald,[d] who was one of our best informed writers on Scotish music, proposed it as a sort of enigma for the solution of the Scotish antiquary. Under these circumstances, it would ill become any one to obtrude his own particular opinion with a feeling of confidence; but after having given the matter all the attention in our power, we see as little reason, on the other hand, to vacillate as to the interpretation which we have given.

[a] Pennant's Tour to the Hebrides, p. 302.

[b] Topog. Hib. lib. ii. c. 2.

[c] Vol. ii. p. 370.

[d] Essay on the Influence of Music on the Scotish Highlanders.

In Mr Strutt's "Manners and Customs of the English,"[a] there are certain drawings of old instruments, "so very imperfect, (as Mr Strutt observes,) that he fears their use will not be very readily discovered." Fortunately, however, as in the case of sign-painters, who feel the inadequacy of their daubs to represent the intended objects, they are accompanied with written explanations or definitions. Underneath two of these we find the following words, "Corus est pellis simplex cum duabus cicutis." This inscription serves to give a certain degree of distinctness to images otherwise too vague to be at all intelligible; and the result is, that we see before us the outlines of two figures which appear to correspond with this description; one of which has, to all appearance, two, and the other three, tubes or pipes attached to it. The definition given, and the delineation, appear to indicate the simplest form of bagpipe.[b] In the next place, we turn to the Epistle to Dardanus, attributed to St Jerome, where he says—"Synagogæ antiquis temporibus, FUIT *chorus* quoque simplex, pellis cum duobus cicutis aeriis, et per primam inspiratur, secunda vocem emittit;" that is to say, "At the synagogue, in ancient times, there was also a simple species of bagpipe, being a skin, (or leather bag,) with two pipes, through one of which the bag was inflated, the other emitted the sound." We can see room for no other interpretation of words which, in themselves, give rise to no ambiguity; and if any doubt could be started, we should at once consider it as set at rest by the passage in the MS. which we have above cited, which embodies all the material part of the description given in the Epistle,—and that, too, in the shape of an express definition of the word "chorus." Singularly enough, however, it has so happened, that a learned Italian, Signor Maccari, the author of a celebrated Dissertation on the ancient "*tibia utricolaris*," or bagpipe,[c] has attempted to extract another meaning from

[a] Vol. i. plate 21, pp. 50,109.

[b] We should mention that these drawings and descriptions are in Mr Strutt's oldest series of Saxon Antiquities, taken, as he informs us, from a MS. in the British Museum marked Tiber, c. vi.

[c] Saggi di Dissertazion iaccademiche pubblicamente lette nella nobile accademia Etrusca dell

it, not only different from, but totally at variance with, the plain and obvious signification of the words, as they stand in the original. According to *his* translation, these words import, that in the synagogue, in former times, there was a "chorus," meaning thereby "a chorus of singers," and also a single skin, with two brass pipes, &c.[a] But assuming the words "chorus" and "pellis" to have been two separate nominatives, and not one conjunct nominative, as they distinctly appear to be, Signor Maccari does not think it necessary to explain how the verb should happen to be in the singular number; he seems altogether to forget that he cuts rather than unties the Gordian knot, and that he endeavours to obtrude upon his readers a version of his own, in direct opposition to the grammatical construction of the passage.

The cause of this attempt to contort, what must appear to all to be a very simple proposition, was not the difficulty of establishing the fact that "chorus" was occasionally used as synonymous with "tibia utricularis,"—but an ardent desire, on the part of the writer, to secure an additional illustration in behalf of another and a different argument, and one which being well supported in many other ways, required no such aid. The subject of the dissertation is a Grecian or Roman antique, representing a shepherd holding one of these instruments on his left arm, and great part of it is occupied in proving that the Greek "Pythaules," who performed at the public games, were "Otricolarii," an opinion maintained by Vossius, Du Çange, and Bianchini, and which the dissertation of Signor Maccari tends strongly to confirm. In the course of this elucidation, although the use of the word "chorus," in the sense of "tibia

antichissima citta di Cortona, vol. vii. See Walker's Memoirs of the Irish Bards, Appendix, p. 41.

[a] Mersenne (de Instr. Harm. lib. ii. prop. xi.) speaks of the bagpipe as having been sometimes employed by the French peasantry, at mass and vespers, in the chapels and churches of villages, in order to supply the want of organs. He adds, that he has no doubt that the Jews made the same use of it at their marriage feasts;—but says nothing as to its having been introduced into the synagogue—a fact, which, notwithstanding the statement contained in the supposititious letter of St Jerome, would appear from a subsequent authority (see p. 125, Note) to be somewhat questionable.

utricularis," seems never to have entered the mind of the author, so much light is casually reflected upon that point, that we must be pardoned for shortly alluding to it. The principal authority quoted by Maccari is Inginus, in his 253d fable, in which he says, " Pythaules qui Pythia cantaverat septem habuit palliatos, unde postea appellatus est Choraules." The words " qui Pythia cantaverat" have been rejected as an interpolation of an ignorant transcriber, and they are clearly out of place, for two reasons;—1st, Inginus is here speaking not of the Pythian, but of the Nemean Games, at which the " Pythia," or Hymn to Apollo, was not introduced. 2dly, The word " Pythaules" has no connexion whatever with " Pythia," but is compounded of πίθος, " dolium," and αὐλός, " tibia." It is certain, therefore, as Maccari remarks, that the " Choraules" and the " Pythaules" were identical; and that the " otricolarii" had, each of them, a chorus of seven men, habited in " pallia," or cloaks. We may observe, in passing, that it is at this stage of the discussion that Maccari has thought proper to refer to the passage in the Epistle attributed to St Jerome; from which he endeavours to make it appear, that the " chorus," and the " tibia utricularis," had been employed in the same manner in the Jewish Synagogue as at the Grecian Games.

We have shortly recapitulated a part of this discussion, because the error into which Signor Maccari has fallen as to the meaning of the word " chorus" in this passage, has contributed much to unsettle the opinions of those who have written on this subject. The circumstances also which he has advanced in order to prove the identity of the " pithaules" with the " otricolarii," afford us more insight into the original cause of the employment of the word " chorus" in the signification in which we have applied it, than any thing we have elsewhere seen. The term " choraules" being derived from χορος, chorus, and αυλος, a pipe, was a name strictly designative of his office of " piper to the chorus;" after which, the word " chorus" may have come to signify " bagpipe" itself, by an easy and natural transition. There is still another derivation which may be noticed. The Greek word δορὸς signifies a leather bag; for which reason, it has been suggested by Salmasius, in his notes on Flavius Volpiscus, that the word "chorus," in the passage in question, should be converted into "dorus." With two terms which are mutually convertible by a mere shade of difference in the pronunciation, one could scarcely desire a nearer approach to the radical etymology of the word.[a]

Thus, it appears that the Scots cultivated the bagpipe in the twelfth century, and the representation in the carved work of Melrose Abbey, erected about that time, is confirmatory of the fact. How long prior to this they possessed that instrument, we know not; neither can we say from what source they received the invention. There is a tradition in the Highlands, that it was derived from the Danes and Norwegians;[b] others, again, think that it might have been communicated to the Scots by the Britons or Welsh, who probably acquired it from the Romans. With

[a] The learned and accomplished gentleman by whom the Skene MS. has been translated, and whose contributions and counsel have been of the greatest importance in the preparation of this Dissertation, after perusing the Editor's remarks upon this subject, has kindly subjoined the following additional authorities, which ought to have the effect of setting this *questio vexata* at rest for ever:—

"Walafridus Strabo, a Benedictine monk, (who wrote, in the ninth century, a Latin Commentary on the Scriptures, and other works, which were published at Paris in 1624,) describes 'the chorus' as 'a single skin with two pipes.' See his Comm. in cap. 15. Exod.

"Farther, regarding the 'chorus,' I find reference made to a book printed at Lyons in 1672, and called 'Traité de la musette avec une nouvelle methode,' &c. from which it would seem that the 'bagpipe' and the 'chorus' were then considered the same instrument.

"J. Bartoloccius, a Cistertian monk of the 17th century, in his 'Bibliotheca Magna Rabbinica,' &c. does not admit the 'chorus' among the sacred *instruments* used in the sanctuary. P. i. p. 192.

"Nicholas de Lyranus, a Franciscan monk, who died in 1340, in his Commentaries on the Bible, published at Rome in 1472, (in 7 vols. folio,) referring to Psalm 150, v. 4, observes, 'Dicunt aliqui, quod *chorus* est instrumentum de *corio* factum; et habet duas fistulas de ligno, unam per quam inflatur et aliam per quam emittit sonum, et vocatur Gallice *cheurette*,' &c. 'Credo tamen magis quod, hic accipiatur chorus, pro laudantium societate.' Thus, although this writer does not think that a bagpipe was meant in the scriptural passage in question, but a chorus of singers, his allusion to the word 'chorus,' as the name of a 'bagpipe,' is, along with the other authorities, perfectly conclusive as to its having been occasionally used in that acceptation. The barbarous corruptions of Latin, too, were so frequent, that there is no saying but somebody may have distorted even *corium* (a skin) into *chorus*; and this is the more likely, as it is occasionally spelt '*corus*;' see Gerbertus de Musica Sacra, plate 34; Strutt's Manners and Customs, vol. i. pp. 50, 109. The French word 'chevrette' means the doe of the roe-deer. Was its skin used in making the bag of the bagpipe?"

[b] Macdonald's Essay, p. 12.

the latter, and the Greeks, it appears at one time to have held a higher rank than with any other nation; though, during the later periods of their history, we see it, as in modern times, almost entirely in the hands of the peasantry.

In Scotland, the use of the bagpipe seems to have gradually superseded that of the harp;[a] but this process, we should think, must have taken place chiefly within the last two hundred years,—previous to which, we doubt very much whether the natives of North Britain were more distinguished for their partiality for the bagpipe than their southern neighbours. Even Shakspeare, although he talks of the "drone of a Lincolnshire bagpipe," and of "a Yorkshire bagpiper," has no where associated that instrument with the Scots: and when we go back several centuries anterior to this, we find it used in both countries by the same class of persons. Chaucer's Miller played upon it.—

> "A bagpipe well couth he blowe and sowne;"

and "Will Swane," "the meikle miller man," in our "Peblis to the Play," calls for it to assist in the festivities of the day.

> "Giff I sall dance, have doune, lat se
> Blaw up the bagpyp than."

Indeed, although we are justly proud of our ancient proficiency on the harp, and adhere unhesitatingly to our claims to supremacy on that head, we are much disposed, upon a candid consideration of the facts, to resign to the English the palm of superiority in this less refined description of music, about the time to which we refer. The pipers who are

[a] The Highland Society of Scotland has been much and justly applauded for having, by annual premiums, kept up the great *military* instrument of the Highlanders; but why should they have allowed to sink into oblivion their great *musical* instrument—that for which all their oldest and most exquisite airs were composed? Why has there been no attempt to revive these, and along with them the recollection of the time when "the shell went round, the bards sung, and the soft hand of the virgins trembled on the strings of the harp?"

mentioned in the Lord High Treasurer's accounts seem almost uniformly to have been natives of England. Thus, 10th July 1489, there is a payment of eight pounds eight shillings " to *Inglis pyparis* that com to the castel yet and playit to the king." Again, in 1505, there is another payment to " the *Inglis pipar* with the drone." It should be added, that, while the " bagpiper" formed part of the musical establishment of the English sovereigns and noblemen, during the sixteenth century,[a] we find no such musician retained at the Scotish court. Our monarchs had probably not much relish for this sort of pipe music, and although the result of our investigation of the word " chorus" has had the effect of clearly convicting our first James of being a performer upon that most unprincely instrument, (for which, the only precedent we can find in history is that of the Emperor Nero,[b]) we should remember that he had most probably acquired that, as well as his other accomplishments, in England, where he received the rest of his education. We do not conceive, upon the whole, that the bagpipe has ever been a very popular instrument in Scotland, except in the Highland districts; and we may state this with some confidence, as to one part of the country,—a royal burgh, which we have already had occasion to name, and where the magistrates actually prohibited the common piper from going his rounds, in terms by no means complimentary of the instrument. Our readers will be the less surprised at the superior refinement here exhibited, when they are informed that these were the " musical magistrates" of the city of Aberdeen, whose praises have been so loudly trumpeted by Forbes, the publisher of the " Cantus," in his dedication of that work. " 26th May 1630. The magistrates discharge the common piper of all going through the toun at nycht, or in the morning, in tyme coming, with his pype,—*it being an incivill forme to be usit within sic a famous burghe, and being often fund fault with, als weill be sundrie nichtbouris of the toune as be strangeris.*"[c]

[a] Burney's Hist. vol. iii. pp. 4, 16; also Ritson's Scotish Songs, p. 114.

[b] It is mentioned by Suetonius, that when the Emperor Nero heard of the revolt by which he lost his empire and his life, he made a solemn vow, that if it should please the gods to extricate him from his difficulties, he would perform in public on the bagpipe.

[c] Aberdeen Town Council Register. See Analecta Scotica, vol. ii. p. 322.

This instrument must have been the great Highland bagpipe, blown with the mouth; and all who have experienced its deafening effects will concur in the wisdom and good taste of the above regulation. Critically speaking, and holding it in the highest possible estimation for its utility in rousing the energies of the Highland soldiery—the sounds which it emits are certainly of a nature much better calculated to excite alarm and consternation, than to diffuse pleasure—and they are perhaps better illustrated by the following anecdote than any thing else that we could mention:—"As a Scotch bagpiper was traversing the mountains of Ulster, he was, one evening, encountered by a hungry starved Irish wolf. In this distress, the poor man could think of nothing better than to open his wallet, and try the effects of his hospitality. He did so, and the savage swallowed all that was thrown him with so improving a voracity, as if his appetite was but just coming to him. The whole stock of provisions, you may be sure, was soon spent: and now his only recourse was to the virtue of the bagpipe, which the monster no sooner heard than he took to the mountains with the same precipitation that he had come down. The poor piper could not so perfectly enjoy his deliverance, but that with an angry look at parting, he shook his head, and said, '*Ay! are these your tricks? Had I known your humour, you should have had your music before supper.*'"[a]

Whether this was the instrument upon which the English were such eminent performers in the fifteenth and sixteenth centuries,—or whether *their* bagpipe had been inflated by a bellows, similar to the Yorkshire, the Northumberland, the Irish, and the Lowland Scotish pipes, we have no data to enable us to decide. It has generally been supposed, that these were of somewhat more recent introduction, and the pilgrim miller of Chaucer, in one of the rude cuts of Caxton's edition, is represented as blowing the pipe with his mouth. Farther, we find it stated by Mr Beauford,[b] that it was at "*the close of the sixteenth century*, when considerable improvements were made by taking the pipe from the mouth, and

[a] Remarks on several occasions. See Walker's Irish Bards.

[b] Ledwich's Antiquities of Ireland, p. 249.

causing the bag to be filled by a small pair of bellows on compression by the elbow." Leyden,[a] however, speaks of the instrument of John Hastie, the hereditary town piper of Jedburgh, as being decidedly the Lowland bagpipe; and after mentioning that he himself had seen the original bagpipe in the possession of Hastie's descendant, he adds—" The tradition of the family, of the town of Jedburgh, and of the country in its vicinity, strongly avers this to have been the identical bagpipe which his ancestor bore to animate the Borderers at the battle of Flodden." For such an instrument as this, the tune of " The Souters of Selkirk," said to be coeval with this event, seems to be naturally adapted. In the " Skene MS." there are some of a similar character, and among these, " Pitt on your Shirt (*i. e.* coat of mail) on Monday," which has much the appearance of having been a Border " gathering," or muster-tune. The tradition, therefore, of which Dr Leyden speaks, is not without foundation. Ritson[b] says, that this sort of bagpipe was probably " introduced (into Scotland) out of England, where it is a very ancient, as it was once, a very common instrument." If there were any proof of this assertion as to the antiquity of the instrument in England, we should be inclined to concur in the observation that the Scots might have borrowed it from that country, since it has been principally used in the vicinity of the Borders; but, failing this, the principles of its construction being the same with those of the French *musette* and the Irish pipes, there are still two other alternatives, and it is quite possible that we may have derived it from one or other of the last mentioned nations.

Before concluding our remarks on the musical instruments, a few words are still necessary as to those which prevailed among the Scotish peasantry; though less will require to be said on this subject, after the full consideration which we have given to the more ingenious and artificial description of instruments which were used by the higher classes, and the inhabitants of the towns. In fact, when we come to speak of the former, it is like resolving the latter into their primitive elements.

[a] Introduction to Complaynt of Scotland, p. 142.

[b] Ritson's Scotish Songs, p. 114.

Pastoral life is necessarily much the same in all ages and in all countries. The ῥαπατη or καλαμις of the Greeks—the *calamus*, *stipula*, or *tenuis avena* of the Latins—the *zampogna* of the modern Italians—the *chalumeau* of the French—the pipes "maid of grene corne" of Chaucer's shepherd boys—and the "corne-pipe," mentioned in the "Complaynt of Scotland," are all one and the same instrument—the first untaught effort of pastoral invention. The "quhissel," or whistle, "formed of different substances, from the perforated elder, (or borit bour-tree,[a]) to the green willow bough, part of the bark of which is skilfully taken off, and afterwards superinduced, when the ligneous part of the instrument is prepared,"[b] and the goat's or cow's horn, are others of equal simplicity.

The genius of the rustic now goes a degree farther, and endeavours to improve the tone and effect of these rude instruments by combination. He discovers that a fuller and mellower expression of sound is produced by inserting the reed or pipe into a horn, and by this means he creates what is called the "stock and horn," or "buck-horne," the instrument alluded to by Ramsay in the Gentle Shepherd.

> "When I begin to tune my *stock and horn*,
> With a' her face she shaws a cauldrife scorn."

And this is, probably, the same with the "pipe maid of ane gait horne," mentioned in the "Complaynt." The "horn-pipe," called by the Welsh the "pib-corn," and said to be played by the shepherds of Anglesey,[c] is a degree more complicated. It has a horn at both extremities, and a concealed reed in that into which the air is blown.

Another of these combinations is that of the reed and the bladder, a process so simple that it admits of being accomplished by the shepherd boys themselves, without even the aid of the village artizan. From this springs the bagpipe with its chord of drones, and all those other appur-

[a] See Cockelbie Sow.

[b] Leyden's Complaynt of Scotland, Introduction, p. 169.

[c] Jones' Welsh Bards, p. 116.

tenances which demand the skill and the turning-loom of the finished mechanic.

What we have stated in this place, and in the preceding pages, may serve to render intelligible the following description, with which, as it contains in itself a tolerably correct enumeration of the pastoral instruments in use in this country, we shall conclude what we have felt it necessary to submit to our readers on this branch of our subject. Of the eight shepherds mentioned in the work last referred to, (the learned and curious illustrations of which, by the late Dr Leyden, have been of much advantage to us in the conduct of this enquiry,) "the fyrst hed *ane drone bag-pipe*, the nyxt *hed ane pipe maid of ane bleddir and of ane reid*, the thrid playit on *ane trump*, the feyrd on *ane corne pipe*, the fyft playit on *ane pipe maid of ane gait horne*, the sext playt on *ane recordar*, the sevint plait on *ane fiddil*, and the last plait on *ane quhissel*."

One word as to the "trump," *i.e.* the Jew's harp. This is said to have been the only musical instrument of the inhabitants of St Kilda, and to be still used by the peasantry in some parts of Scotland, though, we fear, with a success very inferior to that of the celebrated "Eulenstein," whose triumph over its imperfections shews what may be done by the hand of genius, even when destitute of those "means and appliances" which only exist in an age of mechanical invention and a highly improved state of the art.[a] And ought not the same consideration to lead us to pause, before we condemn, by wholesale, the wild and undisciplined efforts of our ancestors? Though art, which is confined to certain periods and

[a] Having mentioned the name of "Eulenstein," it is right that we should not altogether pass over that of "Geilles Duncane," the only noted performer on the Jew's harp who figures in Scotish story, and whose performance seems not only to have met the approval of a numerous audience of witches, but to have been repeated in the august presence of royalty, by command of his most gracious Majesty King James VI.—Agnes Sampson being brought before the King's Majesty and his council, confessed "that upon the night of All-Holloweven last, shee was accompanied as well with the persons aforesaide, as also with a great many other witches, to the number of two hundreth; and that all they together went to sea, each one in a riddle or cive, and went into the same very substantially, with flaggons of wine, making merrie, and drinking by the way, in the same riddles or cives to the kirke of North Barrick, in Lowthian; and that after they had

places, is ours—"creation's heirs," (as Goldsmith says,)—nature and genius, which are universal, were theirs. Genius, and particularly that of music, as has been proved in a variety of instances, is ever ready to burst the fetters that bind it. Let the instrument, therefore, be what it may, where a soul for music exists, there will always be a way of producing pleasing effects; nay, what is more extraordinary, it has been so ordained, that, even without the aid and beyond the influence of art itself, man should give expression to his feelings and sentiments in music, and sometimes in poetry, not only gratifying in the highest degree to the most cultivated taste, but which school-taught skill has vainly endeavoured to equal. Hence the origin of many of our finest Scotish airs. But this is a subject reserved for a future part of the discussion, and into which we here forbear to enter.

It is time now to put the question, if such are the wrecks of our ancient lyrical poetry, and such were the instruments which our ancestors were in the custom of using—"What was the particular style and character of the music performed by these instruments, and the songs which they accompanied?" "This," says our latest historian,[a] "it is now impossible to determine; and in the total want of authentic documents, it would be idle to hazard a conjecture upon the airs or melodies of Scotland, at the remote period of which we now write." Such also was the

landed, tooke handes on the lande, and daunced this reill or short daunce, singing all with one voice,

Commer goe ye before, commer goe ye,
Gif ye will not goe before, commer let me.

At which time, shee confessed that this Geillis Duncan (a servant girl) did goe before them, playing this reill or daunce uppon a small trumpe, called a Jewes trump, untill they entred into the kirk of North Barrick. These confessions made the King in a wonderfull admiration, and sent for the saide Geillis Duncane, who upon the like trump did play the saide daunce before the Kinges Maiestie; who, in respect of the strangenes of these matters, tooke great delight to be present at their examinations."—Newes from Scotland, &c. 1591.

Tytler's History of Scotland, vol. ii. p. 375.

language of our historians of the last century. Dr Henry[a] expresses himself to the same effect,—that although the words of the poems, songs, and ballads, are, some of them, preserved, "the tunes to which many of them were originally sung are now unknown; and the most diligent enquirers have been able to discover only a very few specimnse of the popular music of this period." Nor is the want of documents, illustrative of ancient popular music, confined to Scotland. Dr Burney[b] confesses that he had never "been so fortunate as to meet with a single tune to an English song or dance, in all the libraries and manuscripts which he had consulted, so ancient as the fourteenth century;" and Mr Ritson,[c] in commenting upon this observation, says, that "it is perhaps impossible to produce even the bare name of a song or dance tune in use before the year 1500;" and that the oldest known is Sellinger's,[d] (St Legers,) which may be traced back to nearly the time of Henry VIII.

It is certainly not a little extraordinary, that songs and melodies, which for ages had been universally sung and played throughout the land, forming the occasional recreation of all classes from the prince to the peasant, should thus have been allowed to die away, and "leave no sign." There is reason to believe that in the fifteenth and sixteenth centuries, if not before, the best of them had been committed to notation, and the ravages of time, alone, are scarcely sufficient to account for their disappearance. We must add to these, the temper, manners, and circumstances of the times. In Scotland, about the year 1550,[e] the active measures which were resorted to by the ecclesiastical and civil power for putting down all rhymes and ballads reflecting upon the Roman Catholic hierarchy and its members, and by which every Ordinary was empowered to search his diocese for all books and papers of that nature, must, in their operation, have occasioned the destruction of many valuable collections and pieces of popular music with which the offensive productions

[a] History of Britain, vol. v. p. 492.

[b] Hist. vol. ii. p. 381.

[c] Ritson's Ancient Songs, Introduction, p. 37.

[d] Hawkins's Hist. vol. ii. p. 92.

[e] Stat. Conc. 1549, c. 43, 48. Acta Parl. 1551, c. 35.

had been, either casually or intentionally, associated. And in the era immediately succeeding the Reformation, some idea may be formed of the extent to which this species of composition was discountenanced by the dominant Church party, from the "Compendium of Godly and Spiritual Songs," of which we have treated in another place.[a] The next century exhibits the spectacle of an almost universal severity of manners, the consequence of these austere and fanatical notions;—music, along with dancing and every innocent amusement, prohibited as dangerous and sinful, and indiscriminately thrust into the same category with vices and profligacy of the worst description.[b] When we look back to the character and habits of the people during this part of our history; farther, when we take into view the great questions which successively agitated the public mind during the period to which we refer,—Popery and Protestantism—Prelacy and Presbytery—King and Commonwealth—and, finally, the establishment of our constitutional rights and privileges;—we need not wonder, that there should have been little leisure and less inclination to record or preserve the light and fleeting effusions of musical genius, and that it should have been reserved for an age of greater freedom from austerity and intolerance, to revive and awaken the cultivation of this art, and with it, the almost forgotten strains of former ages.

For these reasons, when, about fifty or sixty years ago, the melodies of Scotland, from their increasing celebrity, came to be a topic of anti-

[a] *Supra*, p. 30.

[b] The records of our church judicatories (a branch of our antiquities which has been too much neglected) are capable of throwing much light upon matters of this nature; take as examples the following excerpts from the Minutes of the Presbytery of St Andrews, (presented to the Abbotsford Club by Geo. R. Kinloch, Esq. 1837:)—

November 19, (1656.)—*Mure, Pyper.*—The quhilk day compeired John Mure, quho was rebuiked for being the author of much disorder by his *pypeing;* and warned, that if he sall be found afterward making dissorder in any congregation within these bounds, recourse will be had to the civile magistrate, for taking order with him.—P. 72.

(*Sept.* 1, 1658.)—*Mure, Pyper.*—The quhilk day, diverse brethren complained that John Mure, pyper, is occasion of much dissorder in ther congregations, *by his pypeing at brythells and vnseasonable drinkings.* The said John compeiring, *the Presbyterie discharged him to play at any brythells, or at drunken lawings;* with certification, if he be found to contraveene, he will be proceided against with the highest censures of the kirk.—P. 74.

quarian discussion, it is not too much to say, that their history was found to be nearly as mysterious as that of the music of the Greeks; with this advantage, however, on its side, that, as we still possessed a good many specimens of what might be, reasonably enough, presumed to be the musical progeny of our ancestors, though removed, by a good many degrees, from the parent stock,—we had some idea of its essence or *substratum*—of the elements of which it was composed;—we knew, in short, rather more than that "it was something with which mankind was extremely delighted."[a] And yet, from the multiplicity of treatises which have been from time to time published on the music of the ancients, one would suppose that it had been considered a simpler task to expound and illustrate this portion of the history of a people, who had lived upwards of two thousand years ago, and of whose compositions not one well authenticated remnant had survived to the present times, than to give a tolerably plausible account of a set of national airs, as they existed two or three centuries back, the successors or remote descendants of which were still floating around us. Thus, Dr Burney, after devoting a whole quarto volume, the preparation of which cost him several years of his life, to the investigation of the former of these topics,[b] sums up his observations on the music of Scotland by remarking, that it would hereafter be proved to be of a much higher antiquity than has generally been imagined.[c] But, unfortunately for his readers and the world, this able writer either forgot, or felt himself unable to redeem his pledge, as he never afterwards makes any allusion to the subject. Let us presume the latter, and that he had not data to bear out his conclusion.

Mr Tytler's Dissertation, as we have already noticed, appeared in 1779; and in 1794, the history of Scotish music was so fortunate as to

[a] This is Dr Burney's definition of ancient music:—"What the ancient music really was, it is not now easy to determine; but of this we are certain, that it was something with which mankind was extremely delighted," &c.

[b] Although quite as successful as any other writer on this very obscure subject, Dr Burney has candidly confessed that the greater portion of his labours in this field of enquiry appeared to him to resemble those of "a wretch in the street raking the kennels for an old rusty nail!"

[c] Burney's History, vol. i. p. 38.

engage the attention of the late Mr Ritson, the most sceptical and scrupulously exact of antiquaries, who, in the Essay prefixed to his Collection of Scotish Songs, did much to disentangle it from the extraneous and apocryphal matter with which it had become involved, and to furnish an analysis of all the authentic particulars which, at that time, could be collected in regard to it. The result of his enquiries as to the antiquity of our national music is given in the following words:—[a]" No direct evidence, it is believed, can be produced *of the existence* of any Scotish tune, now known, prior to the year 1660, exclusive of such as are already mentioned;" (almost all of these have been named in the course of the preceding pages;) "*nor is any one even of these to be found noted, either in print or manuscript, before that period.*" We have no doubt that this observation, at the time it was made, was substantially correct; nay, it was even within the truth as to Scotish printed music;[b] and if Mr Ritson had not been misled by the publication of Forbes's Cantus, which he supposed to contain tunes peculiar to this country, he would probably have said that none of them had appeared in a printed form till about the end of the seventeenth century. In regard to MSS. we may congratulate ourselves that our optical powers, in the present age, are so much more apt in discerning these things than those of our ancestors; and since the time when Mr Ritson made this remark, and his visual orbs expanded over the *supposed* resuscitation (for it was nothing more)

[a] Essay, p. 105.

[b] We had made the above remark before we discovered the following notice in Dr Burney's History, (vol. iii. p. 262,) from which it appears that *some of the Scotish dance tunes had actually been published in Paris, in the year* 1564. " John D'Etrée, a performer on the hautbois, in the service of Charles IX., published four books of *Danseries*, first, writing down the common lively tunes which, till then, had been probably learned by the ear, and played by memory, about the several countries specified in the title." In a note to the above, the Doctor adds—" The editor of these books tells us that they contained ' Les chant (chants) des branles communs, gais, de Champagne, de Bourgogne, de Poitou, *d'Ecosse*, de Malte, des Sabots, de la Guerre, et autres gaillardes, ballets, voltes, basses dances, hauberrois, allemandes.' Printed at Paris, 1564. From the manner in which the work is here referred to, there can be little doubt that Dr Burney had seen it; but whether it will ever be recovered seems now to be somewhat uncertain, as it has hitherto eluded the most diligent search in the public libraries of France and Britain.

of " The Banks of Helicon,"[a] we have not only been so fortunate as to recover the valuable collection which forms the subject of the present publication, but several others of considerable interest and antiquity. They are written in the same kind of literal notation or tablature with the Skene MS.,—a circumstance which, as it most probably has had the effect of withholding them from general use, and from being introduced into other collections of a modern date, at this distant period serves greatly to enhance their value. When fully revealed, they cannot fail to put the public in possession of a large fund of ancient popular melody, which has long been considered as lost, and which, but for them, would have been irretrievable. The manner in which some of these MSS. have emerged has strongly impressed the Editor with the conviction, that, notwithstanding the acknowledged scarcity of such documents, *if the archives of some of our ancient families were well and diligently sifted, other original MSS. of a similar kind might still be brought to light.* And it is not one of the least pleasing anticipations of those who have interested themselves in the present work, that, besides the fine old airs which the Skene MS. has been the means of reviving, and the information which it affords as to the style of music which prevailed in Scotland during the sixteenth century, it will, in all probability, lead to a future series of accessions to our stock of Scotish melody from other quarters; while, along with these accessions, it cannot fail to shed a few glimmering lights over the early history of our literature, the manners and customs of our forefathers, and many features in their private lives and characters which, though not delineated in the pages of the historian, are not the less interesting to us who live at a time so remote, and in a state of society so different, from theirs.

[a] *Supra*, p. 4. The genuine copy of this tune is in a MS. formerly belonging to the late Mr Alexander Campbell, (the author of Albyn's Anthology, &c.) afterwards to Mr Heber, and now to the Advocates' Library, bearing date 1639. That of which Mr Ritson spoke was given to him by one Edward Williams, a Welshman, and had probably been noted by the latter from memory, as in a letter to Mr Campbell, 1st March 1801, Mr Ritson allows that the two were essentially different, and that the former, " if noted in an ancient MS. promised to be the genuine air." It will be found in Dr Irving and Mr Laing's edition of Alexander Montgomery's Poems, p. 308. Edinburgh, 1821.

We can only spare room for a brief account of some of these MSS. and their leading contents. The earliest is certainly not more recent than the Skene Collection. It belonged to Sir William Mure of Rowallan, the author of "The True Crucifixe for True Catholickes," (Edin. 1629, 12mo,) and of several minor poems; and is partly, if not wholly, written by him, in lute tablature, upon a stave of six lines. Sir William Mure was born in 1594, and died in 1657; and from various circumstances with which we need not detain our readers, this small volume, which only extends to fifty pages, was most probably noted some time between the years 1612 and 1628. Its contents are too briefly told.—"For kissing, for clapping, for loving, for proving, set to the lute by me, W. Mure"—"Mary Beatoun's Row"[a]—"Corn yards"—"Battel of Harlaw"[b]

[a] "Row" is not a term known in music. Perhaps it may be a *literal* mistake for 'Roun," which signified a song; (see Ritson's Ancient Songs, pp. 26, 31,)—and Knox, in his History, (p. 374,) says, "It was well known that shame hasted marriage betwixt John Sempill, called the Dancer, and Mary Livingston, sirnamed the Lusty; what bruit the *Maries* and the rest of the dancers of the Court had, the ballads of that age did witnesse, which we for modestie's sake omit." Mary Beatoun is well known to have been one of the Queen's Maries, and this may be the tune of one of the ballads above spoken of by Knox, the words of which have been lost. There is a full-length portrait of this Mary Beatoun at Balfour House in Fifeshire, and several of Buchanan's Epigrams are addressed to her; (see Monteith's Translation of these, p. 65.) She is mentioned as one of the four young ladies of noble families who accompanied Queen Mary to France, and afterwards returned to Scotland in her train. Their surnames were Livingston, Fleming, Seton, and Beatoun; but, as Sir Walter Scott (Border Minstrelsy, vol. iii. p. 302, ed. 1833) has remarked, from the accounts given by Knox, "they formed a corps which could hardly have subsisted without occasional recruits;" and in the ballad of "Marie Hamilton," although "Marie Beatoun" is introduced, the names of Livingston and Fleming are superseded by those of Hamilton and Carmichael.

"Yestreen the Queen had four Maries,
The nicht she has but three:
There was Marie Seton, and Marie Beatoun,
And Marie Carmichael, and me."

[b] This very sanguinary conflict was fought betwixt the Highland forces under Donald of the Isles and the Lowland toops under the Earl of Mar, on the 24th July 1411, at the village of Harlaw near Inverury, in Aberdeenshire, with all the old and deep-rooted hostility of the Celtic and Saxon race. "It fixed itself," says Mr Tytler, in his History, (vol. ii. p. 177,) "in the music and the poetry of Scotland; a march, called the Battle of Harlaw, continued to be a popular air down to the time of Drummond of Hawthornden; and a spirited ballad, on the same event, is still re-

—" Magge Ramsay"[a]—" Cummer tried"[b]—" Ouir the dek (dyke?) Davy"[c]—" Katherine Bairdie"[d]—" Ane Scottish Dance"—several Volts, Currants, Gavots,—a " Spynelet"[e]—another called " Spynelet reforme"—" La Voici"—" Sibit Sant Nikla,"[f] &c. and a few airs with no name attached to them.

A considerable interval occurs between this and the next MS. which we proceed to notice; and to which, from its wanting a nominal, we are obliged, as in regard to some of the rest, to assign a conjectural date,—not earlier, we should say, than 1670, or later than 1675 or 1680. It is only within these few months, and since these enquiries were instituted,

peated in our own age, describing the meeting of the armies, and the deaths of the chiefs," &c. Motherwell, in his " Minstrelsy," (Introduction, p. 62,) having seen the Rowallan MS., speaks of the tune there given as that of the ballad. This is a mistake. It is the march, or rather pibroch, alluded to in the above passage in Mr Tytler's History, and which Drummond introduces among the " notes of preparation" to his " Polemo-Middinia," in a passage which has been already quoted, (*supra*, p. 120.) As one of those fast and furious movements descriptive of the onslaught of a battle such as that of Harlaw, it is well calculated to heighten the " hurly-burly" of the scene which the poet so amusingly describes. The air of the ballad will be found in Johnson's Museum, (vol. vi. p. 528,) though what may be its pretensions to antiquity, it is difficult to tell; especially, as it has been doubted whether the ballad itself, that is to say, the copy of it which we possess, though decidedly old, was coeval with the event.

a We suppose that this must be a Scottish version of the " Peg-a-Ramsey," alluded to in Sir Toby Belch's drunken ejaculation,—" My lady's a Catayan, we are politicians, Malvolio's a ' Peg-a-Ramsey,'" and " Three merry men we be"—(Twelfth Night, act 2d, scene 3d.) " Little Pegge of Ramsie" is one of the tunes contained in the MSS. of Dr Bull, which formed a part of Dr Pepusch's Library. See Ward's Lives of the Professors of Gresham College, (1740.) In " D'Urfey's Pills," (vol. v. p. 139,) there is a song of this name beginning—

" Bonny Peggy Ramsey, that any man may see,
And bonny was her face, with a fair freckled eye."

The tune there given is the same with that of " Our Polly is a sad slut," in the Beggar's Opera; but that given in the Rowallan MS. is different.

b *i. e.* " Tried friend."

c This tune bears a striking resemblance to " Tullochgorum.'

d See " Kette Bairdie" in Skene MS.

e Probably a piece for the spinet.

f Probably misspelt for " Sibyl St Nicholas." " Sibyl" is the name of a tune. See Jones's Welsh Bards, p. 158. See also a tune called " The Old Cebell," in Hawkins, Hist. vol. v. p. 482. In Skene MS. there is an allemande called " Alman Nicholas."

that this collection accidentally presented itself to the attention of one whose perspicacity it was not very likely to have escaped, David Laing, Esquire, the Secretary of the Bannatyne Club—we say accidentally—because it would have required something very little short of the second-sight for which some of our bardic ancestors have been so celebrated, to discover it in the corner where it had nestled—viz. in the midst of a little volume of very closely written notes of sermons preached by the well-known James Guthrie, the Covenanting minister, who was executed in 1661 for declining the jurisdiction of the king and council—" a true copie of his last words on the scaffold at the Cross of Edinburgh"—a series of texts from Scripture, and notes and memoranda, " ex thesibus theologicis a Doctoribus et Professoribus in Academia Leidensi Conscriptis,"[a] &c. In this singular juxta-position we find nearly fifty of the

[a] The only copy of verses in this MS. is the following, which we here insert, not only as being a curiosity in its way, but that our Presbyterian neighbours may compare the anti-prelatical spirit here displayed with the very different feeling manifested in our times, when the most eloquent of Scottish Divines prefaces his lectures on church establishments by reading the collect of the day!

" Great newes we lately heard from Court,
A ruler great was turned out;
Draw billets.
Another did succeed his place,
He lost his lordship and got grace;
Take time o'd.
The ladies that the Court resort,
Ye know for what they seek the sport;
Whip towdies.
The black coats they are sitting high,
The Crown itself they sit it nigh;
Sit sicker.
There is a coath that rides full sharp,
I heard a fidler play on harp,
Trot cozie.
There was a pyper could not play,
It is not half an hour to-day,
Its coming.
Sunday will be another day;
This week's near spent, and we'l away;
Provide yow.

popular melodies of Scotland, noted in tablature like the foregoing, of which we have spoken. Had they been of the "grave and sweet order" described by Mr Geddes, the author of "The Saints' Recreation," we should have supposed that the individual who inserted them had been like that reverend gentleman, an author or amateur of sacred parodies; but they are rather of too miscellaneous a character to have been intended for any such purpose, and it is extremely doubtful whether the

A man on wadger lost a groat,
Alledging some had turned their coat,
Per inde.
Good morrow, Covenant, adieu!
The Covenant is both false and true;
Subscribers.
If Presbyters, they had no greid,
Mixt with the pride, they had no neid
Of Deacons.
I saw a priest carry a bend
Episcopall, it had an end
Papisticall.
Look to our churches the debate,
And to our Court its staggering state;
Wine glasses.
When fools do wake, and wise men sleep,
And wolves do get the lambs to keep;
Sad tidings.
Ah, behold our paroch priest,
With not a button on his briest;
New fashion;
Nixt the pedant he must say
Amen, stand up and give a cry;
Brave doings.
He is most cal'ed up that playes the knave,
Advanced a step above the lave;
The gallows.
In every state some looks for gain.
Stollen dewgs make Talyors vain;
Ill conquest.
Others know what I do mean.
I may speak what I have seen;
Save treason.
FINIS CORONAT OPUS."

music was written by the same individual by whom the sacred contents of the volume were penned. We have here, among others,—" Green grows the rashes[a]—Owr late among the broom—Bonny Jean[b]—The Gee Wife[c]—Corn Bunting[d]—Get ye gone from me—Skip Jon Waker wantonlie—The malt grinds well—Ostend[e]—God be with my bonnie love—Fain would I be married—Long a-growing[f]—Hold her going[g]—Ketron Ogie[h]—Bonnie Maidlen Wedderburn—My Ladie Binnies Lilt or Urania[i]—Bessy Bell—Ranting Ladie—It's brave sailing here[k]—Clout the Cauldron[l]—I love my love in secret—The Shoemaker[m]—Jon Robison's Park—If the Kirk would let me be[n]—The Blench of Midlbie[o]—The Bonnie Broom[p]—The Windie Writer[q]—The High Court of Justice

[a] To this day a favourite and well-known air.

[b] Query—of Aberdeen?

[c] " The gee wife," *i.e.* The pettish wife. The Scotish song, " My wife has taen the gee," though evidently derived from this, would seem to be more modern. (See Ritson's Scotish Songs, vol. i. p. 90.)

[d] The *Emberiza Miliaria* is in Mearns and Aberdeenshire called the " corn-buntlin."—Dr Jamieson's Supplement, *voce* Buntlin. The tune is now better known as Tullochgorum.

[e] In the Skene MS.

[f] " Long a-growing." See a ballad in the " North Country Garland," entitled, " My bonny love is long of growing."

[g] " Haud her gaun." Still well known in modern collections, under the name of " Steer her up, and haud her gaun."

[h] See *supra*, p. 17.

[i] Most probably Lady Binnie of that Ilk.

[k] The title of this song reminds us of the one mentioned in Gawin Douglas's Prologue to Book xii. of Virgil.

> " The schip salis over the salt fame,
> Will bring thir merchandis and my lemane hame ;"

but we do not pretend to trace any connection betweeu the two.

[l] See Chambers's Scotish Songs, vol. ii. p. 542.

[m] We find a copy of this tune in a MS. belonging to Mr Waterston, of 1715. Whether the words are extant, we are not aware. " The gallant shoemaker" is one of the songs mentioned in Mr Ritson's list of those which, in his time, had not been recovered. (Ritson's Letters to Paton, p. 24.)

[n] See Chambers's Scotish Songs, vol. i. p. 134.

[o] See " Weel bobbit blench of Middlebie," in Riddell of Glenriddell's Collection.

[p] " The bonny broom." This, if not the same with " The broom of the Cowdenknows," which is certainly one of the finest of our pastorals, most probably suggested the idea. Chambers's Scotish Songs, vol. i. p. 247.

[q] The windie (*i. e.* swaggering or blustering) writer. A friend has kindly furnished us with the

—Sweet Willie[a]—If thou wert my own thing—My love hath left me sick, sick, sick—Stollen away when I was sleeping—Kety thinks not long to play with Peter at Evin—The gown made—Yonder grows the tanzie—Jockie drunken bable—Bonny Christian—Levin's Rant—Joy to the personne of my love—Good night, and God be with you."

Mr Andrew Blaikie, engraver, Paisley, who has, for many years, taken great pains to collect and preserve all the specimens, traditionary as well as recorded, which he could find, of our genuine Scotish melodies, is in possession of a volume, bearing date 1692, which contains a great number of tunes written in tablature for the *Viol da Gamba*, most, if not all, of which he has himself reduced to modern notation. This is the volume mentioned by Mr Robert Chambers[b] and Mr R. A. Smith,[c] along with another dated 1683. The last, however, Mr Blaikie some years ago had the misfortune to lose, but not until he had nearly rendered himself independent of any such casualty by a translation of the principal airs. Another circumstance lessened the importance of this loss: the tunes, with a very few exceptions, were the same with those contained in the volume which is preserved. It may be mentioned, also, that, although Mr Blaikie procured these MSS. at different times, and from different individuals, they were both written in the same hand, and their respective contents arranged nearly in the same order. Great part of the collection consists of popular English songs and dances, which we need not enumerate.[d] The following are among those of which Scotland may claim the parentage:—

words of this song, as taken down from the recitation of a lady in Edinburgh: but they are little worthy of preservation. *Ex uno disce omnes.*

> "There lives a lass just at the Cross,
> Her face is like the paper,
> And she's forsaken lairds and lords,
> And ta'en a windy writer."

a Probably the tune of the pretty old ballad, "Sweet Willie and fair Annie."

b Introduction to Scotish Songs, p. 44.

c Preface to Scotish Minstrel.

d It would be somewhat singular if this collection and that of 1670, belonging to Mr Laing, had

"A health to Betty[a]—Down Tweedside[b]—Honest Luckie[c]—King James's march to Ireland[d]—Meggie, I must love (thee)[e]—Where Helen lies[f]—Tow to spin[g]—Sweet Willie—Robin and Jonnet[h]—Highland Laddie—Franklin is fled far away—For lake of gold she left me—Abbayhill's Rant[i]—Bonny roaring Willie[k]—O'er the muir to Maggy—My dearie, if thou dye—When the King enjoys his own again—The last time I came over the moor—The new way of owing (wooing)[l]—The Bed to me—The ladd's gane—Binny's Jig[m]—Sheugare-Candie—Phillporter's Lament—Do Rant—New Cornriggs—Montrose's Lynes—Maclean's Scots Measure—Lord Aboyne's Air—Lady Binny's Lilt—John, come kiss

been written by Englishmen; but from the anglicised phraseology and othography adopted in both, there can be little doubt either that this was the case, or that they were written by natives of this country, who preferred the English mode of diction and spelling to that of their vernacular tongue.

a The air, "My mother's ae glowerin o'er me."

b "Tweedside." It is worthy of remark, that this air was introduced with variations by the famous Italian violinist, Veracini, in his solos for the violin, printed in 1744.

c This is in some respects a memorable tune. Mr Blaikie, the owner of the musical MS., relates, that some time before the appearance of Redgauntlet, he happened to make Sir Walter Scott a present of a MS. (not musical) of the 17th century, written by a person who had been resident in the neighbourhood of Edinburgh, and containing some curious details relative to his reconversion to the Roman Catholic faith, in consequence of a vision he had on a mountain in Spain. Among other matters of reproach to the Presbyterians, from whom he had separated, he mentions that one of their preachers said one day in the pulpit, "I hear you have a tune among you called 'Weel hoddled Luckie,' if I hear ony mair of this, I'll hoddle the best of you." "Soon after this," (says Mr Blaikie,) "I began deciphering my musical MS., and sent Sir Walter some of the tunes, and among the rest, 'Honest Luckie,' which I said was probably the tune that had offended the Presbyterian minister, with a more passable name." It is therefore not one of the least characteristic passages in "Wandering Willie's Tale," when Sir Robert Redgauntlet, at his "appointed place," in the lower regions, says to Willie's grandfather, in answer to his demand for the receipt, "ye shall hae that for a tune on the pipes, Steenie. Play us up, 'Weel hoddled Luckie.'"

d "Lochaber no more."

e "Peggy, I must love thee."

f Chambers's Songs, vol. i. p. 144.

g "Nancy's to the greenwood gane."

h "My jo Janet."

i "O this is no my ain house."

k Rattlin roarin Willie? Chambers's Songs, vol. ii. p. 605.

l "Carle now the king's come."

m "The Dusty Miller."

me now—Jockie went to the wood[a]—Joy to the person—Allan Water—Ballow—Bonie Nanie—Bonie Lassie—Jock, the laird's brother[b]—Hold away from me, Donald—Hey how, Robin, quoth she—Bonny Christon—Drumlanrick's Ayr—Duke of Lennox Port—Gerard's Mistress—I pray your love turn to me[c]—In January last—Jockie wod a owing (wooing) go—My Ladie Monteith's Lament[d]—Jockie drunken bable—Mackbeth—My Lady Errol's Lament[e]—The bonny brow—The Nightingale." Among

[a] This tune, a copy of which will be found in the Musical Appendix of this work, is not what we would have expected from the name,—of a Scotish cast, but decidedly Welsh in its structure,—obviously a harp tune, and substantially identical with a Welsh air called "Reged," p. 150, Jones's Welsh Bards. As "Jockie" is but a familiar impersonation of the male sex, the name "Jockie went to the wood," precisely corresponds with the "Hie ruff sang"—"Ane man fur to the holt," in "Peblis to the Play;"—(*supra*, p. 45;) and if the two airs could be identified, it would lead to the singular result, that harp songs like this were in vogue among the populace, in Scotland, during the 15th century. We know that the harp was the most popular instrument in Britain at this time. It was the one on which James I. chiefly excelled, and "at the coronation of Henry V., in 1413, we hear of no other instruments than harps, and one of that Prince's historians (Thomas de Elmham) tells us that their number in the hall was prodigious." (Burney's Hist. vol. ii. p. 382.) In Scotland, however, we consider that at this time the popular style of melody was something very different from that which prevailed in Wales or England; and we cannot conceive that an air so refined and regular as "Jockie went to the wood" could ever have been described as a rough song. At the same time, if the enquiry were instituted, as to whether or not the tunes of the Welsh or early Britons had formed the basis of *some* of our popular airs, we should be inclined to say, that there could be no doubt of the fact, however distinct and different the melodies of the two countries in reality are. Let any one, for example, compare the Welsh air "Pen Rhaw" with "John, come kiss me now," and the latter with the lively air, "There's nae luck about the house," and he will see that they all spring from the same parent source. But we here only present our readers with the germ of an enquiry, which we leave to others to bring to maturity.

[b] "There's auld Rob Morris."

[c] "Turn thee, sweet Will, to me?" Complaynt of Scotland, see *supra*, p. 53.

[d] "Whistle o'er the lave o't."

[e] The incident to which this tune related was an action of divorce, brought, in 1658–59, by Lady Erroll, a daughter of the Earl of Southesk, against her husband, upon a similar ground to that which first proclaimed the infamy of the Countess of Essex, in the reign of James VI. If, however, any reliance can be placed on the ballads and traditions of the country, the plea was not here urged with the same success as in the case of the English countess. Our judicial records, so far as they have been investigated, are said to be silent on the subject; but a letter from Keith of Barholm to Captain Brown at Paris, dated 22d February 1659, which Mr Sharpe quotes in his Ballad Book, goes far to corroborate the general truth of the story, and the tune, "Lady Erroll's

the dances there are—"The Canaries"—"The Seamen's dance," &c.

Dr Leyden, in his Introduction to the Complaynt, (p. 285,) refers to a MS. collection of airs written soon after the Revolution, and adapted to the Lyra-viol. Whether this volume is still extant, the Editor is not aware, but from the names mentioned by Leyden, it must have contained many of those to be found in Mr Blaikie's collection of 1692, and, besides them, the following:—"The Lady's Goune[a]—Strick upon a Strogin—Hallowevin—The new kirk gavell—When she cam ben (she bobit)—Full fa my eyes—When the bryd cam ben she becked—The Colleyrs Daughter—Foull take the wars[b]—The bonie brookit lassie, blew beneath the eyes[c]—The milkein pell."

We find, also, in a very small MS. belonging to Mr Laing, probably not older than the early part of the eighteenth century, and written partly in common notation, and partly in a species of notation, for the flute or flageolet, consisting of *dots*, the following among others:—"The wind has blown my plaid away[d]—Willie Winkie's dead away[e]—Gilliecrankie—Robin laddie—Foull fa' the wars—Widow, art thou wakin—Findlay came to my bed-stock[f]—King James's March to

Lament," in this MS. of Mr Blaikie, may be deemed an additional confirmation. See Mr Maidment's "North Country Garland," Mr Kinloch's "Ballad Book," and "Lamont's Diary;" entry, January 7, 1658.

[a] Although it might puzzle many a Scotch lawyer of the present day to explain the legal signification of "The Lady's Gown," the term appears formerly to have been applied to a certain gratuity or pecuniary gratification, which was paid to a wife when she gave her consent to the alienation of her husband's lands over which her liferent extended. Fountainhall's Decisions, vol. ii. p. 519.

[b] "Deil tak the wars."

[c] Chambers's Songs, vol. ii. p. 544.

[d] "Over the hills and far away."

[e] Probably "Willie Winkie's Testament:" but these words do not occur in the verses which Herd has furnished in his Collection in 1776.

[f] Burns has a song founded on this. It begins—

"Wha is that at my bower's door?
Wha is it but Finlay."

Dublin—Jamaica[a]—Galloway's Lament," &c. We may add, that there are at present lying before us, in common notation, a MS. belonging to the Advocates' Library, dated 1704; another to Mr Laing, 1706; and a third of 1715 to Mr Waterston, stationer in Edinburgh.

With these documents, besides that of which we here furnish a translation, we are now amply fortified against the attacks of Mr Ritson's scepticism; and our readers will recollect that these MSS. are merely such as have fallen within the scope of *our* personal observation.[b] In a letter which Mr Ritson addressed to Mr Walker, the author of the Memoirs of the Irish Bards, in 1791, several years before the publication of the Essay on Scotish Song,[c] after noticing the apparent want of all direct evidence of the existence of our favourite airs, prior to the Restoration, he puts the question—" Upon what foundation, then, do we talk of the antiquity of Scotish music?" Indeed, we have been taunted on this subject in more than one quarter. Jones tells us that we have " no such thing as an ancient and authentic MS. like what the Irish or the Welsh have."[d] Now, although we have no inclination whatever to provoke a national contest upon this or any other point, or to challenge the antiquity of many celebrated Welsh and Irish airs; yet, believing, as we do, the real state of the fact to be this, that neither the Welsh nor the Irish can produce any authentic collections of their national music of so old a date, and containing so many popular melodies, as the MSS. of Scotish airs which we have above described, we cannot allow the observation to pass unnoticed. We are not aware that Mr Morris's MSS.,—said to be of the eleventh century, but which Dr Burney[e] thought much more recent—though filled with harp music, arranged in harmony or coun-

[a] As Jamaica was taken by the English from the Spaniards, in 1655, this may be assigned as the date of the tune. Many of the above songs will be found in Hogg's Jacobite Relics.

[b] That more of the same sort are still extant, we have little doubt. Gordon's Lute Book, noted at Aberdeen in 1627, which contains, among other things, the air of " Greysteil," is mentioned as having been the property of Dr Burney, (see *supra*, p. 84,) who probably may have collected other MSS. of Scotish music, especially from his having undertaken to prove that it was of higher antiquity than generally supposed.

[c] Letters of Ritson, vol. i. p. 190.

[d] Welsh Bards, p. 99.

[e] Hist. vol. ii. p. 110.

terpoint, contain any Welsh air known at the present day. In Jones's Collection, two or three airs are copied from MSS.; but of these the age is not mentioned; and the Editor expressly styles his work[a] a Collection of Welsh National Melodies, which "have been handed down by tradition," and which he collected "from hearing the old musicians or minstrels play them on their instruments, and from their being chanted by the peasantry."

In the same way, the first collection of ancient Irish airs was formed by Mr Bunting, being noted at the meeting of harpers in 1792 at Belfast, and afterwards taken down from their performance, and from the singing of the people in different parts of the country.

In short, the authentication of these airs by MSS. is a thing which appears never to have been dreamt of either in Wales or in Ireland, and the best evidence which Mr Bunting obtained on the point of antiquity will appear from the following extract from his preface:—"Most of the performers convened at the meeting above mentioned were men advanced in life, and they all concurred in one *opinion* respecting the *reputed* antiquity of those airs which *they called ancient*. They smiled, on being interrogated concerning the era of such compositions, saying, 'They were more ancient than any to which our popular traditions extended.'"[b] So much for the assertion that, in Scotland, we have no such thing as an ancient and authentic MS. such as the Irish and Welsh have!

But, besides their rarity, we can scarcely regard these MSS. with indifference, even in an historical and literary point of view. No doubt, so far as relates to the poetry—the titles, and sometimes the first lines of the songs, are all that are there preserved; and, we may add, all that, in most cases, are known to be extant; but these are not only interesting from personal and local associations, and as illustrations, however slight, of the manners of a bygone age, but they denote the former existence, and, to a certain extent, mark out the individual character, of a great

[a] Welsh Bards, p. 122.

[b] It seems to be admitted on all hands, that the old music of the Irish bards and minstrels is purely traditionary. "Though musical notation (says Mr Walker, Irish Bards, p. 66) was not known amongst the aborigines of this island, remains of their music have been handed down to us *by tradition*, in its original simplicity."

many songs and ballads, some of which (if written copies of them are no longer to be found) may still survive in the memories of the present generation. It is not unlikely, therefore, that the bare mention of their names may lead to their discovery. Of their restoration by the hands of any of our "North-countrie" minstrels of the nineteenth century, we are not so sanguine;—a task which so perfectly fitted the genius of Burns does not so readily adapt itself to the capacity of ordinary men. There are relics, however, particularly in the Skene MS. which, together with the music,—from the images and associations they suggest,—are well calculated, we should think, to awaken the pathos, the simplicity, and the humour of the Scotish muse.

The interest attached to their musical contents can best be appreciated by those who, like ourselves, have taken pains to enquire into the history of Scotish music, and who, not being able to go farther back than the beginning of the last century, have been tempted, in their unavailing search after the strains of preceding ages, to exclaim—

"Where should this music be?—i' the air or the earth?"

Has it altogether ceased to exist? Has it quitted this terrestrial sphere, or does it still continue to hover around us, in some of those gentle, breathing forms which the creative genius of man has, from time to time, imparted to it? If so, what are the forms in which we are most likely to recognise it? Were those ancient songs which have reached us, along with their reputed melodies, originally chanted to the same tunes with which we now find them associated? What has been the nature of the changes which they have undergone in passing through the trying ordeal of oral communication? Have they been improved or deteriorated in consequence? Have they been casually altered by the ignorance of the multitude, or wilfully changed and perverted by the crude attempts of inexperienced amateurs, or the injudicious efforts of tasteless and pedantic composers, to polish and improve them? For these, and other such questions, an answer is now provided, which, so far as it goes, may be relied on as authentic and indisputable.

With all these documents at our disposal, and the most unreserved privilege of publication liberally conceded to us by their respective owners, we confess that we, at one time, felt much inclined to include in the present volume copious extracts from the music, and a complete commentary upon the whole of these MSS. Upon consideration, however, it was found that the execution of such a project would have increased the letter-press and engraving to a degree not only beyond the limits, but incompatible with the plan, of a dissertation which professed to treat simply of the Skene MS.—a subject which, when combined with those general views of the history of Scotish music which naturally spring out of it, is, of itself, sufficiently voluminous. We resolved, therefore, to content ourselves with introducing these ancient collections to the notice of our readers in the cursory manner we have here done, and, in the course of our observations, to avail ourselves of their materials, at all times when they were likely to prove serviceable for the purpose of illustration.

In what farther remains, we confine our remarks tc the more immediate object of the present enquiry.

The most gratifying result which arises from the discovery of the Skene MS. is the proof which it affords of the antiquity of some of our most celebrated Scotish airs, and of those striking national peculiarities by which the music of this country has been so long distinguished. In the same spirit with the observations of Ritson, Mr Pinkerton,[a] in 1783, referring to the names of the songs given in the Complaynt of Scotland, observes—"This list, which is of exceeding curiosity, may teach us that not one of our Scotish popular airs is so ancient as 1548." But, although the Skene MS. is upwards of half a century more recent than the Complaynt of Scotland, it contains sufficient internal evidence to refute this opinion,—if, indeed, (resting upon so weak a foundation,) it may be thought to require any refutation. In a rhapsody such as the Complaynt, where "ane rustic pastour, distitut of urbanite and of speculatione of natural

[a] Select Songs, vol. ii. p. 32.

philosophe, indoctrynes his nychtbours as he hed studeit Ptholome, Averois, Aristotel, Galen, Ypocrites or Cicero, quhilk var expert practicians in methamatic art,"—we are not to look for historical evidence as to the music which was popular in Scotland at the epoch of its publication. In fact, "the sweit melodious sangis of the natural music of the antiquitie" there named, appear, most of them, to have been, like the philosophy which the shepherd inculcated, of the scholastic order; and they are described in the narrative as having been sung in parts,—"in gude accordis and reportis of dyapason, prolations, and diatesseron,"—so that the music attached to them had been, most probably, the works of English composers, and served up in this Scotish pasticcio with the same regard to consistency, with which the author has introduced the nightingale, singing her sweet notes all the night long, although it is well known that she was never a native of these less favoured climes.

We have now before us direct and incontrovertible proof that many melodies which have come down to the present day are two hundred, and, in some instances, upwards of two hundred, years old; and, farther than this, we are enabled to ascend many years beyond the commencement of the seventeenth century, upon grounds which, though circumstantial and presumptive, are, in some respects, not the less satisfactory and convincing.

As may be expected in all such collections, none of the tunes in the Skene MS. bear either a date or the name of their author. Nay, we have not even the satisfaction of an observation of the copyist, very common in our day, (though often misapplied,) that this or that was "a very ancient melody." Neither do any of the titles of the tunes correspond with the names or description of the ancient lyrics alluded to in the chronicles and poems which we have above particularized. In regard to some of these, had they appeared in this collection, the known dates of the works in which they were mentioned would have carried back their antiquity for centuries beyond the time when the MS. was written; others, such as—"God sen the Duc had bidden in France, and de la Beauté had neuer come hame," by being interwoven with historical events, would have at once fixed their own era,—that is to say, the most *recent* term of their existence,—though the custom, which has at all times prevailed, of adapting new songs to old, favourite airs, would have left, still undetermined, their age *prior* to that period. It is to be regretted, therefore, that none of these recorded historical songs appear in the MS. There is one, however, which, though handed down to us by tradition alone, till within a comparatively short period, commemorates an event in our history too disastrous—too deeply engraven on the hearts of Scotsmen—ever to be forgotten,—"The Flowers of the Forest;" and it is no small satisfaction to be able, at last, to point to the original strain which deplored the desolating effects of the Battle of Flodden,—the very accents in which the simple inhabitants of Etterick Forest so pathetically bewailed their griefs. Sir Walter Scott[a] has told us that the words of this song,—with the exception of the first and last line of the first stanza,[b] together with another brief fragment,—were written by a lady of Roxburghshire, about the middle of last century, (Mrs Elliott,) and that these were the only genuine remains of the ancient ditty; for which reason, some of our hypercritical antiquaries (who err, perhaps, nearly as much on the side of scepticism as our too credulous ancestors did in the opposite extreme) have thrown out doubts as to whether those remains actually related to the event in question. For ourselves, we could never see any reason for withholding our assent from an universally accredited local tradition, associated with words which, though figurative and poetical, confessedly admitted of no other application than that which had been popularly assigned to them; and if any additional ray of light could render still more palpable the link of connection between the two, it

[a] Border Minstrelsy, vol. ii. p. 156.

[b] These are,

I've heard them lilting at the ewes milking.
. . . . .
The flowers of the forest are a' wede away.
. . . . .
I ride single on my saddle.
The flowers of the forest are a' wede away.

would be the mournful, touching flow of the original air, which adapts itself, in so perfect a manner, to the fragments that remain:

"And chaunts, in solemn strain, the dirge of Flodden-field."

It is curious to note the coincidence of two historical documents of an ancient date, where one is brought to light two or three centuries posterior to the other; but where the ever-varying, and often, it must be confessed, the delusive voice of tradition is re-echoed by an unlooked-for discovery, such as the MS. before us, we hail their mutual recognition with a double feeling of satisfaction and pleasure.[a] It was with no slight curiosity, therefore, that we scanned the pages of this collection for many an air rumoured to have sprung up in the olden time; and, in some cases, our researches were attended with success, while, in others, (as might be expected,) we have been disappointed. We have not been so fortunate as to meet with "The Souters of Selkirk," a tune supposed to be coeval with "The Flowers of the Forest," nor "Gilderoy," of the

a The most singular instance of any coincidence of this kind which has, perhaps, ever occurred, relates to the Irish air, "The summer is coming," better known by Moore's words, "Rich and rare." When this was taken down by Mr Bunting, in 1792, from the performance of the Irish harpers, at the meeting at Belfast, it was discovered to be the same with the vocal composition in score for six voices, beginning—

"Sumer is i cumin
Lhude sing cuccu,"

preserved in a Harleian MS. and inserted by Hawkins and Burney, in their respective works, as the oldest *English song* extant, (in parts.) It is referred by them to the middle of the 15th century; but Ritson says, "there cannot be a doubt that it is two hundred years older, *i.e.* of the latter part of the reign of Henry III." (1260 to 1270.) In this case the MS. copy will be upwards of 500 years older than the traditional version. They still, however, resemble each other in all material respects, while the name being the same, leaves no doubt of their original identity; and as little can there be any question as to the purely traditional character of the Irish melody. It is said that "to those who have resided among the peasantry of the southern and western parts of Ireland, where the national manners are most unadulterated, it is at this day perfectly familiar, and that it has been sung by the people of that nation, from time immemorial, at the approach of spring." (Should this not be summer?) Hardiman's Irish Minstrelsy, vol. i. p. 354, (edit. 1831.)

age of James V. "The Jolly Beggar" and "The Gaberlunzie Man," also of the same age, and reported, but without any evidence of the fact, to have been the productions of that monarch, do not appear among the number neither by name nor according to the airs to which they are now sung. They remain as apocryphal as ever both as regards the author and the date. "The Bonny Earl of Murray," whose assassination took place in 1592, is similarly situated. Neither are there any vestiges of "O Bothwell Bank, thou bloomest fair." To make amends, however, for these and other disappointments, we have our old favourite, "John Anderson," of whose antiquity there was no *written* testimony; and, among those which have carried down their original appellatives, with slight modifications, to the present day, we find "The last time I came o'er the moor," under the more emphatic name of "Alas! that I came o'er the moor."—"Bonny Dundee," also under the preferable cognomen of "Adieu, Dundee."—"Johny Faa," under the title of "Lady Cassilis Lilt."—"My Jo, Janet," under that of "Long er onie old man,"—"Good night, and joy be wi' you a'," (Good night, and God be with you.)—"Janet drinks na water."—"Sa merry as we ha' been," and others. Besides these, several airs with which we have been long familiar will be found figuring in their old, though possibly not their *most* ancient characters, to say nothing of occasional resemblances, which, in some cases, are so decided as to moot a question as to the originality of compositions which were never previously suspected.

It is not to be presumed of any collection of national airs that they are coeval with the period when the collection was formed. An individual who sits down to a task of this nature, has no inducement to give the preference to such as have been most recently composed. On the contrary, he rather looks back to former ages. It is—"the voice of years that are gone that roll before him with their deeds,"—the airs which are endeared to him by national and family association, and embalmed in his memory by the consecrating power of time, in which he chiefly delights, and which he is most anxious to secure from oblivion. To suppose, therefore, that the greater part of the Scottish melodies contained in this MS. are not of a much earlier date than the reign of James VI., would be, to say the least of it, a gross violation of probability. Farther, a document has transpired, in the course of our researches, from which it distinctly appears that the Scotish music most highly appreciated at that time was not the composition of that age, but of a period long anterior to it. This is a paper styled "Information touching the Chappell-Royall of Scotland," the original of which is deposited in the General Register House. It is dated at Whitehall, 24th January 1631, and bears to be signed by Edward Kellie, who, as appears from a writ under the Privy Seal, was appointed "Receiver of the fees" of the said chapel, 26th November 1629. But, before introducing it to our readers, we shall take the liberty of digressing so far as to notice some particulars in the history of the Scotish Chapel-royal, concerning which very little has been said by any of our historians.

This institution was originally founded at Stirling by James III. The building formed one of the most conspicuous ornaments of its romantic castle rock, and is commemorated by Sir David Lyndsay, in the well known lines in which he makes his Papingo exclaim,

"Adew, fair Snawdoun, with thy towris hie,
Thy chapell-royall, park, and tabill round;
May, June, and July wald I dwell in thee,
War I ane man, to heir the birdis sound,
Quhilk doth again thy royall rocke rebound."

The foundation was enlarged by James IV. in 1501, at which time the establishment consisted of sixteen canons, nine prebendaries, and six boys.[a] This was exclusive of the dean, an office which was originally vested in the Bishop of Galloway, the Queen's confessor.[b] Among the

[a] See an original MS. headed "Information anent the first and present estait of the King's Majestie's Chapel-Royal," in a volume entitled "Church Affairs from the zeire of God 1610 to the zeir 1625." Balfour MSS., Advocates' Library.

[b] See Spottiswood's Religious Houses, p. 527. Keith's Scotish Bishops, p. 288. There is, or was, a painting at Kensington Palace, supposed to have been executed from 1482 to 1484; and to have been intended for an altar-piece to the Chapel-Royal of Scotland. It extends to three

sixteen canons there were various functionaries, viz. the sub-dean, the sacristour, the chanter, the thesaurer, the maister of the bairnis, and the chancellor. These were called the "sax dignities." There were also musical retainers of an inferior grade. In the MS. from which we have obtained the above information, we see mention of a "trumpeter;" and in the Privy Seal Register (May 14, 1601[a]) Mr William Chalmer is admitted to the office of "lwter" of the chapel-royal. For the sustentation of this establishment, revenues were provided from various priories, prebendaries, kirks, and lands, and confirmed to it by Papal bulls. These (we quote from the MS. of 1610) were reckoned "to have payit to the chapell then, in the 1501 ȝeir, 2000 lib. ȝeirly, which is more than ten thousand lib. now."

A curious feature of the old institution, mentioned by Pitscottie, should not be omitted.[b] He says that the original founder doubled the number of the musicians, "for that effect, that the one half should ever be ready to sing and play with him, and hold him merrie; the other half to remain at home, to sing and pray for him and his successioun."[c] This was independent of the ordinary musicians of the royal household, some account of whom has already been given.

When the rites of the Catholic Church were abolished at the Reformation, this splendid establishment was, as a matter of course, allowed to sink into dilapidation and ruin. Its rents were either withheld or con-

compartments, and represents James III. and his son; besides other figures and members of the royal family, including his queen and an ecclesiastic in an act of devotion. Pinkerton gives an engraving of this picture in his "Iconographia Scotica," and supposes the latter personage to have been intended for the Dean of the Chapel-Royal, the Bishop of Galloway, or "Sir William Rogers, the great English musician, (the Sir being often applied to ecclesiastics,) or some other eminent foreigner." Sir William Rogers, however, was not an ecclesiastic, he was a layman; and Ferrerius, Drummond, and other authorities, concur in stating, that he was promoted by the king to the honour of knighthood.

[a] Fol. lxxiii. 232.

[b] Vol. i. p. 210, Dalyell's edit.

[c] A similar regulation prevailed in the Chapel-Royal of Edward IV., a part of the musicians belonging to it being, in like manner, retained for the king's private amusement, as well as the religious service of the chapel; from which, and other circumstances we have already hinted, (*supra*, p. 106,) that James III. had probably borrowed the idea of the Scotish establishment from his brother of England. See Hawkins's History, vol. ii. p. 290.

veyed away in grants of titularity to laymen; and individuals were appointed to the different offices who were non-resident, and incapable of serving,—a circumstance of less moment, as the choral service, and all instrumental music, having been forbidden, their occupation was, in fact, at an end, and no farther duty remained. In this state of things, we observe,[a] that in 1586, "Thomas Hudson, musician, maister of his Majestie's chaipell-royall," was "appointed, with power to him to searche and try the auld foundatioun of the said chaipell-royall; and all superstitioun and idolatrie being abolist, to follow and embrace the form, so far as it aggreis with Goddes worde, and religioun presentlie profest within the realme." We find, accordingly, that in 1610 the service was reduced to the simple and naked psalmody of the Presbyterian Church; and its situation at this period, in this and other respects, is described in the "Information" already referred to, as follows:—"The sax boys had 90 merkis among them, whareof there is none this day, and of all the sixteen chanonis and nyn prebendis, only sevin attendis and hes no means, so that only they sing the common tune of a psalme, and being so few as skarse knowen."

After the accession of James VI. to the throne of the three kingdoms, the restoration of the chapel-royal was one of the steps in the progress of this monarch's ill-advised and disastrous undertaking to bring the religious institutions of Scotland into a state of conformity with those of England—an undertaking, the obstinate and reckless prosecution of which was attended with such fatal results to his son and successor. In 1606, the foundation revenues and privileges of the chapel-royal were ratified by Act of Parliament:[b] and, in 1612,[c] Maister William Birnie (minister) was appointed its dean, "with speciall power to the said Mr Williame, to chuse ane sufficient number of prebendares, skeilful in musick, being apt and qualifiet for uthir divine service," and to confer upon the benefices belonging to them "according to the first institution;"—the place of residence to be "at Halyrudhous, the palice of the samyn, and the

[a] Privy Seal Register, 5th June 1586.

[b] Acta Parl. p. 299.

[c] Privy Seal Register, 20th Sept. 1612, Present. to Benefices, fol. 8.

chappell not to be called the chappell-royall of Striveling, as heretofore, but 'his majesties chapell-royall of Scotland;' and the members to attend his majesty in whatever part of Scotland he may happen to be." In pursuance of these objects, in 1629 an annual pension of L.2000 was granted by Charles I. to the musicians of the chapel;[a] and for several years previous to his coronation in Scotland, in 1633, exertions appear to have been made by remodelling its arrangements, and appointing efficient persons for the discharge of its various duties, in order that, upon this occasion, and the contemplated introduction of Episcopacy by the authority of the legislature, which took place immediately afterwards, the religious service should be there celebrated according to the form of the Church of England.[b] The nature of these arrangements is circumstantially set forth in the "Information" by Kellie, which has given rise to this digression, and from which, in this place, we subjoin the following extract, as more particularly relating to the object for which we have had occasion to refer to it:[c]—

"Therafter your majestie was gratiously pleased, by your letters under your highnes privie seall, with consent of the dean of your said chappel-royall, to constitute mee collector and distributer of the rents pertayning to your said chappell, and to see such good orders established in the same, as the service therein might be well and faithfully done, and that none but persons sufficiently qualified should have any place there, and that they should be all keept at daily practise; and, for that effect, your majestie appointed mee ane chamber within your pallace of Halyrudehouse, wherein I have provided and sett upp an organe, two flutes, two pandores, with violls and other instruments, with all sorts of English, French, Dutch, Spaynish, Latine,[d] Italian, and OLD SCOTCH MUSICK,

[a] Privy Seal Register, Feb. 18, 1629.

[b] Besides these preparations from some documents that have come under our notice, particularly "the accompt of James Murray of Kilbabertoun, Master of Wark to our Sovereign Lord, 1628," (General Register House,) and MS. notes to Sibbald's History of Fife, Advocates' Library,—it would appear that about this time, considerable sums were laid out in repairing the Royal Chapels at Stirling and Falkland.

[c] The reader will find the whole of this "Information" printed entire in the Appendix.

[d] We suppose that the "Latine" music here mentioned consisted either of masses or church

vocall and instrumentall. In the said chamber the said organist and the boyes doe remain, and the remanent musicians and under officers doe meet therein twice a week to practice and to receive directions for the next service," &c.

From this, it appears that the musicians of the chapel-royal were "kept at daily practice" in all sorts of vocal and instrumental music, including English, French, Dutch, Spanish, Latin, Italian, and OLD SCOTISH MUSIC. There can be no doubt that this last expression referred to the popular national music of Scotland. That sacred music was here not meant is sufficiently obvious; the metrical psalmody of the Reformed Scotish Church was not *old*, and the music of the church in Scotland before the Reformation was identical with that of Rome, and therefore not *Scotish*. Again, we are told that the music provided by Kellie was of "all sorts"—secular, of course, as well as sacred; nor is there any thing very extraordinary in this, when we see that from its outset—from the time that the original founder of this institution required that a portion of the "musicians of the chapel" should ever be ready to "sing and play with him, and hold him merrie," they had been in the custom of extending their cultivation of music to all its different departments. Charles I., who (as Playford remarks in his Introduction) was "not behind any of his predecessors in his love and promotion of this science," and who was himself a tolerable performer on the viol da gamba,[a] in seeking to revive the ancient usages of the institution, was not likely to have omitted one which was calculated to contribute so much to his own personal gratification.

Farther, the mention of old Scotish music is not a little interesting from the particular manner in which it is here introduced. The music of other countries is simply designated as English, French, &c.; that of Scotland (*par excellence*) OLD Scotish music—a circumstance quite decisive as to the description of national melody which was then most in repute,—that it was not of a contemporaneous, but of an ancient date. Allan Ramsay, in his preface to his "Tea Table Miscellany," (1724,)

services, motets, hymns, or songs of a sacred or serious character, of which there were many with Latin words.

a Burney's History, vol. iii. p. 361. Hawkins's do. vol. iv. p. 14.

observes—"What further adds to the esteem we have for them (the Scotish airs) is their antiquity, and their being universally known;" and this Mr Ritson[a] notices as "the earliest testimony hitherto met with of the excellence and antiquity of Scotish music." Here, therefore, we have a testimony one hundred years older than that of Ramsay. But the truth is, that this observation of Mr Ritson was not made with that scrupulous attention to accuracy, so common with this author; other authorities on this point can be appealed to, and, among them, the well-known dictum of the Italian poet, Tassoni, who, in the Tenth Book of his "Pensieri Diversi," (a portion of that work which first appeared in 1620,) observes—"We, again, may reckon among us moderns, James King of Scotland, who not only composed many sacred pieces of vocal music, but also, of himself, invented a new kind of music, plaintive and melancholy, different from all other, in which he has been imitated by Carlo Gesualdo, Prince of Venosa, who, in our age, has improved music with new and admirable inventions."[b] Ever since this passage was, first of all, publicly noticed by Lord Kaimes, in his Sketches, in 1774, and commented upon by Mr Tytler, in his Dissertation, in 1779, it has been hailed as the most unanswerable proof which could be adduced of the ancient celebrity of our Scotish airs, and it has ever and anon given rise to the most triumphant ebullitions of national congratulation. We are sorry, however, to be constrained to take a different view of it from that which our countrymen have hitherto done. We confess, that its sole importance appears to us to lie in this,—that, in the words, "a new kind of music, plaintive and melancholy, different from all other music," the peculiar expression and style of the Scotish melody, as known at the present day, are so distinctly marked, as to lead to the inference that it was, at this time, prized and celebrated in the more distant parts of Europe for the same national characteristics which it still continues to pos-

[a] Historical Essay on Scotish Song, p. 105.

[b] "Noi ancora possiamo connumerar trà nostri Jacopo re di Scozia che non pùr cose sacre compose in canto, ma trovò, dà se stesso, una nuova musica lamentevole é mesta, differente da tutte l'altre. Nèl che poi é stato imitato da Carlo Gesualdo, principe de Venosa, che, in questa nostra età, hà illustrata anch'egli la musica con nuove mirabili invenzioni." P. 436.

sess. Mr Tytler, however, the author of the Dissertation on Scotish Music, taking it for granted that it was meant to imply that the Scotish music had been imitated in the compositions of the Prince of Venosa, exclaims, in a burst of enthusiasm, "What an illustrious testimony to their excellency! Some of the dilettanti in the Italian music of the present times may perhaps sneer at being told that the Italians, the restorers of music, owe the improvement of their music to the early introduction of Scotish melody into it; yet nothing is more certain, not only from the candid acknowledgment of Tassoni, but from the testimony of the Italian music itself, before the Prince of Venosa's time, as I shall attempt to illustrate." And forthwith he proceeds to show us that the Italian music of the sixteenth century, even that of the sublime Palestrina himself, however admirable for its harmony and the contexture of its parts, being deficient in melody, this deficiency had happily been supplied by an infusion of the music of Scotland. "In the above state of music in Italy," says this author, "we may suppose the Scotish melodies of King James I. had found their way into that country. Is it then to be wondered at that such a genius as the Prince of Venosa should be struck with the genuine simplicity of strains which spake directly to the heart, and that he should imitate and adopt such new and affecting melodies, which he found wanting in the music of his own country?" That the melodies of Scotland should have performed such a distinguished service to the general interests of music, was an announcement not a little gratifying to all Scotsmen, and, since Mr Tytler's time, few of our countrymen have shown any disposition to disclaim the very high honour here conferred upon them. But, although we may, in consequence, draw down the disapproval of such (if such there be) who, in the words of Johnson, "love Scotland better than truth," we must endeavour to put an end to this delusion. Had the melody of Italy been in the least degree tinctured with the national peculiarities for which that of Scotland is so remarkable, their effect would have been very distinctly discernible in the music of the former country. But every one at all acquainted with the subject knows, that that is not the case. The groundwork of those exquisite strains which sprung up in Italy in the seventeenth century, in consequence of the establishment of the lyrical drama,[a] and which have, since that time, diffused themselves over the whole of the civilized world, was, and still is, essentially and purely Italian. And with a people so finely organized for music, and a climate so well suited for its indulgence, what part of the world is so rich in popular native melody as Italy?[b] Along with it, no doubt, were blended the congenial airs of Sicily; and Della Valle, the celebrated traveller, who, in his account of the state of music in Italy at this epoch,[c] has some observations upon this very point—the introduction into that country of foreign national airs—although he speaks of the dance tunes of Spain and Portugal as having already (in 1611) found their way into the popular music of Italy, and adds, that he himself had made a collection of Persian, Turkish, Arabian, and Indian tunes, says nothing whatever as to those

[a] We have said "in consequence" of the establishment of the Lyrical drama. So incredibly slow, however, was the progress of Song even upon the Italian stage, that Burney, (vol. iv. p. 60,) after having carefully examined all the published Italian operas from "Euridice," which originally appeared in 1600, downwards, remarks that for the first fifty years they proceeded with mere recitative, and afterwards for fifty years more "with little assistance from measured air or melody."

[b] In an interesting essay by M. Mainzer, which appeared some years ago in the Revue de Deux Mondes, entitled "Les Chants Populaires de l'Italie," the districts of that country where the national music is principally located are said to be "Venice, the Tiburtine, Sabine, and Albanese Mountains, the coasts of Salerno and Sorrento, the neighbouring islands, and the country which extends to Terracina by Benevento, and the Mountains of Apulia to the coasts of the Adriatic." To prevent ambiguity we may here state, that by "national music" we, in Britain, mean what the French call exclusively "chants populaires." With them "national music" has a more limited signification, and is confined entirely to that which refers to the historical and political events of a people, which is also sometimes (though not usually) the case with us, as when we speak of our "national anthem."

[c] This was published in the second volume of the works of Giovanni Battista Doni at Florence in 1763. See Burney's Hist. vol. iv. p. 35. In addition to what is here stated, it may be mentioned, that G. B. Doni, in his Trattato della Musica Scenica, p. 131, a work originally published in 1631, and which contains some observations on national melody, while he recommends to composers the study of Italian, French, Spanish, Portuguese, Sicilian, *English*, and German airs, makes no mention of those of Scotland; and as he holds out the *English* and German airs as worthy of imitation, merely on account of their "bold and military conceptions," one would scarcely suppose that he meant to comprehend under such a description the Scotish or the Irish, or that, from his total silence in regard to them, he had been aware of their excellence. See Essay on the Theory and Practice of Musical Composition, by George Farquhar Graham, Esq., p. 16.

of Scotland. The Prince of Venosa, therefore, if he had ever, in his compositions, imitated the modulation of our fine plaintive melodies, may have done no more than other Italian composers since his time,—written an occasional "aria alla Scozzese;" although we are inclined to think that there is no proper basis even for such an idea. Dr Burney examined a portion of the works of this eminent dilettante; viz. six books of madrigals, and after a very attentive perusal of them he says,[a] "I was utterly unable to discover the least similitude or imitation of Caledonian airs in any one of them; which, so far from Scots melodies, seem to contain no melodies at all; nor, when scored, can we discover the least regularity of design, phraseology, system, or, indeed, any thing remarkable in these madrigals except unprincipled modulation, and the perpetual embarrassments and inexperience of an amateur in the arrangement and filling up of the parts." But, besides these six books of madrigals, Serassi, in his Life of Tasso,[b] remarks that there were twenty-five others preserved in MS. in one of the principal libraries in Naples; so that the Prince's imitations of the Scotish music may possibly be contained in these; and the doctor's reasoning upon that point, which proceeded on the assumption that Gesualdo had produced no more than the printed works which had fallen under his observation, is altogether inconclusive, and must fall to the ground. We are disposed, however, to agree with the learned historian, in an interpretation which he puts on the passage in Tassoni, and which, if adopted, must have the effect of entirely removing the point at issue. Tassoni's real meaning may have been entirely misapprehended. He may never have meant it to be understood that Gesualdo had imitated the melodies of King James, but only (to use Burney's words) "that these princely dilettanti were equally cultivators and inventors of music." Tassoni, it will be observed, is not here expatiating upon the history and progress of the art; he is enumerating, in a chapter of his work, entitled "Musici Antichi e Moderni,"[c] the illustrious

[a] Burney's Hist. vol. iii. p. 219.

[b] Vita del Tasso, p. 487.

[c] "Connumerare" is the word used by Tassoni.

persons in ancient and modern times by whom it has been cultivated and adorned. And it is in this way that he alludes to the Prince of Venosa, who, contrary to the views of Burney, has been described by his own countrymen, and after them by Sir John Hawkins, as an author "admirable for fine contrivance, original harmony, and the sweetest modulation conceivable,"[a]—as a fit parallel to James I. of Scotland, whom he considered to have invented the music of that country. This topic is touched upon by the late Mr Joseph Cooper Walker, in his Memoirs of Tassoni; and we are surprised that this view of the true meaning of the passage seems never to have struck him. On the contrary, he says,[b] "Unless we impeach the veracity of Tassoni, whose fidelity as an historian has not, except in the present instance, been questioned, we must admit that 'the music invented by James King of Scotland has been imitated by Carlo Gesualdo, Prince of Venosa,' a fact which has not been denied by any Italian writer of respectability." The same opinion has been occasionally expressed by others, and thus the Italians have been held to have tacitly admitted the truth of the remark. But did it never occur to Mr Walker, or to those who have adopted this somewhat narrow view of the question, that if the musical historians of Italy had quietly permitted a statement so material as affecting the very history of the art itself, to pass without comment or explanation, this could only have proceeded from their apprehending it in a totally different sense from that in which it had been understood by *them?*—And, in this sense, the one which we have above pointed out, we actually find it embodied in one of their treatises—in how many more we know not. This is the "Miscellanea Musicale" of Berardi, published at Bologna in 1689, in a chapter "Delle lode e Nobiltà della Musica." It is there given *literatim* in the words of Tassoni, though without acknowledgment, in a paragraph which commences, "In ogni tempo, fra Prencipi e Cavalieri, si sono trovati bellissimi ingegni," and ends, "D. Pompeo Colonna ancor lui fù versatissimo nella professione armonica."

[a] Hawkins's Hist. vol. iii. p. 212.

[b] Memoir of Alessandro Tassoni, p. 103.

If we are right in holding that "the plaintive and melancholy kind of music, different from all other," which is here spoken of, was a description which could only have been meant to apply to the national music of Scotland, James I.[a] is pronounced by Tassoni to have been its inventor; and this idea seems to have prevailed, even till within a recent period.[b] But whatever obligations we owe to this most talented and patriotic monarch, we should just as soon think of ascribing to him the invention of our language as of our music; and, considering that he was only thirteen years of age when he was taken prisoner on his voyage to France, his subsequent absence of eighteen years, and his English education,—we should regard it as much more probable that he had *learned* the better part of both from his Scotish subjects, after his return to his native kingdom. In reality, the question is not who were the inventors, but who were the improvers, of the music of Scotland? Mr Tytler has not hesitated to affirm that James I. was one of these. In his Life of that monarch,[c] he says, that he is justly reckoned the first reformer, if not the inventor, of the Scotish vocal music; and, in his Dissertation, he holds it as "scarce to be doubted," that his original Scotish melodies "are still remaining," and form a part of our finest airs, "though they, probably, pass undistinguished under other names, and are adapted to modern words." And yet, where is there any authority for holding that he ever composed a single Scotish tune, or at all directed his attention to the

a James the First's pre-eminence as a musician would seem to us to place it beyond question, that he was the monarch here alluded to, and this is also the opinion of Lord Kaimes. (Sketches, vol. i. p. 166.) Nevertheless, Pinkerton has supposed it to have been James V., for which no valid reason can be assigned; and Ritson (Historical Essay on Scotish Song, pp. 94, 96) has endeavoured to make it appear that it was James VI. who, he says, was a writer of madrigals, (*i. e.* of the words.) We should really have liked to put the question to the last of these learned antiquaries, when he penned these comments, whether he was serious in supposing that Tassoni who wrote, or for the first time printed these remarks in 1620, was very likely to have referred to the sovereign of *England* under the name of James, King of *Scotland*?

b In the exhibition at Somerset House, 1793, there was a portrait of James playing on the harp, and in the moulding of the frame, the inscription. "King James I. The original inventor of Scotch music." Eastcott on Music, p. 44.

c Tytler's Life and Remains of James I., p. 6.

improvement of the national music of his country?[a] The nearest approach to any thing of the kind is Tassoni's remark as to his having invented the plaintive style of melody which has already been referred to. But whatever this may mean, and its real import has never yet been explained, it is not borne out by the evidence of any historian. Neither Bower, who was James's contemporary, nor Boethius, nor Major, both of whom wrote nearly a hundred years after his death, and who successively treat of his musical skill and accomplishments, say one word which would lead us to suppose that he cultivated or composed Scotish music. Boethius[b] says, that he instituted regular choirs in the churches, and introduced, into the cathedrals and abbeys, organs of an improved construction; and Major's observations, which our readers will find at the bottom of the page,[c] and which have been sometimes misapprehended, and supposed to relate to the composition of music, obviously point to his literary, and not to his musical works. King James's composition of Scotish tunes, therefore, and his reformation of the Scotish music, are purely conjectural.

Having said thus much to distinguish between historical fact and

[a] The same author tells us that "Fordun has a whole chapter, the 29th of his History, on King James's learning and knowledge in the ancient Greek, as well as in the modern, scales of music, which, for its curiosity, is worthy to be read by the modern theorists in music,"—a circumstance which, if true, (as the scale upon which the Scotish music is composed is said to resemble that of the Greeks,) would go very far to fortify the remarkable assertion of Tassoni, as to his having been its inventor. As Fordun is supposed to have concluded his history about twenty years before James was born, the work referred to here is, of course, the continuation of Fordun by Bower, who was a contemporary of that prince; but our modern theorists, if they expect to be illuminated in regard to his knowledge of the Greek and modern scales of music by any thing which they may find in this or in any other part of this historian's works, will be wofully disappointed. There is not a word about the Greek scales within the four corners of this 29th chapter; nor any thing there stated, from which we should be warranted to infer that James was in the most remote degree acquainted with them. It consists almost entirely of a transcript of the well-known passage in Giraldus Cambrensis's Topographia Hiberniæ, in praise of the Irish and Scotish music of the twelfth century!

[b] Hist. Lib. xvii.

[c] "In vernacula lingua artificiosissimus compositor, cujus codices plurimi et cantilenæ memoriter adhuc apud Scotos inter primos habentur. Artificiosam cantilenam (composuit) *Yas Sen.*, &c. et jucundum artificiosumque illum cantum at Beltayn quem alii de Dalketh et Gargeil mutare studuerunt, quiâ in arce aut camerâ clausus servabatur, in qua mulier cum matre habitabat."

hypothesis, we would add, that, as an hypothesis or conjecture, the idea that this monarch had composed Scotish airs, and improved the music of his kingdom, would appear to be by no means ill-founded. Considerng his extraordinary musical taste and acquirements, if our national music had been ameliorated in his time, no one was, perhaps, so well qualified for the task;[a] and who was more likely to have felt and appreciated the high-toned expression of feeling which pervades the more pathetic of our airs, or to have entered with greater keenness and zest into their more animated strains, than the elegant author of "The Queen's Quhair," or the graphic and truly characteristic delineator of those humorous scenes of rustic festivity and merriment, which were never, perhaps, exhibited in greater perfection than in his "Christ Kirk on the Green," and his "Peblis to the Play?"

In all our enquiries regarding the history of Scotish music, we have to encounter this difficulty, that none of our historians ever distinguish between the music of the nation, which, from the first, must have possessed certain peculiar traits, and that which was cultivated by those who devoted themselves to the practice of the art, and which may be said to have comprised the regular, artificial music in use throughout the greater part of Europe. Our historians seem to be always discovering some "illustrious testimony of the excellency" of the Scotish music; and, were we to trust to what Dr Henry[b] has stated, it must have found admirers in Italy, even in the early part of the sixteenth century. "James III. (says the reverend historian) being no less fond of music than the other fine arts, invited the most famous musicians to his court, and loaded them with favours. Sir William Rogers, a musician, was one of his six unhappy favourites, who were put to death at Lauder, 1482. Ferrerius, an Italian, who wrote the history of the Prince, acquaints us that he had conversed with several celebrated musicians in Italy, who spoke in high terms of Scotch music, and the munificence of James III. These musicians, probably, had belonged to that numerous

[a] Boethius says of him, "Musicam exacte tenebat ac quicquid illi arti affinebatur peritissime,"—Buchanan, "In musicis curiosius quam regem vel deceat vel expediat."

[b] History of Great Britain, vol. v. p. 496.

choir which King James established in the chapel of his palace in the Castle of Stirling, and had returned into their own country after the death of their royal patron, and carried with them the knowledge of the Scotch music." But what says Ferrerius, from whose history Dr Henry has felt himself authorised to deduce the above statement? He says, that William Rogers, a famous musician of that age, whom Edward IV. had sent into Scotland, along with some others, upon an embassy, in order to negotiate a truce with that country of twenty years' duration, had, by his exquisite singing, and performance on various instruments, so captivated James III., that, at the close of the embassy, the latter retained Rogers, nothing loath, (non invitum,) and, shortly afterwards, promoted him to the honour of knighthood. Farther, he mentions, that, under this individual, so celebrated in his art, many persons at the Scottish court became such proficients in music, that, a few years before Ferrerius wrote his history, several distinguished characters were still living who, in his hearing, had boasted of their having been benefited by the instructions or schola of Rogers, and that the time here alluded to was the year 1529.[a]

From this it does not appear either that these musicians who lauded the instructions of Rogers were Italians, or that the conversation spoken of took place in Italy. On the contrary, while Ferrerius does not speak of his informants as being his own countrymen, the circumstance to which he alludes could only have taken place in Scotland, where, and not in Italy, Ferrerius was resident in the year 1529.[b] There were, however, as we have formerly had occasion to notice, several Italian musicians retained

[a] Gulielmum quoque Roger, Anglum, insignem ea etate musicum quem Edwardus ejus nominis quartus, Anglorum rex, una cum aliquot aliis viris, legatum, ut supra docuimus, pro induciis viginti annorum impetrandis, in Scotiam miserat, ubi modulantem concinne et variis instrumentis musicis dexterrime personantem, vidisset, ita dilexit, ut, absoluta ea legatione, non invitum, apud se retinuerit, quem, paulo post, locupletatum, valde ad equestris ordinis honorem, evexit. Sub hoc autem viro, in arte sua percelebri, adeo multi in aula Scotiæ perfecti musici evasere, ut proximis annis nonnulli viri insignes adhuc extiterint qui de illius schola, se prodiisse, nobis audientibus, gloriarentur scilicet anno Domini 1529. Ferrerius' Continuation of Boethius's History, (Edit. 1574,) pp. 391–2.

[b] See a Sketch of his Life in Pinkerton's History of Scotland, vol. ii. p. 422. Ferrerius's History was written in Italy in 1564.

by the Scottish sovereign at this time,[a] one of whom, "Bestiane Drummonth," is entered in the Treasurer's Books in 1515, as having received ten pounds "to help his expens by his wages abuffwritten, because he past with licence to visy his frendes in Itale." There might also have been a music school connected with the royal household for training the king's musicians, and this, very probably, had been instituted by Sir William Rogers, and may have been the "schola" referred to by Ferrerius in the passage above quoted, as we observe another entry in the Treasurer's Accounts for 1512, "to foure *scolaris menstralis*, be the kingis command, to by thame instrumentis in Flandris, vij li. gret, answerand in Scottis money to xxi li., and help thair expensis and fraucht, lvj s.; and, therefter, becaus thai plenyeit thai gat our litill expens and fraucht, deliverit uther lvj, . . . xxxvj li. xij s."

In the next place, it will be remarked that the observations of Ferrerius say literally nothing with respect to the national music of Scotland, whatever light they may throw upon the history of the art of music in this country, during the reign of James III., and for some time afterwards. The arrival of Rogers had, no doubt, been an era in its progress similar to the return of James I. Ferrerius[b] styles him "*rarissimus musicus ex Anglia;*" and we may naturally suppose that he would have imparted to the Scots a knowledge of all the leading improvements of his country, which, according to Erasmus, about that time challenged the prerogative of being the most accomplished of any in the art of music.[c]

Hamboys was one of the most eminent musicians during the reign of Edward IV.[d] He was the author of a musical work entitled "Can-

[a] *Supra*, p. 75.

[b] P. 395.

[c] They also laid claim to two other distinctions, which, though not relating to music, should not be omitted, viz. that they possessed the handsomest women, and kept the best tables. "Natura ut singulis mortalibus suam, ita singulis nationibus, ac pene civitatibus communem quandam insevisse Philantium; atque huic fieri Britanni præter alia, formam, musicam et lautas mensas proprie sibi vindicent." Erasmi Moriæ Encomium. See also Holinshed, vol. ii. p. 1355, and Morley's Introduction, p. 151.

[d] Hawkins's History, vol. ii. p. 345.

tionum Artificialium Diversi Generis," and is supposed to have been the first person upon whom the degree of Doctor of Music was conferred. He flourished about 1470, the very time when Rogers had been imbibing the elements of his musical education. We may presume, therefore, as no particulars regarding the latter have reached us, beyond what have been above mentioned, that he was a musician of this class, though, most probably, more distinguished for his practical than his theoretical attainments.

In another view, these circumstances lend a few scattered rays to illuminate the " darkness visible" in which the history of the Scotish airs is enveloped. We are not here speaking of their origin; that is a question upon which we shall afterwards enter; but of their improvement by the hands of composers; and that most of them had been subjected to a process of this kind at a very early period, there can be no doubt. Many tunes, also, may have been composed in imitation of the artless primitive airs of the country. In speaking of the Neapolitan rustic and street tunes, Dr Burney observes,[a] " The first secular music in parts, after the invention of counterpoint, that I have been able to discover on the Continent, is the harmony that was set to the rustic and street tunes of the kingdom of Naples; and these under the several denominations of arie, canzonette, villotte and villanelle, alla Napolitana, were as much in fashion all over Europe during the sixteenth century, as Provençal songs were in preceding times, and Venetian ballads have been since. Besides the old tunes which were collected, and published in four parts, others were composed not only by the natives, but in imitation of these short familiar airs, by almost all the principal composers of other places, of which innumerable volumes were printed at Venice, Antwerp, and elsewhere, under the same titles." We have never heard of any publication of Scotish airs during the sixteenth century, in the shape here mentioned; but with so many accomplished musicians as we appear then to have possessed,—to say nothing of harpers, luters, violars, pipers, flute and cornet players, &c., it is impossible but that a large proportion of the

[a] Burney's History, vol. iii. p. 214.

music which was then composed and performed had been of a national kind, or, as the Information touching the chapel-royal (which of itself, from the regulation there specified, furnishes indubitable proof of its early popularity and excellence) expresses it, "Old Scotish Music." With so many individuals who could not fail to have been attracted by its many pleasing traits, and whose professional talents would naturally have been exercised in exhibiting it to the best advantage, what are we to think of the absurd conjectures which, without a particle of evidence, would ascribe the composition of our finest airs, nay, the very invention of the Scotish melody itself, to James I. and David Rizzio? The former of these we have already considered; and with respect to the latter very little will require to be said. It seems, indeed, to have been little better than one of those foolish popular traditions, which would have died a natural death had it not been brought forward on all occasions, less for the purpose of being entertained than of being confuted. Even Burney intended to have added himself to the list of combatants in this field of contention, although he deferred doing so till the Greek kalends.[a] "The controverted point (says the learned historian) of Rizzio having been the author of the Scots tunes which go under his name, will be discussed hereafter, when national music comes to be considered." The real cause of this *questio vexata* seems to have been, that Thomson, the editor of the "Orpheus Caledonius," and Oswald, in order that they might give additional celebrity to certain tunes in their respective collections, had pointed them out as having been composed by Rizzio.[b] As for the fact itself, no well-informed writer ever averred him to have been the author of a single Scotish tune; and history is wholly silent, both as to this, and as to his having been the reformer or polisher of our

[a] Burney's History, vol. ii. p. 576.

[b] It has often been thought that Oswald himself was the author of several of the tunes said to have been composed by Rizzio, but we have never till now seen any thing approaching to evidence of the fact. Appended to one of his collections, in the possession of David Laing, Esq., there is the following memorandum:—"The airs in this volume, with the name of David Rizo affix'd, *are all Oswald's*. I state this on the authority of Mrs Alexander Cumming and my mother, —*his daughter and sister*. (Signed) "H. O. Weatherley."

melody. It is even doubtful how far he was qualified for such a task; and the subordinate capacity in which he was originally introduced into the queen's service would not lead us to form a very lofty estimate of his musical acquirements. " Queen Mary (says Sir James Melville)[a] had three valets, who sang three parts, and she wanted a person to sing a bass, or fourth part. David Rizzio, who had come to France with the Ambassador of Savoy, was recommended as one fit to make the fourth in concert, and thus he was drawn in to sing *sometimes* with the rest; and afterwards, when her French Secretary retired himself to France, this David obtained the said office."

It was this sudden elevation to the dangerous post of secretary and confidential adviser of the queen, (which, considering his ignoble birth and station, must be allowed to have been an act of no ordinary indiscretion,) and its consequences, especially the tragical and barbarous manner of his death, which, as Dr Robertson gravely remarks—" obliges history to descend from its dignity, and to record his adventures." Had he continued merely to exercise the calling which formed his passport to the notice of his royal mistress, we may reasonably conjecture that the name of David Rizzio—an obscure musician—would no more have been known to posterity than those of the three valets, his associates, who were very probably quite his equals in musical skill.[b] It should be remembered, also, that the period of his sojourn in this country did not altogether extend to three years, the one half of which was occupied in the anxious

[a] Memoirs, p. 54.

[b] We may here have underrated the musical capabilities of Rizzio. Regard, perhaps, ought to be had to one so nearly a contemporary as Birrel, who, in his Diary, describes him as a man well skilled in poetry and music; and Irvin, in his Nomenclatura, which was written towards the middle of the seventeenth century, calls him " a Savoyard, well acquainted with state policy, and a great musician;" adding, however, that when murdered, he was in the 71st year of his age, whereas there can be no doubt that he was a much younger man. It appears, also, that he was educated in France, and that the French ascribe to him the composition of several of *their* popular airs of uncertain parentage,—with what truth we know not. " Rizzo est l'auteur d'un grand nombre d'airs que tout le monde chante, sans qu'on sache de qui ils sont, comme ' M. le Prevôt des marchands,' Notre curé ne veut donc pas," &c. Laborde's Essai sur la Musique. Tom. iii. p. 530.

and harassing cares of office. If, therefore, we are to conclude that Scotish music owes any thing to Italian art, it would be more rational to refer our obligations to the Italian musicians mentioned in the Treasurer's Accounts, who, for at least fifty years previous to the time of Rizzio, were regular and constant retainers of the royal household.

But have we any means of distinguishing between such airs as are of indigenous growth, and such as are of foreign and artificial production? Referring to the sister arts of poetry and painting, where the best judges are at all times apt to be deceived by well executed copies and imitations, we should conceive that the erection of any thing like a standard or test by which the genuine could be discriminated from the counterfeit—the modern from the *veritable* antique—in national music—a department where the spirit and character are so easily caught—was, *a priori*, altogether hopeless. And yet, the attempt has been made, and certain rules have been laid down, by which we are to be enabled to discover, with unerring certainty, not only the authenticity of our most favourite melodies, but the particular epoch in our history when they were composed. In this branch of enquiry Mr Tytler has rendered himself particularly prominent, although we will do him the justice to say, that he has not urged his opinions in the spirit of a dogmatist, but as mere matter of probability, and in order, as he states, to "lead others to a more direct road." The general rule which he adopted was "to select a few of the most undoubted ancient melodies, such as may be supposed to be the production of the simplest instrument, of the most limited scale, as the shepherd's reed; and thence to trace them gradually downward to more varied, artful, and regular modulations, the compositions of more polished times, and suitable to instruments of a more extended scale." And there may be some truth in the general proposition, that the most ancient songs are expressed in a simpler and more artless form than those of modern times; but that simplicity, and even the rudeness and imperfection of instruments, are the concomitants of the *condition* of a people as well as of the *age;* and in a country so thinly peopled, and so uncultivated, as Scotland, there are, both in the

Highlands and Lowlands, districts where the sounds of artificial music have, till within these few years, but rarely penetrated,—where the simple inhabitants still continue to lighten their toil, and to beguile their leisure, with the same lilts and dances which have been in use amongst them for centuries; and where, it is possible, that an original, artless air, may still spring up spontaneously, as it did of old. It is needless to add, that no faith can be attached to any such criterion; and the result of its application has, accordingly, been a series of conjectures which have not even the merit of plausibility to recommend them, and which are liable to be overturned by the first original document which presents itself. In the Skene MS., for example, we find " The last time I came o'er the moor," and " Sa merry as we ha' been"—tunes which are classed by Mr Tytler as among those which, " from their more regular measure, and more modern air, we may *almost with certainty* pronounce" to have been composed " between the Restoration and the Union!" It were idle to go into an examination of theories such as these; and we shall only notice another of this author's postulates which the same MS. affords us the means of refuting.[a] He says, that the old airs " consist of one measure only, and have no second part, as the later and more modern airs have." As " rhymes the rudders are of verses," so are they, occasionally, of melodies; and those, of course, which are adapted to words, partake of their irregularities. The rythmus or structure of the verse may, therefore, sometimes render the continuation of the air to a second measure unnecessary. But these cases are rare; and, so far is Mr Tytler's notion from deriving the least support from the Skene MS., that, from beginnning to end of it, there are scarcely any instances where tunes are wanting in a second part, and none whatever where it merely consists, as he says, of a repetition of the first an octave above.

The peculiar scale upon which the Scotish music is constructed has also been founded on as a means of separating the old from the new, and of

[a] Logan, in his " Scotish Gael," (vol. ii. p. 257,) makes the same remark, that the most ancient vocal airs had only one measure.

ascertaining what may have been the primary form of the original airs. This has been made the groundwork of much ingenious speculation in a Dissertation prefixed to Thomson's Select Melodies of Scotland,[a] in which the structure of the tunes is very ably analyzed and illustrated, although we cannot concur in many of the opinions there expressed, or the conclusions to which the learned author has arrived. The old music of Scotland belongs to a different scale from the regular music of modern times, which is founded either upon the diatonic or chromatic series; whereas that upon which most—some authors will have it *all*—of our national music is written, has been described to be the same with the modern diatonic, with two exceptions,—viz. that it wants the fourth and the seventh in such keys as resemble our major modes, and the second and sixth in those which we would characterize as minor. We express ourselves thus guardedly, because the two great arrangements of tones and semi-tones, which we denominate major and minor, are of modern invention, and having been introduced not earlier than the sixteenth century, do not admit of being applied to compositions anterior to that period, with the same critical precision as to those of the present day. But it has been observed, in the quarter to which we have just now referred, that, although the melodies are often equivocal in regard to key, making rapid transitions from one to another, they are, in reality, constructed upon one scale or series of sounds; and that the reason why they have the appearance of being composed in different keys, and in different modes, and of the singular wildness and variety of their effect, is the freedom with which they wander up and down the scale, and every now and then rest upon certain parts of it, which, for the time, become principal or leading notes. The following, for example, is the diatonic scale divested of the fourth and seventh; and to this series of notes, but extending their range, when necessary, beyond the octave here given, all the ancient Scotish melodies are referred, whatever may be the varieties of their mode and character:—

[a] Quarto edition, 1822.

As the first note is here followed by two full tones, an air beginning and ending upon the above series would have the appearance of having been written on the key of C major; and this, accordingly, has been considered as the Scotish major mode. But, if the composition began and ended on A, although it ran through the same series with the key of C, the flat third would give it all the effect of A minor, and the key would possess the characteristics ascribed to the Scotish minor, viz. the want of the second and the sixth. Thus,—

The same series will give rise to other varieties of key, simply by adopting a different final note, without deviating from the original scale; and these, though they are not supposed to occur with us so frequently as the former, savour strongly of the Scotish character,—a consequence which has been remarked as attendant on the habitual omission of particular notes of the scale, especially those which produce skips of thirds.[a]

This has been regarded as the general system of tones upon which the Scotish melody is framed, and so rigidly has it been adhered to by some critics that no air has been admitted as genuine, which does not come within its scope, with one exception, and that is where the flat seventh is introduced.[b] This is described as being done in two ways, either "as a note of great emphasis and expression," as in "Waly, waly,"—"The Flowers of the Forest,"—"Lochaber," &c.; or "as the primary note of a new series of sounds, or, in modern language, the fundamental of a new key"—(to which might have been added, its frequent employment in rising to the final-note at a close.) But of this it is said that very few instances occur. It is even hinted, that in one of these tunes, "Locha-

[a] Burney's Hist. vol. i. p. 41.

[b] Dissertation prefixed to Thomson's Collection, p. 7.

ber," the use of the flat seventh may be a modern innovation, as it is not to be found in the copy of that air given in the "Orpheus Caledonius;" but the antiquity of the practice is now fully established by the original version of the "Flowers of the Forest," as it stands in the Skene MS. And in regard to the use of the flat seventh, as a direct and unprepared transition from the tonic, we would observe in passing, that, so far from being of rare occurrence, it constitutes one of the most striking features of Scotish melody. We do not merely refer to its introduction in a minor key, as in "Adieu, Dundee," where its effect is exceedingly pleasing, but to its use, as a transition from the major series, instances of which are so abundant that we shall not stop to refer to them. In fact, nothing connected with Scotish music is better understood; and we may appeal to the well-known fact, that our reels and strathspeys seldom receive any other accompaniment than the tonic and the full tone immediately under it.

With these exceptions, it has been represented that all our ancient airs are constructed according to the scale which has been above described, that "they do not contain a single note which is foreign to it." In particular, it has been repeatedly asserted that "they contain *no semitones whatever;*" that our primitive musicians "could no more introduce minuter divisions of the scale, or sounds not comprehended in it, than a musician of the present day could introduce sounds not to be found in the scale to which his ear had been accustomed."[a] Afterwards we find this proposition restricted to airs purely vocal, (those for the bagpipe and harp being usually in the full diatonic scale,) and from any thing that we have seen to the contrary, we suspect that it will require to be yet still farther restricted, as it cannot be said but that semitones are of very frequent occurrence throughout the vocal melodies here presented to the public,—a fact which we leave to the adherents of this theory to explain as they best can.

For ourselves, although we disclaim all intention of theorising, (however desirous we may be to furnish materials for the theories of others,) we con-

[a] Dissertation prefixed to Thomson's Collection, p. 4.

fess that we have been induced to adopt views in some degree at variance with the above, and with other opinions which have been very generally circulated with respect to the formation of our national music; and these views, involving many points of a technical nature upon which we should have adventured with no slight diffidence, we felt it to be our duty to bring forward—embracing, as they did, some of the most prominent topics which had occurred in the course of the present enquiry. But from this part of our undertaking we have fortunately been relieved in a way which, we have no doubt, will prove quite as satisfactory to our readers as it has been gratifying to ourselves. Before closing the Dissertation, we became aware of the fact, that many of our opinions were shared, and had been much more than anticipated, by a musical professor of eminence, a native of Scotland, who had, for several years, greatly distinguished himself by his admirable arrangements of our national melodies, and who, in a spirit of the most ardent enthusiasm, had applied himself to the investigation of their structure, during the short intervals of leisure which the duties of a laborious profession had left him. Many of this gentleman's notions had been matured before he had had an opportunity of seeing the Skene MS., but this document having been submitted to him, he at once did us the honour to agree to our proposal of making the present work their vehicle of publicity, and of availing himself of such illustrations as the contents of that MS. are calculated to afford. To his observations[a] we here gladly refer our readers; nor is it too much to say, that they contain the most able and complete analysis, scientific and critical, of the Scotish music which has hitherto appeared.

Perhaps its most novel feature is the singular analogy which it exhibits between the Scotish music and the Canto fermo, or plain chant of the Romish Church. Not that the Canto fermo is to be considered as consisting of melody,—being destitute of time, measure, and rythm. It is in the succession of its intervals, and the medial and final closes found in it on sounds other than the tonic, that the resemblance is chiefly to be traced. Why this should have been the case, we cannot tell. Why a peo-

[a] Appendix, No. I.

ple, never much distinguished for a scrupulous adherence to the forms and discipline of the Roman Catholic Church, and, far less, for any blind subserviency to its power, and who, at the Reformation, flung from them, with a degree of rage approaching to frenzy, its doctrines, rites, and usages,

. . . . its eremites and friars,
White, black, and grey, with all their trumpery,

should have been, perhaps, the only nation in the world which adhered to the strict rules of the Gregorian chant in the modulation of their popular airs, and why they should have clung to these vestiges of their ancient faith with a zeal and a pertinacity which neither the subversion of the Romish hierarchy, nor all the rancour of the most deadly hatred, could mitigate or extinguish—is a problem which we leave to the solution of others. We profess to do no more than to bring the fact under the reader's attention.[a]

The resemblance between the church chants and the Scotish melodies is casually noticed by Ritson. A friend of his observes[b]—"When I was in Italy, it struck me very forcibly that the plain chants which are sung by the friars or priests bore a great resemblance to some of the oldest of the Scotish melodies. If a number of bass voices were to sing the air of 'Barbara Allan' in the ecclesiastical manner, the likeness would appear

[a] The use of the flat, instead of the sharp, seventh for the penultimate note, is an ancient ecclesiastical practice of long standing, the remains of which still subsist in the psalm—and even in the ballad—singing of the uneducated, in all parts of the country; and in some cases in Scotland, where anti-catholic prejudices run high, it almost provokes a smile to see people, who so thoroughly detest Popish forms and usages, continuing (though unknown to themselves) to put in practice so undoubted and venerable a portion of the Romish Ritual. Dr Burney (vol. iii. p. 273) has a similar observation in speaking of the compositions of Claudin le Jeune, one of the authors of the reformed Protestant psalmody,—"Though the melody manifestly begins and ends in the chord of G, yet by keeping F constantly natural, there is a stronger impression throughout of the key of C than of any other. This was still adhering to the ancient modes of the church, and may be called a *rag* of *Popery*, for, however reformed the author may have thought himself in religion, his music was still Papistical."

[b] Historical Essay on Scotish Song, p. 102.

so great to a person who is not accustomed to hear the former frequently, that he would imagine the one to be a slight variation on the other." But Ritson, Campbell, and Tytler, all concur in deprecating the idea of our popular airs having sprung from the music of the church. The former expresses himself to the following effect:—"No vestige of any Scotish melody ever was, or ever will be, found in the old Scotish church service, which did not, (for one of their service books is preserved,[a]) and could not, possibly differ from that of other Catholic countries, and must, therefore, have consisted entirely of chant and counterpoint. We may, therefore, safely conclude, that the Scotish Song owes nothing to the church music of the cathedrals and abbeys before the Reformation; and that nothing can be more opposite than such harmonic compositions to the genius of song, which consists in the simple melody of one single part."—"It is a received tradition in Scotland," says Dr Percy, "that, at the time of the Reformation, ridiculous and obscene songs were composed, to be sung by the rabble, to the tunes of the most favourite hymns in the Latin service. 'Green sleeves and pudding pies,' (designed to ridicule the Popish clergy,) is said to be one of those metamorphosed hymns; 'Maggy Lauder' was another; 'John Anderson, my jo,' was a third. The original music of all these burlesque sonnets was very fine." Mr Tytler adds to these, the tunes of "John, come kiss me now," and "Kind Robin lo'es me." We know not what credit is attachable to these traditions; but there are many circumstances which would lead us to believe, that, at the Reformation, and for many years before it, the adaptation to secular purposes of the hymns and Canto fermo of the Romish Church was no novelty in Scotland.[b] As Mr Ged-

[a] This is the "Antiphonarium" of the Abbey of Scone, which belongs to the Advocates' Library. In the College at Edinburgh there is another of these ancient service books, viz. a Collection of Roman Catholic Hymns, supposed to have belonged to the church of Dunkeld before the Reformation.

[b] A friend of ours mentions the following fragment of a song which used to be sung to a very aged relative of his when a child:—

"I have a true love beyond the sea,
Para mee dicksa do mee nee;

des, the editor of "The Saints' Recreation," observes[a]—"It is possible and probable" that our "graue sweet tunes" had been "surreptitiously borrowed from spiritual hymns and songs;" and we have often thought that the solemnity of the ecclesiastical tones, every now and then pealing upon the ear, powerfully contributes to the production of those wild, plaintive, and pathetic effects, for which our slow airs are so celebrated.

A little examination will serve to explain why the ecclesiastical modes should have intermingled so largely with our ancient popular music. Whatever might have been the national melodies of our Celtic and Gothic ancestors, and of the ancient nations of Europe, they seem gradually to have receded before the all-powerful influence of the church; and although they are said to have taken refuge with the humble and ignorant, it is a remarkable fact, that the music popular among the lower, as well as the higher ranks, during the middle ages, is invariably described by our musical historians, as differing very little from that which was dedicated to the service of religion. Numerous testimonies may be appealed to in corroboration of this remark, a few of which we shall here take the liberty of quoting. "We may fairly conclude," says Hawkins,[b] "that the knowledge of music was then (during the middle ages) in great measure confined to the clergy; and that they, for the most part, were the authors and composers of those songs and ballads, with the tunes adapted to them, which were the ordinary amusement of the common people." And in casually alluding to the same topic, Dr Burney[c] assures us, that the melodies not only of England, but of all the rest of Europe, "had no other model than the chants of the church till the cultivation of the musical drama; whence, all the rythm, accent, and grace of modern music have manifestly been derived." In

And mony a love-token he sends to me,
With a rattum, pattum,
Para mee dicksa do mee nee."

The "para me, dixi, Domine," is an obvious adaptation of a part of the service; and we have no doubt that other relics of the same sort could be pointed out.

[a] *Supra*, p. 38.

[b] History, vol. ii. p. 88.

[c] Vol. iii. p. 88.

another place[a] he assures us, that during "the thirteenth century, the songs in vogue were of various kinds, moral, merry, and amorous; and at that time melody seems to have been little more than plain song or chanting." Even the far-famed songs of the Troubadours, although they appear to us to have been of a lighter and more airy character, are stated by M. Perne to have been cast in the same mould. "Toute composition musicale depuis les bas siecles avoit pour base et type de melodie les tons ou modes du chant Gregorien, vulgairement appelé plain-chant, modes d'origine Grecque, d'apres lesquels les modernes ont formé leurs modes majeurs et leurs mineurs," &c.[b] In addition to what has been here stated, and in order to show the extent to which the ecclesiastical tones found their way into popular music, and how long it was doomed to wander within the stationary and limited routine of keys and scales laid down for the guidance of composers in those days, we shall here cite a passage from Berardi's Miscellanea Musicale, published in 1689, its details on this point being more copious and satisfactory than any that we have elsewhere seen.[c]—"Musicians have begun to separate their style as much as possible from that of the ancients, in order to give such expression to the words as was best calculated to move the passions, which our ancestors did not attempt, as they only made use of one style and one common system in their consonances and dissonances, which may be proved from their different publications. If we take Palestrina, the chief and father of music, as an author not very ancient, we shall find that there is little difference between his madrigals and his motets, in so far as regards their respective styles. If we look at the popular French and Dutch works, such as the Twenty-six 'Chansons Musicales,' also the Thirteenth Book, containing twenty-two new songs for six and eight parts, printed in the years 1545, 46, and 49, 1550 and 1552, the compositions of different authors, such as Crequilon, Janluys,[d] Petit, Jaude-

[a] Vol. ii. p. 262.

[b] Chansons du Chatelein de Coucy, par Messieurs Michél et Perne. Paris, 1830, p. 146.

[c] P. 40.

[d] We transcribe these names as they stand in the original, the Bologna edition of 1689, though they are evidently misprinted.

latére, Jaques Vaet, Vulnerant, Baston, Clemenz Morel, Clemens non Papa, (this is to contradistinguish him from Pope Clement,) Jusquin, Jan Gerard, Simon Cardon, Ricourt, Adriano, Noel Baldwin, Jan Ockenheim, Verdelot, and many others of different nations whom we omit to mention; with respect to their compositions there is no difference between the ecclesiastical and the popular melody, if we except some, the modulation of which is somewhat more sprightly, such as 'La Bella Margarita'—'La Girometta'—'La Battaglia de Clem. Jan,' and that of Verdelot; and this occurs where the words are humorous and gay, but where they are serious there is little or no difference between the motets, masses, and madrigals, in the style and arrangement of the consonances and dissonances. So that we plainly see that our ancestors had only one style and rule of composition."

Every where, in short, do we find the ecclesiastical chant and style of composition usurping the place of the old national music. The songs of the Gondolieri, at Venice, are described by Burney[a] as little better than a species of Canto fermo; and Eximeno[b] speaks of the tunes of the Spanish romances as "monotonous and tiresome," and believes them to be remnants of Moorish melody, or else sprouts of Canto fermo. As for England, so eagerly were the modes of the church followed up in that country in the time of the Anglo-Saxons, that, as far back as authentic history extends, they appear to have swept away the last vestiges of their national music, so as to leave it a matter of question whether or not that nation ever possessed any—of a marked and peculiar character. The manner in which this was effected is thus described by Dr Ledwich:[c] —"It was the policy of the Church of Rome, from the first entrance of her missionaries into Britain, to decry and depreciate the ancient rites and ceremonies of the natives, and to exalt the efficacy and perfection of her own. Arguments, however, were in vain; power soon decided the controversy in favour of the latter. We are informed by Bede, that

[a] Vol. ii. p. 32.

[b] Trattato de l'origine della Musica, 1774.

[c] Appendix to Walker's Irish Bards, p. 25.

James the deacon instructed the clergy of York in singing after the Romish manner, as Stephen did the northern ecclesiastics. Pope Agatho thought the establishment of the Gregorian chant so important an affair, that he sent John his precentor hither for that purpose. These efforts of the Papal See, seconded by the favour of the British princes, soon extinguished every spark of our (the English) ancient music, and confirmed the slow, spacious, and unisonous melody of plain song. The perpetual use of it to both clergy and laity was secured by canons, and when it became a commutation for sins and fasting, the practice of it must have been universal. 'Tis then no wonder that the taste of the nation accommodated itself to this chant;—a dull and heavy modulation succeeded, well fitted to a state of spiritual thraldom, and to express the dismal tales of minstrelsy."[a]

In Scotland, where the same ecclesiastical institutions and regulations prevailed as in other Catholic countries, the original vocal music of the people must have been overlaid by that of the church in the same manner, though not, perhaps, to the same extent. In one shape or other, it must all, more or less, have passed through the hands of ecclesiastics themselves, or of their pupils; that is to say, of persons who had been trained up in the ecclesiastical tones; for, from the time that the Gregorian chant first found its way into Great Britain in the seventh century, it was taught (as has been noticed in an early part of this Dissertation)[b] gratuitously to the poor, in connection with our collegiate churches, monasteries, and other religious houses.[c] The music of the common people, therefore,

[a] Such was also the fate of the Anglo-Saxon literature—" It is not unreasonable," says Ritson, " to attribute the suppression of the romantic poems and popular songs of the Saxons to the monks, who seem not only to have refused to commit them to writing, which few others were capable of doing, but to have given no quarter to any thing of the kind which fell into their hands. Hence it is, that except the Saxon chronicle, and a few other traditional fragments, together with many of their laws and a number of charters, deeds, &c. all which are, to be sure, of some consequence, we have little or nothing original in the language, but lying legends, glosses, homilies, charms, and such like things, which evidently show the people, from their conversion, at least, to have been gloomy, superstitious, and priest-ridden." Ritson's Essay on National Song, p. 45.

[b] *Supra*, p. 28, note.

[c] The training of our youth in the Gregorian Chant continued till the Reformation. " It was

would naturally resemble that with which they had been familiar from their infancy, and which they had been instructed to consider as the only legitimate and regular style of melody.[a]

It is impossible not to feel that the very general adoption of the plain chant in the singing of popular songs and ballads, and the use of the ecclesiastical formulæ in the composition of many of our favourite airs, (of which the airs themselves afford undoubted internal evidence,) are circumstances which tend to impinge a little upon the originality of our ancient vocal music, insomuch as almost to raise a question as to the antiquity of

required (says Dr M'Crie, in his Life of Andrew Melville, vol. i. p. 221) of those who were admitted to St Leonard's College, that besides being of good character, acquainted with grammar, and skilled in writing, they should be sufficiently instructed in the Gregorian Song. (Cantuque Gregoriano sufficienter instructum.) Papers of University. The religious of the Priory of St Andrews were always celebrated for their skill in music, and singing formed one of the regular exercises of the students." Boetii Aberdon. Episcop. Vitæ, F. xxvi. In another place, (*supra*, p. 27,) it has been shown that the music schools were continued in Scotland after the Reformation, even till the middle of the last century. In England, this does not seem to have been the case, as we find old Thomas Mace, in his work entitled "Musick's Monument," published in 1676, recommending to the adoption of his countrymen the very method which was at that time in full operation in Scotland. (See Hawkins's Hist. vol. iv. p. 453.) This occurs in the course of certain remarks, in which he proposes to point out how psalms may be performed in churches without the organ. Probably the want of these instruments to guide the voices of our congregations in Scotland, rendered it inexpedient to dispense with the training and tuition which the music schools afforded, and thus led to their continuation here longer than in the sister country; but as that plain and obvious *ratio* of utility still subsists in full force, why have they ceased to exist?

[a] Such are the charms of novelty in music, as well as in other things, that the *conventional*, wherever it enters, is sure to succeed in displacing the *natural;* a truth which should never be lost sight of, in reasoning upon national music. If in Italy, at the present day, the primitive airs of the people are dispelled at the presence of the more artful and luxuriant, but scarcely more elegant and tasteful, strains of the musical drama, we may imagine how difficult it must have been at a time when no regular system of music existed, except the dull, heavy, monotonous modes of the church, for the natural melody of a nation to extricate itself from the pressure of the superincumbent mass. Upon this point, M. Mainzer, in his ingenious Essay on the Chants Populaires de l'Italie, has the following observations :—"In proportion as the primitive character of a people is effaced and disappears, when brought into daily contact with the stranger, are effaced and disappear also their genuine popular songs, soon supplanted by foreign melodies, and the songs which, till then, confined within the precincts of halls and theatres, at last reach the streets. . . . . An opera was established at Sorrento, and in this country so abundantly supplied with popular songs, I searched long before finding any; because, wherever the doors of the theatre are opened, the natural is sacrificed to the conventional—the music of the people is dumb before that of the scientific world."

a style of modulation which has generally been considered as separate and distinct from the music of other nations. The same author,[a] who discards as utterly preposterous and incredible the tradition that two or three of our popular tunes were derived from the Catholic ritual, has ventured (in spite of the monstrous inconsistency which the proposition involves) to throw out a doubt whether the music to which our secular songs had been anciently sung consisted of *any thing but the music of the church*. "As we have seen, the Scots had songs in the fourteenth century, so no doubt had they tunes or music to them; but of what nature, and how far, if at all, resembling their now celebrated melodies, *or if, indeed, any thing more than the plain church chant,* is at present almost beyond the reach of conjecture." But, although time and other causes may have conspired to rob us of any thing like written evidence as to the actual state of our melody at this period, we see no reason why a few conjectures may not be hazarded on the subject. Since the time of Mr Ritson,—the Skene MS., the Information touching the chapel-royal, and other documents, have furnished us with data which may assist in enabling us to gratify our curiosity in points of this nature. From what has been stated,[b] the regulation requiring the musicians of the chapel-royal to exercise themselves in "OLD Scotish music," has very much the appearance of having been a restoration of a much more ancient usage; and the very expression *old* which is here used, (in the year 1631,) may, of itself, be a sufficient answer to those who would argue that our melody was of modern invention. But, what particular revolution in the manners, taste, and habits of the people, would sanction the idea that our national style of melody had sprung up posterior to the fourteenth century? We know of none;—nor can we very readily conceive any change which was likely to be attended with such an effect. Wherever national music exists, we should consider it to be indigenous—based in the natural constitution and temperament of a nation—"growing with its growth, and strengthening with its strength"—liable to be modified by circumstances, but so deeply rooted and intertwined in its very essence, as to be

[a] Mr Ritson,—Historical Essay on Scotish Song, p. 91.

[b] *Supra*, p. 156.

nearly indelible by any revolution of time, government, or education. It is bequeathed by fathers to their children, and passes with the inheritance of the family. And why? Because it sinks deep into the heart, endeared to us by associations of home and kindred, and consecrated by many of the warmest, the kindliest, and the most virtuous feelings of our nature. " The peasant (says Leyden[a]) has not learned his favourite airs from a music-master or in a scientific manner; but he has acquired them in his infancy, in the bosom of his family; and in their tones he hears the voice of his mother, of his sister, of his youthful love. There is no fibre of his heart which does not vibrate to some of his well-known strains; —you cannot improve them to him; you cannot restore him the tones of affection which he loses by any alteration. Even if he has heard those martial airs which celebrated the deeds of his ancestors, sung by their descendants, his own relations, who are now no more,—would he change those rude barbarous strains for the most delectable harmony which ever flowed to the enraptured ear of mortals? No! The peasant will not change or modify his ancient musical airs, till you drive him into civilized life, and obliterate the vestiges of ancient tradition." If we look for the origin of these airs, we need not expect to find it in " nook monastic," or in " cloisters' pale,"—neither in courts nor in camps,—but apart from the haunts of learning and the busy hum of men, in the recesses, and amidst the beauties and sublimities of nature, in the valleys, in the woods, and on the mountain tops. These are the airs which Burney[b] has correctly stated to be " as natural to the common people as warbling is to birds in a state of nature:" always expressive, and often beautiful without art, they are the songs of which the people were originally the poets as well as the musicians; and, as such, they have an origin coeval with that of our history,—far higher in point of antiquity than the music of the Christian Church. To use the words of Mason, in his Caractacus, they are

" . . . . the ancientest of all our rhymes,
Whose birth tradition notes not, nor who framed
Their lofty strains."

[a] Complaynt of Scotland, p. 275.

[b] History, vol. ii. p. 220.

This species of melody, possessed more or less by almost every nation, and varying in each, according to their particular genius, taste, and character,[a] together with such airs as were composed for the regulation of the movement of the dance,[b] we are to regard as the primary source of the "rythm, accent, and grace of modern music," which Dr Burney, in a passage above quoted, has more immediately ascribed to the progress of the musical drama.[c] And to the same cause, and the use which modern composers have so frequently made of the *chants populaires* of different countries, in every department except that of the church, we are chiefly to refer what has been called the *ideal* system of modern music,—a system at once scientific and pleasing, and which we find carried to its highest pitch in some of the symphonial compositions of Haydn, Mozart, and Beethoven, which not only delight us with the richness and the brilliancy of their harmony and instrumentation, but transport us into regions of enchantment by the variety of characteristic associations to which they give rise, and by awakening our imaginative faculties, conjoin with what may be termed the organic pleasures of the art, all the higher enjoyment of which the poetical part of our nature has rendered us capable.[d]

[a] "Every nation," says M. Choron, "has its own peculiar style of music. Italy has the *canzonette*, the *villanelle*, the *estrambotte*, *&c.*; Spain, the *bolero*, *&c.*; France, the *romance*, the *vaudeville*, *&c.* The history of this branch, though apparently of slight importance, is, however, as respects the art in general, of much greater interest than would be at first imagined. First, because the musical character of every nation is expressed in its songs; and, secondly, because it is in this kind of music that is to be found, as we have already noticed, the foundation of the ideal style, and the elements of the modern system." Summary of the History of Music, by Alexander Choron.

[b] For the proper adjustment of measure, rythm, and the more minute subdivisions of time, accent, &c. we are mostly indebted to the "airs de danse," where these points were sooner perfected than in any other branch of the musical art. There was a book of dance tunes published in Venice, in 1581, (Il Ballerino di M. Fabritio Caroso da Sermoneta,) where the tunes were "well accented, phrazed, and divided into an equal number of bars, with as much symmetry as those of the present times," a circumstance which Burney says he had not remarked with any music of the 16th century, that he had seen. Hist. vol. iii. p. 297.

[c] *Supra*, p. 181.

[d] In the opera, there is a peculiar appropriateness in the introduction of national melodies, according to the scene where the action is laid; indeed, we see no reason why the same rule should not hold here as in regard to costume. They have both, however, been singularly neglected, es-

It has been thought that the whole body of modern music may be traced to the musical ideas of the ancient nations of Europe, and the remains of the music of the Greeks, which are supposed to have been embodied in the early psalms and hymns of the Christian Church, and particularly in the Ambrosian and Gregorian chants, the former of which was instituted about the end of the fourth, and the latter at the end of the sixth century.[a] What was the character, and what the peculiar tonality of the ancient Celtic music, we have no means of ascertaining. We cannot even form an idea as to whether it was the same with, or different from, the music of the church, and it may be wrong to hazard even a conjecture upon a matter so uncertain and so obscure. But we cannot refrain from noticing a fact, from which it may be inferred, with some degree of plausibility, that the style of the two, respectively, resembled each other. The leading peculiarity, the omission of the fourth and seventh, was most probably common to both. Wind instruments, as they have been found much more frequently among savage nations than those of the stringed sort, are supposed to have been of earlier introduction.[b] On these instruments there is a difficulty in the intonation of the fourth and the seventh. On the chanter of the bagpipe and the flute *à bec*, the fourth, which is made by keeping up the second, third, and fourth fingers of the lower hand, is too sharp;—the seventh, again, which is produced by keeping up the whole of the fingers except the upper one and the thumb, is too flat. We have here, therefore, a circumstance (independently of the plain chant, where the omission of these notes is so frequently observable) to which we may ascribe the origin of this

pecially on the Italian stage. With all the exuberance of fancy which Rossini has lavished on his "Donna del Lago," we could never reconcile our minds to the un-Scotish style and character of the music. Rossini, himself, must have been conscious that he had here committed an error, as he has not repeated the offence in "Guillaume Tell," a more perfect production in many ways, but in which nothing has been more admired than the characteristic vein of Swiss melody which pervades it.

[a] See Choron's Sommaire, p. 21. Also Paper by M. Fetis Revue Musicale, v[me]. annee, No. 18.

[b] Wind instruments seem also to be among the last which are destined to arrive at perfection, as, notwithstanding the improvements of modern times, they are still defective in their intonation.

peculiarity in our music;[a] and, as its effect is not unpleasing to the ear, when once it becomes blended with family and national recollections, it is not difficult to imagine a people contracting a partiality for such a succession of intervals.[b] At the same time, we do not pretend to offer any explanation of the causes which may determine a nation in the choice of its musical intervals. "One may be prejudiced by long habit to a major scale, another to a minor; as well as to certain skips in their melody, like the Scots; and to a certain measure, like the Poles."[c] Nations, as well as individuals, have their peculiar habits and idiosyncrasies, originating in circumstances incident to their temperament and history, of which it often happens that they themselves possess no knowledge or recollection, and which no investigation, however minute and curious, can elicit. Although, therefore, we have alluded to the imperfection of wind instruments, as one of the causes to which the omission of the fourth and seventh may be attributed, and although we have noticed the resemblance between the chief characteristics of the Scottish melodies and the chants of the Romish Church, and have suggested some reasons to explain the intimate connection which formerly subsisted between the two, and the manner in which they may have come to be assimilated, we are far from supposing that any of these causes is sufficient to account for the preference which the Scots have given to music of this particular style and character. The use of the Catholic ritual in Scotland was no reason why the popular music of the Scots should have been more deeply tinctured with its essential qualities than that of other countries, where the

[a] It also serves to account for this peculiarity that the fourth and seventh are comparatively difficult of intonation in singing. But when we see nations, the most barbarous, giving utterance to successions of notes so chromatic, that, to execute them with precision, (a thing, however, of which they have seldom any idea,) would demand the skill of a finished vocalist; this is a circumstance on which we are not disposed to lay much stress, in determining the causes which led to the avoidance of these sounds.

[b] Plutarch, in his Dialogue on Music, in explaining the old enharmonic of the Greeks, which has been supposed to have been the same with what has been called the Scotish scale, describes its inventor, Olympus, as having formed it from choice, in consequence of having observed the agreeable effect produced by his missing the third of every tetrachord in ascending. Burney's Hist. vol. i. p. 21.

[c] Burney's Hist. vol. i. p. 57.

same institutions and usages were equally, if not still more prevalent. In like manner, if we are to suppose that the occasional omission of certain notes of the scale arose from the imperfection of the ancient wind instruments, we refer to a cause which, though of almost universal application, has only in a few instances been attended with the same effect. The specimens of Norwegian melodies, given by La Borde in his Essai, instead of being defective in the fourth and seventh, are singularly chromatic in the succession of their intervals. A collection of the airs of Sweden,[a] which we have lately examined, appear, with respect to the scale on which they are composed, to be precisely the same with the regular music of the present day; and the same observation holds with regard to a publication of Danish songs and ballads, which appeared at Copenhagen in 1814.[b] We may also refer to the music of Russia and of Turkey. The last is said to possess not only all the sounds of ours but the quarter tones. The music of the Egyptians is full of semitones, and the Arabians " in singing are accustomed to ascend or to descend from one determinate sound to another chromatically, or by still smaller intervals than semitonic ones."[c] The music of the Persians and the Hindoos, also, is said to owe much of its effect to the skilful management of the chromatic and enharmonic tones both in singing and playing.

[a] Svenska Folk-Visor Fran Forntiden, Samlade och Utgifne af Fr. Geijer och Arv. Aug. Afzelius. Stockholm, 1814.

[b] Udvalgte Danske Visor fra Middelalderen, Copenhagen, 1814.—In the preface to this work, it is stated that the tunes there given are genuine relics of antiquity, noted by a native of the Faröe Islands, where, and not in Norway and Denmark, it is said, that the ancient airs of these countries are now to be found. The editor observes, " In Norway, as well as in Denmark, the modern songs have superseded so completely those venerable simple airs, that after having descended from the palaces and castles to the cottages of the Danish peasantry, they have been at last expelled even from these asylums, and forced to fly to a part of the world so remote as the Faröe Islands." Mr Jamieson, in his " Northern Antiquities," (p. 370,) notices the existence of such a belief, although he is not disposed to put much faith in it; and yet, considering the quarter from which it comes, it is unquestionably worthy of credence. " According to the best information received in Copenhagen, from men equally distinguished for their extensive learning and deep research in northern antiquities, there now exist no ancient popular ballads or national airs, among the people either in Denmark or in Norway."

[c] New Edinburgh Review, vol. ii. p. 158.

From an idea that the notes most difficult to execute with the voice are those which involve semitones, it has been assumed that the scale most natural to nations, in a rude and primitive state of society, is one similar to the so-called Scotish scale.[a] But, although we are not much versed in the music of savage nations, we must say that, in any specimens of their melody, if melody it can be called, which have fallen under our attention, we have seen no evidence of the truth of this assertion; but, on the contrary, a great deal to bring our minds to an opposite conclusion,—viz. that the chromatic series is the succession of intervals which appears to be most agreeable to the taste of an uncivilized people. We cannot here spare room for illustration, but our readers will find one memorable example in Mr Graham's Essay on the Theory and Practice of Musical Composition,[b]—viz. a song and chorus of Cannibals, consisting almost entirely in a passage which slides through very small intervals from E to G. The following, which we extract from one of our last books of travels, Captain Alexander's "Voyage of Observation among the Colonies of Western Africa in 1835,"[c] published in 1837, will serve for another. It consists of a Fingo War-Song.

With these facts before our eyes, we feel it to be utterly impossible to concur in the generally received opinion as to the existence of "a

[a] Speaking of the ecclesiastical chants, Burney says, (vol. i. p. 21,) "For want of semitones, cadences are made from the flat seventh, rising a whole tone, in the same manner as *among the Canadians and other savage people.*" Upon what authority did Dr Burney make this statement, and in what quarter was he informed that the Canadians and other savage nations made their cadences from the flat seventh?

[b] Plate 384, No. 18.

[c] Vol. ii. p. 112.

primitive national scale," consisting of certain "elementary tones prompted by nature,"[a] and from which the fourth and the seventh of the key are excluded; which is not only said to be "the same in the most remote and unconnected parts of the world,"[b] and "natural to the human voice in an uncultivated state,"[c] but to furnish us with such an infallible test of antiquity, that, "in proportion as a melody approaches (to it) it is to be reckoned genuine and ancient."[d]

Dr Burney originated this error, for error it unquestionably seems to be. He was naturally much struck with the coincidence between the tonality of the Scotish tunes and a Chinese scale of six notes mentioned by Rameau, with a specimen of Chinese music in Rousseau's Dictionary, both of which wanted the fourth and the seventh of the key; and finding a resemblance between this scale and the description given of the old Enharmonic of Olympus, he was led to conclude,[e] not that the Scots borrowed their music from the Chinese, or that either of these nations was indebted to ancient Greece for its melody, but that, as the Chinese were extremely tenacious of old customs, and equally enemies to innovation with the ancient Egyptians, there was a presumption in favour of the high antiquity of this kind of music, and that it was natural to a people of simple manners during the infancy of civilization and art. Burney had also seen one of the Chinese musical instruments, which wanted the means of producing semitones. But the Chinese, according to Staunton, possess "a vast variety of musical instruments formed upon the same principles, and with a view to produce the same effect with those of Europe."[f]—"The scale Máravì of Soma," (says a learned Reviewer,[g]) "as well as a certain Chinese scale, shows that the Indians knew, like the ancient Greeks, how to give a peculiar character to a mode by diminishing the number of its primitive sounds. But they were not, on that account,

[a] Dissertation prefixed to Thomson's Melodies, p. 10.
[b] *Ibid.* p. 1.
[c] *Ibid.* p. 17.
[d] Campbell's Introduction to History of Scotish Poetry, p. 6.
[e] Burney's History, vol. i. p. 41.
[f] See New Edinburgh Review, vol. ii. p. 526.
[g] *Ibid.* p. 523.

ignorant of semitones, and of even smaller intervals, as has been stated by modern musical historians. Need we mention that the very same *artifice* (if it be one) of omitting certain sounds in the diapason of a particular mode, in order to produce a peculiar character of melody, occurs in numberless passages of the best modern composers?" To this citation, we cannot refrain from adding a few more observations from the pen of the same author, Mr George Farquhar Graham, as they place this matter of the scales in what we conceive to be their only legitimate point of view. We transcribe them from his recently published "Essay on the Theory and Practice of Musical Composition,"[a] a work of which it may be said, that, within the same space, a larger body of sound, varied, and practical information, was never condensed by a more masterly hand. "We must not mistake (these) fragmentary formulæ for entire and peculiar scales independent of the general system of sounds . . . .
Some peculiarities that have been observed in certain national tunes, as the omission, in some instances, of the fourth and seventh of the key, have been referred to scales of a particular kind, while it seems more reasonable to refer them merely to the imperfections of some of the musical instruments employed; for instance, the ancient flageolet, and the chalumeau, &c. Scales, seemingly anomalous, may arise from such causes, or from caprice, or conventional usage; but all such scales are only fragments of that general system of sounds which comprehends all manner of appreciable intervals, many of which last are much smaller than is commonly believed. It has been denied that the ancient Scottish music contained any semitones; but that this is an error is proved by the Skene MS., in the Advocates' Library, Edinburgh."

If any thing could be named as likely to have had the effect of rendering the Scottish and Irish music more light, airy, and animated, than that of England, and of rescuing it, in a great degree, from the drawling monotony of plain chant, we think it must have been the superior attention which was bestowed, in these countries, on the cultivation of instrumental music. The instrumental and the vocal music of a nation are

[a] P. 9. Messrs Black. Edinburgh, 1838. 4to.

sure to react upon each other. The singer (as we know, from experience, in our own times, where the practice is often carried to a baneful excess) delights in imitating the effects and aping the fantastic tricks of the instrumental performer; and as human nature is the same in all ages, we are not to suppose that our progenitors were altogether free from that fault. With them, however, it could not fail to have been attended with the advantage of enlivening their melody, and of adding to a somewhat limited stock of musical ideas. The early proficiency of the Scots and Irish on the harp has been already noticed; and it is impossible (especially as that instrument is supposed to have been chiefly used as an accompaniment to the voice[a]) altogether to separate any description which has come down to us of the style of their instrumental from that of their vocal music. The two, in fact, were too nearly allied to have been otherwise than homogeneous in their principal qualities. That we have such a description in the works of Giraldus Cambrensis is well known; and, what is even more to our present purpose, it contains a comparison between the music of Ireland and Scotland and that of England, of so distinct and explicit a nature, as, in our estimation, to go far to settle the question as to the existence of our national style of melody, not merely in the fourteenth, but as far back as the twelfth century. This musica criticism, quite as eloquent as any that, ever and anon, fall from the pens of our periodical writers when they wax warm in their panegyrics on Paganini or Thalberg, and not unlike the whole style and tenor of their phraseology, forms a part of a work which was read by the venerable Archdeacon himself in the year 1187, before the University of Oxford, in full convocation, at the most magnificent festival which had ever been given at that renowned seminary of learning, " rivalling (as he expresses it) the times of the ancient classic poetry, and wholly unknown in England either in the past or present age." It should be premised, that Giraldus was not only an excellent musician, but, having travelled a good deal abroad, his opinion on such matters must have been the result of extensive observation. Speaking of the Irish nation, he says[b]—" It is in

[a] *Supra*, p. 90.

[b] Topographia Hiberniæ, lib. iii. cap. 2, p. 739.

the cultivation of instrumental music alone that I consider the proficiency of this people to be worthy of commendation; and, in this, their skill is beyond all comparison superior to that of any nation I have ever seen; for theirs is not a slow and heavy style of melody, like that of the instrumental music of Britain, to which we are accustomed, but rapid and abrupt, yet, at the same time, sweet and pleasing in its effects.[a] It is wonderful how, in such precipitate rapidity of the fingers, the musical proportions are preserved, and, by their art, faultless throughout, in the midst of the most complicated modulation, and most intricate arrangement of notes; by a velocity so pleasing, a regularity so diversified, a concord so discordant, the harmony is expressed, and the melody is perfected; and whether a passage or transition is performed in a sequence of fourths or of fifths, (by diatesseron or by diapente,) it is always begun in a soft and delicate manner, and ended in the same, so that all may be perfected in the sweetness of delicious sounds. They enter on and again leave their modulations with so much subtlety, and the vibrations of the smaller strings of the treble sport with so much articulation and brilliancy along with the deep notes of the bass; they delight with so much delicacy, and soothe so charmingly, that the greatest excellency of their art appears to lie in the perfect concealment of the art by which it is accomplished.

"It is to be observed, however, that both Scotland and Wales, the former from intercourse and affinity of blood, the latter from instruction derived from the Irish, exert themselves with the greatest emulation to rival Ireland in musical excellence. In the opinion of many, however, Scotland has not only attained to the excellence of Ireland, but has even, in musical science and ability, far surpassed it, insomuch that it is to that country they now resort as to the genuine source of the art."

[a] "Non enim in his, sicut in Britanicis (quibus assueti sumus) instrumentis, tarda et morosa est modulatio, verum velox et preceps, suavis tamen et jucunda sonoritas." This slow and sluggish style seems to have pervaded all the music of England, even to the very beat of their drum; although upon this point it must be allowed that the reply of the Welsh officer, Sir Roger Williams, in the reign of Queen Elizabeth, to Marshal Biron, the French General, when he spoke disparagingly of the slow movement of the English march, was "a hit—a very palpable hit."—"True," said the Briton, "but slow as it is, it has traversed your master's country from one end to the other."

Fortified by the authority of Giraldus, whom the late Sir Richard Colt Hoare, his biographer, has described as "one of the brightest luminaries of the twelfth century," we may say, without fear of contradiction, that, at this time, the Scots and Irish possessed a species of melody very different from the plain chant, to which most of the songs and carols throughout Europe were then sung. But if the question were put, whether, at this time, or for several centuries posterior to this, the English possessed a species of vocal melody of a characteristic or national kind, distinct from that of the church, we should be much disposed to answer it in the negative.

The same author whom we have just now quoted furnishes us with some of the earliest information as to the practice of the English nation of singing in harmony, in which they seem to have been quite as eminent as the Scots and Irish were in music of an instrumental kind. And this very practice, while the Scots probably confined themselves more to single voice parts in their vocal pieces, would have naturally tended to round off their melody, to divest it of any abrupt and startling changes of key, and thus gradually to accommodate it to those improvements in the use of the scales and keys which were, from time to time, taking place, and which ultimately led to the formation of the modern system. "They (the Welsh) sing not uniformly,[a] as elsewhere, but in various ways, and in many keys and tones; so that in a crowd of singers, which is their custom, you hear as many parts and different voices as you see heads, all closing with exquisite softness, and blended together in one rich harmonious strain. In the northern parts, also, of Great Britain, beyond the Humber, and on the confines of Yorkshire, the English who inhabit those parts, in singing, adopt a similar symphoniac kind of harmony, but only in two different tones and voices,—the one murmuring the lower, and the other, in an equally soft and pleasing manner, warbling the higher part. Nor is it by art only, but by ancient use, and as if now converted into nature by constant habit, that the people of either of these countries have acquired this peculiar faculty; for, so far has it extended, and such deep root has it taken in each, that no melody is wont to be sung singly, but either in many parts, as among

[a] We suppose that by this Giraldus meant that they did not sing in the ecclesiastical tones.

the former, or in, at least, two parts, as among the latter. And what is still more extraordinary,—the boys, and even those who are little more than infants, (when they first begin to break out from cries into songs,) adopt the same manner of singing."[a] We must admit, that so obvious an exaggeration as this last mentioned circumstance casts a shade of suspicion over the venerable author's testimony, and that, like many musical critics of our own day, his language is too often vague and inflated. But we see no reason to doubt the general truth of his statement as to the ancient superiority of the English in vocal harmony. This is evinced by many early specimens of their composition, the oldest of which is the song for six voices already referred to,[b] "Sumer is icumen," which shows that in the latter part of the reign of Henry III. (1270) they wrote vocal music according to the strict rules of counterpoint. J. Stafford Smith's Collection of Songs in Score, before the year 1500, furnish many other specimens, the general character of which leaves no doubt that these *cantiones artificiales*, as Hamboys calls them, had got into common use among the people, and that they preferred the pleasure of singing roundelays and canons in the unison, and of "rouzing the night-owl in a catch," to the charms of simple melody. Indeed, if we except dance tunes, one would suppose that such a thing as simple melody was scarcely known to form a part of the ancient music of England. Alluding to the "songs and ballads, with easy tunes adapted to them," Hawkins[c] says, "hardly any of these, with the music of them, are at this day to be met with, and those few that are yet extant are only to be found in *odd-part* books," &c. Ritson[d] cannot conceive "what common popular tunes had to do in odd-part books;" but if he had been at all acquainted with music, of which he candidly confessed himself to be wholly ignorant, he would have seen that Hawkins here meant it to be implied that the common popular tunes of the English were all composed to be sung in parts; and in his own "Ancient Songs," we see none which do not answer that description,—with one exception, and that consists of a class of songs without harmony,

a Cambriæ Descriptio, c. 13.

b *Supra*, p. 153.

c Hist. vol. iii. p. 2.

d Ancient Songs, Introduction, p. 37.

and, we may add, at the same time, without grace, animation, accent, or rhythm. Such, for example, as the following :—

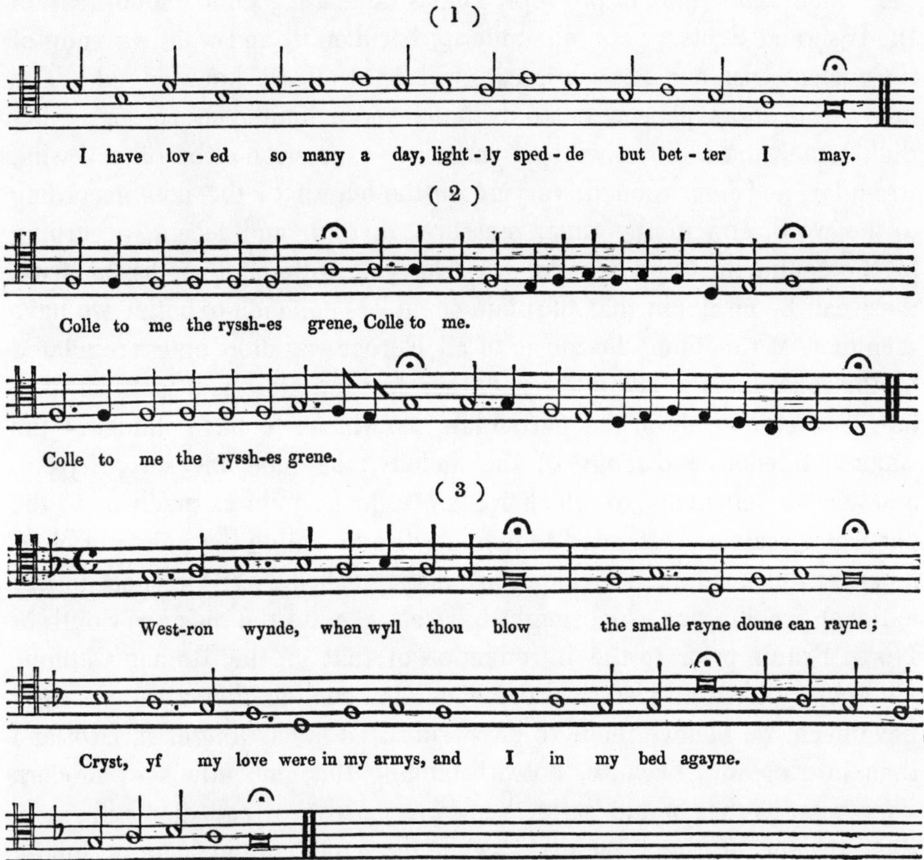

These we extract from the last mentioned work, as being about the oldest extant.[a] The first, says Ritson, was taken from a MS. written, "partly at least," in the times of Richard II. and Henry IV. (1377 to 1433.) The second and third are copied from a MS. of the reign of Henry VIII.,[b] and all of them, together with other ancient songs contained in Ritson's and other collections, are of the heavy, drawling char-

[a] Ritson, *ibid.*

[b] "Colle to me" is supposed to be the same with "Cou thou me," mentioned in the Complaynt of Scotland, *supra*, pp. 54, 55.

acter ascribed to the English music by Giraldus in the remarks above quoted, where he pointedly contrasts it with the more enlivening strains—the " modulatio velox et præceps, suavis tamen et jucunda sonoritas" of the Irish and Scots. The dissimilarity between it, and what we know of the ancient Irish and Scotish music, will be at once acknowledged. The one seems to have been not only much more limited in compass, but dull, tame, and tedious, without variety or expression; the other—wild, irregular, and impassioned, varying in the length of the note according to the word, and in the time, measure, rhythm, and accent, according to the sentiment to be expressed. And yet, with all this dissimilarity, there can be no doubt that the plain chant was common to both: we have seen that, at this time, the music of all Europe was more or less regulated by the tonal laws. The difference, therefore, striking as it is, must have lain almost entirely in the particulars to which we have alluded,—the superior freedom and range of the melody, the time, measure, rhythm, and accent—elements to which we are to look, quite as much as to the particular scale or system of sounds, in discriminating the points of character by which different melodies are distinguished. With respect to any national peculiarities which might have attached to the music of South or North Britain prior to the introduction of that of the Roman Catholic Church, we have no historical evidence; but such as they were, or might have been, we believe them to have subsisted much longer in Scotland than in England, because, notwithstanding the innovations of modern *improvers*, as they would style themselves, many of *our* airs still retain their ancient form and tonality;—while those of England seem no longer to carry with them any traits of melody which can strictly be denominated either national or ancient; so that, at the present day, it becomes difficult, if not impossible, to point out the peculiar characteristics in which they differ from the regular music of modern Europe.

The preservation of our national music may perhaps, in some degree, be attributed to the comparatively tardy progress of civilization in Scotland. The love of music and poetry is often the concomitant of barbarism. " Where" (says Sir Walter Scott[a]) " the feelings are frequently stretched to the highest tone by the vicissitudes of a life of danger and

[a] Border Minstrelsy, vol. i. p. 91.

military adventure, the predisposition of a savage people to admire their own rude poetry and music is heightened, and its tone becomes peculiarly determined." And, again, in speaking of the Borderers, from whom, perhaps, the largest portion of our melodies has emanated, he says[a]—"The tales of tradition, the song, with the pipe or harp of the minstrel, were probably the sole resources against *ennui* during the short intervals of repose from military adventure." The season when (to use the words of Shakspeare, for where can we find words so expressive?) "grim-visaged war has closed his wrinkled front,"—when "stern alarums are changed to merry meetings," and "dreadful marches to delighted measures,"—is not the least propitious for the full and perfect enjoyment of music and the dance; and it is probable that some of our best airs have been composed during the short intervals of repose of a hardy and warlike people, who were almost incessantly agitated by fierce and bitter contentions. Much of it also may have sprung from districts, where rumour "of unsuccessful or successful war" seldom, if ever, penetrated; indeed, so many of our fine national melodies carry with them the very echo of our mountains and waterfalls, our glens and our loanings,—and the wild and artless notes of the shepherd's pipe are so often discernible in the sweet and plaintive succession of their sounds, as, of themselves, to demonstrate that much of our music must have been the produce of those extensive tracts of pastoral country which, even yet, cover so large an extent of Scotish ground. In the southern parts of Scotland, in particular, says Dr Beattie, in his Essay on Poetry and Music[b]—"Smooth and lofty hills covered with verdure; clear streams winding through long and beautiful valleys; trees produced without culture, here straggling or single, and there crowding into little groves and bowers; with other circumstances peculiar to the districts I allude to, render them fit for pasturage, and favourable to romantic leisure and tender passions. Several of the old Scotish songs take their names from

[a] Border Minstrelsy, vol. i. p. 89.
[b] P. 173.

the rivulets, villages, and hills adjoining to the Tweed near Melrose;[a] a region distinguished by many charming varieties of rural scenery, and which, whether we consider the face of the country, or the genius of the people, may, properly enough, be termed the Arcadia of Scotland. And all these songs are sweetly and powerfully expressive of love and tenderness, and other emotions suited to the tranquillity of pastoral life." The Highlands, again,[b] "are a picturesque, but in general a melancholy country. Long tracts of mountainous desert, covered with dark heath, and often obscured by misty weather; narrow valleys, thinly inhabited, and bounded by precipices resounding with the fall of torrents; a soil so rugged, and a climate so dreary, as in many parts to admit neither the amusements of pasturage, nor the labours of agriculture; the mournful dashing of waves along the friths and lakes that intersect the country; the portentous noises which every change of the wind, and every increase or diminution of the waters, is apt to raise, in a lonely region, full of echoes, and rocks, and caverns; the grotesque and ghastly appearance of such a landscape by the light of the moon;—objects like these diffuse a gloom over the fancy, which may be compatible enough with occasional and social merriment, but cannot fail to tincture the thoughts of a native in the hour of silence and solitude." . . . .

"What, then, would it be reasonable to expect from the fanciful tribe, from the musicians and poets, of such a region? Strains expressive of joy, tranquillity, or the softer passions? No: their style must have been better suited to their circumstances; and so we find, in fact, that their music is. The wildest irregularity appears in its composition; the expression is warlike and melancholy, and approaches even to the terrible.[c]

[a] Cowdenknows, Galashiels, Gala Water, Ettrick Banks, Braes of Yarrow, Bush above Traquair, &c.

[b] Essay on Poetry and Music, pp. 169, 173.

[c] The very titles of the Highland airs are sufficient to evince the truth of this remark. Take some of those in Macdonald's Collection, for example, "Wet is the night and cold"—"Many are the cries and shrieks of woe"—"My cheeks are furrowed"—"This casts a gloom upon my soul"—"The death of Dermid"—"The vale of Keppoch is become desolate"—"Sad and cold are my people," &c.

There is, no doubt, a considerable difference between the Highland and the Lowland melody, although we think that Dr Beattie has overrated it, when he says that it is as great as that which exists "between the Irish or the Erse language, and the English or Scotch." The difference, in reality, is one of style and expression, rather than of *genus*, both being composed according to the same scale. The old Irish vocal airs are also characterized by a similar succession of intervals to the Scotish, but those of a more modern date are chiefly of a diatonic or chromatic structure, arising, it is supposed, from the harp having continued in use in that country to a greater extent, and for a longer period, than with us. Chalmers has said, that "the Welsh, the Scots, and the Irish, have all melodies of a simple sort, which, as they are connected together by cognate marks, evince, at once, their relationship and antiquity."[a] Such, however, is the regularity of the Welsh airs, and their conformity to modern scales and keys, that we search in vain for any internal evidence of the affinity here spoken of. Their more modern character has been sometimes ascribed to the exclusive preference which the Welsh have always shown for music of an instrumental kind, and a still more plausible exposition may be arrived at when the regulations of the Eistedvodd come to be more fully investigated, and better understood. But into these matters it is no part of our present purpose to enter; the unexpected length to which our observations have run, renders it imperative in us to avoid all topics except those which are immediately and necessarily connected with that under consideration. And yet we are conscious that the full and perfect developement of this subject depends upon the carrying out of a great variety of collateral enquiries, which, of themselves, would demand no ordinary labour and thought. Much still requires to be done before the history and progress of Scotish music can be elucidated with certainty and precision; and in one department, in particular, it has been a matter of regret, that we have had no opportunity of adding to the stock of information which we already possess. That the northern nations by whom this country was invaded and peopled during the earlier periods of our his-

[a] Caledonia, vol. i. p. 476.

tory, had, along with their manners, customs, and language, imported into Scotland their music, both vocal and instrumental, we have no reason to doubt; and to trace the coincidence of their national airs with ours, is a task which could scarcely fail to be attended with success. But the difficulty which we have experienced in obtaining access to authentic collections of Danish, Swedish, and Norwegian airs, must prevent us from expressing a positive opinion upon this point. We were certainly much struck with the circumstance, that the second section of the very first Swedish air which presented itself in the collection which we have above named, and the corresponding part of "John Anderson, my Jo," should appear to be almost identical.[a] But we find few other features of resemblance to the Scotish music in the rest of the volume, or among the Danish airs which we have examined. On the other hand, we know nothing for certain as to the genuineness and antiquity of these collections; and we may mention, that when the celebrated Norwegian violinist, Ole Bull, visited Edinburgh, in Spring 1837, upon being shown some of the Scotish airs, he at once recognised them as of the same character with those of his own country; and we, ourselves, heard him perform several of them in public, with a spirit and an expression which might almost be termed instinctive.

Before closing our notice of the ancient Scotish music, perhaps it is not too much to deduce another observation from the memorable *critique*, by Giraldus Cambrensis, on the Irish and Scotish music of the twelfth century. He has represented its style as lively and rapid, and contrasted it with the dull heavy spirit of the English airs. Is it not probable, therefore, that our oldest tunes were of the lively sort, and our slow airs (and these possess the most decided ecclesiastical peculiarities) of more recent origin? We merely start the conjecture, and yet it is one which we have sometimes thought strengthened by other considerations. We have the evidence of Tassoni that, at the beginning of the seventeenth century, Scotland was distinguished for its plaintive melodies; but, at this time, or anterior to this, we scarcely find any other instance where

[a] See Appendix.

this part of our music is mentioned with approbation, or commented upon in any kind of way, while the dance tunes appear to have been very much in vogue. The only reference to Scotish music in Morley's Introduction is where he says—" I dare boldly affirme that, looke which is hee who thinketh himself the best descanter of all his neighbours, enjoyne him to make but a *Scotish jygge*, he will grossly erre in the true nature and qualitie of it."[a] In like manner, the only notice with which Shakspeare has honoured the music of Scotland, relates to the same kind of tune. It is in " Much Ado about Nothing,"[b] where Beatrice says, " Wooing, wedding, and repenting, is as a *Scotch jig*, a measure and a cinque pace; the first suit is hot and hasty, like *a Scotch jig*, and full as fantastical; the wedding, mannerly modest, as a measure full of state and ancientry; and then comes repentance, and, with his bad legs, falls into the cinque pace faster and faster, till he sink into his grave." Then, we have the " chants des branles communs gais," published in Paris in 1564—the *chefs d'œuvre* probably of " Cabrach," and the other violars or " fithelaris" of the court of the Jameses—the Gows and Marshalls of the sixteenth century, and no less eminent, we dare say, for the spirit and vivacity with which they gave effect to the movement of the dance, at times, when the joyous character of the Scots was wont to break forth with equal, if not greater, hilarity than in the present day.

The slow, drawling, and monotonous style of many of the Scotish melodies which were popular during the last century, is certainly something very different from the description given by the Cambrian churchman of our ancient airs, and not a little at variance, we should say, with the spirit and character of the nation,[c]—the *perfervidum ingenium*—the effervescent enthusiasm of our countrymen. Some of these airs were composed, and most of those which had been handed down from antiquity were

[a] P. 182, edit. 1597.

[b] Act ii. scene 1.

[c] Speaking of our pronunciation, which he contrasts with the " too slow and grave style" of the English, Sir George Mackenzie says that that of the Scots is " like themselves, fiery, abrupt, sprightly, and bold." Essay on the Eloquence of the Bar. Mackenzie's Pleadings, p. 17.

essentially altered, by Oswald and others, especially by the former, a person, whose taste in music, although he unquestionably possessed some inventive talent, (would that he had possessed less!) was too much perverted by the age in which he lived, for him to relish the simple notes of our primitive melodies; and who, accordingly, so far from taking any pains to preserve them in their original form, generally contrived to adapt them to a formula of his own, in which phrases, the sole merit of which lay in their being unaffected and pleasing, were exchanged for passages of embellishment invented, in order to display the skill of the singer or the performer, and artificial closes or shakes, substituted for the natural, broken, and often touching cadences of the original.[a]

Of this, we are enabled to speak the more confidently, with the Skene MS. before us. The favourable contrast which many of the Scotish airs, therein contained, present to the dull, tiresome, and meretricious productions, which, from time to time, have been palmed off upon the public, under that name, and the vitiated copies of the same tunes which have been handed down by tradition alone, are among the most gratifying results of its discovery. We are now no longer at a loss for a standard by which we can test the genuineness of our national music, distinguish the true from the false, and separate the pure ore from all admixture of baser metal. Whether or not they come from "the well of (Scotish) genius undefiled"—we cannot say; but they are a distance of one hundred years nearer the fountainhead than any with which the public have previously been acquainted. And it is also worthy of remark, (we speak here of the principal Scotish airs,) that they are not cast in the formal and elaborate mould which characterizes the artificial compositions of the age when the collection was formed. They are animated, chaste and simple in their style and expression, and though "old and plain," and more remarkable for spirit and originality than for elegance,

[a] In certain practical remarks as to the manner in which Scotish airs ought to be sung, Mr Tytler, in his Dissertation, recommends singers, by all means, to acquire the embellishment of a *shake* by which they are to wind up the melody. *Tempora mutantur, et nos mutamur in illis.* Were a young lady, now-a-days, to conclude a Scotish air in the way here proposed, it would occasion nearly as much surprise as if she were to enter the room in her grandmother's hoop and high-heeled shoes.

it may be said of them, as of the poetical relics of ancient minstrelsy,

> " With rough majestic force they move the heart,
> And strength and nature make amends for art."

At the same time, we will not do them the injustice to say that they are less smooth and flowing than the Scotish airs of a more recent date. On the contrary, there are perhaps fewer of those sudden and unexpected leaps in the melody which we find in the latter,[a] and of this any one may satisfy himself who will take the trouble of comparing the original copies here given of " The Flowers of the Forest"—" Alas! that I came o'er the Moor"—and " Adieu, Dundee," with the modern versions of the same tunes. They will also see that tradition, and still more, the unscrupulous treatment which they have received at the hands of composers, have tended to injure, and not by any means to improve, the originals, frittering away their simplicity by notes of *remplissage* and variations, and, in some instances, divesting them of the leading points and characteristics upon which their effect and expression depended. But this is a subject on which it is not our intention to expatiate. It is not for us to presume to arbitrate in matters of taste, or to prejudge the public, to whom this Collection is now submitted, and who will form their own opinion of its excellencies and its defects. Whatever these may be, it will be remembered that it possesses more than one recommendation, altogether independent of its musical merits. It comes fresh from the hands of our forefathers of the sixteenth and seventeenth centuries, with all the features of their musical genius, style, taste, and ideas, such as they were, fully impressed upon it. Farther, it is well known, and has been pointed out in the course of the present enquiry, that the original versions of our ancient and most celebrated Scotish airs were lost, and that they have for many years been given up

a It may be added, that the " catch," as Burney calls it, (vol. iv. p. 457,) or custom of " cutting short the first of two notes in a melody," which certainly forms one of the most abrupt features of Scotish music,—so far as we can judge from the Skene MS., where its existence can scarcely be traced, is not chargeable against the ancient music of Scotland.

as irrecoverable.[a] Contrary to all expectation, however, several of them have been preserved by the Skene MS.; and it ought, we think, to afford satisfaction to every lover of Scotish melody and of Scotland, that relics so precious should at last have been saved from destruction, and thrown into a form which may go far to prevent the occurrence of such casualties in future. Besides the airs that are known to us, the collection contains others of great beauty which have not been heard for many years, and which are now awakened into new life, to run, it is to be hoped, a new career of existence. To this extent, the bounds of Scotish melody have been enlarged—in the only way in which, as appears to us, any legitimate enlargement is practicable—and, through the other musical MSS. which we have enumerated, and such as may hereafter offer themselves, now that we have been led into a track hitherto unexplored, more contributions of this nature may not unreasonably be expected. Traditional sources, though secondary to these, should also be kept in view; and we are assured by Mr Blaikie, who has most laudably and successfully exerted himself in this department, as well as by others, that many fine original airs still admit of being recovered in the more secluded districts of the country. But the selection here is a matter which requires more than ordinary discrimination and judgment. There is much truth in the following observation of an author whom we have frequently had occasion to quote,[b] and who, whatever may have been the infirmities of his temper, was seldom wanting in acuteness and sagacity. "The era of Scotish music and Scotish song is now passed. The pastoral simplicity and natural genius of former ages no longer exist: a total change

[a] Sir John Hawkins, (vol. iv. p. 6,) after stating that the ancient Scotish melodies had been committed to writing at the time when they were originally composed, observes, that "there are no genuine copies of any of the Scotish tunes now remaining, they having for a series of years been propagated by tradition, and till lately subsisted in the memory of the inhabitants of that kingdom;" and Mr George Thomson, a gentleman to whom the music and lyrical poetry of Scotland are largely indebted, has remarked in the preface to his Scotish Melodies, "What their precise original form might have been cannot now be ascertained. Although we go back to the earliest printed collection, it is far from certain that the melodies are there presented to us as they come from the composers; for they had been preserved, we know not how long, by oral tradition, and thus were liable to changes before being collected."

[b] Mr Ritson—Essay on Scotish Song, pp. 110, 111.

of manners has taken place in all parts of the country, and servile imitation (has) usurped the place of original invention. All, therefore, which now remains to be wished is, that industry should exert itself to retrieve and illustrate the reliques of departed genius."

The Editor has hitherto deferred to notice the obligations which he owes to those gentlemen, through whose assistance he has been enabled to accomplish the task which he has here undertaken; and, were it a mere matter of private consideration, he might have reserved the expression of his acknowledgments to the intercourse of private friendship, the chief source from which their communications have emanated. But, as they have contributed to render a service to the public, this is scarcely enough; and although he trusts that he may, without impropriety, avoid particularizing, in this conspicuous manner, the aid which he has derived from some of the individuals by whom his enquiries have been occasionally promoted, there are others, in regard to whom he cannot do less than take this opportunity of briefly recording the grateful sense which he entertains of their kindness, and the zeal which they have manifested in the prosecution of the work. Without the co-operation of one gentleman of distinguished literary and musical attainments, it would have been abandoned as hopeless. The Editor refers to Mr George Farquhar Graham, the author of an Essay on the Theory and Practice of Musical Composition, and other works,—by whom the MS. has been reduced to modern notation, and who has, from time to time, given him the benefit not only of his suggestions, but of his information, scientific as well as historical, which, in all matters of this nature, is known to be as accurate and extensive as it is varied and minute. The Essay on the structure of the Scotish Airs, so creditable to the talents of the writer, speaks for itself, as to the extent of the Editor's obligations to Mr Finlay Dun. He has also to acknowledge the assistance of two gentlemen, whose intimate acquaintance with all that relates to our national antiquities has been of the highest utility—Mr David Laing, Librarian to the Society of Writers to the Signet, and Secretary to the Bannatyne Club, and Mr Alexander M'Donald, Keeper of the Register of Deeds and Protests in the General Register House, and Curator of the Museum of the Society of Antiquaries. By the former, he has been shown a great many scarce and curious documents, and had his attention directed to many channels of intelligence which would otherwise have escaped him; while it has not been one of the least of his privileges that he has had it in his power to consult Mr Laing at all times, when necessary, in the course of his researches. To Mr M'Donald he has been indebted for the "Information touching the Chapel-Royal," the extracts from the treasurer's accounts, and other papers belonging to the public records, which were suggested and rendered accessible through his friendly zeal and attention. Several of the ancient musical MSS. referred to in the course of this Dissertation, have been obtained through the kindness of Mr Blaikie of Paisley, who had exercised his ingenuity in deciphering the tablature long before it ever came under the attention of the Editor, and who, in the most liberal manner, not only conceded to him the unrestricted use of the original documents, but, of his own accord, put the Editor into entire possession of the result of his labours—a favour much greater than any that he ever could have looked for, far less solicited; and which, together with Mr Blaikie's personal communications, has done much to enhance the value of this publication. Other MSS. have been obligingly communicated by Mr Thomas Lyle, Surgeon at Airth, the author of several pleasing and popular lyrical pieces, and editor of a volume of "Ancient Ballads and Songs;"[a] and by Mr Waterston, Stationer in Edinburgh.

In conclusion, the Editor has great pleasure in stating how much this undertaking has owed to Mr John Bayne, W.S., Lecturer on Law to the Juridical Society, whose professional avocations have not extinguished his love of the arts. Had it not been for the ardour which this gentleman evinced for unravelling the contents of the Skene MS., it is more than probable that it would still have continued to slumber, along with many of its unedited contemporaries, in the silent depository to which it had been consigned.

[a] London, 1827.

FAC-SIMILE OF THE SKENE MS.

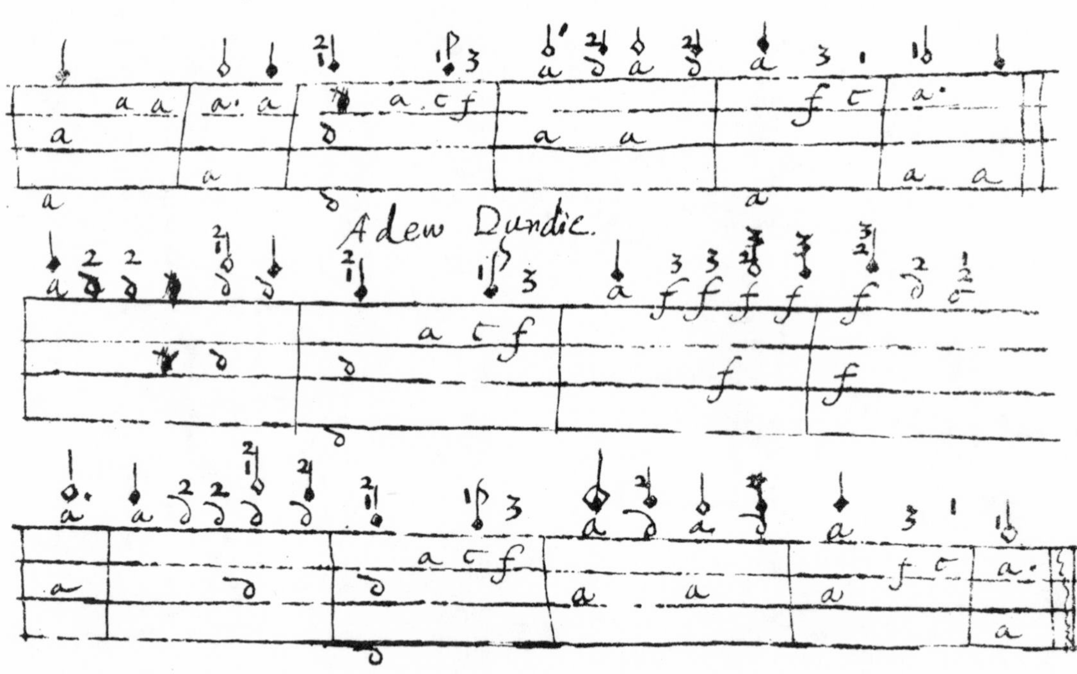

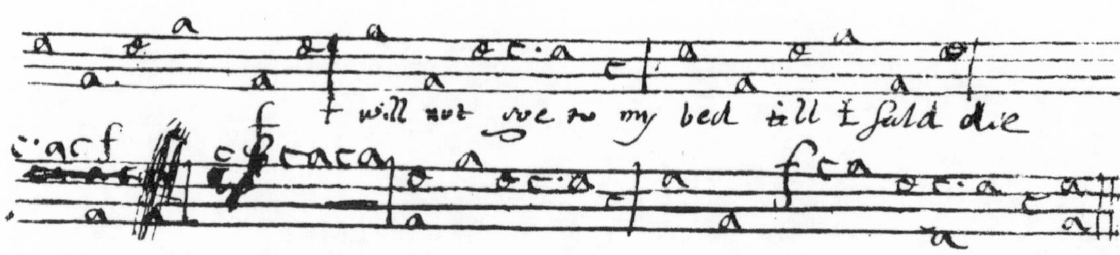

Leith & Smith, lithog.

EXPLANATION OF THE TABLATURE AND MODE OF INTERPRETATION EMPLOYED.

The tablature or *literal* form of notation in which the Skene MS. is written, although it has been in disuse for many years, was formerly the customary and established method of noting music for instruments of the Lute species, besides being sometimes adapted for the Viol.

The notes are expressed by the letters a, b, c, &c. These letters, however, are not used like ordinary musical characters to denote the intervals of the diatonic scale or gamut, but the semitones of the chromatic scale, ascending in regular progression from each of the open strings of the instrument. The strings are indicated by the different lines of the stave, and above each of the lines is placed the alphabetical character by which the particular note is represented. A, is always used to signify the open string; b, the semitone above that; c, the semitone above that again, and so on. Indeed, as the necks of these instruments were *fretted* by small strings tied round them at distances denoting a semitonic interval, and the frets were marked b, c, d, e, f, g, h, i, &c., these characters were just the representatives of the frets. The duration of the sounds is expressed by minims, crotchets, quavers, &c., placed above the stave, and immediately over the letter or letters which they are intended to affect; and each of the musical notes is held to apply to the letters immediately following, making them of the same length with the first, until some new note occurs.

It will be observed, that, although the stave of the Skene MS. has only four lines, the mandora or mandour, a kind of small lute, for which it was written, must have had at least five strings. This appears from the circumstance that the letters occasionally go *under* the fourth line, in all which cases they refer to a string of the instrument lower than the fourth. See Hawkins's Hist. vol. iii. p. 163.

A necessary consequence of writing music in tablature is, that the relations of the sounds expressed by the letters must vary according to the *accordatura* or tuning of the instrument, which was not always the same; and in the Skene MS. two different adjustments of this nature appear to have been employed.

One of these adjustments was equivalent to the following,— and the expression of its scale in letters would be as below:—

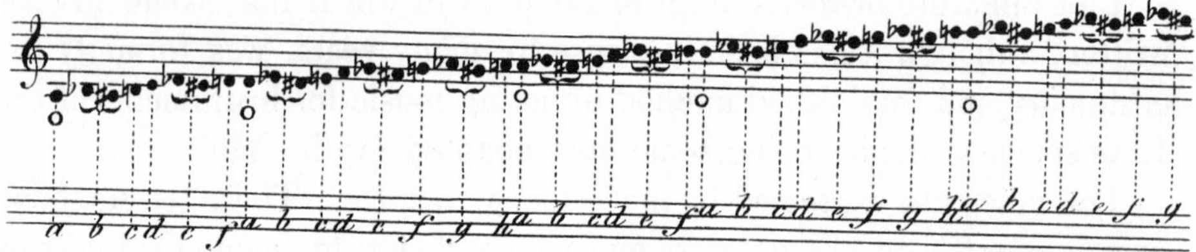

The other was what was called in the MS. the "Old Tune" (accordatura) of the Lute,—in common notation as follows,— and in tablature thus:—

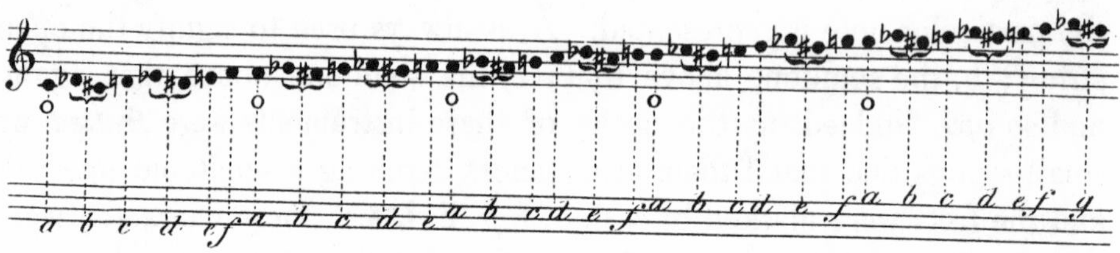

In these diagrams the modern notes above, on the stave of five lines, represent the equivalents of the letters written below on the stave of four lines, as in the Skene MS. The o marks the position of the open strings.

Speaking of the specimens of French airs of the sixteenth and seventeenth centuries, which La Borde has given in his "Essai," Dr Burney observes[a]—"When we see how they are tricked up by the Editor with

[a] Hist. vol. iii. p. 595.

all the chromatic learning of modern times in the accompaniment and taste, in the appoggiaturas and embellishments, it destroys all the reverence and respect which, in their native simple garb, they would have inspired. This want of fidelity in copying throws a doubt upon all the manuscripts and representations of ancient things that come from France.[a] In the history of an art, nothing can ascertain its state and progress at different periods of its cultivation, or satisfy a careful enquirer, but the most genuine fac-similes."

Impressed with the justness of this principle, and the correctness of the views here expressed, although it would have been an easy task to have furnished the airs of the Skene MS. with piano-forte accompaniments, and even some of them with words, and thus to have adapted them to popular use, it was felt that this could not be done without encroaching upon that authenticity and fidelity of translation which the public were entitled to expect in a work of this nature, and which would alone enable them to point to these airs as the ancient music of Scotland without any intermixture of modern ideas. For this reason, it was deemed advisable to adopt as strict a mode of interpretation as practicable; representing the notes in modern characters, exactly as they appear on the face of the MS. Nor is it any exception from this rule, that the semibreves and minims should be exchanged for crotchets and quavers, the same proportion being preserved throughout, and the last mentioned symbols in modern notation being equivalent to the two former in that of an older date. It should be mentioned, however, that the ignorance of rhythm which prevailed at the time when the MS. was written having occasioned some irregularities in that part of the transcription, the translator has some-

[a] We are afraid that even M. Michel's elegant work, the "Chansons du Chatelain de Coucy," however satisfying in a literary point of view, will scarcely, in so far as the music is concerned, redeem his countrymen from the slur which Dr Burney has here cast upon them, (somewhat more sweepingly, perhaps, than was fully warranted.) But the late M. Perne, by whom the airs were deciphered, and who was a composer of great learning, from certain admissions which he has made, (p. 148,) leads us to infer that he had adjusted the melody to the modern scale; while his accompaniments are not only modern in their style, but artificial, chromatic, and not accommodated so much to the character of the melodies as to the taste of the present day.

times required to exercise his judgment with respect to the duration of the particular sounds; as well as the division of the series of these by means of bars, so as to distinguish the different phrases of the melody.[a] It was also thought right to prefix to the different airs the measure of the time, and the signature of the *apparent* key, neither of which has been done in the original. To give the precise pitch upon which the melodies are set has not been attempted, as we have no certain knowledge of the diapason or concert-pitch of the age when the MS. was written. And this can be of little consequence, as the process of transposition would still have been necessary with most of the airs, from their having been removed from their original keys, on being transferred to the MS., in order to accommodate them to the instrument for which they are there arranged.

[a] No liberty has ever been taken in substituting one note for another, except in a few cases where a clerical error in the MS. has been corrected; and when these occur, the nature of the mistake has been explained at the foot of the page.

THE SKENE MANUSCRIPT.

ALACE YAT I CAME OWR THE MOOR & LEFT MY LOVE BEHIND ME

PEGGIE IS OVER YE SIE WI'YE SOULDIER.

TO DANCE ABOUT THE BAILZEIS DUBB.

† Error in M. S. C♯ instead of C♮.

LADIE ROTHEMAYIS LILT.

No. 4. SLOW.

I LOVE MY LOVE FOR LOVE AGAIN.

No. 5.

BLEW RIBBENN AT THE BOUND ROD

No. 6.

JOHNE ANDERSONNE MY JO

MY DEAREST SUEATE IS FARDEST FRA ME

PRETTIE WEILL BEGANN MAN.

LONG ER ONIE OLD MAN.

KILT THY COAT MAGGIE.

† Error in M. S. D instead of G.

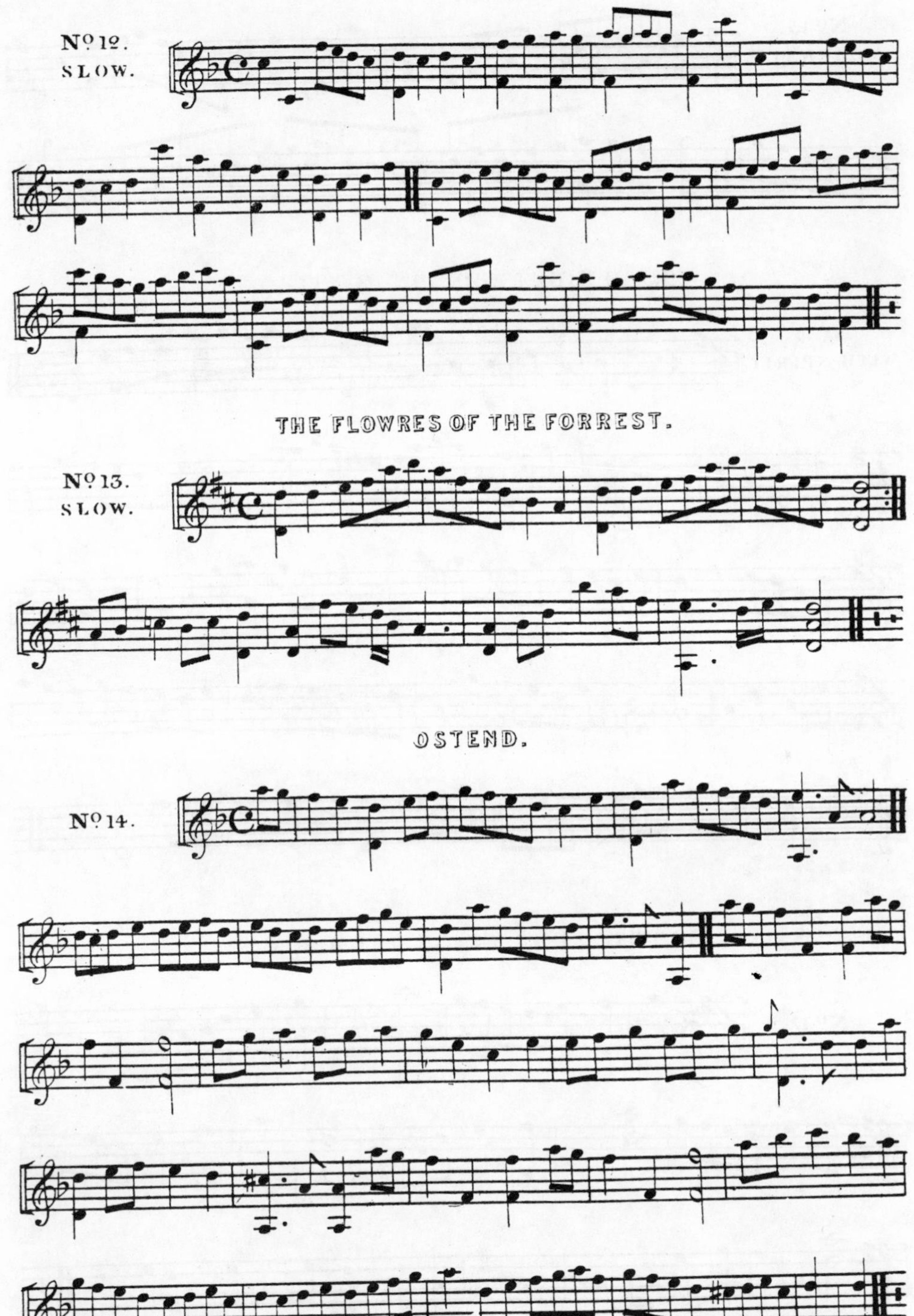
ALACE THIS NIGHT YAT WE SULD SINDER.
Nº 12.
SLOW.
THE FLOWRES OF THE FORREST.
Nº 13.
SLOW.
OSTEND.
Nº 14.

MY LADIE LAUDIANS LILT.

No. 15.
MODERATE.

GOOD NIGHT AND GOD BE WITH YOU.

No. 16.
WITH SPIRIT.

MY LOVE SHOE WINNS NOT HER AWAY.

No. 17.

JENNET DRINKS NO WATER.

No. 18
WITH SPIRIT.

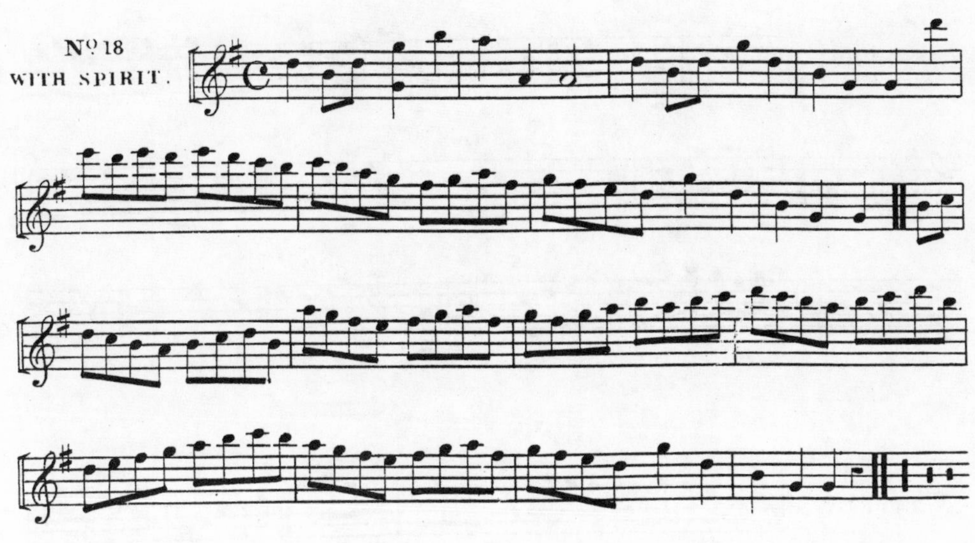

REMEMBER ME AT EVENINGE.

No. 19.

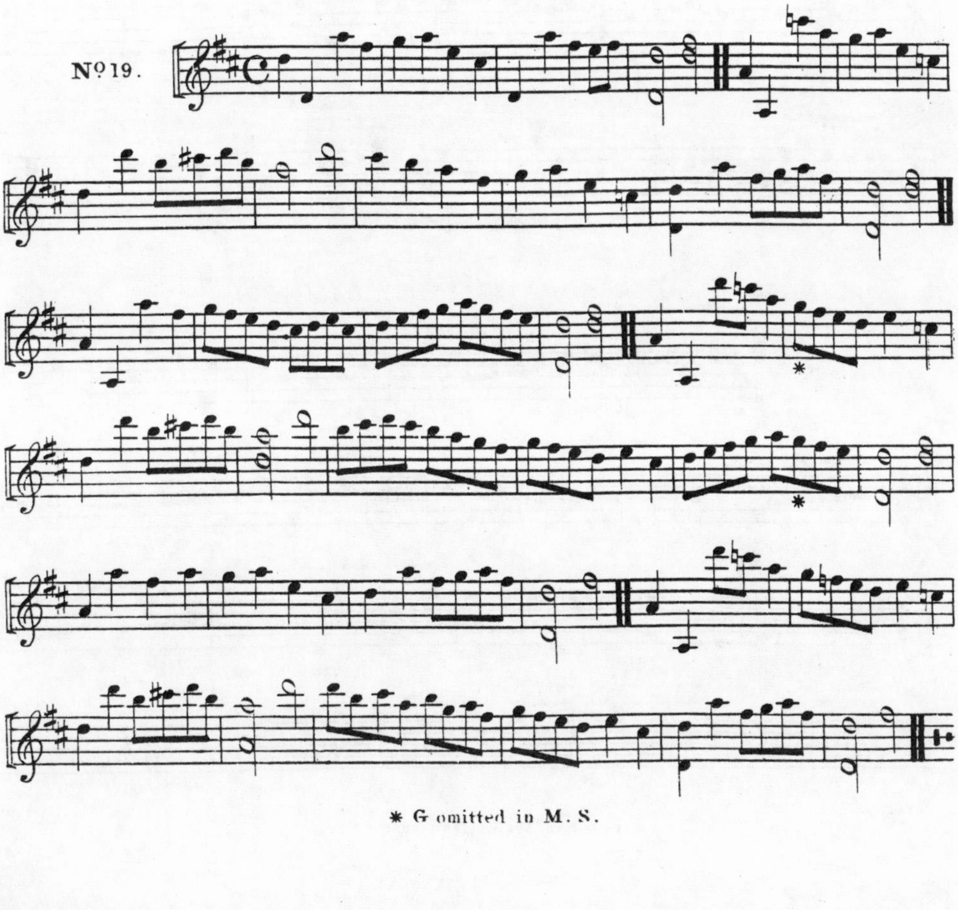

* G omitted in M. S.

I METT HER IN THE MEDOWE.

BLEW BREIKS.

I CANNOT LIVE AND WANT THEE.

* Error in M.S. D instead of A.

I DOWE NOT QUNNE COLD.

No. 23.

ADEW DUNDEE.

No. 24.

** In M. S. E. G. instead of G. E.

SHOE LOOKS AS SHOE WOLD LETT ME.

No. 25.

I DARE NOT VOWE I LOVE THEE.

No. 26.

* Error in M. S. C♯ instead of C♮.

† D°

LETT NEVER CRUELTIE DISHONOUR BEWTIE.

No. 27.

ALACE I LIE MY ALON, I'M LIK TO DIE AWLD.

No. 28.

** These Notes A & B are erroneously repeated in the M. S.

THE KEIKING GLASSE.

Nº 29.

LADIE CASSILLES LILT.

Nº 30.
SLOW

THRIE SHEIPS SKINNS.

Nº 31.

No. 32.

MY MISTRES BLUSH IS BONIE.

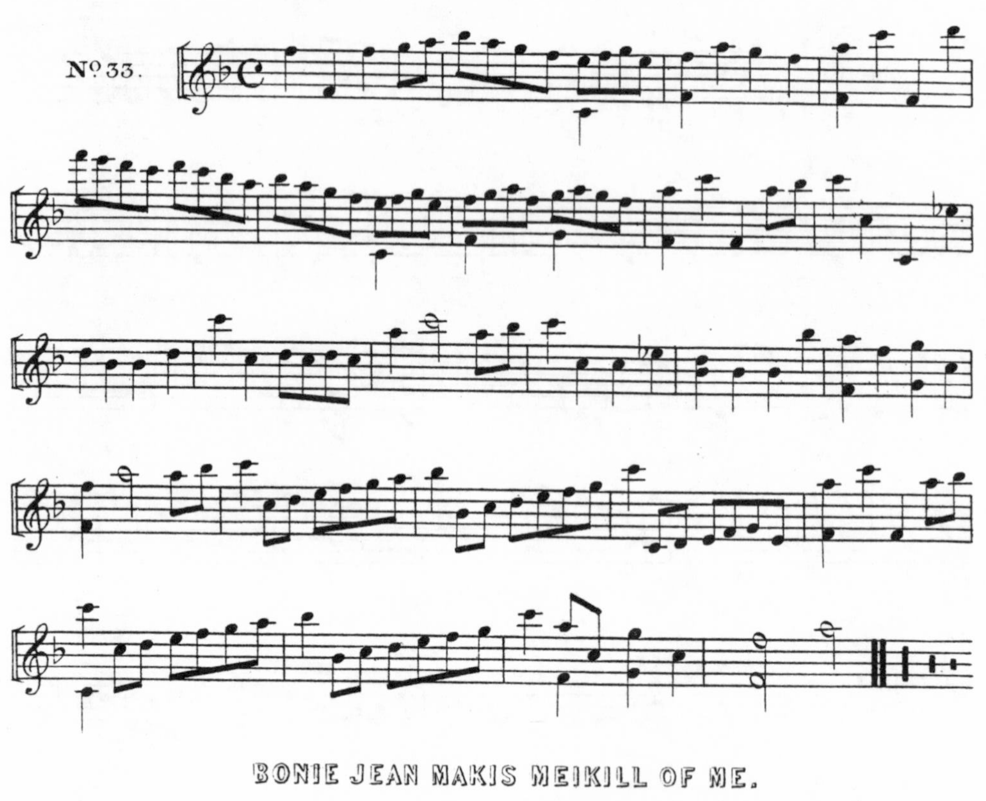

BONIE JEAN MAKIS MEIKILL OF ME.

Nº 34.
LIVELY.

* Should probably be B.

† Error in M. S. C♮ instead of E.

LESLIES LILT.

No 35.

JOHNE DEVISONN'S PINT OF WIN.

No 36.

THE LASS O GLASGOWE.

DOUN IN YON BANKE.

✱ A bar wanting here to complete the rhythm.

BLEW CAPPE.

No. 43.

GILCREICH'S LILT.

No. 44.

No 45.
HUNTERS CARRIER.
No 46.
KETTE BAIRDIE.
No 47.

I WILL NOT GOE TO MY BED TILL I SULD DIE.

Nº 48.

I SERVE A WORTHIE LADIE.

Nº 49.

SHE MOWPITT IT COMMING OWR THE LIE.

WHO LEARNED YOW TO DANCE AND A TOWDLE.

OMNIA VINCIT AMOR.

No. 52.

PANTALONE.

No. 53.

SIR JOHN HOPES CURRANT.

No. 54.

MARIE ME MARIE ME QUOTH THE BONIE LASS.

* Error in M. S. C♮ instead of B.

No. 58.

No. 59.

JOY TO THE PERSONNE.

THEN WILT THOU GOE AND LEAVE ME HER.

COME LOVE LETT US WALK INTO THE SPRINGE.

THE SPANISHE LADIE.

N° 63.

FROGGIS GALZIARD.

N° 64.

CHRICHTON'S GUD NIGHT.

* The first three notes of this bar are erroneously repeated in M.S.

* Error in M. S. D instead of A.

WHAT IF A DAY.

Nº 70.

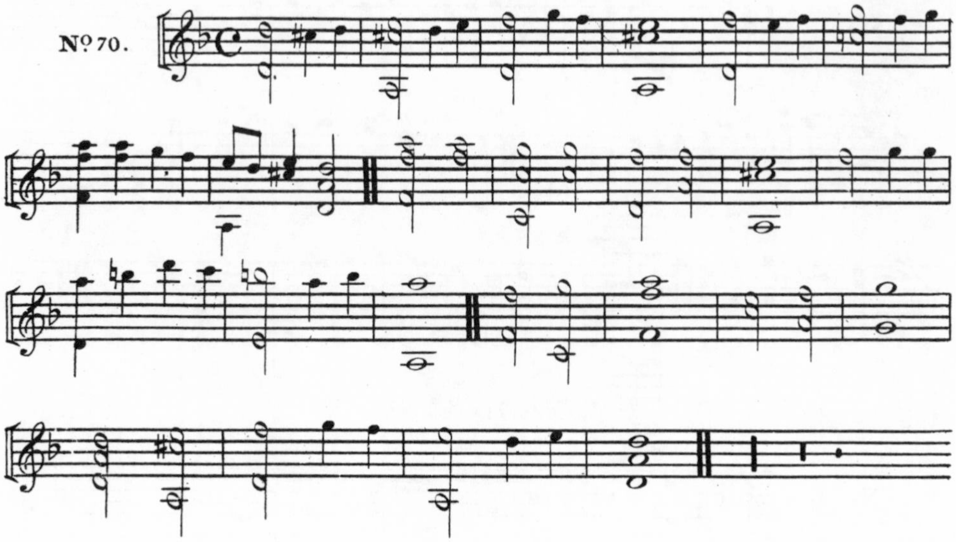

SCERDUSTIS.

Nº 71.

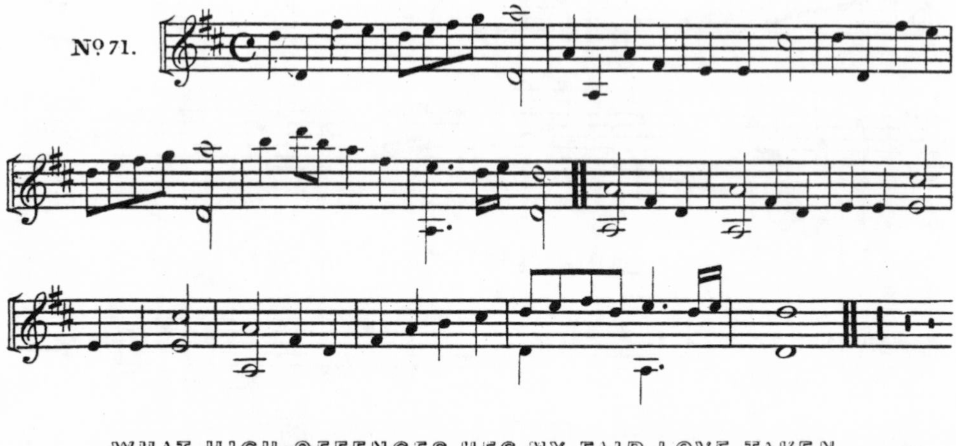

WHAT HIGH OFFENCES HES MY FAIR LOVE TAKEN.

Nº 72.

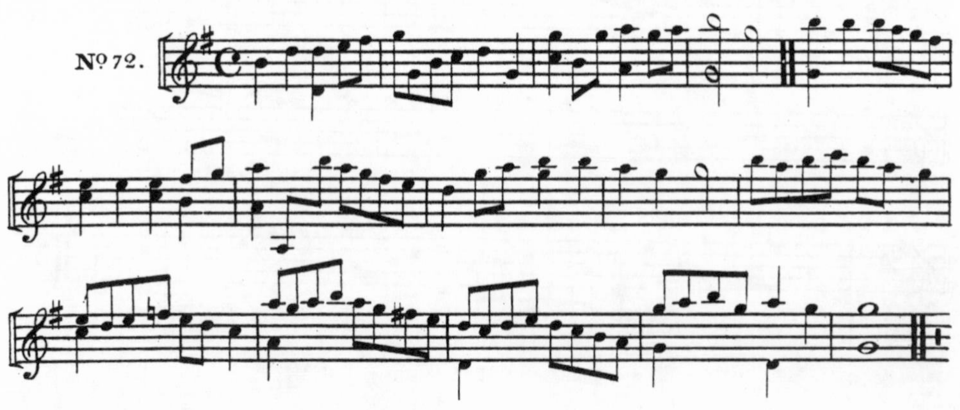

Nº 73.

THE WILLOW TRIE.

Nº 74.

SHIPEHERD SAW THOU NOT.

Nº 75.

O SILLIE SOUL ALACE.

Nº 76.

* Error in M. S.

+ A [illegible] wanting here to complete the rhythm.

CANARIES.

No. 80.

SCULLIONE.

No. 81.

THE FOURTH MEASUR OF THE BUFFINS, A FRAGMENT

No. 82.

* Error in M. S. C♮ for C♯.

+ Do. F♮ for F♯.

BRANGILL OF POICTU.

No. 83.

A FRENCHE

No. 84.

TRUMPETERS CURRAND.

No. 85.

*This bar erroneously repeated in M. S.

NOTES AND ILLUSTRATIONS.

No. I.—" ALACE YAT I CAME OWR THE MOOR, AND LEFT MY LOVE BEHIND ME."

" Ramsay," says Burns, " *found the first line of this song*, which had been preserved as the title of the charming air, and then composed the rest of the verses to suit that line. This has always a finer effect than composing English words, or words with an idea foreign to the spirit of the old title. Where old titles of songs convey any idea at all, it will generally be found to be quite in the spirit of the air."[a] It appears, however, that Ramsay was scarcely so fortunate. What he found was something much less poetical—" The last time I came o'er the moor"—but a poor substitute for the empassioned ejaculation—" Alas! that I came o'er the moor;" and therefore not very inspiring to the genius of the poet, who has certainly not educed from it any thing more than a very namby-pamby sort of ditty. The subject was one which would have better suited the ardent temperament of Burns; and had he known the original title, and the expressive melody with which it was associated, they would, doubtless, have elicited one of his most spirited and pathetic effusions.[b]

It will be at once perceived that the same deteriorating influence which has defaced the title has extended itself to the air; and if tradition has been truly represented to be a species of alchemy, which converts gold into metal of an inferior quality, the proposition could hardly be better illustrated than by comparing the genuine copy of this beautiful and characteristic melody with the modern version.[c]

a Cromek's Select Songs, vol. i. p. 22.

b Even before Ramsay's time, " The last time I came o'er the moor" appears to have superseded the old title, as we find the air under the former name in Mr Blaikie's MS. of 1692.

c The reader will find a copy of the modern air in the Appendix.

In the latter, while the general outlines are retained, all the finer traits of the modulation have disappeared. Our musical readers will at once perceive to what we allude. In the ancient melody, which appears to consist of the first sixteen bars, (the rest being a sort of symphony,) the first measure, from the outset, may be considered to be in the relative minor of the key to which the air properly belongs—a strain admirably expressive of the sentiment of the song—it then rises into the dominant, at the commencement of the second part, and concludes in the tonic; while, in the modern version, the empassioned tones with which the original song commences are exchanged for a few unmeaning notes, and, throughout, little more is perceptible than the ordinary modulation between the dominant and the tonic. The flow of the ancient melody is also more smooth and equable, and perfectly free from the formality of the modern, which looks as if it had been got up by some songwright of the last century, who, being totally insensible to its natural beauties, had reconstructed it upon a plan of his own, concluding, in the artificial manner of the day, by a regular cadence and *shake*,—a style of embellishment now happily dispensed with in these artless compositions, and reserved for music of a scientific character.

No. II.—" PEGGIE IS OVER YE SIE WITH THE SOULDIER."

The modulation of this air is perfectly national, and in the second part it bears a resemblance to the lively Scotish tune, " Hey Jenny come down to Jock." The words, if it ever had any, are no longer extant.

No. III.—" TO DANCE ABOUT THE BAILZEI'S DUBB."

Contrary to what might be expected from the name, this does not seem to have been a dance-tune, but a slow air, and one which, strangely enough, re-appears in the collections of the last century under the name of " Wae's my heart that we should sunder;" though, according to custom, protracted to double its original length. Still more singularly, the air in the Skene MS. (No. XII.) called, " Alas this night that we should sinder," though it corresponds in name with that now mentioned, is essentially different, and, like many others in this collection, perfectly new to the present age. From this we may learn how unsafe it is, in enquiries of this sort, to infer the antiquity of a *tune* from that of the *words*.

No. IV.—" LADYE ROTHEMAYIS LILT."

We believe this to be the air of one of the most poetical and interesting of our ballads,—that upon the burning of the castle of Frendraught. It was first printed in a complete form in " The North Country Garland," in 1824, a small volume, which was only intended for private distribution; so that we should have been inclined to have inserted it entire, had it not been that, since that time, it has appeared in two different collections, illustrated with very full historical notes, to which we refer our readers for the details of the story. These are Motherwell's Minstrelsy, (1827,) pp. 161, &c. and Chambers's Scottish Ballads, (1829,) pp. 85, &c. It commences—

" The eighteenth of October
A dismal tale to hear,
How good Lord John and Rothiemay
Was both burnt in the fire.

" When steeds was saddled and well bridled,
And ready for to ride,
Then out came her and false Frendraught,
Inviting them to bide."

Being in the common ballad metre, the perfect correspondence of these verses with the first and second measure of the tune, to which they adapt themselves with peculiar felicity, is a circumstance which goes but a short way to establish their mutual connection. The manner in which they become more particularly associated is, that the mother of John Gordon of Rothiemay, a youth, who, upon this occasion, perished in the flames, along with the young Viscount of Aboyne, was the Lady Rothiemay—the wife of William Gordon of Rothiemay, who was slain in a fray with Frendraught, on 1st January 1630. The fire of Frendraught, a mysterious and horrible transaction, which was never fully explained, took place in October of that year.

From the presumed date of the Skene MS., this tune must have received the name of " Lady Rothiemay's Lilt," several years previous to 1630, probably on the occasion of her marriage;[a] for in the state of affliction into which that family were thrown, by the catastrophe of Frendraught, we cannot suppose it to have sprung up after that event.

Another air in the Skene MS. is similarly situated, " Lady Cassilles' Lilt," which turns out to be the identical tune to which the ballad of " Johny Faa, or the Gipsy Laddie," founded upon the supposed elopement of that celebrated personage with this lady, has, from time immemorial, been actually sung.[b] We have here direct evidence of the fact, the popularity of the tune and the ballad having both been continued to the present day. In the one now under consideration, we are left to infer their mutual connection from the circumstances which we have above pointed out; and one of these embraces a fact which, so far as we know, has never hitherto been noticed,—viz. that the ballad-mongers of these days were in the custom of adapting their verses, when they related to the members of a particular family, to any popular lilt or tune which might happen to bear their name.

No. V.—" I LOVE MY LOVE FOR LOVE AGAIN."

This is the prototype of the tune of " Jenny Nettles," though somewhat wilder and more chromatic in its modulation. When played fast, the latter makes an excellent reel, and it is our belief that to this it owes its celebrity. The words of the song, " O, saw ye Jenny Nettles," have no merit, poetical or otherwise, to recommend them. It must, therefore, have been the music which cast its magic spell over the memory of this person; for Jenny was not formed of " the stuff that dreams are made of," but a real character of flesh and blood, a native of Falkland in Fife, and flourished in the early part of the last century; and her fate, though sufficiently melancholy, was, in reality, no more than what has happened to many a hapless maiden before and since her time, whom the genius of song has passed over in silence. She was betrayed by a gay deceiver who figures under (what we

[a] There is a fine strain of pastoral simplicity in the air itself, which would lead us to suppose it to be of considerable antiquity.

[b] See No. XXX.

presume to have been) the fictitious name of "Robin Rattles," and committed a certain rash act very common in these cases. The scene of the catastrophe was about a mile from Falkland, on the side of the road leading to Strathmiglo, and the tree upon which she was found suspended—one of the last survivors of the king's forest—was in existence, and continued to be pointed out by the neighbours, till within these few years. They also tell a story of two farmers who got a sad fright on the occasion of Jenny's suicide. It was a fine moonlight evening, and as they were returning from the market to their homes in the neighbourhood of Strathmiglo, the clearness of their vision somewhat dimmed by the manner in which they had concluded the transactions of the day, they descried their old acquaintance on the side of the road, but in such a position that they were not at all aware of what had happened. The weight of her body had bent down the branch of the tree from which she was dangling, so that her feet rested upon the ground, and she had all the appearance of being in a half-sitting posture. One of the men gave her a push with the butt-end of his whip, and called out, "Stand up, Jenny Nettles," when the body swung back in a manner so awful, as at once to convince them of the horrible truth, and to throw them into such a state of consternation, that they both galloped off, never daring to look back until they reached their own firesides, and, as the people in that quarter say, had "got into their beds between their wives and the wall."

The body of Jenny was carried off to the grave exactly in the state in which it was found, and buried about two miles from the spot where her death had taken place. Like those of other memorable characters, her remains have since been disinterred; and although they were for the most part decayed, some of the ornaments of her person, and several coins which were supposed to have been left in her pockets, were found in the grave. The former consisted of twenty-six beads which had once encircled her fair neck, and two gold ear-rings, each about an inch and a half in diameter, and apparently of French manufacture, the gifts, no doubt, of the faithless "Robin Rattles," who is said to have been one of a party of soldiers who were stationed for some time at Falkland Palace, and who, after ruining, had deserted her. The ear-rings and one of the beads may be seen in the possession of Mr Fraser, Lapidary, South St Andrew Street, Edinburgh, whose museum contains many curious antiquarian relics, and objects of natural history.

No. VI.—" BLEW RIBBENN AT THE BOUND ROD."

We find this tune in Gow's Complete Repository (Part II. p. 4) under the name of " The Blue Ribbon, Scotish measure," and that our readers may compare it with the old version now produced, we have inserted a copy of the former in the Appendix. Upon the whole, considering the great interval of time which has elapsed since the air was played in the form in which it appears in the MS., it is surprising that the difference between the two should be so slight. The Gows have certainly been reflected upon with no ordinary injustice for not having given our Scotish airs in their characteristic manner, (see Logan's Scotish Gael, vol. ii. p. 259.) So far as we have observed, there is not only much fidelity, but there are very strong traits of nationality, in the airs which have been preserved and composed by the late Neil and Nathaniel Gow, Marshall, and others of that class.

As to the meaning of the term " Blue ribbon at the bound rod," we have no difficulty in recognising " blue ribbon" as the national cognisance. " Blue" is said to have been the favourite colour of the Britons from the earliest times, and the Lowland Scots, as their " blue bonnets" to this day testify, have always shown a more than common partiality for it. " Blue" was the livery of the Covenanters, and, to go farther back, in the Chartulary of the City of Edinburgh, (vol. i. p. 33,) there is particular mention of a " banner" called the " Blue Blanket," which was employed about the end of the fifteenth century in calling out the train bands of the metropolis.[a]

In regard to the expression " Bound Rod," we have a choice of conjectures. It was certainly a term used to signify a place of rendezvous for the military,—and it is not improbable, that the " blue ribbon at the bound rod" might have consisted of a rod or pole, with blue streamers attached to it, forming a banner or flag-staff, to indicate the place of muster,—in other words, the place where soldiers were required to make themselves " boun;" *i. e.* " prepared," or, in modern phraseology, to hold themselves in readiness,—an instance of which we notice in Kennedy's Annals of Aberdeen, (vol. i. p. 209,) where it is stated that on the 1st May 1639, the magistrates were ordered to furnish every fourth man completely armed to the " bound rod" at Edinburgh. It is most likely, therefore, that this air was a Scotish national gathering or muster-tune.

[a] See Tytler's History of Scotland, vol. iv. p. 280.

"Bound Rod," or "road," has also a more limited signification. It is the boundary road or line of demarcation which separates the independent burgh of Berwick-upon-Tweed from the territories of Scotland, forming the base of the triangle which circumscribes the confines of that burgh, and of which the German Ocean and the River Tweed compose the other two sides. In the charter by James VI., (30th April 1604,) by which that monarch established the neutrality of Berwick, and its independence of both realms, we see the "Bound road" referred to as one of its ancient and accustomed limits. Previous to this, the town of Berwick had been the subject of many fierce conflicts between the English and Scots, although it had remained in the exclusive possession of the former from the year 1482, when it was taken by the Duke of Gloster, afterwards Richard III. If, therefore, we are to presume this to have been a tune which bore relation to any military triumph of the Scots at the "Bound rod" at Berwick, we throw back its antiquity to a very remote period.

No. VII.—"JOHNE ANDERSONNE, MY JO."

Although this celebrated air has often been talked of as ancient, its discovery in this MS. is the first evidence which has transpired of its antiquity. Tradition has in this instance been more than usually faithful, and there is scarcely any essential point of difference between the *old* and the *new*, except in the introduction into the former of the sharp third towards the close of the air. This manner of concluding minor movements in the *major* is called the "Tierce de Picardie,"—owing, as Burney says,[a] to the number of cathedrals in that province, where the practice, as he states, continued even at the time he wrote. It is still occasionally had recourse to; and in the grave and severe style it is not objectionable. But although Padre Martini[b] recommends it for general adoption, his views have not met with the approbation of modern composers, and its effect has been confined to music of an ecclesiastical order, except in a few rare instances, some of which we have casually noticed in the secular compositions of Beethoven, Weber, Nëukomm, and others, but where the object seems to have been rather to produce a *piquante* effect, and to surprise, than to gratify the ear. As long as the secular music continued to be governed by the ecclesiastical, it was of course very common. Thus it makes its appearance in

[a] Vol. iii. p. 114.

[b] Saggio di Contrappunto. Prima parte, 23.

the "Alman" of old Robert Jhonson, (quoted by Burney, vol. iii. p. 118.) The favourite glee, "We be soldiers three," as given by Hawkins, vol. iv. p. 22, concludes in the same way; and in the Skene MS. there are other instances where it is introduced, besides the subject of the present note; we would particularise "I love my love for love again," No. V.; and "Shipeherd, saw thou not," No. LXXV.

"John Anderson" has been already referred to (Dissertation, p. 181) as one of the songs which were composed in order to ridicule the Popish clergy at the Reformation; and Dr Percy, by whom that circumstance is mentioned, gives the following as the words of the original ballad:—

WOMAN.

"John Anderson, my jo, cum in as ȝe gae bye,
And ȝe sall get a sheip's heid weel baken in a pye,
Weel baken in a pye, and the haggis in a pat:
John Anderson, my jo, cum in and ȝe's get that."

MAN.

"And how do ȝe, cummer? And how hae ȝe threven?
And how mony bairns hae ȝe? Wom. Cummer, I hae seven.
Man. Are they to ȝour awin guidman? Wom. Na, cummer, na;
For five of them were gotten quhan he was awa."[a]

One of the most characteristic features of the air appears in the Swedish ballad tune which we have given in the Appendix. It is also curious to observe the same air, "John Anderson, my Jo," lurking among some ancient English popular dances under the title of "Paul's Steeple," in Hawkins's Hist. vol. v. p. 469;[b] and from a musical MS. belonging to the Advocates' Library, (dated 1704,) we learn that in Scotland it was formerly used as a country dance. It is here expressly arranged as such, and after an explanation of the figure, we have the following note, which throws a new light on the manners of the day:—"The tune is to be played even through once over every time: *so the first couple has time to take their drink.* To be danced with as many pairs as you please."

[a] The point here is said to be that the "seven bairns" are intended to represent the seven sacraments, five of which are the illegitimate offspring of Mother Church.

[b] We reckon the old favourite country dance, "Roger de Coverly," which Hawkins gives in the page immediately following that now referred to, (p. 470,) another Scottish tune with an English name. It has been long known in this country under the title of "The Maltman comes on Monday;" and, as such, now lies before us in a MS. collection belonging to Mr Laing, dated 1706. The date of Sir John Hawkins's copy is not given.

No. VIII.—" MY DEAREST SUEATE IS FARDEST FRA ME."

It is much to be wished that collectors would keep in view the ancient titles of these popular songs, as they form a clue which may sometimes lead to the recovery of the songs themselves.

No. IX.—" PRETTIE WEIL BEGANN, MAN."

This is a very pure specimen of Scotish pastoral melody, bearing a resemblance to some of the beautiful Swiss and Tyrolese airs.

No. X.—" LONG ER ONIE OLD MAN."

This tune is the same with that known to us under the name of " My Jo, Janet," the words of which first appeared in Ramsay's Tea-Table Miscellany in 1724, and do not seem, from their style and phraseology, to have been much older. Of the original song, " Long er onie old man," we have no trace; but as " The Bridegroom greets when the Sun gaes down," was the ancient name of the air of " Auld Robin Gray," and no doubt suggested the modern ballad, it is not improbable that the very humorous song of " My Jo, Janet," and " Long er onie old man," were allied by some such significant bond of connection. See Cromek's Select Songs, vol. ii. p. 26; also Chambers's Scottish Songs, vol. ii. p. 392.

No. XI.—" KILT THY COAT, MAGGIE."

In speaking of the song of " Saw ye nae my Peggy," Burns[a] says—" There is another set of the words, much older still, and which I take to be the original one;

[a] Cromek's Select Songs, vol. i. p. 12.

but though it has a very great deal of merit, it is not quite lady's reading." The verses here referred to commence "Saw ye my Maggie;" but we suspect the true version to have begun as in the Skene MS.—"Kilt thy coat, Maggie"—to which the music there given (which is quite different from the modern air of "Saw ye nae my Peggy") perfectly corresponds. It is also mentioned in the trial of John Douglas and eight women (belonging to Tranent) for witchcraft, on 3d May 1659,[a] where the pannels confessed, among other things, that they had had certain merry meetings with the devil, at which they were entertained with music, John Douglas being their piper; and that two of the tunes to which they danced were "Kilt thy coat, Maggie," and "Come this way with me," &c.

No. XII.—"ALACE, THIS NIGHT YAT WE SULD SINDER."

See No. III.

No. XIII.—"THE FLOWRES OF THE FORREST."

We have here the ancient air in its original purity, and any thing more solemn or pathetic is not to be found in the whole range of Scotish melody. Adapted to Miss Elliott's words, the effect is perfect; so much better than when sung with the vitiated modern version, that we almost think they had been composed for the air in its genuine form.[b] Mr Allan Cunningham very justly applauds these verses of Miss Elliott, as an astonishing restoration of the antique.—"The most acute poetic antiquary (he observes) could not, I think, single out, except by chance, the ancient lines which are woven into the song—the simulation is so perfect. The line with which it commences—'I've heard a lilting at our ewes milking'—is old; and so is the often recurring line which presses on our hearts the desolation of the forest. Now, admitting these lines to be old, can we say that the remainder of the song has not, in every line, in language and image, and sentiment, the same antique hue, spirit, and sound? The whole comes with a cry on our ears, as from the survivors of Flodden Field; and when it is sung, we owe little to imagination

[a] Abstract Records of Justiciary, (Advocates' Library,) p. 466.

[b] We have inserted in the Appendix a copy of the modern version, that the two may be compared.

when we associate it with the desolation of the forest, and hear the ancient wail of the maids and matrons."[a]

The other words—" I've seen the smiling of fortune beguiling," &c.—have enjoyed an extended popularity. They are tender and highly poetical, though not for a moment to be compared to those of Miss Elliott. " Although they were both," says Cunningham, " imagined for a while to be old compositions, there was no need to call antiquity to the aid of two such touching songs; and I have not heard that even an antiquary withdrew his admiration on discovering them to be modern."[b]

No. XIV.—" OSTEND."

This tune points to an event nearly contemporary with the MS.—the Siege of Ostend, which, after a contest of three years and three months, during which it is said that upwards of 70,000 men fell on each side, was taken from the United Provinces by the Marquis Spinola, Commander-in-chief to Philip III. of Spain, in 1604. The obstinate resistance of the Dutch, on this occasion, was the cause of much disappointment to the assailants, and to none more than to Isabella Eugenia, Governante of the Netherlands, with respect to whom, it is related, that having taken upon herself a vow that she would not change her under-garments until the town had surrendered, the ladies of the court were latterly obliged to *dye theirs*, in order to keep their vice-regal mistress in countenance.

By his success in the capture of Ostend and other feats, the name of Spinola became so formidable, that apprehensions of an invasion, to be conducted by him on the part of Spain and France, were afterwards entertained, in England at least. —See Howell's Letters, vol. i. § 5, Lett. 13; also Ben Jonson's " Staple of News," iii. 2. That Scotland looked on with considerable interest during this sanguinary and long protracted siege is evinced by the tune. Drummond, also, in his Polemo-Middinia, makes an allusion to Spinola in the following passage:—

" . . . . . . et sic turba horrida mustrat.
Haud aliter quam si cum multis, Spinola, troupis
Proudus ad Ostendam marchasset fortiter urbem."

a The Songs of Scotland, vol. i. p. 209.
b See Dissertation, pp. 152, 153.

No. XV.—" MY LADIE LAUDIAN'S LILT."

This was probably Lady Lothian, spouse of Mark Kerr, Commendator of Newbottle, who was created Earl of Lothian in 1606, and died in 1609. There was also a Lady Loudon at this time, (daughter of the Master of Loudon,) who was married to Sir John Campbell of Sawers, one of the Glenurchy family, in 1620. But as the name " Laudian"—the common way at that time of spelling Lothian—is very distinctly written in the MS., the former was most likely to have been the person to whom the air related.

No. XVI.—" GOOD NIGHT, AND GOD BE WITH YOW."

To this tune, which has been long popular in Scotland, there are attached the following verses, under the name of " Armstrong's Good night," said by Sir Walter Scott to have been composed by one of that predatory clan of Borderers who was executed for the murder of Sir John Carmichael of Edrom, Warden of the Middle Marches, on 14th November 1600.[a]—

" This night is my departing night,
  For here na langer must I stay;
There's neither friend nor foe o' mine
  But wishes me away.

" What I have done through lack of wit,
  I never, never, can recall;
I hope ye're a' my friends as yet,
  Good night, and joy be with you all!"

Sir Walter, however, does not vouch for the originality of the words, and they are obviously too general to have a definite application to any one. Farther, if the tune had been publicly known as that to which " Armstrong's Good night" was sung about the year 1615, when the Skene MS. is supposed to have been written, it

[a] Border Minstrelsy, vol. i. pp. 183 and 105.

would most probably have been entered in the collection under that name; instead of which, it is styled simply "Good night, and God be with you;" which, in modern usage, has been converted into "Good night, and *joy* be with you."

No. XVII.—"MY LOVE SHOE WINNS NOT HER AWAY."

Anglice—"My love she dwells not hereabouts." All that we need say of this air is, that it is new to us; and that, although it possesses various antique characteristics, yet, contrary to the *non-semitonic* theory, it is not marked by any avoidance of half notes—an observation, however, which applies to so many of the tunes, that we need not repeat it.

No. XVIII.—"JENNET DRINKS NA WATER."

We think that we can perceive more spirit and originality in this tune in its pristine than in its modern form, and we have accordingly given the latter in the Appendix; though the slight change which it has undergone, during so long an interval, is the circumstance most worthy of notice. The second part seems to have been a sort of popular Scotish ritornello, as we find the same passage attached to several other tunes in the MS.

No. XIX.—"REMEMBER ME AT EVENINGE."

The nearest approach to the title of this air that we observe upon ancient record is "Lait, lait in evinnynges," mentioned among the tunes in Cockelbie Sow, (1450,) Dissertation, p. 46. The character and leading ideas of the air resemble the well-known tune of "Dainty Davie" more than any with which we are acquainted, and this last appears in Durfey's Collection, (1700.)

No. XX.—" I METT HER IN THE MEDOWE."

There is an old tune—" Down in yon meadow"—which Gay introduces into his Opera of Polly; but it is not the same.

No. XXI.—" BLEW BREIKS."

A dance tune.

No. XXII.—" I CANNOT LIVE AND WANT THEE."

A wild and curious melody in the true Scotish style.

No. XXIII.—" I DOWE NOT QUNNE (*i. e.* WHEN) COLD."

No. XXIV.—" ADEW, DUNDIE."

A comparison between the ancient and modern version of this tune is certainly much to the advantage of the former.[a] The name itself—" Adieu, Dundee," bespeaks an air of sentiment and emotion; and here we have one which gives

" —— a very echo to the seat
Where love is throned."

The modern tune may be well enough fitted to the words—

" O whare did ye get that havermeal bannock ?
O sillie auld body, O dinna ye see ?"

[a] To satisfy such of our readers as may not remember the modern air, we have given it in the Appendix.

And Hector Macneill has done the most for it in his "Saw ye my wee thing," a justly popular ballad. But for the other, we desiderate vocal poetry of a higher class, —something which, while it responded to the simple, affecting, and characteristic modulation of the melody, would bring before our minds the scenes and images which the ancient name of the air most naturally suggests. The recovery of the old words would be better than all; but that is now hopeless, and we know of no historical event or tradition connected with Dundee on which they were likely to have been founded.

The variations to this air merit attention. They are appropriate, and rather a graceful specimen of the composition of an age when, in all matters of this sort, art was too often permitted to stifle the voice of nature.

No. XXV.—"SHOE LOOKS AS SHOE WOLD LETT ME."

This seems to be a pipe tune. It concludes with the "ritornello" alluded to in No. XVIII.

No. XXVI.—"I DARE NOT VOWE I LOVE THEE."

This fine air has all the appearance of having been composed for the harp.

No. XXVII.—"LETT NEVER CRUELTIE DISHONOUR BEWTIE."

No. XXVIII.—"ALACE, I LIE MY ALON, I'M LIK TO DIE AWLD."

i.e. I am likely to die an old maid! This air strongly reminds us of Marshall's well-known tune, "Of a' the airts the wind can blaw."

No. XXIX.—"THE KEIKING GLASSE."

In the style of the masque tunes of the reign of James VI.; without any tincture of Scotish melody.

No. XXX.—"LADIE CASSILLES LILT."

It has been mentioned,[a] that this air is the same with that which is popularly known by the name of "Johnie Faa," and to which the ballad descriptive of the Countess of Cassillis' supposed elopement with that personage is sung. It is not for us to repeat in this place any thing so well known. It will be enough to bring to the recollection of our readers the opening verses,—

"The gypsies they came to my Lord Cassillis' yett,
And O! but they sang bonnie;
They sang sae sweet, and sae complete,
That doun came our fair ladie.
"She came tripping doun the stairs,
And all her maids before her,
As soon as they saw her weel fa'ured face,
They coost their glamourie owre her."

The only essential difference between the old and the new is to be found in the last two bars, where the ancient copy is remarkable for a wailing, *mordendo* sort of close, similar to what may be found in some of the other Scotish Melodies in this Collection. As this concluding passage has been laid aside in modern times, and does not readily admit of being adapted to the words of the ballad, it affords an additional presumption that the air was known under the denomination of "Lady Cassilles' Lilt" anterior to the composition of the verses, and the circumstances which gave rise to them.[b] In that case, "Lady

[a] See No. IV.

[b] There is a tune called "The Gypsy's Lilt" in the Rowallan MS., (which is of the same age with the Skene MS.,) but it bears no resemblance whatever to Lady Cassillis' Lilt.

Cassillis' Lilt" may have been a family tune for many generations before the Countess of "gypsy" notoriety saw the light. She is supposed to have been Lady Jean Hamilton, daughter of Thomas, first Earl of Haddington, and the wife of John, the *sixth* Earl of Cassillis. We observe, in the Scots Magazine for November 1817, a lively and agreeable paper on this subject from the pen of a distinguished antiquary, together with a portrait of the lady herself, taken from an original picture at Culzean House, and a copy of the ballad, somewhat different from that which occurs in the common collections, and to which we would refer our readers. There are two editions of the story,—one the poetical, and the other the prose version. In the first, to use the words of the writer immediately referred to—" A very numerous jury of matrons"—spinsters and knitters in the sun—" pronounce the fair Countess guilty of having eloped with a genuine gypsy, though compelled in some degree to that low-lived indiscretion by certain wicked charms and philtres, of which Faa and his party are said to have possessed the secret." And the scene concludes with the whole party being intercepted by the Earl, and taken back to Cassillis Castle, where fifteen of them are executed, leaving only one of their number, who, in the common way in which the verses run, is supposed to " tell the tale." The prose tradition, again, if not altogether exculpatory of the lady's virtue, is at least somewhat less derogatory to her taste, her seducer being represented not as a real, but a feigned gypsy, in the person of Sir John Faa of Dunbar. Her affections are said to have been engaged to this gentleman before she was married, contrary to her wishes, to " the grave and solemn" Earl of Cassillis, (as he was called,)—a stern Covenanter, who took a prominent part in his country's politics, having been a delegate to the Assembly of Divines at Westminster on the ratification of the Solemn League and Covenant in 1643. It is stated to have been at this time, and while the Earl was absent on this very mission, that Sir John Faa repaired to Cassillis Castle, disguised as a gypsy, and attended by a band of these desperadoes, when the lady agreed to elope with him;—that the Earl returned home in time to set out with his followers and overtake the party before they had crossed the Border; and, having captured, brought them back to Cassillis, where he hanged all of them, including Sir John, upon " the dule tree"—" a splendid and most umbrageous plane which yet flourishes in front of the castle gate."[a] The Countess, after having been compelled to witness the death scene from the window of an apartment still called " The Countess's Room," is said, after a short confinement in that

[a] Chambers's Scotish Ballads, p. 144.

apartment, to have been immured in the house belonging to the family at Maybole, which was fitted up for her reception, by the addition of a fine projecting stair-case, upon which there are still to be seen a set of carved heads representing the effigies of her lover and his attendant gypsies. It seems, however, that there are a number of carved heads in the windows of the upper flat of Cassillis Castle regarding which *tradition is silent;* and another circumstance tells still more unfavourably for the truth of the story. This Lady Cassillis, who had two daughters, one of whom was married to Lord Dundonald, and the other to Bishop Burnet, could not have been less than *thirty-seven* years of age at this time, viz. in 1643, as she was born in 1607. Farther, the ingenious author of the article in the Scots Magazine has informed us that he has seen a letter or letters from the Covenanting Lord addressed to this very person, *after* the event is said to have taken place, in which he expresses himself in such terms as to show that the utmost mutual confidence and affection continued to subsist. Neither does the tapestry work still preserved at Culzean House, and said to have been wrought by her, throw any additional light upon the story. It merely represents a lady gorgeously attired on a superb white charger, and surrounded by a set of persons bearing no resemblance whatever to gypsies. Upon the whole, therefore, we are inclined to think that the popular traditions and rhymes of the country have done great injustice to the memory of a lady, who, for any thing we *know* to the contrary, may have been one of the most virtuous and exemplary of her sex. Ballads, it is well known, were a common mode of revenge in those days, and as such they must have been the vehicles of all manner of calumny and falsehood. When Falstaff quarrels with his comrades at Gadshill, he exclaims—" An I have not *ballads* made on you all, and sung to filthy tunes, let a cup of sack be my poison." And really the case of Lady Cassillis is not singular. Few, perhaps, will read the details of the Frendraught tragedy without coming to the conclusion that Sir James Chrichton of Frendraught and his spouse were wholly innocent of the foul and atrocious crime which the ballad so pointedly lays to their charge.[a]

[a] Mr Finlay, in his " Scottish Ballads," also adopts the opinion, that the whole story, relative to Lady Cassillis' elopement, was an invention of some feudal or political rival, to hurt the character and feelings of an opponent.

No. XXXI.—" THRIE SHEIPS SKINNS."

In a song in ridicule of the Popish hierarchy which we have quoted, (Dissertation, p. 32,) a passage occurs in allusion to something of this kind—

" Remission of sins in *auld sheep skins,*
Our sauls to bring from grace ;"

—and it is possible that this tune (if a song had ever been attached to it) had sprung up in some such way, among the ballads which were levelled against the Catholic clergy at the time of the Reformation. But for these many years it has been known as one of the trades' tunes; and we find a copy of it in Oswald's Pocket Companion, vol. vii. p. 10, very little altered from that in the MS. The worshipful body who lay claim to it are, as may be supposed from the name, the incorporation of " Skinners ;" and we are told that it used to be played on the bells of St Giles's Church on the day on which they had their annual procession. " Clout the Caldron," a tune so like this, that it is difficult to distinguish the one from the other, is appropriated to the Hammermen.

No. XXXII.—" PORT BALLANGOWNE."

" To the wandering harpers" (says Mr Tytler, in his Dissertation on Scotish Music) " we are certainly indebted for that species of music which is now scarcely known—I mean *the port*. Almost every great family had a port that went by the name of the family. Of the few that are still preserved are Port Lennox, Port Gordon, Port Seton, and Port Athole, which are all of them excellent in their kind. The port is not of the martial strain of the *march*, as some have conjectured; those above named being all in the plaintive strain, and modulated for the harp." " Port Ballangowne," therefore, may be regarded with some interest as by much the oldest recorded copy of this very rare description of music which has hitherto been published.

No. XXXIII.—" MY MISTRES BLUSH IS BONIE."

No. XXXIV.—" BONIE JEAN MAKIS MEIKLE OF ME."

No. XXXV.—" LESLIE'S LILT."

There were various families of this name in the early part of the seventeenth century, so that to fix upon any one in particular to whom this lilt related is impossible.

No. XXXVI.—" JOHNE DEVISONN'S PINT OF WIN."

The tune which bears this name appears to be a French Volt. See No. LXXXV.

No. XXXVII.—" THE LASS O' GLASGOWE."

No. XXXVIII.—" MALE SIMME."

Few persons versed in matters of this sort will have forgotten the ballad which relates the luckless fate of the king's daughter, whom her sister drowned in the mill-dam; and the number of ingenious ways in which the miller contrived to dispose of her remains. One of the most fanciful of these is explained in the following distich:

" What did he do with her two shins?
Unto the viol they danced *Moll Syms*."

At first it was thought that this might be the tune here celebrated, but, on farther consideration, there was something in the grave majestic strain of "Male Simme" which forbade the idea that it could be the "Moll Syms" of popular notoriety. It was again considered how far this "Male Simme" might claim propinquity with "Symme and his Bruder," the Scotish Tartuffes of the sixteenth century, and of whom the reader may learn some particulars in Lord Hailes's Notes to his published selections from the Bannatyne MS., but no satisfactory evidence could be obtained on that head. Finally, it was resolved, that, looking to the general features of the air, its regular structure, and certain imitative passages which are very common in harp tunes—it was a native of Wales—the forgotten favourite of some of the old Welsh Bards. The Editor, however, has not hitherto been so fortunate as to find it in any collection of Welsh airs; and the only work besides the Skene MS. where he has met with it is a collection of old and new Dutch Rustic Songs and Country Dances —"Oude en nieuve Hollantse Boeren Lietes en Contre Dansen," printed at Amsterdam about the end of the seventeenth century, and containing nearly a thousand airs of different countries. Here it figures under the name of "Malle Sÿmen."

No. XXXIX.—"SHACKLE OF HAY."

No. XL.—"DOUN IN YON BANKE."

The words of this song have not been recovered, and the nearest approximation to its name which we can find is "By a bank as I lay," one of the "bunch of ballets and songs, all auncient," belonging to Captain Cox, and enumerated in Laneham's Letter, describing the entertainment to Queen Elizabeth, at Killingworth, in 1575. It is said to be preserved along with the music, among the books of the Royal Library in the British Museum, (17, B. 43,) where we have not had an opportunity of seeing it; but Ritson, who, however, was no judge of music, calls it "a love song, without any other merit than antiquity." The air in the Skene MS., though slightly defective in the second part, is one of the most beautiful and expressive we have any where seen.[a]

[a] Ritson's Ancient Songs, p. 59.

No. XLI.

No. XLII.—"ADERNEI'S LILT."

No. XLIII.—"BLEW CAPPE."

The tune of the Anglo-Scotish ballad, "Blue cap for me,"[a] which begins as follows:—

"Come hither the merri'st of all the Nine,
  Come sit thee down by me, and let vs be jolly;
And in a full cup of Apollo's wine
  Wee'll drowne our old enemy, mad melancholy:
Which, when wee have done, wee'll betweene vs deuise
  A dainty new ditty, with art to comprise;
And of this new ditty the matter shall be,
  Gif ever I have a man, Blew cap for me.

"There liues a blithe lasse in Falkeland towne,
  And shee had some suitors, I wot not how many;
But her resolution shee had set downe
  That shee'd haue a Blew cap, gif ere she had any.
An Englishman, when our good king was there,
  Came often unto her, and loued her deare:
But still she replide, 'Sir, I pray let me be;
  Gif ever I have a man, Blew cap for me.'"

After this, a Welshman, a Frenchman, an Irishman, a Spaniard, a German, and a Netherlander, successively pay their addresses.

[a] See Evans's Old Ballads, vol. iv. p. 264.

"These sundry suitors of seueral lands
Did daily solicite this lasse for her fauour,
And euery one of them alike vnderstands,
That to win the prize, they in vain did endeauour:
For shee had resolued (as I before said)
To haue bonny Blew cap, or else dee a maid.
Unto au her suppliants still replide she,
'Gif ever I have a man, Blew cap for mee.'

"At last came a Scottish man (with a blew cap),
And he was the party for whom she had tarry'd,
To get this blithe bonny lasse 'twas his gude hap,
They gang'd to the kirk, and were presently marry'd:
I ken not weel whether it were lord or leard,
They caude him some sike a like name, as I heard;
To chuse him from all she did gladly agree,
And still shee cry'd, Blew cap, th'art welcome to mee."

"Blue cap" was formerly a very common designation of the Scots. Dryden uses it in an address to the University of Oxford, on the part of the actors of the London company, the half of whom had been drafted off to perform at Edinburgh, during the Duke of York's (afterwards James II.) residence at Holyrood House.

"Our brethren have from Thames to Tweed departed,
And of our sisters all the kinder hearted,
To Edinburgh gone, or coach'd, or carted,
With bonny *Blew cap* there they act all night,
For Scots half-crowns, in English—threepence height."

And to distinguish them by this appellation was natural enough. "The husbandmen in Scotland, (says Morrison in his Itinerary, 1598,)[a] the servants, and *almost all the country*, did wear coarse cloth made at home, of grey or sky colour, and *flat blew caps, very broad*." The expression in the second verse, "when our good king was there," would fix the date of this ballad to be sometime posterior to 1617, the year of James's visit to Scotland, when he spent a short time at Falkland, in the enjoyment of his favourite amusement of hunting: and if so, it had been inserted in the MS. during the season of its popularity. But it was so common to vary

[a] See Arnot's History of Edinburgh, p. 56.

old versions of ballads and songs, as well as tunes, that it would be more consistent with the presumed age of the MS. to hold that the tune " Blew cappe," which we find there, referred to some previous set of verses on the same theme. In " Wit Restored," vol. i. p. 118, there is another song " to the tune of Blue cap," beginning—

" Come hither the maddest of all the land."

No. XLIV.—" GILCREICH'S LILT."

No. XLV.—" SA MIRRIE AS WE HAUE BEEN."

One of the Scotish melodies which still retains its popularity, and which Mr Tytler conjectured to have been composed *between the Restoration and the Union!* The version here given is essentially different from the traditional copy, but such is the indistinctness of the notation, that, although we have given it a place in the present publication, we cannot vouch for its perfect accuracy.

No. XLVI.—" HUNTER'S CARRIER."

Not Scotish.

No. XLVII.—" KETTE BAIRDIE."

So well did Sir Walter Scott know that this was a popular dance during the reign of James VI. (though from what source he obtained that information, we have no idea, as we do not believe that the Skene MS. was ever submitted to his attention,) that true to nature, as he always is in his historical delineations, he introduces it in the " Fortunes of Nigel;" with this difference, that it is there called " Chrichty

Bairdie"—a name not precisely identical with that here given; but as "Kit" is a diminutive of "Christopher," it is not difficult to perceive how the two came to be confounded. "An action," says King James, (addressing his Privy Council on the subject of Lord Glenvarloch's misdemeanour within the precincts of the court,) "may be inconsequential or even meritorious *quoad hominem*; that is, as touching him upon whom it is acted, and yet most criminal *quoad locum*, or considering the place wherein it is done, as a man may lawfully dance *Chrichty Bairdie*, or any other dance, in a tavern, but not *inter parietes ecclesiæ*."

We find the same tune in the Rowallan MS., where it is called "Catherine Bairdie."[a] "Kitty Bairdie" is also the heroine of a nursery rhyme in the recollection of most people.

"Kitty Bairdie had a cow,
Black and white about the mou,
Wasn't that a dainty cow,
Dance Kitty Bairdie.

"Kitty Bairdie had a grice,
It could skate upon the ice,
Wasn't that a dainty grice,
Dance Kitty Bairdie," &c. &c.

No. XLVIII.—"I WILL NOT GOE TO MY BED TILL I SULD DIE."

A wild, plaintive strain, of a pastoral and strictly Scottish character.

No. XLIX.—"I SERVE A WORTHIE LADIE."

In a musical MS. belonging to Mr Laing, bearing date 1706, this air appears under the kindred name of "I lov'd a handsome lady;"—but in modern times it is

[a] See Dissertation, p. 139.

better known as "Dumbarton Drums"—a song which (as Mr Robert Chambers has pointed out in his "Scottish Songs," vol. i. p. 66) does not refer to the *town* of that name, but to the Earl of Dumbarton, commander of the Royal Forces in Scotland during the reigns of Charles II. and James II., who suppressed the rebellion of Argyle, in 1685, and accompanied the last mentioned monarch to France at the Revolution. The song "Dumbarton's Drums" first appeared in the "Tea Table Miscellany."

No. L.—"SHE MOWPIT IT, COMING O'ER THE LIE," (LEA.)

To "mowp," in Scotish, is to eat like children and old people, who have few teeth. It is expressed, or nearly so, by the English word "munch."

No. LI.—"WHO LEARNED YOU TO DANCE AND A TOWDLE."

Apparently the same with the Cushion Dance, which is well known to be of considerable antiquity. See extract from Selden's Table Talk, No. 83.

No. LII.—"OMNIA VINCIT AMOR."

An air called "Omnia vincit amor" appears in "Oswald's Pocket Companion," but in different time, of a different character, and decidedly inferior to this in style and modulation.

No. LIII.—"PANTALONE."

The reader will find a dance tune very similar to this, and obviously of the same school, in the extracts which Dr Burney gives (Hist. vol. iii. p. 282) from "Le

Ballet Comique de la Royne," published by Baltazar de Beaujoyeulx, in 1582,—the music of which was composed "par les sieurs Beaulieu et Salmon," by command of Henry III. of France, on occasion of the nuptials of the Duke de Joyeuse. Baltazar calls it "un son fort gai nommé la clochette."

No. LIV.—"SIR JOHN HOPE'S CURRANT."

See Dissertation, p. 11.

No. LV.—"MARIE ME, MARIE ME, QUOTH THE BONIE LASS."

The tune of an unrecovered ballad, very probably English, and though not exactly the same, apparently the ground-work of what Ritson[a] calls "the most famous and popular air ever heard of in this country,"—"The King shall enjoy his own again."—"Invented," says this author, "to support the declining interest of the royal martyr, it served afterwards, with more success, to keep up the spirits of the Cavaliers, and promote the restoration of his son; an event it was employed to celebrate all over the kingdom. At the Revolution it of course became an adherent of the exiled family, whose cause it never deserted. And as a tune, it is said to have been a principal mean of depriving King James of the crown. This very air, upon two memorable occasions, was very near being equally instrumental in replacing it on the head of his son. It is believed to be a fact, that nothing fed the enthusiasm of the Jacobites, down almost to the present reign, in every corner of Great Britain, more than 'The King shall enjoy his own again;' and even the great orator of the party, in that celebrated harangue, which furnished the present Laureate with the subject of one of his happiest and finest poems, was always thought to have alluded to it in his remarkable quotation from Virgil of

"Carmina tum melius cum venerit ipse canemus."

[a] Ancient Songs, p. 229.

No. LVI.—" ALMAN DELORNE."

After describing the Galliard, which is a lively Italian dance in $\frac{3}{4}$ time, Morley[a] says—" The Alman (which is of German origin) is a more heavie dance than this, (fitlie representing the nature of the people whose name it carrieth,) so that no extraordinary motions are used in dancing of it." In Scotland, it seems to have been common during the sixteenth century, as we find the " Alman Haye" mentioned in the " Complaynt of Scotland," and another " Alman Nicholas" occurs in the Skene MS. " It was," says the quaint author of the Complaynt, " ane celest recreation to behald ther lycht lopene, galmonding,[b] stendling bakuart and forduart,[c] dansand base dansis, pauvans, galzardis, turdions, braulis and branglis, buffons, vitht mony uthir lycht dances, the quhilk ar over prolixt to be rehersit." The names of several of these, however, are given, although we cannot here spare room for their insertion; and these names, denoting the particular airs, are, as Leyden remarks,[d] all Scotish. Ritson[e] expresses his regret that " not one of the dance tunes here named should be known to exist at this moment;" and even yet, it can scarcely be said that any have been recovered corresponding in designation with the national Scotish dances there specified. But there are several dance tunes in the Skene MS. which answer to the general description, such as galliards, branles, buffons, &c., and most of these appear to have been French. In this matter Scotland seems in an especial manner to have affected the fashions of foreign countries.

" Sum usit the dancis to dance
Of Cipres and Boheme,
Sum the faitis full yarne
Of Portugal and Naverne;

[a] Introduction, p. 181. Edition 1597.

[b] " Galmonding."

" Now, boy, for joy and mirth I dance,
Tak thair ane *gamond* of France."

SIR DAVID LYNDSAY.

[c] See " Platfute," " Backfute," and " Futebefore," " Ourfute," and " Orliance," mentioned in " Dissertation," p. 46; also, " Lang platfut of Gariau," another of the dances specified in the " Complaynt."

[d] P. 130.

[e] Historical Essay, p. 100.

Sum counterfutit the Gyis of Spayne,
Sum Italy, sum Almayne;
Sum noisit Napillis anone,
And uyir sum of Arragone;
Sum 'The Cane of Tartary,'
Sum 'The Soldane of Surry,' (Syria,)
Than all arrayit in a ring,
Dansit 'my deir derling."[a]

The favourite dances in use, however, were French; and of these many of this age are still extant. We have been favoured with the perusal of a MS. volume belonging to Mr Lyle, Surgeon at Airth, written in tablature for the lute of seven strings, and which had been the property of Sir William Mure of Rowallan about the year 1620. It is in excellent preservation, extends to about forty pages, and contains a great variety of these dances, including Currants—Basse Dances—Voltes—Bourrées[b]—Sarabandes—Passameze—Ballete—Canaries—La Robinette—Branles, &c.—and has not yet been deciphered.

No. LVII.—"AN ALMAN MOREISS."

This may be interpreted a German morris dance, but we should rather think that it must have meant a particular kind of allemande in use among morris dancers.

The earliest notice we have of the morris dance in Scotland is in James the First's "Christ Kirk on the Green."—

"He use himself as man discreet,
And up tuk 'moreis dance.'"

In its simplest form, it seems to have been danced by a number of youths, with bells at their feet,[c] and ribbons of various colours tied round their arms, and slung across their shoulders.[d] Whether it was a dance of Moorish invention seems to be very doubtful. According to Junius,[e] its name originated in a pastime in which it was

[a] "Cockelbie Sow."
[b] A lively dance, believed to have originated in Auvergne.
[c] See Dissertation, p. 45.
[d] Hawkins, vol. ii. p. 135.
[e] Tripudium Mauritanicum, *nam* faciem plerum queinficiunt fuligne et peregrinum vestium cul-

customary for the performers to blacken their faces and put on a foreign costume, in order to appear like Moors, or persons who had come from a distant part of the world, and had brought with them a new species of recreation. But, when performed at festivals, the characters were not usually such as here described. On May-day, in particular, one of the party consisted of a boy dressed up like a girl, to represent "Maid Marian," Robin Hood's mistress; and she, again, was accompanied by a gentleman usher—Friar Tuck—a hobby-horse—foreigners or Moors—fools, jesters, and other characters, an enumeration of which will be found in Mr Tollet's account of a painted window, subjoined to the First Part of Henry IV., in Steevens' Edition of Shakspeare, (1778.)[a]

No. LVIII.—"PITT ON YOUR SHIRT ON MONDAY."

It must not be supposed by our brethren on the other side of the Tweed, that the name of this tune imported an injunction to the people of Scotland to change their linen on Monday more than on any other day of the week; and far less that they were in the habit of dispensing with so important an article, except on that particular day. The true meaning of it was, that they were to buckle on their armour or coat of mail on Monday; and a regulation in our Statute Book sufficiently explains why Monday should have been selected for that purpose, while it fixes an era when it is probable that the tune had been composed.

Musters, or military rendezvous called weapon-schawings, were customary in Scotland from an early period. They took place annually, at stated times, and were summoned by the sheriffs and magistrates of the counties, who, in conjunction with commissioners appointed by the king, superintended the raising of the troops, divided them into companies, and appointed their captains. Persons in all stations were obliged to bear a part on these occasions, and to appear equipped in military array according to their rank. Having been disused for some years, these weapon-schawings were revived by James V. in a series of consecutive acts,—1540,

tum assumunt qui ludicris talibus indulgent, ut Mauri esse videantur aut e longius remota patria credantur advolasse, atque insolens recreationis genus advexisse.

Junii Etymologicon, *v.* Morris Dance.

[a] See Malone's Edition of Shakspeare, (1821,) vol. xvi. p. 419; also Mr Douce's Illustrations of Shakspeare.

c. 85, 86, 87, 88, 89, 90, 91; by the first of which, c. 85, it is "thocht expedient that the samin (*i. e.* the weapon-schawings) be made thrise for the first yeir; and the first time to be *on the morne after Law-Sunday* (*i. e.* Low-Sunday, the first Sunday after Easter) nixt-to-cum." And, again, by c. 87, "because it is understandin that their weapons and harnesse may not be compleitlie gotten at the first weapon-schawing, that is to say, *on the morne after Law-Sunday nixt-to-cum:* Therefore it is dispensed be the kingis grace, that they make their schawinges and mustures with sik harnesse and weapones as they haue, or may convenientlie get against the said day." It was also appointed, by c. 90, that "the lieges be warned to the saidis weapon-schawinges, upon fourtie daies warning, for the first time; and yeirlie at every time thereafter, upon twentie daies."

"Pitt on your shirt on Monday" is a brisk, lively, and highly original bagpipe tune, in the style of a march or gathering, and excellently adapted to be played by the common pipers to warn the people of their duty during the period of premonition here mentioned.

No. LIX.

No. LX.—"JOY TO THE PERSONNE."

Nos. LX., LXI., LXII., LXX., LXXIV., LXXV., LXXVI., and LXXVII., are not Scotish airs, but regular vocal compositions to which were adapted, *selon les règles*, fashionable songs and sonnets of the sixteenth century, to be sung in three, four, five, and six parts. Their grave, psalmodic character, and the monotony of their modulation, seldom leaving the key-note, present a singular contrast to the wild, varied, and animated strains of the Scotish minstrels. Most of them were written by English composers of the reign of Queen Elizabeth, and there can be no doubt that their popularity was quite as lasting in Scotland as it was in England. In the former country, these songs, along with others of the same stamp, were taught in the different music schools throughout the whole of the seventeenth century—a fact which appears not only from Forbes's "Cantus, Songs, and Fancies," printed at Aberdeen in 1662, 1666, and 1682,[a] (and which, with the exception of No. LXI., contains every one of the above airs, and all of them but one—No. LXXVI.—set to words the same with those indicated by the title given in the Skene MS.;) but from another book of songs, dated 1639, belonging to the Advocates' Library, and which is filled with the same description of vocal pieces, including several of those here specified. This volume was the property of the late Dr Leyden, who was informed that it had belonged to a schoolmaster on the Border. There is also another MS., called "Constable's Cantus," (from its having been the property of the late Mr Constable the bookseller,) the contents of which appear to be nearly the same.

Considering these and the numerous collections of madrigals and songs in parts, which are extant both in print and MS., of the age of Queen Elizabeth and James VI., and in which these "ayres," and others little distinguishable from them, are to be found, it might almost seem a work of supererogation to republish them on the present occasion. But they may still be a novelty to such of our readers as are not versed in the music of that age; and even Forbes's Cantus has become so scarce, that the insertion of the verses to which they were sung may not be unacceptable to some,—while others would, no doubt, regard their non-insertion as a culpable omission on the part of the Editor.

"JOY TO THE PERSON."

"Joy to the person of my love,
Although she me disdain;
Fixt are my thoughts, and may not move,
But yet I love in vain.
Shal I lose the sight
Of my joy and heart's delight?
Or shal I leave my sute?
Shal I strive to touch?
Oh! no, it were too much;
She is the forbidden fruit.
Oh! wo is me that ever I did see
The beauty that did me bewitch;
Yet out, alace! I must forgo that face,
The treasour I esteemed so much.

[a] See this work noticed in Dissertation, pp. 28, 29.

"O! shall I rage into some dale?
Or to the mountains mourn?
Sad echoes shal resound my tale;
Or whither shal I turn?
Shal I buy that love,
No life to me will give,
But deeply wounds my heart?
If I flee away,
She will not to me say, stay,
My sorrows to convert.
O! no, no, no, she will not once say so;
But comfortless I must be gone:
Yet though she be so thrawart unto me,
I'le love her, or I shal love none.

"O! that I might but understand
The reasons of her hate,
To him would be at her command,
In love, in life, in state:
Then should I no more
In heart be griev'd so sore,
Nor sad with discontent.
But since that I have lov'd
A maid that so hath prov'd
Unworthie, I do repent.
Something unkind hath setled in her mind,
That caused her to leave me so:
Sweet, seem to me but half so kind to be,
Or let me the occasion know.

"Thousand fortunes fall to her share,
Though she rejected me,
And fill'd my heart full of despair,
Yet shal I constant be.
For she is the dame
My tongue shal ever name,
Fair branch of modestie,
Chaste of heart and mind.
Oh! were she half so kind,
Then would she pity me.

Sweet, turn at last, be kind as thou art chaste,
  And let me in thy bosom dwell;
So shall we gain the pleasure of love's pain:
  Till then, my dearest love, farewell."

Forbes's Cantus.

No. LXI.—"THOW WILT NOT GOE AND LEAVE ME HEIR."

"Thow wilt not goe and leave me heir,
O do not so, my dearest deir;
The sune's departing clouds the sky,
Bot thy depairting maks me die.

"Thow can'st not goe, my deirest heart,
Bot I must quyt my choisest pairt;
For with two hearts thow must be gone,
And I sall stay at home with none.

"Meane whill, my pairt sall be to murne,
Telling the houres whill thow returne;
My eyes sall be but eyes to weip,
And nether eyes to sie nor sleipe.

"Prevent the hazard of this ill,
Goe not at all, stay with me still;
I'lle bath thy lips with kisses then,
And look for mor ease back againe.

"Since thou will needs goe, weill away!
Leave, leave one hart with me to stay;
Take mine, lett thine in pane remaine,
That quicklie thou may come againe.

"Fairweill, deir heart, since it must be,
That thow wilt not remain with me;
My greatest greife it still sall be,
I love a love that loves not me."

MS. Advocates' Library, 1639.

No. LXII.—"COME, LOUE, LETT US WALK INTO THE SPRINGE."

"Come, love, let's walk in yonder spring,
Where we shal hear the blackbird sing,
The robin-red-breast and the thrush;
The nightingale in thorny bush:
The mavis sweetly caroling,
This to my love, this to my love,
Content will bring.

"In yonder dale grows fragrant flowrs,
With many sweet and shady bowrs:
A pearly brook, whose silver streams
Are beautified with Phebus's beams,
Still stealing through the trees so fair;
Because Diana, because Diana,
Batheth her there.

"Behold the nymph, with all her train,
Comes tripping through the park amain:
And in this grove she here will stay,
At barly-break to sport and play;
Where we shall sit us down and see
Fair beautie mixt, fair beautie mixt,
With chastitie.

"All her delight is, as you see,
Here for to sport, and here to be,
Delighting in this silver stream,
Only to bath herself therein;
Until Acteon her espy'd,
Then to the thicket, then to the thicket,
She her hyed.

"And there by magick art she wrought,
Which in her heart she first had thought,

By secret speed away to flee,
Whilst he a hart was turn'd to be.
Thus whilst he view'd Diana's train,
His life he lost, his life he lost,
Her love to gain."

Forbes's Cantus.

No. LXIII.—" THE SPANISHE LADYE."

This is the original tune of the Spanish Lady's Love, an English ballad, which, Dr Percy says,[a] most probably took its rise from one of the descents made upon the Spanish coast, during the reign of Queen Elizabeth, in 1596, under the command of Lord Howard and the Earl of Essex. In Ritson's English Songs (vol. ii.) the ballad is given as having been sung " to a pleasant *new* tune." Hence the present version, taken down so near the event, may be depended upon as genuine and uncorrupted; and the syllabic precision with which it gives effect to the words would of itself leave no doubt of the fact. Ritson states that the tune was " *not known;*" but although this may have been the case in England, in Scotland, Mr Blaikie has furnished us with a traditional version which he took down from the singing of a lady in Renfrewshire, who died at an advanced age about eleven years ago: and this we have inserted in the Appendix, as another specimen of the deteriorating influence of tradition upon ancient melodies. We regret that we have not room for more than the commencement of the ballad; but it is well known, and will be found in most of the English Collections.

" THE SPANISH LADY'S LOVE."

" Will you hear a Spanish lady,
How she woo'd an English man?
Garments gay, as rich as may be,
Deck'd with jewels had she on:
Of a comely countenance and grace was she,
Both by birth of parentage and high degree.

" As his prisoner there he kept her,
In his bands her life did lie,
Cupid's bands did tie them faster,
By the liking of an eye.

[a] Reliques, vol. ii. pp. 223 and 229.

In his courteous company was all her joy,
To favour him in any thing she was not coy.

"But at last there came commandment
For to set all ladies free,
With their jewels still adorned,
None to do them injury.
O, then, said this ladie gay, full woe is me!
O, let me still sustain this kind captivity.

"Gallant Captain, show some pity
To a lady in distress;
Leave me not within this city,
For to die in heaviness:
Thou hast set, this present day, my body free,
But my heart in prison still remains with thee," &c. &c.

No. LXIV.—"FROGGIS GALZIARD."

This is a sort of fantasia for the mandour, in which it is very difficult to discover any melody at all; but the *motivo*, whatever it is, may be presumed to have related to the very old nursery song about the wedding of the frog and mouse, mentioned in the "Complaynt of Scotland," in 1548, under the name—"The Frog cam to the myl dur;" and carried down to the present day in the children's still favourite rhyme—"A Frog he would a wooing go." Ravenscroft has given it along with the music in his "Melismata, Musicall Phansies, fitting the court, citie, and countrey humours, to three, four, and five voices," published in 1611. It commences—

"It was the frogge in the well,
Humble dum, humble dum,
And the merry mouse in the mill,
Tweedle, tweedle, twino."

The tune in the "Melismata" is totally different from that which appears to have formed the theme of the Froggys Gagliard in the Skene MS.; but singularly enough, the former is nearly the same with the favourite Scotish air—" Saw ye Johnny coming."[a]

No. LXV.—" CRICHTON'S GUD NIGHT."

" Justice Shallow," says Falstaff, " came ever in the rearward of the fashion; and sung those tunes to the over-scutcht huswives that he heard the carmen whistle, and sware they were his Fancies or his *Good-nights.*" These " Good-nights" were generally " a species of minor poem of the ballad kind;"[b] such as " Armstrong's Good-night"[c]—" Essex's Good-night"—" Lord Maxwell's Good-night"[d]—containing the " dying speech and confession" of some criminal of distinction upon the occasion of his final exit. But the passage in Shakspeare refers to *tunes* without poetry; and the air, " Chrichton's Good-night," in the Skene MS., is a specimen of this sort of composition, being evidently of the instrumental class, and the production of some English composer.

We have no difficulty in recognizing the individual to whom this " Good-night" related to have been Robert Chrichton, Lord Sanquhar, an accomplished Scotish nobleman, who was executed at London, in 1612, for the murder of Turner, a fencing-master, under circumstances which, though well known, are so curious in themselves, and so illustrative of the manners of the time, that we may perhaps be excused for briefly alluding to them.

Robert, sixth Lord Sanquhar, was a man of distinguished family, being the lineal descendant and representative of one of the most eminent characters who flourished in Scotland during the fifteenth century, Sir William Chrichton, Master of the Household to James I., and afterwards Chancellor of the Kingdom, and to whose efforts the House of Stuart were perhaps more indebted than to those of any other individual for withstanding the encroachments of the powerful family of Douglas during the most precarious period of their career. The Chrichtons were even allied

[a] See Dissertation, p. 53.

[b] See Nare's Glossary.

[c] No. XVI.

[d] Border Minstrelsy, vol. i. p. 194.

to royalty, a son of the Chancellor having married a daughter of James II. And yet the life of this young man was forfeited to the law—and that, too, for an offence which, though in reality an odious and base act of assassination,—a nation only emerging from the barbarism of the Middle Ages might have regarded in a more venial light; and to which, but for particular circumstances, the royal mercy would have been extended.

The young Lord had met Turner, in 1605, at the house of an English nobleman, Lord Norreys', in Oxfordshire; and in the course of a *bout d'armes,* owing to some mismanagement, most probably the impetuosity of the youth, the foil of the fencing-master entered Lord Sanquhar's eye, and he was, for several days, in danger of his life.[a] Notwithstanding the accidental nature of the occurrence, Chrichton seems, from that moment, to have cherished a settled purpose of revenge, although the fatal blow was suspended over the head of his victim for no less than seven years, when he hired two ruffians, who, on the 11th May 1612, called upon Turner at his lodgings in White-Friars, and while the latter was entirely off his guard, and making them a proffer of his hospitality, shot him through the heart. The two men were executed; and Lord Sanquhar, after having absconded, was also apprehended, and being arraigned as a commoner at the King's Bench, on 27th June 1612, made a full confession of his guilt. Some idea of the sentiments prevalent among the gallants of this day may be gathered from the terms in which a part of this confession was couched:—"Another aspersion," says Lord Sanquhar, "is laid upon me that this was God's judgment, for that I was an ill-natured fellow, ever revengeful, and delighted in blood. To the first I confess I was never willing to put up a wrong, when, upon terms of honour, I might right myself; *nor never willing to pardon where I had a power of revenge.*" Upon this part of his character the great Lord Bacon, (who, as Attorney-General, conducted the prosecution,) in his grave, philosophical spirit, remarked—"All passions are assuaged with time; love, hatred, grief, and all fire burns out with time, if no fewel be put to it; for *you* to have been in the gall of bitterness so long, and to have been in a restless case for his blood, is a strange example. And, I must tell you plainly, that I conceive you have sucked these affections of dwelling in malice, rather out of Italy, and outlandish manners, where you have conversed, than out of any part of this island of England and Scotland."

A circumstance, however, is related, but for which the embers of the young nobleman's wrath might, very possibly, have smouldered away; and although it

[a] Cobbett's State Trials, vol. i. p. 746.

was not mentioned by him at his trial, there is no reason to suppose on that account that it was not perfectly true. Happening to be at the Court of France, in which country he was resident several years previous to the murder, Henry IV. one day casually asked him how he had lost his eye ; to which he answered, " By the thrust of a sword," when the King, supposing that he had received the injury in some affair of honour, emphatically exclaimed, " Does the man yet live!" Nothing more passed, but these words are said to have inflamed Lord Sanquhar's desire of vengeance to such a pitch, that he immediately resolved to lose no time in carrying it into effect.

His ready confession, the address which he delivered, and his whole demeanour at the trial, indicated a pretty confident reliance on the King's leniency, to which family considerations, in his case, added a more than ordinary claim. But, although intercession was made for him by the Archbishop of Canterbury and others of great influence, James is said to have considered an example necessary in order " to curb the insolence of the Scots,"—and Lord Sanquhar died the death of a felon in Palace-Yard, Westminster, on 29th June 1612. To judge from the following epitaph by Drummond of Hawthornden,[a] his fate was not a topic of much commiseration :—

" Sancher, whom this earth scarce could containe,
Having seen Italie, France, and Spaine,
To finish his travelles, a spectacle rare,
Was bound towards Heaven, but dyed in the aire."

James obtained no small credit for the firmness with which he allowed the law to take its course in this instance ;[b] but it is somewhat doubtful whether this sovereign, whose general conduct so little entitled him to be considered as a rigid dispenser of justice, did not receive more praise for his inflexibility in this particular than he deserved. In the year 1760, during the excitement produced by the trial of Earl Ferrers for the murder of his steward, a good deal of discussion took place in the public journals as to the execution of noblemen for felony; and the case of Lord Sanquhar having been brought to recollection, a letter appeared in the " Edinburgh Chronicle," from a descendant of the Chrichton family, which goes very far

[a] Archæologia Scotica, vol. iv. p. 110.

[b] Lord Bacon called it " the most exemplary piece of justice that ever came forth in any king's reign."—State Trials, vol. vii. p. 86.

to explain what has hitherto been deemed an anomaly in James's history, and exhibits what may perhaps be considered to have been the real feeling by which his majesty was actuated. The writer, whose name is unknown, professes to have been "let into the secret by a person of quality," (the Honourable William Carmichael,) "who was himself related to that family," and "whose polite learning and curious knowledge of anecdotes of this nature were known to every body."

"The story is this—When the Duke of Sully was sent over upon that famous embassy, of which he has given us an account in his letters, King James gave him the most solemn promises, that he would support Henry with all that vigour and gallant magnanimity with which the glorious Elizabeth had done; and that he would enter into all the heroic schemes projected between them two, for breaking the power of the House of Austria, then so justly formidable to all Europe: but instead of all this, Sully was hardly out of England, when James made peace with Spain, and continued their dupe ever after. This entirely ruined his reputation in France. Numberless were the jokes, the sarcasms, and epigrams, that were made upon him; of which that famous one which begins, *Quand Elisabeth fut Roi*, was one. In the meantime, at home, King James's flatterers called him the Solomon of the age. It happened that one day Lord Sanquhar was in a merry company at Paris, when one of them said, it was no wonder he was called Solomon, since he was the son of David, alluding to the story of David Rizzio. This Lord Creighton did not resent, but joined in the laugh. James was told of this by some malicious whisperer; and this was the true reason of his letting him suffer death," &c.[a]

The information contained in this letter is worthy of regard, since it appears to have come from a relation of the family; but the circumstance itself was not so much of the nature of a "secret" as the anonymous correspondent of the "Edinburgh Chronicle" seems to have thought. As an *on dit*, it was sufficiently well known, and is related by Osborne in his "Traditionall Memoyres on the Raigne of King James I." with this difference, that the individual who threw out the sarcasm is there described as having been Henry IV. himself, which, if true, would the more easily account for the fact of its afterwards having reached the ears of James; while the additional circumstance there alluded to, that Chrichton was personally attached to the French monarch, would have served to abate, in no slight degree, the interest which his own sovereign might otherwise have felt in his behalf. By the death of Lord Sanquhar, says Osborne, "the King satisfied in part the people, and *wholly himself*; it being

[a] "The Chronicle of Perth," presented to the Maitland Club by James Maidment, Esq., 1831.

thought he hated him for his love to the King of France, and not making any reply when he said in his presence to one that called our James a second Solomon, that he hoped he was not David the fidler's son: Thus doe princes abuse one another."—See "Secret History of the Court of James I." vol. i. p. 231, and vol. ii. p. 397; also "State Trials," vol. vii. p. 86; and Wood's Peerage, vol. i. p. 450.

No. LXVI.—"THE NIGHTINGALE."

The Nightingale has always been so favourite a theme with our lyrical poets, that we shall not attempt to say to what words this air had been originally adapted. "So sweetly sings the Nightingale" is one of the scraps introduced into the medley in the "Pleugh Song" contained in Forbes's Cantus, 1666. Leyden[a] cites the air among a number of others in a MS. collection adapted to the Lyra-viol, and written soon after the Revolution, and it will be found in Durfey's Pills, vol. v. p. 87. Considering the nature of the melody, it can scarcely be worth while to pursue the enquiry farther; but should any one wish to do so, he will find a Welsh harper's version of the same air taken from a manuscript in Jones's Welsh Bards, p. 181.

No. LXVII.—"PRINCE HENREI'S MASKE."

No. LXVIII.—"COMŒDIANS MASKE."

No. LXIX.—"LADIE ELIZABETH'S MASKE."

These three airs, together with No. LXXVIII., (Sommerset's Maske,) had, no doubt, formed part of the music which was performed at those magnificent perform-

[a] Introduction to "Complaynt of Scotland," p. 285.

ances called masques, for which the court of King James VI., after his accession to the English throne, became so celebrated. With respect to "Comœdians Masque," we have no information; but the others can be distinctly traced. On Monday, 4th June 1610, Prince Henry, then in his sixteenth year, was created Prince of Wales with extraordinary pomp and solemnity. On the next day (Tuesday) the beautiful masque of "Oberon" was performed, and on Wednesday "The Barriers" or Tilting. Both these pieces were written by Ben Jonson, and personated in presence, and partly by the aid, of the queen, ladies, and nobles of the court.[a] Lady Elizabeth's Masque was celebrated on the 14th February 1613, at Whitehall, by the Society of Lincoln's Inn, in honour of her marriage with Frederick the Elector Palatine or Palsgrave; and that of the Earl of Somerset took place at the Banqueting Room at Whitehall, on St Stephen's Night, (26th December) 1614, on occasion of the inauspicious nuptials of this nobleman with the divorced Countess of Essex.

The words of the masque last named were written by Dr Campion; the music by Nicholas Laniere, a native of Italy, and John Cooper, an Englishman, who, having received his musical education in Italy, usually styled himself Coperario. Alfonzo Ferrabosco, born at Greenwich, the son of a distinguished Italian composer of the same name, was also greatly patronized at this time, and most probably wrote the dramatic music of the other masques to which we have here alluded.[b] To these composers, and Laniere, is ascribed the importation into England of the *Stilo Recitativo*, which had, not long before, been introduced upon the Italian stage. Mr Hogarth observes,[c] "From the directions given in the printed copies, in Jonson's Works, as to the manner of performing some of the masques which Laniere set to music, it is evident that, having newly arrived from Italy, he followed the Italian mode of the day; setting the dialogues in *stilo recitativo*, and intermingling them with airs for single voices and choruses. Indeed, the masques of Ben Jonson, as set by Ferrabosco and Laniere, bore a much closer resemblance to the regular Italian opera than the pieces called operas which prevailed on the English stage during the greater part of the last century."[d]

For a circumstantial account of these costly and elegant entertainments, the

a Gifford's Jonson's Works, vol. vii. p. 160.

b Hawkins's Hist. vol. iii. p. 380. Burney, Hist. vol. iii. p. 346.

c Vol. i. p. 86.

d Memoirs of the Musical Drama, vol. i. p. 86.

reader will do well to consult the attractive pages of Mr Hogarth's recently published "Memoirs of the Musical Drama."—"I have no doubt," says Lord Orford, "that the celebrated festivals of Louis XIV. were copied from the shows exhibited at Whitehall, in its time the most polite court in Europe. Ben Jonson was the laureate; Inigo Jones the inventor of the decorations; Laniere and Ferrabosco composed the symphonies; the king, the queen, and the young nobility, danced in the interludes."

The masque tunes in the Skene MS. appear to have been a sort of *arie di marcia;* but, in a musical point of view, they are, perhaps, neither very curious nor very important. No doubt, Dr Burney has said that it would now be difficult to produce many specimens of the dramatic music of these composers;[a] but several examples are to be found in Playford's Works, in the Second Part of the "Musical Companion," (1667,) and a set of "Ayres" published by A. Ferrabosco in 1609. There are also many songs by Laniere to be found in the collections published during the reign of Charles I.; and a good many compositions of Coperario still extant in MS.[b] The latter was music-master to the royal family; and, among other works, published in 1613—"Songs of Mourning, bewailing the untimely death of Prince Henry, worded by Dr Campion, and set forth to be sung with one voice to the lute or viol."

A degree of historical interest, however, is attachable to the tunes, considering the personages and events to which they relate. The premature death of Prince Henry in his nineteenth year will always be considered as one of the greatest national calamities that ever befel this country.[c] His manly, straightforward, and virtuous character shone conspicuously in the midst of the dissimulation, intrigue, and licentiousness, with which he was surrounded, and led the people, who idolized him, to prognosticate a career as advantageous for the kingdom, as it would have been brilliant for himself. Nor is it easy to over-estimate the prosperity which this country might have enjoyed, or the rapid strides which it might have made in the

[a] Burney's Hist. vol. iii. p. 446.

[b] Hawkins's Hist. vol. iii. pp. 315, 380.

[c] The great regret felt at the death of this prince, who was cut off by a fever, after a few days' illness—the apprehensions entertained of the designs of the Papists, to whom he was supposed to be unfriendly, and the slight concern manifested by some of his own relatives, concurred, with other circumstances, in giving rise to the suspicion that he had been poisoned. But of this there was no real probability, and the *post mortem* examination of the body, conducted in presence of members of the Privy Council and of many medical men, gave no countenance whatever to the supposition.

great march of civilization, under a prince possessed of his qualities of mind and disposition. It pleased Providence, however, to disappoint the hopes of the nation, and to place the inhabitants of Britain under the rule of a sovereign whose bigotry, intolerance, and self-will, not only plunged them into all the horrors of civil war, but, in the event, may be said to have retarded their social advancement for nearly a century. Knowing, as we do, the melancholy issue of all the splendid pageantry with which this music was associated, we almost look back upon it with fear and trembling—with a feeling akin to that with which the Egyptians beheld the emblems of mortality obtruded upon them in their festive moments. And surely no stronger proof of the hollowness and vanity of human grandeur can be imagined, than when we follow up these scenes of mirth and revelry with those of an opposite character by which they were destined to be succeeded;—not only the premature death of the Prince, and Charles's melancholy fate—but the ruin of the Palsgrave and his family, and their final expulsion from the kingdom of Bohemia. Add to these, the atrocious murder of Overbury, which so soon followed the odious nuptials of the guilty Somerset and his wife—the execution of the perpetrators, and the condemnation and disgrace of the principals, who, although, through the weakness of James, their lives were spared, and they were even enabled to live in splendour,[a] only lingered out the remainder of their days in misery and remorse, shunned by every one—mutually hating each other with a hatred so intense and implacable, that though dwelling for years in the same house, they were never seen to exchange a single word—and dying covered with execration and infamy.

No. LXX.—" WHAT IF A DAY."

" What if a day, or a month, or a year,
Crown thy delights with a thousand wisht contentings?
May not the change of a night, or an hour,
Cross thy delights with as many sad tormentings?
Fortune, honour, beauty, youth,
Are but blossoms dying;
Wanton pleasures, doting love,
Are but shadows flying.

[a] King James added to his pardon a pension of no less than L.4000 per annum.

All our joyes are but toyes,
Idle thoughts deceiving,
None hath power of an hour,
Of his life's bereaving.

" Th' earth's but a point of the world, and a man
Is but a point of the earth's compared centure;
Shal then the point of a point be so vain,
As to triumph in a silly point's adventure?
All is hazard that we have,
Here is nothing byding;
Days of pleasure are as streams
Through fair meadows gliding.
Well or wo, time doth go,
Time hath no returning.
Secret Fates guide our States
Both in mirth and mourning.

" What if a smile, or a beck, or a look,
Feed thy fond thoughts with many vain conceivings:
May not that smile, or that beck, or that look,
Tell thee as well they are all but false deceivings?
Why should Beautie be so proud,
In things of no surmounting?
All her wealth is but a shrewd,
Nothing of accounting.
Then in this ther's no bliss,
Which is vain and idle,
Beauties flowrs have their hours,
Time doth hold the bridle.

" What if the world, with a lure of its wealth,
Raise thy degree to great place of hie advancing:
May not the world, by a check of that wealth,
Bring thee again to as low despised changing?
While the sun of wealth doth shine,
Thou shalt have friends plentie;
But come want, they repine,
Not one abides of twentie.
Wealth and friends holds and ends,
As thy fortunes rise and fall:
Up and down, smile and frown,
Certain is no state at all.

"What if a grip, or a strain, or a fit,
Pinch thee with pain of the feeling pangs of sickness :
May not that grip, or that strain, or that fit,
Shew thee the form of thine own true perfect liekness ?
Health is but a glance of joy,
Subject to all changes ;
Mirth is but a silly toy,
Which mishap estranges.
Tell me then, silly man,
Why art thou so weak of wit,
As to be in jeopardie,
When thou mayst in quiet sit."

Forbes's Cantus.

No. LXXI.—"SCERDUSTIS."

The meaning of this term is not easily explained, and the only conjecture that we can offer is, that it may be a corruption of *Surdastrum*, the old name of a drum (or perhaps a tabour) used to accompany a shepherd's pipe in a dance, which was supposed to render harmless the bite of the tarantola spider. The tarantola is so named from Tarento in Italy, which is said to be infested with these really innocuous insects. The Latin word *Surdaster* means deafish. *Erat Surdaster M. Crassus*, Cic. 5, Tusc. c. 40. The air itself appears to have latterly merged into the Scotish tune, "Steer her up, and haud her gaun."

No. LXXII.—"WHAT HIGH OFFENCES HES MY FAIR LOVE TAKEN."

No. LXXIII.—"SINCOPAS."

Sincopas, or *Cinque pas*, as its name implies, was a dance regulated by the number *five*, which will be perceived at once by running over the notes of the air.

Five was the number of the musics feet,
Which still the dance did with *five* paces meet.[a]

Sir John Davies's Poem on Dancing.

This is the only copy of the *cinquepas* which we have seen; and now that we have had an opportunity of inspecting it, it is amusing to observe how closely it tallies with Shakspeare's description of this dance, in the passage in "Much Ado About Nothing," where Beatrice compares wooing, wedding, and repenting, to a Scotish jig, a measure, and a *cinquepace*:—"And then comes repentance, and, with his *bad legs*, falls into the *cinquepace faster and faster*, till he *sink* into his *grave*."[b] It would now seem as if the "bad legs" had referred to the tottering fabric of the tune—the "faster and faster" to the acceleration of its movement towards the close—the *sinking* "into his *grave*" to the slow and solemn strain of the finale. Indeed, it is not improbable that Shakspeare might have intended an additional play upon the word *grave*, as being a musical term used to denote a slow movement of the *grave* kind; but, without descending to such *minutiæ*, or attempting to follow the example of some annotators, and diving into latent and obscure meanings which may never have entered even the fertile imagination of the poet himself, the correspondence between his description and the general cast and features of the air is too obvious to escape notice, or to admit of dispute; and it is *something*—if, in this instance, the Skene MS.—a contemporaneous document—should have been the means of illustrating even so slight a portion of the text of our great dramatist. Here, the passage is such that nothing perhaps but the production of the particular tune could have rendered his meaning intelligible.

Shakspeare has made another allusion to the same dance in Twelfth Night, Act I. Scene 3; and many other notices of it by authors of the same period might be cited.

"Now do your *sinquepace* cleanly."

Microcosmus.

'He fronts me with some spruce, neat *sinquepace*."

Marston, Sat. 1.

&c., &c.

[a] The *cinquepas* is spoken of as if it were the same with the Galliard; but the Galliard was a dance of various kinds and figures, and it has only been in the *cinquepas* properly so called that we have observed the *five paces* distinctly traced out in the *rhythmus* of the air. See Hawkins's Hist. vol. iv. p. 386.

[b] Act II. Scene I.

No. LXXIV.—" THE WILLOW TREE."

" How now, shepherd, what means that?
Why wearst thou willow in thy hat?
Are thy scarfs of red and yellow
Turned to branches of green willow?
They are changed, so am I;
Sorrows live when joys do die:
It is Phylis only she,
That makes me wear the willow tree.

" Is't the lass that loved thee long?
Is it she that doth thee wrong?
She who loved thee long and best,
Is her love now turned to jest?
She who loved me long and best,
Bids me set my mind at rest:
She loves a new love, loves not me,
Which makes me wear the willow tree.

" Come now, shepherd, let us join,
Since thy love is like to mine;
For even she I thought most true
Hath also changed me for a new.
Herdsman, if thy hap be so,
Thou art partner of my wo;
Thy ill hap doth mine appease,
Company doth sorrow ease.

" Is it she who lov'd thee now,
And swore her oath with solemn vow?
Faith and truth so truly plight,
Cannot be so soon neglect.
Faith and truth, vows and oaths,
Are forgot and broken both:
Cruel Phylis, false to me,
Which makes me wear the willow tree.

" Courage, man, and do not mourn
For her who holds thy love in scorn;
Respect not them who loves not thee,
But cast away the willow tree.

For thee shal I live in pain,
Phylis once was true love mine,
Which shal ne're forgotten be,
Although I wear the willow tree.

" Shepherd, be thou rul'd by me,
Cast away the willow tree;
For thy sorrows her content,
And she is pleased if thou lament.
Herdsman, I'le be rul'd by thee,
Here lyes grief and willow tree;
Henceforth I will be as they,
That loves a new love every day."

Forbes's Cantus.

No. LXXV.—" SHEPHERD, SAW THOU NOT."

" Shepherd, saw thou not my fair lovely Phylis.
Walking on yon mountain, or in yonder plain?
She is gone this way to Dianaes fountain,
And hath left me wounded with her high disdain.
Ay, she is so fair, and without compare:
Sorrow comes to sit with me.
Love is full of fear, love is full of care:
Love without this cannot be.
Thus my passions pain me,
And my love hath slain me,
Gentle shepherd, play apart.
Pray to Cupid's mother,
For I know no other
That can ease me of my smart.

" Shepherd, I have seen thy fair lovely Phylis,
Where her flocks are feeding by the river side:
Ah! I much admire, she is fair exceeding,
In surpassing beauty, should surpass in pride:
But, alace! I find they are all unkind:
Beauty knows her power too well:
When they list they love, when they please they move;
Thus they turn their heaven to hell.

Where their fair eyes glancing,
Like to cupids dancing,
Rules well for to deceive us,
With vain hopes deluding,
Still their praise concluding,
Thus they love, thus they leave us.

"Thus I do despair, love her I shal never,
If she be so coy, lost is all my love;
But she is so fair, I will love her ever.
All my pain is joy, which for her I prove.
If I should her love, and she should deny,
Heavy heart with me would break:
Though against my will, tongue thou must be still,
For she will not hear thee speak.
Then with kisses move her,
They shal show I love her;
Lovely love, be thou my guide:
But I'le sore complain me,
She will still disdain me;
Beauty is so full of pride."

Forbes's Cantus.

No. LXXVI.—"O, SILLIE SOUL, ALACE."

We have not discovered the words of this sonnet; but the tune possesses some interest in consequence of its being that to which the song "Farewell, dear heart, since thou must needs be gone," (which Shakspeare introduces in the scene with Sir Toby Belch, Sir Andrew Aguecheek, and the Clown,) was sung. The original words of the sonnet "Farewell, dear heart," have been published by Dr Percy. They are also to be found in the MS. Music Book of 1639, formerly noticed as belonging to the Advocates' Library.[a]

[a] See Dissertation, pp. 29, 30.

No. LXXVII.—"FLOODIS OF TEARES."

"If floods of tears could change my follies past,
Or smoak of sighs could sacrifice for sin:
If groaning cryes could free my fault at last,
Or endless moan for ever pardon win;
Then would I weep, sigh, cry, and ever groan,
For follies, faults, for sins and errors done.

"I see my hopes are blasted in their bud,
And find men's favours are like fading flowers:
I find too late that words can do no good,
But loss of time, and languishing of hours.
Thus since I see, I sigh, and say therefore,
Hopes, favors, words, begone, beguile no more.

"Since man is nothing but a mass of clay,
Our days not else but shadows on the wall:
Trust in the Lord, who lives and lasts for ay;
Whose favour find will neither fade nor fail.
My God, to thee I resign my mouth and mind:
No trust in youth, nor faith in age I find."

Forbes's Cantus.

No. LXXVIII.—"SOMMERSET'S MASKE."

See No. LXIX.

No. LXXIX.—"VEZE SETTA."

The tune appears to be some kind of dance, probably French. The name which it bears we are unable to explain.

No. LXXX.—"CANARIES."

Hawkins[a] considers the "Canaries" to have been a dance of English invention, and has described it from a specimen which occurs in Purcell's opera of Dioclesian, as a movement of two strains, with eight bars in each, and three quavers in a bar. These, however, appear sometimes to have been followed up by variations, as in a copy of the "Canaries" in Mr Blaikie's MS. of 1692, there are several strains in addition to the two first. The version of this tune given in La Borde's Essai, vol. ii. p. 178, contains nearly the same notes with those in the Skene MS. but in $\frac{2}{4}$ time, which does not correspond with any copy or description of the tune which we have elsewhere seen. We suspect, therefore, that there must here have been some mistake in the transcription, which, if the tune had been taken (as is not improbable) from the Lute Tablature, was very likely to occur to an inexperienced translator. As it stands, with the halting effect produced by this alteration of the time, it would be a more fit accompaniment to a *St Vitus'* dance than to one like this, where the feet are said to have been moved with great rapidity. By a very strange coincidence, in the same page of La Borde's work where the "Canaries" appear, we find the fragment No. 82 called "The fourth measure of the Buffins." In La Borde it forms the second part of what he calls "Le Branle de l'Official;" and the "air des Buffons," also on the same page, is completely different from the fragment in the Skene MS. The French author does not mention the quarter from which he obtained these specimens of the music of the sixteenth century, but it would almost seem as if he in 1780, and Mr Skene in 1615, had borrowed their materials from the same source; and we should suppose that in 1780, and even at the present day, some of the numerous collections of "Danseries," which were made in France during the sixteenth century, were still extant.

"Canaries" was the most rapid and animated of all the old dances. Mr Douce says it was performed to a tabour and pipe, and Shakspeare characterizes it in the following passage:—

"I have seen a medicine
That's able to breathe life into a stone;
Quicken a rock, and make you dance Canary
With sprightly fire and motion." [b]

[a] Vol. iv. p. 391. Hawkins, however, may be mistaken. "El Canario" is described in old Spanish Dictionaries as "an old Spanish dance."

[b] "All's Well that ends Well." Act II. Scene 1.

No. LXXXI.—" SCULLIONE."

This was probably the name of a tune to a particular figure of dance, like " Pantalone."

No. LXXXII.—" THE FOURTH MEASURE OF THE BUFFINS."

We have here only one strain of the tune. It appears from the " Complaynt," that in Scotland, about the middle of the sixteenth century, we had a dance of this name; but in regard to its particular nature we can give no information. See No. LVI. An " Air de Bouffons" occurs in La Borde's " Essai," vol. ii. p. 178; also in the Dutch book referred to, No. XXXVIII.

No. LXXXIII.—" THE BRANGILL OF POICTU."

Speaking of the music of the Brangill or Branle, and the style and manner of its composition, Morley[a] says—" Like unto this (the Alman) is the French *Branle*, (which they call *Branle-simple*,) which goeth somewhat rounder in time than this; otherwise, the measure is all one. The ' *Branle de Poictu*,' or *Branle-double*, is more quick in time, (as being in a round *tripla*,) but the strain is longer, containing most usually twelve whole strokes." As for the figure of the dance—

[a] Introduction, p. 181.

" Why, 'tis but two singles on the left, two on the right, three-doubles forward, a traverse of six round: do this twice, three singles side, gagliard trick of twenty, curranto pace; a figure of eight, three singles broken down, come up, meet two doubles, fall back, and then honour."

The reader will find this very minute but somewhat embarrassing description in Marston's " Malcontent." (Act IV. Scene 2.) The figure, however, is said to have been a particular kind of Branle called *Bianca's Brawl* or *Branle;* for the two terms were synonymous, or nearly so. It may be more comprehensible to modern understandings to be informed that the Branle bore a pretty close resemblance to a *Cotillon*, or a country-dance, and it has been described as consisting of a dance in which a number of persons danced together in a ring, and sometimes at length, holding each other by the hand.[a]

It will surprise musical people to find that this Branle of Poictu should be, after all, something with which they have long been familiar—the theme of the still favourite glee of " We be three poor mariners," said to have been *composed*,—and, doubtless, *adapted*, by Thomas Ravenscroft, the author of several works in the reign of James VI., and, among others, of " Musick's Melodie, or Melodious Musicke: of Pleasant Roundelaies, Freemen's Songs, and such delightful Catches," published in 1609. This is depriving him of one of his choicest laurels; but if he has hitherto been figuring in borrowed plumes, we may rest assured that these had not been awarded to him by his contemporaries, who must have known perfectly that he was not the *author*, but merely the *harmonizer*, of that composition; and it is not likely that he ever laid claim to any higher distinction than that of having selected the subject,—which, having so nobly stood the test of time, does nearly as much honour to his judgment, as the actual authorship would have done to his invention.[b]

As the popularity of so fine a glee could not fail to have commenced with its first appearance, which must have been very early in the seventeenth century, the insertion of the air under its ancient name may be appealed to as an additional proof, if such were wanting, of the antiquity of the Skene MS.

Sir Walter Scott, with his usual attention to historical accuracy, (in the Abbot, vol. iii. c. 4,) introduces Queen Mary commanding her lady in waiting to tell her " where she led the last *Branle*."

[a] See Hawkins, vol. ii. p. 133; also Cotgrave.

[b] The words of the glee, " Shall we go dance the rounde," had obviously related to the Branle, which, as we have above seen, was a circular form of dance, similar to the " Rounde," or " Roundelay."

Of the fashionable dances of this age, the most solemn and pompous was the Pavan, (supposed to be of Spanish origin.) This was performed by princes in their mantles, nobles and gentlemen with a cap and sword, lawyers in their robes,[a] and by ladies in gowns with long trains; the motion of which was supposed to resemble the tail of a peacock, from the Latin name of which, *Pavo*, the term *Pavan* is said to have been derived.[b] During the reign of Charles I., Selden, in his Table Talk, (title "King of England,") humorously complains that "the Court of England is much altered. At a solemn dancing, first you had the Grave Measures, then the Corantoes and the Galliards, and this kept up with ceremony;[c] and at length to Trenchmore and the Cushion-dance: then all the company dances, lord and groom, lady and kitchen-maid, no distinction. So, in our Court in Queen Elizabeth's time, gravity and state were kept up. In King James's time, things were pretty

[a] Gentlemen of the long robe may smile when they look back upon the antics of their predecessors, at a time when it was thought not inconsistent with the decorum of the bar, and even the dignity of the bench, for the learned society of Lincoln's Inn, at certain seasons, to take the lead in the masques and public pageants, the sports, recreations, and particularly the *dancings* of the day. It may be, however, that time has brought with it an accession of gravity without any corresponding accession of wisdom.

"It is not many years (says Hawkins in his History, vol. ii. p. 137) since the Judges, in compliance with ancient custom, *danced* annually on Candlemas-day, in the Hall of Serjeant's Inn, Chancery Lane. Dugdale, speaking of the revels at Lincoln's Inn, gives the following account of them:—'And that nothing might be wanting for their encouragement in this excellent study, (the law,) they have very anciently had dancings for their recreations and delight, commonly called revels, allowed at certain seasons; and that by special order of the society, as appeareth in 9 Henry VI. viz. that there should be four revels that year, and no more; one at the feast of All-Hallow'n; another at the feast of St Erkenwald; the third at the feast of the Purification of our Lady; and the fourth at Midsummer-day, one person yearly elected of the society being made choice of for director in those pastimes, called the Master of the Revels, which sports were long before then used.' And, again, he says, 'Nor were these exercises of dancing merely permitted, but thought very necessary, as it seems, and much conducing to the making of gentlemen more fit for their books at other times; for by an order made 6th Feb., 7 Jac., it appears that the under barristers were, by decimation, put out of commons for example's sake, because the whole bar offended by not dancing on Candlemas-day preceding, according to the ancient order of this Society, when the Judges were present; with this, that if the like fault were committed afterwards, they should be fined or disbarred.'" Dugd. Orig. Jurid. cap. 64.

[b] Hawkins, Hist. vol. ii. p. 134. Although no "Pavans" occur in the Skene MS., specimens of them are by no means uncommon; and we have not deemed any of sufficient rarity to merit insertion.

[c] That this was precisely the order of the proceeding appears from Ben Jonson's Stage directions, of which this is one—"Then followed the *Measures*, *Corantos*, *Galliards*, &c. till Phosphorus, the Day Star, appeared, and called them away," &c.—Masque of Oberon, Gifford's Jonson, vol. vii. p. 194.

well. But in King Charles's time, there has been nothing but Trenchmore and the Cushion-dance, omnium-gatherum, tolly polly, hoite come toite." This distinguished lawyer and antiquary died in 1654. Had he lived a few years longer, it might have been his fortune to have witnessed the restoration of these ancient usages, along with others which would have afforded him less satisfaction. In Pepys's Memoirs we have the following account of a Court Ball during the reign of Charles II.:—" 31 December 1662.—By and bye comes the King and Queene, the Duke and Duchesse, and all the great ones: and after seating themselves, the King takes out the Duchesse of Yorke, and the Duke the Duchesse of Buckingham; the Duke of Monmouth, my Lady Castlemaine; and so, other lords, ladies: and they danced the *Brantle*. After that the King led a lady a single Coranto; and then, the rest of the lords, one after another, other ladies: very noble it was, and great pleasure to see. Then, the Country dances, (Contre-danses,) the King leading the first, which he called for; which was, says he, ' Cuckolds all awry,' the old dance of England."[a]

No. LXXXIV.—" A FRENCHE."

A French dance.

No. LXXXV.—" TRUMPETER'S CURRAND."

Besides this and No. LIV. the MS. contains several other *currants*, or *corantoes* —" Aberdein's currant,"—" My Lord Hayis currant,"—" My Lord Dingwall's currant,"—" Queen's currant,"—" Sir John Moreson's currant." But from the two which we have inserted, the reader will be able to judge as to the nature of this dance, specimens of which are sufficiently abundant. Morley[b] says, that voltes and courants are both in the same measure, but " danced after sundry fashions; the *volte* rising

[a] Vol. i. p. 359.
[b] Introduction, p. 181.

and leaping, the *courante* travising and running;"[a]—and Hawkins,[b] that the air of the latter consists of three crotchets in a bar, moving by quavers in the measure of $\frac{3}{4}$. He adds, that of dance tunes it is said to be the most solemn.

Those who are curious with respect to these old dances will find much information regarding them in the valuable historical work of the author to whom we have last referred, whose five volumes form little short of a library of musical history, and one nearly as interesting to the general student as to the musical reader. Its value, however, is much lessened by its not being accompanied with a proper index, of which it stands the more in need, as Sir John Hawkins, though most laborious in his researches, has taken so little pains in the arrangement of his matter, that one can never be certain that he has possessed himself of all the information which the work contains upon any given subject, until he has traversed it to its full extent—a range of 2574 quarto pages. The work of Burney, though not liable to a like objection in point of method, is even still more defective with respect to index, and can scarcely be said to have any means of reference whatever.

We make these observations chiefly in the hope that some one may, even yet, be induced to supply these deficiencies by furnishing a clear synopsis of the contents of these bulky volumes, which, we are persuaded, would supply an important desideratum in our musical literature. We would wish also to take this opportunity of recording the high sense we entertain of the value of these works, especially of the Musical History of Dr Burney; and we had thought that that sentiment was fully participated in by all who have directed their attention to these subjects. Certain it is, that abroad, among the critics of France, Germany, and Italy, only one opinion is entertained on that point; but we have sometimes seen a disposition on the part of Englishmen to depreciate the merits of this eminent writer. Faults he had, and these have been prominently brought forward; while his excellencies have not been always so readily acknowledged, even by those who have availed themselves of his labours as the ground-work of their own. The mass of valuable opinions, not only on music, but on general art and literature, which his various writings contain, has been too much overlooked. It would seem sometimes to have been forgotten that few, besides himself, ever combined, in so remark-

[a] The *Volte*, though generally alluded to as French, and much practised by that nation, was, in reality, an old Italian dance, "La volta," in which the male dancer turned his partner round several times, and then assisted her to take a leap in the air. It was particularly common among the people of Provence.

[b] Hist. vol. iv. p. 387.

able a degree, the theoretical and practical attainments of the professional musician, with the qualifications and accomplishments of the gentleman and the scholar. Whatever errors he may have committed—and what historian and critic was ever exempt from errors?—Burney is an author of whom his country will ever have reason to be proud; and, taken as a whole, we have never yet seen cause to dissent from the high eulogium pronounced upon his History by Dr Samuel Johnson, when he declared it to be his opinion that it was "*one of the most correct books in the English language.*"[a]

Considering the extreme rarity of all early specimens of Scotish national music, it may be satisfactory to state, that in the preceding pages the reader will find all the airs of this kind which the Skene MS. contains, with the single exception of No. LVII. of the Contents, the translation of which, from the looseness of the notation, was deemed too unsatisfactory to be presented to the public. It was also found necessary to leave out No. XXV., "Lady wilt thou love me," which turned out, upon examination, to consist of a mere fragment, wholly unintelligible.

Nos. VIII., X., XIX., XXXVI., XLIX., LVI., LIX., LXXIX., LXXXV., C., CX., and CXIV., have been omitted, because they consisted of Gagliards, Volts, Sarabands, Currants, and Allemandes, of which it was thought to be enough to furnish one or two specimens.

No. LXXVII., "Love is a labour in vaine," has also been omitted. It is an English composition, (of the same age with the MS.,) to which no interest whatever attaches; and Nos. CXI. and CXII. have been withheld for a similar reason, besides which, they appear in Forbes's Cantus. In regard to No. CXI., "Lyk as the dum Solsequium," (or Sun Flower,) no one who has seen the melody to which it was sung will have reason to regret its non-appearance in this publication; but as the words, by Alexander Montgomery, possess considerable merit, they are here subjoined.

"THE SOLSEQUIUM."

I.

Lyk as the dum Solsequium, with cair ou'rcum,
And sorou, vhen the sun goes out of sight,
Hings doun his head, and droups as dead, and will not spread;
Bot louks his leavis, throu langour of the nicht,
Till folish Phaeton ryse, with vhip in hand,
To cleir the cristall skyis, and light the land:

[a] See Eastcott on Music, Bath, 1793.

Birds in thair bour luiks for that hour,
And to thair Prince ane glaid good-morou givis;
Fra thyn, that flour cist not to lour,
But laughis on Phœbus lousing out his leives:

II.

Sa fairis with me, except I be vhair I may se
My lamp of licht,—my Lady and my Love.
Fra scho depairts, ten thousand dairts, in syndrie airts,
Thirlis throu my hevy hart, but rest or rove;
My countenance declairs my inward grief;
Good hope almaist dispairs to find relief.
I dye,—I duyn,—play does me pyn,—
I loth on euiry thing I look,—alace!
Till Titan myne vpone me shyne,
That I revive throu favour of hir face.

III.

Fra she appeir [into hir spheir,] begins to cleir,
The dauing of my long desyrit day:
Then Curage cryis on Hope to ryse, fra he espyis
My noysome nicht of absence worne auay.
No wo, vhen I aualk, may me impesh;
Bot on my staitly stalk, I flourish fresh.
I spring,—I sprout;—my leivis ly out;
My color changes in ane hartsum hew.
No more I lout, but stands vp stout,
As glade of hir, for vhom I only greu.

IV.

O happie day! go not auay. Apollo! stay
Thy chair from going doun into the west:
Of me thou mak thy Zodiak, that I may tak
My plesur, to behold vhom I love best.
Thy presence me restores to lyf from d[eath;]
Thy absence also shores to cut my breath.
I wish, in vain, thee to remane,
Sen *primum mobile* sayis aluayis nay;
At leist thy wane turn soon agane.
[Fareweill, with patience perforce, till day.]

Montgomery's Poems, edited by Dr Irving and Mr Laing.—Edinburgh, 1821.

APPENDIX.

APPENDIX.

No. I.

ANALYSIS OF THE STRUCTURE OF THE MUSIC OF SCOTLAND.

BY MR FINLAY DUN, TEACHER OF SINGING, &c., IN EDINBURGH.

The national music of Scotland will always occupy a distinguished place in the history of music, on account of its remarkable structure and peculiar style, as well as its great popularity. It is generally considered to be of high antiquity. Its history, however, seems to be involved in obscurity.

When, and by whom, the early Scotish melodies were composed, and how long they continued to be handed down, by tradition, from one generation to another, are questions not easily answered at the present day, from the absence of positive historical evidence. There may exist unpublished documents, however, to which we have not had access, and which may yet throw light upon this subject; but the vague and unsatisfactory accounts given by our early historians, and their common practice of indiscriminately confounding with each other the poetry and the music of the Scotish songs, render it a task of no ordinary difficulty to trace the history and progress of our national melodies.

Judging from the music itself, there is every reason to believe that it originated in a remote age. The few notes upon which the oldest (at least those considered as such) of the Scotish melodies turn, lead us to infer, either that these melodies were composed at a time when the musical scale and musical instruments of the country were yet in an infant state; or, that they were formed upon models of an early period, which had continued to be imitated in after times, even when the musical scale had become enlarged, and musical instruments improved. And whatever changes, in the course of time, may have taken place upon their external form, it is undoubtedly from these early models that our melodies derive their essential and peculiar character.

Independently, altogether, of the poetry of the Scotish songs, and the powerful associations connected with it in the heart of every Scotsman, there is something remarkable in the music of these songs. It is like no other music of the present day. Its wild irregular strains speak of times long past. It may not be uninteresting, therefore, to endeavour to ascertain, by an analysis of the music itself, what it is which produces such pleasurable effects, not only upon the native, but upon the stranger, unacquainted alike with the poetry and associations of the country. Such an enquiry, also, may be attended with the farther result of establishing a standard of reference as to the real nature and form of the music, which being once ascertained, would prevent, either in composition or performance, the introduction of any ill-advised changes and innovations, or admixture of incongruous matter, and so preserve entire the purity and simplicity of the inspirations of the olden time. That such changes have been made, from time to time, upon our melodies, may be easily proved by examining and comparing the various versions of them published in different collections. Several of them, however, seem to have retained, even to the present day, their primitive form, unchanged and uncorrupted; while others in their style and structure furnish as decided internal evidence of the changes and innovations which have been made upon their original form, by the prevailing fashions of successive generations. Notes foreign to the native character of the music have been substituted for the true and legitimate ones; others have been added which had no place in the originals, besides modes of expression and embellishments peculiar to other countries. In short, through mistaken attempts at refinement and modernization, many of our melodies have already been almost entirely deprived of their national and characteristic form; and should such attempts be continued, it is not difficult to foresee that a period may arrive when the music of Scotland may be so completely blended and incorporated with that of other countries, as to lose all title to a distinctive and national character.[a]

In the hope of guarding against such an event, we, some years ago, entered upon an analysis of the Scotish airs, founding our observations on the structure of such as were reputed to be most ancient and authentic; and we propose, in this place, to present the reader with a brief sketch of the views which then occurred to us. These

[a] That such a result has actually taken place, from similar causes, in the national music of France, may be learnt from the following passage of M. Fétis. After speaking of the old French airs previous to the year 1596, he adds:—"Les *vaux-de-vire* ou *vaudevilles* et les *romances* ont insensiblement fait disparaître tous ces anciens airs, et le *mélange* de quelques-unes des *formes Italiennes* et *Allemandes* dans les airs populaires français a fini par *ôter* à ceux-ci le *caractère national* qu'on ne retrouve plus que dans quelques provinces, qui sont restées fidèles à leurs souvenirs."

we might have illustrated by referring to the data upon which they were originally formed—the Scotish airs which are currently known to every one; but having subsequently been made acquainted with the contents of the old MS., which has given occasion to this publication; and finding that they tend to enforce and corroborate the ideas which we had previously adopted, we shall endeavour to deduce our examples from the airs in that MS. as well as from others more generally known to the public. In fact, we think it preferable to do so, as the documentary authority upon which they rest is so much more solid and satisfactory than any reliance that can be placed on the antiquity of airs handed down by tradition alone.

We shall begin with the modulation—the melodic forms or traits of melody, and the closes or endings of the airs, which appear to us to contain some of the most remarkable features by which the music of Scotland is distinguished. These subjects we shall examine separately, and it may be proper, at the same time, to furnish a brief explanation of several of the technical terms which we may have occasion to employ.

With respect to

THE MODULATION[a] OF THE SCOTISH AIRS,

we cannot find a more apt illustration to suit our purpose than that which presents itself in the air "Adew, Dundee," No. XXIV. Although this air begins and ends

a Modulation may be said to be the course of the melody. It may be farther explained as the art by which the impression of any given key is made upon the ear, and by which the constitution and establishment of a key is effected. A melody may modulate, or move about, in any way whatever, through a scale, and still continue strictly to be in one key; or it may pass out of one key into another, or through several successive keys. Modulation, accordingly, is twofold. It may be confined either to one key, or extend to two or more keys. The Germans call the first kind *leitergleich*, or *leitertreue*, (like, or true to the scale,) and also *der Tonart treue modulation*, (the true modulation of the key.) The second kind, the passing or transition from one key to another, is what is generally understood by the term modulation, although it may be correctly applied to both kinds. See Gfr. Weber's "Theorie der Tonsetzkunst," Zweiter B.S. 97–8, § 184–5. Also Mr G. F. Graham's admirable "Essay on the Theory and Practice of Musical Composition," just published, from the current edition of the Encyclopædia Britannica. He says, "Modulation signifies, properly, the regular constitution of melody and of harmony, in any given key," &c. &c. Also that "modulation takes place even in the *simplest melody confined to one key*." See p. 31.

in D minor, (speaking according to our modern notions of keys,)[a]—the key in which it is here given—it will be observed that the modulation or progression of the melody is not such as is found in modern tunes in that key, nor are some of the sounds present which constitute that key in modern music. Modern tunes, for instance, have the sixth degree of the scale, B flat in this key, and the seventh, C sharp, in the *ascending* series of sound. Now, these sounds, B and C, as used in "Adew, Dundee," are *natural throughout* the melody: for the two first parts or sections only are to be considered as the real melody, the third and fourth parts being only *variations* upon it. The use of the C natural, at the beginning of the third bar of this air, is particularly worthy of notice. The effect is uncommon, and strange to a modern ear, as the C sharp might have been expected instead. It is, however, of frequent occurrence in Scotish music, and is an example of a modulation to the major second below the key-note, or, by inversion, to the minor seventh above the key-note. It is one of the characteristic modulations of our music, and takes place in *minor* as well as in *major* tunes; although oftener, perhaps, in the former. "Adew, Dundee," is a beautiful specimen of Scotish melody, and the version given of it in the Skene MS. far surpasses the current one in expressive simplicity. Its recovery will doubtless be appreciated by the public.

Another example of a similar progression of melody may be found in "Johne Andersonne," No. VII. This air is also in D minor, and yet the C is natural *throughout*. The sixth of the scale, B, is not introduced. At the fourth bar, there is a close or cadence upon C, the seventh degree of the scale, as in the second bar of "Adew, Dundee;" and at the eighth bar, a cadence upon A, the fifth of the scale, as in "Adew, Dundee," at the eighth bar of the second part. At the fourteenth bar, (two bars before the end of the *first* part of "John Anderson, my Jo," which, in fact, contains the air, the second part being a mere fanciful amplification of what has gone before,) we find F sharp introduced, which converts the previous impression of the key of D minor into that of D major. Another example of this manner of ending is found in "Male Simme," No. XXXVIII.; to which we might add the national music of other countries, especially that of Spain, and also in a certain style of musical composition, which will be afterwards noticed. In No. XXVII. "Lett never crueltie dishonour bewtie," there will be seen another instance of diatonic modulation between the second and third bars—and also between the fourth and fifth, the eighth and ninth, and the twentieth and one-and-twentieth bars.

Many more instances of the same characteristic form of modulation could be

[a] Although it may be questioned whether many of the Scotish melodies can be said to come under the head of, or belong strictly to, any particular major or minor key, as used in modern times

brought forward, not only from the Skene MS., but from the current airs of the day. Those already adduced may be sufficient to point out to the enquirer others of a like description. The sudden transitions, as exhibited in the above examples, from the scale of one key to that of another, one degree higher or lower, (speaking according to our modern notions and phraseology,) would not be so very remarkable, did they not occur so frequently, and form, in fact, so essential a property of the Scotish melody. They may often appear harsh to a modern ear; because they are sudden and unexpected; but still, when judiciously introduced, as in "Adew, Dundee," the effect is bold and striking.

Examples of such modulation are indeed not wanting in modern music; they are used by the best composers, but only occasionally, and almost as exceptions to general practice; whereas, in the music of Scotland their occurrence is so frequent, that they form one of its most prominent and striking characteristics.

Another prevailing course of modulation to be noticed in the Scotish melodies is, that of the alternation of the major key, and its relative minor; the melody moving to and from these keys to the exclusion of every other, and this, too, not unfrequently, at regular distances. Nos. I., II., III., and XX., are examples of this kind of modulation—of these, No. I., "Alace yat I came owr the moor," is a spirited and genuine Scotish air. No. II., "Peggie is over ye sie wi' ye souldier," is also a beautiful and expressive air, in the best style of our national melodies, and deserves to be made known. No. XX.—"I mett her in the medowe"—exhibits this alternate modulation of the minor, and its relative major key exclusively throughout. Of this description, also, are the well-known airs of "Poortith cauld," "Wandering Willie," "Bonnie May," besides many others, which alternate from major to minor, beginning in the former and ending in the latter. We have also instances of modulations at once diatonic and alternating, taking place in the same tune. There is a remarkable specimen of this cômbination in the air of "Blithe, blithe and merry was she."

It may be worthy of remark, that, in these examples of modulation, the *melody*, for the most part, keeps true to the *diatonic* scale of the principal key; and that even when other notes of that scale are, in the course of modulation, used as substituted or temporary key-notes, still, no accidental flats or sharps, foreign to the *principal* key, are introduced in the melody; and that, therefore, the modulations, however varied, are still, in fact, confined to one principal key. This will appear the more clear as we proceed farther. We are quite aware that we are now treading

in modern music, yet, in order to be better understood, we have retained here, in the meantime, the common notions and expressions about major and minor keys. But more of this afterwards.

upon debateable ground; but, in corroboration of our remark, we may, in the meantime, appeal to the evidence of the tunes themselves, not only in the Skene MS., but in the collections previously known to the public, where the tunes have not been altered and *modernized* through the caprice of editors, or for the purpose of accommodation to modern harmony, or otherwise. Besides the published proofs, we may appeal also to the traditional manner of singing and playing these tunes which is practised throughout the country by those skilled in the true style of the national music. But we shall return to this subject afterwards.

Although the diatonic modulation mentioned above—we mean that in which the melody passes from the scale of one key to that of another one degree higher or lower—is decidedly one of their most characteristic modulations,[a] we find that many of these airs modulate out of the scale of the principal key into the scale of another key, not as a substituted, but a principal key, bearing, for the time, its own scale. This kind of modulation, however, must of course be of very short duration in melodies containing at the most but two strains like the Scotish. Every one acquainted with the songs of the "Flowers of the Forest," No. XIII., and "Waly, waly," must have felt the effect of the passages where the *minor* seventh of the *major* scale is introduced;—these passages are beautiful examples of the kind of modulation of which we are speaking. It is this minor seventh, of a *major* scale, that does away with the impression, for a time, of the principal key, and makes one feel that he is passing into a different scale and key. The modulation, in both examples, is made into the *fourth* degree of the principal key.[b] There are several other instances of this modulation in the Skene MS., such as No. XXXIII., "My mistress' blush is bonie;" No. XIX., "Remember me at eveninge;" and No. XXXV., "Leslie's Lilt." The first is a lively pretty tune, in the style of a "measure;" Leslie's Lilt is also pretty and characteristic.

[a] We have witnessed many instances of the effect which this strong feature of our national music has produced upon foreign musicians. Among others, during Paganini's first visit to Scotland, he requested the band, at the rehearsal of one of his concerts, to let him hear some of our Scotish national music. They immediately played some of the strongly marked dance tunes. He appeared much amused with the suddenness and oddity of their modulations, as well as with the style of the performance, and begged a copy of the tunes as musical curiosities. He said they were very "*baroques.*"

[b] Speaking as regards Harmony.

THE MELODIC FORMS, OR TRAITS OF MELODY.

As frequently recurring traits of melody in the Scotish music, we will instance the following:— [musical notation] and [musical notation]
Even these snatches, played or sung to a Scotchman, will instantly bring before his mind his native country, and many associations connected with it. To an Irishman they will have the same effect; for the *old* Irish melodies appear to be constructed upon the same scale as our own. The same passages, in so far as mere successions of intervals are concerned, also occur frequently in a style of music, which will be spoken of by-and-by. To any one acquainted with our music, innumerable examples of such successions of sounds cannot fail to suggest themselves. They will be found in the first page of the Skene MS., Nos. I. and III.; and any of the other pages, where the tunes are Scotish, will afford the same evidence. In the music of Ireland instances will be found, among many others, in the well-known songs of the " Meeting of the Waters,"[a] and " As a beam o'er the face of the waters."[b]

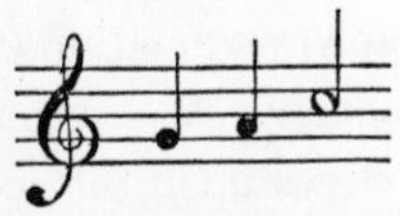

Now, it is evident that the wild and plaintive effect of such passages arises in great measure from the omission or absence of certain sounds which we are accustomed to hear introduced in other styles of music, particularly of a more modern date. Whether the omission of these intervals in much of the Scotish music is referable to an imperfect primitive scale, or to imperfect musical instruments, such as the shepherds' pipe, chalumeau, &c., upon which the music may have been at first composed, it is difficult to determine. But not to mention the human voice, which has the power of expressing not only whole tones, but semitones, and even still more minute musical intervals—there existed in the country, at a very early period, instruments capable of producing the whole series of sounds of a perfect scale. Of this there can be no doubt; and yet the predilection of the people, from whatever cause, was, and still is, in favour of those tunes containing the kind of passages in question with omitted intervals. These passages, in short, exhibit part of the recognised features of the national melody; and all Scotish tunes, ancient as well as modern, which possess any claim to popularity, will be found to have their traits more or less moulded after this form.

[a] Old name, " The young man's dream."

[b] Old name, " Old head of Denis." See Moore's Irish Melodies.

THE CADENCES OR CLOSES.

The close upon the key-note of the melody is common in the music of all countries. The Scotish melodies, however, end upon other degrees of the scale besides the first degree, or key-note; namely, the second, third, fifth, sixth, seventh, and eighth degrees. Examples of closes upon the second and seventh degrees are found principally in the Highland airs. When in a major key, they often close upon the second; and when in a minor, upon the seventh, (the minor seventh of the scale.)[a] "Port Ballangowne," No. XXXII., Skene MS., a curious kind of "Measure," begins and ends on the second degree of the scale. The effect of this ending is wild, and perhaps unsatisfactory to many a modern ear, which would desire something else to follow to make the conclusion more determinately final.

Closes upon the third may be seen in Nos. IV., IX., XV., and XIX., of Skene MS.; the three first of which exhibit true features of Scotish melody: also in "Roy's wife of Aldivalloch," and many others of the common tunes of the country. These are all in major keys; but there are instances of tunes beginning in minor keys, that is, with the minor third of key-note, and ending with the *major* third. See Nos. V., VII., ("Johne Andersonne, my Jo," cited above in reference to modulation;) "Shepherds, saw thou not," a pretty tune, but not of Scotish growth; and XXXVIII., "Male Simme," a remarkable tune in point of modulation, but apparently not Scotish. Besides sacred music, in which such closes are said to have originated, many examples of them are to be found in the different styles of modern music. There is a beautiful specimen, for instance, in the last movement of the second of Mozart's violin quartets; and also in the last Chorus of Furies in the second act of his Don Juan. C. M. Von Weber likewise frequently employs this as well as the first description of close on third. Its effect is generally lively and exciting, and sometimes grand, as in the case of the Chorus in Don Juan just quoted.

Closes on the fifth occur in Nos. VI., VIII., X., XI., XXX., XXXI., and LVIII., of Skene MS. Of these Nos. VI., XI., and XXX., are good samples of Scotish music. The ending of the fifth in these tunes is brought about in various ways. It is sometimes immediately preceded by the key-note, or its octave; sometimes by the third; sometimes by the fourth; sometimes by the sixth; and once,

[a] See "*Celtic Melodies*," published by a Highlander, Edinburgh. Many specimens of modulation, traits of melody, and closes characteristic of our national music, are to be found in this volume. As also in the Rev. P. M'Donald's Collection of Highland Airs, 1781; Captain S. Fraser's Highland Melodies; and Campbell's "Albyn's Anthology."

in No. XXXI., by the seventh of the key. The fifth used as final note preceded by the sixth, as in No. XI., and in the well known airs of "Gala Water," "Aye Waukin, O," "Scots wha hae," and many others, is also much practised in the Scotish and English Church music. This form sounds unsatisfactory as an ending to ears accustomed to other styles of music. They expect something more to follow.

The Swiss and Tyrolese melodies abound with examples of endings on the fifth rising from the key-note, as we have it in the airs of "Highland Mary," "Up in the morning early," &c. Indeed, this appears to be a favourite form of ending in the music of mountainous countries. Its effect is wild but pleasing.

Closes on the sixth take place in Nos. II. and III. The former is a beautiful air. Of this class also are the familiar songs of "Woo'd and married and a," "Birks of Aberfeldie," "Poortith cauld," "Wandering Willie," &c.; and among many others of the Irish songs, "Drink not to her," ends in the same way.

The *eighth*, rising by a leap from the key-note, as in the "Braes aboon Bonaw," is likewise used as a final note. This form is also common to the Swiss, Tyrolese, and Neapolitan melodies. In addition to the usual forms, we find closes upon the *key-note*, preceded by the third above, at Nos. XVIII., XX., XXV., and LIX.; and by the third below, at No. XII., Skene MS. Similar endings occur in Irish tunes.

Of all the closes above mentioned, the most remarkable, on account of their peculiarity, are those upon the *second*, *sixth*, and *seventh* degrees of the scale. Some of those upon the fifth are rare.

We have now examined those parts of our national music which go to form its internal and strongly marked character. And it is in the internal constitution of the music itself that we must look for the cause of the effect which it produces as *music*, independent of the aid of poetry, or even of the style or manner of performance. But when we add these, and measure, rhythm, and accent, the dead mass becomes animated—the bones are "clothed with flesh," and life is inspired into them. We then behold realized that wild, dignified, and expressive character which our melodies so eminently possess.

THE RHYTHM.

We would say a few words here about rhythm;[a] for, although it enters into the

[a] This word is used in music to express the difference of quickness and slowness of sounds, according to any regular order of succession; and also the symmetrical proportion, with respect

structure of all kinds of modern musical composition, except a particular species of church music, its proper office and treatment, as regards Scotish music, have been frequently overlooked or misunderstood.

The rhythm of Scotish melodies, like that of all other national music, is for the most part regular. Indeed, it could not be otherwise; for it is the regular recurrence of the reposes or cadences in the melody which makes the music of the people easily caught and remembered, besides rendering it applicable to their songs and dances. Most of our melodies consist of sentences or phrases of four or eight bars length, which is the *usual* number employed in music; but some of them also consist of three or six bars. Of these last, " Tweedside," " Leezie Lindsay," " The Mucking o' Geordie's byre," and some others, afford examples.[a]

Almost all the tunes in the Skene MS. appear to be regular in regard to rhythm, except a few. The first part of No. XXXIX. contains a rhythm of eight measures or bars, but the second only six. It is, however, a graceful air, but apparently not Scotish. " Come, love, lett us walk into the Springe," at p. 192–3 of original MS., has an uneven rhythm of five bars in the second part. " Joy to the personne," p. 24, also of original MS., contains a rhythm of seven bars in the first and third parts. The effect of the tune is, however, by no means hurt by it. The three last tunes are evidently not Scotish.

In the course of the foregoing remarks we have several times alluded to a style of musical composition in connection with the Scotish melodies—that style is the ancient ecclesiastical music. While prosecuting our enquiries respecting the nature of these melodies, many points of strong resemblance appeared to exist between them and that music. But, although we bring forward proofs of this resemblance, and are also quite aware of the fact, that until about the middle of the seventeenth century all secular music was composed upon the model of the church style,[b] we are still far from asserting that Scotish music derives its constitution from the music of the Romish Church. We speak only to the fact of coincidence between the two. And, indeed, until proofs be adduced of what the music of Scotland was before

to length, of the successive musical sentences or phrases contained in an air. This last the French musicians call " la carrure des phrases," which is the sense in which we use the term rhythm in the above remarks. See G. F. Graham's Essay on Music, p. 18.

[a] It is strange that this peculiarity of rhythm has not been noticed or acted upon by many who have arranged the Scotish songs. We often find the introductory and other symphonies so managed as to impress a totally different rhythm upon the ear, from that which the air really has —the reposes being made to fall upon the even instead of the odd measures. This is surely a great oversight.

[b] See Burney, Hawkins, Berardi, Fétis, &c. and the music previous to that period.

the introduction of the Romish service into the country, the question as to the extent of influence which the latter had on the former must be held in suspense. In order that these points of coincidence may be more fully understood, we shall, in the first place, briefly state what the ancient ecclesiastical music is. The ancient ecclesiastical modes or tones are certain *formulæ*, by which the plain-song, or chant, used in the Romish Church, is regulated. These modes or tones are said to be a relic of the ancient Greek music. They were originally four in number, and were first reduced to fixed laws by St Ambrose, Archbishop of Milan, in the fourth century; and, about two hundred years afterwards, they were increased in number—to eight—by Pope Gregory the First. The first four were called *authentic*, or principal modes; those added by St Gregory were called *plagal*, derivative, oblique, or less principal modes. The plain-song, as improved by him, is, therefore, often called Cantus Gregorianus.[a] This cantus, besides being plain or simple, was *unisonous*, and not in different parts, or, what is technically called, in *harmony*.[b] For it is generally acknowledged that harmony, as we now understand the term, was not known in the time of Gregory the First. The arrangement or disposition of the sounds composing the scales upon which these chants were constructed, was made according to the *natural* or diatonic order of progression, without any accidental alterations of flats or sharps, that is, from D, (the first mode,) upwards, to its octave above; from E, F, G, A, and B, in like manner; employing, in short, in all these scales the same sounds as the moderns do in the scale of C major, (which was also among the number,) but beginning the series from D, E, F, G, A, or B, according to the mode. As in process of time four more modes were added to the eight

[a] In Italy it is called indifferently Canto Fermo—Canto Gregoriano—Canto piano—Canto corale—or Canto Romano. In France, plain-chant, or chant d'Eglise; and the modes are called Modes antiques or ecclésiastiques—Tons d'Eglise, or Tons du plain-chant. In Germany, these are called Alte, griechische, (from their supposed Greek origin,) oder Kirchentonarten; and the melodies composed in them, Cantus firmus, or *choral*, with the addition sometimes of *römischer*, to distinguish the Roman from the Protestant choral, although the latter, for a considerable time after the Reformation, was composed in the ancient church modes. "The psalms, and ancient chants of the Romish Church," says Burney, "were long retained in the Lutheran service, as appears by a book with the following title:—Psalmodia hoc est cantica sacra veteris ecclesiæ selecta, per Lucam Lossium collecta, cum prefactione Phillippi Melancthonis. Wittebergæ, 1561. Becker, printed at Leipsic, 1621, the PSALTRY of *David*, in the German language, with the melodies used in the Lutheran Church." See vol. iii. p. 33; also pp. 30, 31, 34, same vol.

[b] Cardinal Bona, "De Cantu Ecclesiastico."

ancient ones, it became necessary to use one and the same scale for several of the modes, each mode having, however, some peculiar laws to distinguish it from the others. It will easily suggest itself, from the above description of the scales, that taking any of the sounds, D, E, &c. as the starting note, and running through the diatonic scale up to the octave, although using, at the same time, the same sounds as in the modern scale of C major, yet the places of the tones and semitones in each of such scales will be different from each other. See plate, p. 342, containing the scales of the eight modes, with the places of the semitones indicated by black notes; the round notes showing those of the whole tones. The scale of the ninth mode is a repetition of that of the second—the tenth of the third—the eleventh of the fourth and sixth—and the twelfth of the seventh. All these modes may be transposed in any convenient manner to suit voices; the only thing indispensable being to preserve *exactly* the places of the tones and semitones.

There were certain laws observed as to the beginnings of the chants, and as to the middle and final closes or cadences. These are called the *tonal* laws, as belonging to the respective tones or modes. And hence the term *tonality*, which we have but very recently borrowed from continental writers on music. All these laws were made with reference to melody alone, and not to harmony. Now, it is in the character of the melody, and in the peculiar cadences upon various sounds of the modes—cadences initial, medial, and final—that strong points of resemblance may be traced between the ancient Canto Fermo of the Romish Church, and a number of the Scotish airs, particularly those of a graver cast. We are quite aware that such resemblances have been casually noticed by several authors, but it has never yet been shown, so far as we know, wherein the resemblance lies. A few examples of well authenticated chants will illustrate this. The passages particularly worthy of attention in these are indicated by an asterisk followed by a broken line. In examining these specimens, and comparing them with Scotish music, it must be borne in mind that, while the latter possesses both rhythm and measure, and contains long and short notes, the Gregorian chant has neither rhythm nor measure, and consists of equal notes. The Ambrosian chant is, however, in some degree rhythmical, and consists of long and short notes.

It must be mentioned also, that the *distinct intervals* only are given in these printed specimens, the frequent consecutive repetitions of the same sound being left out, as they could serve no purpose here, except adding to the number of music plates. The chants have likewise been transposed from the tenor and other clefs, into the bass and treble clefs, and, in some cases, reduced into modern notation for the facility of reading.

The first example[a] is composed upon the first, or Dorian mode. It begins on F, and ends on D. The C is natural throughout. Observe the many leaps of *thirds*, and the notes before and after them. The cadences take place on A, F, and D; the middle cadence on A, and the final one on D. The scale of this mode is similar to that of the modern one of D minor, except that it has B and C natural in its series of sounds. See what we have said on the modulation of "Adew, Dundee," "John Anderson," &c., at pp. 317-18-19, of "Analysis."

In the second specimen[b] the same features occur. Mark the third note of the melody, C, and the notes leading to and from it. This mode is often transposed into the fourth above, and then it has B flat. We find it here.

No. 3[c] is in the transposed state; the B flat is marked at the beginning. Here the psalmody commences upon C *natural*, and terminates on D.

According to the *tonal* laws of this mode, compositions of Canto Fermo may begin with any of the six following sounds, C, D, E, F, G, A. The regular cadences are in D, A, and F. The middle cadence of the psalmody is in A. The final cadences in D, F, G, A; and even in C. Mark here, that although the psalmody begins in D, it may end in C, the *seventh* of the scale. See No. XXII. of Skene MS. Each of the modes has its own peculiar tonal laws as to the above particulars—the initial intonation—the cadences regular, medial, and final. Our space not permitting us to discuss these modes separately, we must, therefore, refer for farther information on the subject to Padre Martini's Saggio di Contrappunto, and also to Mr G. F. Graham's Essay.

We shall, however, proceed to make some brief remarks upon a few of the specimens. The "Offertorium," No. 5,[d] contains a number of Scotish modulations; also the following "Communion," and the "Audi benigne."[e] All the three have a Scotish sound. They are composed in the second, or Hypo-Dorian mode. The scale of this mode is similar to the modern scale of A minor, except that G, the seventh, and F, the sixth, are natural. It is always transposed a fourth above, and then it has B *flat*.

In No. 8,[f] we have a striking example of a common manner of Scotish ending; the descent by third. See "Analysis," p. 323. The beginning of No. 9,[g] "Hostes Herodes," gives us the feeling of one key, and the ending that of another. This is also common in Scotish music. See p. 319. These two specimens are in the third, or Phrygian mode. A passage in No. 12[h] in the fifth, or Lydian mode, ending by descent of *fifth*, reminds us strongly of similar passages in our own airs. The scale of this mode corresponds to that of the modern F major; except that B is natural. This mode is, however, sometimes transposed, as may be seen in the second ex-

[a] See p. 342. [b] Ibid. [c] See p. 343. [d] Ibid.
[e] See p. 344. [f] Ibid. [g] Ibid. [h] See p. 345.

ample[a] here given of it, (No. 13,) and then it has B *flat*. Compositions in this mode begin upon D, or F, or G, or A, or C. Its regular cadences are in F, or C, or A. The middle cadence of the psalmody is in C. The final cadences are—the Roman in A; and in the other churches in F, G, C, and even B. It will be observed, that among the sounds that may terminate melodies in this mode we find G, the *second* of the scale. A similar termination may also take place in the seventh mode, which corresponds to the modern scale of G major, except that F, the seventh, is natural. We meet with such endings in some of the Scotish tunes, particularly those of the Highlands. See p. 322.

We have one more remark to make upon the cadences in the fifth mode. A is there mentioned as forming not only one of the sounds upon which the final cadence may be made, but also as forming one of the regular cadences in the course of the composition. Now, a modulation of this kind proceeding, for instance, from the key of F major to that of A minor, or from D major to F sharp minor, has been very much employed of late years. Rossini was perhaps among the first who in our day brought it into vogue; but he and his imitators have used it so often, that it has become stale, and even more trivial than the most common modulation. Some other *new* modulations may perhaps be found among the church tones, and extolled as original products of genius by the public, ever greedy after any thing in the shape of novelty. But might we not well say in this case, as in many others, "There is nothing new under the sun?" See another instance of ending by descent of *third* in No. 16,[b] in the eighth, or Hypo-Mixo-Lydian mode. The number before this affords another example of what we moderns would conceive to be beginning in one key, and ending in another. The scale of this mode resembles that of the modern scale of D minor; but the B is natural. This mode is sometimes transposed to the fourth above, beginning on G. Although the scales of the eighth and the first modes consist of the same series of sounds, yet the cadences in each are in some respects different. In the former, the regular cadences are upon G and B, besides D; the middle cadence on C; and the final cadences upon G, C, and A. See above, the cadences in the first mode. In the eighth mode, therefore, cadences can be made upon the fourth, fifth, sixth, and seventh degrees of the scale. See what has been said upon the endings of the Scotish melodies, pp. 322, 323.

The following specimens of Canto Fermo are of the year 400, and from a MS. in the monastery of St Blasius. See Gerbert "De Cantu et Musica Sacra," Vol. I. They are here transposed an octave higher—from the tenor into the treble clef—for the facility of reading. See p. 346.

[a] See p. 345. [b] Ibid.

The first example from Gerbert begins with a bold and striking passage, which will at once remind every Scotsman of the song of "Lord Ronald, my son," where precisely the same passage occurs at the fifth and sixth bars. The other specimens sound in many places very Scotish—particularly the melody set to the "Prosa post Offertorium," No. 19, p. 346, the ending of which is also Scotish. See likewise the five last bars of the "Kyrie," No. 21, in the same page.

We shall now give a few examples of what are called irregular intonations, (Intonazioni dette Irregolari,) as practised by particular churches and certain orders of monks. These bear pretty strongly upon the Scotish melodies in regard to endings, which, although common in them, are unusual in other styles of music.

They are remarkable, viewed abstractedly; but more so, occurring, as they do, in the modes to which they are assigned. The mode to which these cadences respectively belong is indicated by *primo tuono, secondo tuono,* &c. There are several examples given in each mode. These are marked by the figures 1, 2, &c. See pp. 347, 348. The forms of some of these cadences are similar to those in modern use, particularly Nos. 1, 2, and 4, of the *sixth* tone or mode, p. 348.

Before quitting the points of analogy as to structure, which exist in many respects between the Scotish music and the Canto Fermo, we must notice the Dominants, or, as they may be called, the prevailing notes of the modes. In the ancient tonalities the Dominant varies its place in different modes. In the modern tonalities the Dominant is *invariably* the fifth of the key. In the ancient system, supposing we reckon all the twelve modes, six of the modes have their Dominants upon the *sixth* of the key, five of them upon the *fifth*, and one of them (the eighth mode) upon the *seventh* of the key. See what has been said of the prevalence of the modulation to the sixth of the key in the Scotish songs, pp. 319, 323.

The reader will now understand that in the former part of this Analysis, we used the modern terms of *major* and *minor* keys in reference to the Scotish tunes, because we had not then spoken of the ecclesiastical modes with which some of the Scotish tunes have more affinity than with the modern major and minor scales or keys. See note, p. 318.[a]

[a] As to the question regarding the Scotish scale, or the so-called scale of nature, we do not enter into it. We may just remark, however, that the occasional omission or absence of certain sounds in particular keys or modes observable in many Scotish tunes, does not warrant our saying that the Scotish scale *really* wanted such sounds, and was, therefore, imperfect, any more than we should be warranted in saying, that because in a Canto Fermo some particular sounds were not used, the scale upon which it was composed should also want such sounds, and be consequently imperfect. That such a conclusion would be false, is proved by the Canto Fermo, No. 1. It is in the first mode; and although B, the sixth of the scale, is *not* used throughout the melody, yet that interval *is* in the scale of this mode. See plate, p. 342. "John Anderson, my Jo," also

After the reader has examined these specimens of Canto Fermo, and compared them with Scotish music, and drawn his own conclusions from such comparison, we submit the following observations to him. It appears evident that the Canto Fermo was composed originally with the view of constructing a melody consisting of single sounds, without reference to harmony, or music in parts, and that the scales upon which it is constructed, and the *tonal* laws by which its modulations and cadences are regulated, are, in many respects, distinct from those used in modern music. Hence the distinction made by musicians between the ancient and modern tonality.[a] Again, it also appears that much of the Scotish music is composed in the ancient tonality, and that the analogy between it and the Canto Fermo is in many respects very remarkable. However, there are marked differences between the two styles of composition. The occasional resemblances seem to arise from some of the

wants the sixth of the scale, B, (See VII. Skene MS.,) and yet who will say that it is not a beautiful air, and perfect in its kind, whatever the scale may have been upon which it was formed? In fact, we cannot say, with our present scanty information upon the subject, what the Scotish scales *originally* were. But we know to a certainty what the tunes are that have been handed down to us. Some of these, when the notes of which they consist are compared with what is called a regular scale, will, it is true, be found wanting in certain sounds; while others, again, have all the sounds contained in a regular scale; and yet, as we have before observed, Scotish people in general prefer the former description of tunes.

But let it be granted that the music of Scotland was at one time composed according to a limited scale, arising from imperfect instruments, is it incompatible with the fact to say that, even at a time when there existed a regular and perfect scale, and corresponding instruments to perform all sorts of intervals, the omission of particular sounds in certain cases might not be the result of *design* on the part of the composer? Might he not wish to produce a peculiar effect by not using such sounds, although otherwise at his disposal? These sounds might not even suggest themselves to his mind in the act of composition, and yet the melody composed might nevertheless be still quite correct and perfect.

The occasional omission of sounds in melodies appears to us, therefore, not attributable to any peculiar form of scales, but rather to the imperfection of certain instruments, or to design on the part of the author.

[a] Such discrimination is, however, not always made. "There exist, indeed," says Choron, in a note, in his edition of Albrechtsberger, "in composition, two systems of proceeding, which differ singularly from each other, and on the nature of which most professors have but very *confused and inaccurate ideas*."—"We have already shown," he continues, "that two sorts of *tonality* (tonalité) exist in the music of the present age: first, the *ancient* tonality, a relic of that of the Greeks, and still existing in the *plain chant*, otherwise called the Gregorian Chant, in use in the Catholic Church, and principally in the Roman Church; second, the *modern* or common tonality, which is generally in use in all the modern nations of Europe. Now, these two tonalities form the basis of the two systems, or methods of proceeding in musical composition." See *Merrick's* English edition of *Albrechtsberger*, p. 99.

laws as to structure appearing to be common to both. And hence the similarity of impression which they sometimes make upon the mind and feelings. They both partake of a wild and plaintive character, and possess a certain pleasing vagueness of expression, which the imagination delights to follow out in its own way.

This plaintive character may arise, in no small degree, from the peculiar nature of the scales upon which the melodies are constructed. For, when it is considered, that the majority of these scales contain within the octave (the extent to which at least the Canto Fermo is usually confined) a greater proportion of minor thirds than major ones, it will not be wondered at that the music should have a plaintive effect. In some of the scales we find the proportion of four to two in favour of the minor thirds, and in some it is equal; but in none do the major thirds prevail over the minor. As to vagueness of expression, this might indeed be said with more or less propriety of all kinds of music, but of none surely with more truth than of that composed according to the ancient tonality, in which the uncertainty of the key or mode forms so remarkable a feature, and which is sufficient in itself to impart that wandering and apparently irregular style of modulation to this kind of music. And it is this uncertainty which makes it often difficult to say in what particular mode or key, whatever the assumed one may be, a Canto Fermo or a Scotish tune is.[a] This is especially the case with the Canto Fermo; for, besides other causes of uncertainty as to mode, several of the scales are identically the same. Some of the

[a] This puzzling difficulty of distinguishing the ecclesiastical modes has been noticed by several authors. Kircher, in his *Musurgia*, remarks—" Tanta est de Tonorum numero et qualitate inter authores dissentio, ut cui subscribas vix dispicere possis." Lib. v. cap. 7. Fux also observes—" Ad modorum materiem tractandam adniti, perinde est, ac antiquum chaos in ordinem redigere. Tanta enim opinionum diversitas inter auctores, tum antiquos, tum recentiores reperitur, ut ferme quot capita quot sententiæ fuisse videantur." See Fuxius, in " *Gradu ad Parnassum*," Exerc. V. Lect. vii. De modis, p. 221. This difficulty is farther increased by the (to us) unmeaning names of Dorian, Hypo-Dorian, Mixo-Lydian, Hypo-Mixo-Lydian, &c. being affixed to them, purporting thereby that they are the same modes with those used by the ancient Greeks, or at least off-shoots from them. But what do we know of the ancient Greek music? Nothing. We cannot hear it: we cannot see it to compare it with modern music; for, unfortunately, no musical examples were given by the Greek writers in their works. See " Eximeno *Dell'origine e delle regole della musica.*" Many learned men have indeed endeavoured to decipher the few fragments of it which have been found, and which are said to be authentic; but they have all given a different explanation of the notation. The Greek music, as rendered by them, is certainly very uncouth, and most unlike what might be expected from such a people. But, in fact, until a *key* is found to the semēiography, or musical notation, (that hitherto impenetrable mystery,) we can form no clear conception of the real effect of their music. Forkel, in his " *Geschichte der Musik*," says, that we are as much in the dark with regard to the true sound or expression (*wahrenton*) of the ancient music, as we are in regard to the true pronunciation of the dead languages.

Scotish tunes are of a like embarrassing description, and whether one tries to assign to them such a mode or key, either in the ancient or modern tonality, the result is equally unsatisfactory. There is no seeing one's way through the "Lucis egens aër;" and so we fear it must rest, until something more is known of the early history of our native music which may throw light upon the subject. Be this as it may, however, it is perhaps of no great moment in the present enquiry whether a Scotish tune be sometimes found of that doubtful character which makes it difficult to assign it to this or that particular key or mode, provided we have, in the meantime, been able to ascertain, in the absence of earlier information, that much of the Scotish music is constructed upon the ancient tonality, and that in many respects it coincides with the laws of the ecclesiastical modes. These laws have been in operation since the fourth century, and until we find some trace of the principles upon which the Scotish music in early times was composed, it is surely not unreasonable to refer them in the meantime to these laws, particularly when the two styles of melody exhibit so many features of kindred resemblance. This is the point we wished to arrive at. Much difficulty is encountered in attempting to understand and explain the nature of the Scotish music according to the *modern* tonality. Indeed, it is impossible to do so. Every step leads to disappointment. Every thing appears at variance with the practice of that tonality. Every thing seems anomalous. But the moment we refer to the ancient tonality, the difficulties disappear. What before was unusual, irregular, and unaccountable, is sanctioned and explained by the tonal laws.

It may be thought that we have dwelt too long and too minutely on the ancient ecclesiastical music; but we had no other reason for bringing the subject forward here at all, except that it seemed to afford better means of illustrating the nature of Scotish music. The tonal laws which regulate the structure of the Canto Fermo are extant, and are known to musicians of all countries: but still the general reader could not be supposed to be conversant with these laws; and seeing the many points of analogy which existed between the structure of the Scotish music and the Canto Fermo, and not being aware of the existence of any code of rules or laws regarding the composition of the former, it appeared to us necessary to enter thus far into the subject of the tonal laws. Had we merely stated the fact that the forms of melody, the modulations, the cadences, &c. of Scotish music differed in many respects from those used according to the modern system of composition, or the so-called modern tonality, and that they seemed rather to depend on and flow from what is called the ancient tonality; had we done this, without at the same time attempting to explain what was meant by the ancient tonality—or in what the difference between it and the modern tonality consisted, in order that the two might be compared—or what were the points of analogy between the Scotish music and the Canto Fermo, we should, as we conceive, have given the reader no very satisfactory solution of the subject of investigation.

Scotish music shows its antiquity by its connection with the ancient tonality. And it is remarkable that the more antique the Canto Fermo, the more features of resemblance does it seem to have in peculiarities of tonality (progressions of intervals, modulations, cadences, &c.) in common with the ancient Scotish music. And, as these peculiarities do not appear so strongly marked in what is considered as the national music of other parts of Great Britain, this seems to throw back the origin of the ancient Scotish music to a period of more remote antiquity than can easily be assigned to any other popular music of our island. And moreover, if it is true, as many authors assert, that the Canto Fermo is a relic of the old Greek music, or, according to Padre Martini,[a] that it was introduced into the Christian churches by the Apostles, who derived it from the Hebrew synagogues, then we shall find the Scotish music to be of the same lineage as the music of nations of the highest antiquity.

We have said that much of the Scotish music is composed according to the ancient tonality, and that, being of that tonality, it has many striking points of resemblance with the Canto Fermo. And so has the old Irish music, which we have noticed before. But, although such resemblance is inevitable, it does not follow that there should be no difference between the music of the Canto Fermo and the music of Scotland or Ireland. For if that were the case, we might just as well say, that because a school of painters chose to use certain colours, with the exclusion of others, all the individual works of those artists would be little more than mere copies one of the other: or that because modern musical compositions are formed upon the modern tonality, they should be all alike, or nearly so. There are, indeed, *general* laws by which the structure or plan of these compositions is formed, and by which the modulations, cadences, &c. are regulated. This may give to the works, even in opposite styles, of different composers, a certain degree of sameness in many passages. And this is well known to be the case; and yet, although the materials are the same with which they work, the productions of one artist will be different from those of another, in proportion as the genius of each is different. So also in regard to the productions of the ancient system or tonality. Although the composers of the Scotish music and the Canto Fermo, for instance, might work, in a great measure, with the same materials, yet the subjects upon which these were employed being different, and the genius of the individual artists also, as may fairly be presumed, being different,

a Storia della Musica, tomo I. Dissertazione 3.

different results would necessarily be produced. And such is the fact. Nay, indeed, comparing the Scotish music with the Canto Fermo, the difference between them is perhaps still more conspicuous than between any two kinds of composition in the modern tonality. And for this reason, the Scotish music has measure, rhythm, accent, besides a very peculiar manner or style of performance. The Canto Fermo has none of these. They are most powerful engines of expression, and when added to a piece of music, which previously did not possess them, are sufficient so to change that piece as to make it almost irrecognizable. But even without these aids and additions, all powerful as they are, we can safely say, that there is not one single Scotish air we are acquainted with, which throughout can be called a transcript of any known Canto Fermo.

We hope that we have already shown sufficient reasons why the primitive form and style of our national music should be, as far as possible, preserved. But how is this best to be done? Why, by first ascertaining the great leading features of our music, and keeping these untouched;—by preserving the ancient tonality in such tunes as are evidently framed upon it, and repelling all attempts to mix it up and confound it with the modern tonality, which compound must unavoidably produce a perfect jumble—a patch-work of incongruous things. If there are really two kinds of tonalities, and two distinct styles of musical composition resulting from them, why cripple the resources of the art, which has need of all its different means of expression to produce variety of effect, by confounding together the two styles, and reducing them to one only; and particularly when the effect of each is good in its own way? Had the music of the ancient tonality been proved to be bad, then, indeed, it would be time to throw it aside altogether, and employ exclusively that of the modern tonality. But such is not the case. Both, then, should be retained in practice; each acting in its own proper sphere. It is from not going upon this principle, partly, perhaps, from ignorance of the existence of any more than one tonality—the modern—and partly from caprice, that much of the Scotish music has in later years been adulterated by strange mixtures and additions, exhibiting, in many cases,

> " ——— a particoloured dress
> Of patch'd and piebald manufacture."

We have hitherto spoken of Scotish music only as regards its *melodic* character, and for (as we think) the very obvious reason, that the original models at least, if not the whole body of the music, were composed with reference to the laws of melody, and these, too, of the ancient tonality. But before closing these remarks, we wish to say a few words upon the susceptibility of Scotish music for harmonic treatment.

The system of harmony at present in use is based upon the *modern* tonality.

When or where this tonality came first to be introduced into practice, it is difficult precisely to determine; but it is known that even about the middle of the sixteenth century not only the ecclesiastical, but all kinds of secular music, were composed in the ancient tonality, and that no difference was then made between these two styles, and that composers had only one style and one mode of procedure for all their compositions.[a] Even towards the end of the seventeenth century, we find the introduction of certain intervals (such as the diminished fifth, the tritone, the unprepared seventh, &c.) spoken of as novelties, and as belonging to the new mode of procedure, (*la seconda prattica*, as Berardi calls it, in contradistinction to the *prima prattica*, or old practice.) These novelties, as they were then called, besides being introduced gradually, must have taken a considerable time before they came into general use. Upon this *seconda prattica* was built the modern system of composition as regards melody and harmony. When we compare it with the older system, we find the difference to consist in a freer use of all manner of intervals that could be employed in melody and in harmony, and a more determinate establishment of *tonics*, or initial and final key-notes; and this is what is now called the modern tonality.

Now, it must occur to every one, from what has been said as to the distinctive peculiarities of these two tonalities, that it must be a task of no ordinary difficulty to combine the two in one composition, without at the same time sacrificing in great measure the due force and effect of either. Indeed, in many cases it is even questionable whether we should attempt to unite them at all. Let us take a Scotish tune—one containing a greater proportion of minor than of major thirds—" Adew, Dundee,"[b] for instance, and put an accompaniment of *modern* harmony to it for the piano-forte. How is the melody of the third bar to be treated; occurring, as it here does, with C *natural*, where, according to the constitution of the modern key of D minor, C sharp would be used? (See p. 318.)[c] It will be observed, that, even

[a] See Berardi's " *Miscellanea Musicale*," 1689. What Berardi says above refers to the state of music on the Continent only; but when it is remembered that there was but one school and one style of composition followed by composers before and at the period he alludes to—towards the middle of the sixteenth century—his remarks apply with equal force to this country as well as the Continent. A Continental author observes, that it would perhaps be no easy task to discover any difference between the styles of Willhaert, Zarlino, Henry Isaac, Goudimel, or of William Bird. Claudio Monteverde, about the close of the sixteenth century, is said to have been the first innovator upon the ancient tonalities.

[b] No. XXIV. Skene MS.

[c] The fine old French air, " *Vive Henri Quatre*," has a similar modulation at the second bar: D, d d,—c *natural;* and also at the opening of the second part. By-the-by, there is a striking resemblance between the second part of this air and the second part of the Scotish air of " *Bonnie*

in the *variations* of this air, at the second bar before the end of each part, (of the variations,) the c is also *natural,* contrary to the usual modern way, either in harmony or melody, of making closes or cadences in such keys. The closes of Nos. II. and III., among many others of the Skene MS., present similar difficulties to the harmonist. The way in which the *seventh* of the scale is often used in the ancient tonality puts the modern harmonist to a stand. His harmony tells him, and, perhaps, his modern ears also tell him, that that interval ought to be sharp; but the melody before him says no, it must be as it *is,* natural. Then he either

May." Many of the old French airs are composed after the model of the ancient modes, and some of them were actually taken from the church service. The well-known air of the romance "*Charmante Gabrielle,*" for instance, was *originally* a *Christmas Hymn.* On the other hand, popular airs were at one period used as psalm tunes, and as *subjects* or themes for masses and motets. Bayle, article Marot, has some curious passages relative to this practice. He quotes the Sieur de Pours's *Divine Mélodie du St Psalmiste,* where it is said that a Flemish translation of the Psalms, published at Anvers by Simon Cock, in 1540, contains music borrowed from popular songs, and this is indicated at the beginning of each psalm. For example, Psalm 72 is marked to be sung to the tune of "D'où vient cela;" Psalm 81 to "Sur le pont d'Avignon;" Psalm 95 to "Que maudit soit ce faux vieillard;" Psalm 103 to "Languir me faut;" Psalm 113 to "De tristesse et déplaisir;" Psalm 120 to "Madame la Regente ce n' èst pas la façon;" Psalm 128 to "Il me suffit de tous mes maux;" Psalm 135 to "Le berger et la bergère sont à l'ombre d'un buisson," &c.

Florimond de Remond, speaking of Marot's version, says—"On n'en pouvoit tant imprimer qu'il ne s'en debitast d'avantage. Ils ne furent pas lors mis en musique, comme on le voit aujourd'huij, pour estre chantez au presche. Mais chacun y donnoit tel air que bon luy sembloit, et ordinairement des vau-deville. Chacun des Princes et Courtisans en prit un pour soy. Le Roy Henry second aymoit et prit pour le sien le Pseaume, *Ainsi qu'on oyt le cerf bruire,* lequel il chantoit à la chasse. Madame de Valentinois qu'il aymoit prit pour elle, *Du fond de ma pensée,* qu'elle chantoit en volte. La Royne avoit choisi, *Ne veueillez ô sire,* avec un air sur le chant des bouffons. Le Roy de Navarre Anthoine prit, *Revange moy, prens la querelle,* qu'il chantoit en bransle de Poitou, ainsi les autres." Flor. de Rem. p. 70.

Muret, in his "Querela ad Gassendum," &c., has the following passage quoted by Bayle:— . . . . . vixque in indignatione risum teneo, quoties recordationem subit alicubi vidéri sacrorum cantuum rituale, in quo hanc (ut alias omittam omnino turpes) rubricam legere est;

MAGNIFICAT: sur le chant,
Que ne vous requinquez-vous vieille?
Que ne vous requinquez-vous donc?

The fact of there being no music for the express purpose at the time above alluded to, may sufficiently account for, although it cannot excuse, the profane folly of associating sacred words with ridiculous songs. The French psalms, after being completed by Theodore de Beza, were some time afterwards set to suitable music by the ablest masters of the time, and the old way of singing them to popular airs was abandoned.

alters the melody, in spite of its characteristic peculiarities, to accommodate it to the usual routine of his harmony; or, which is certainly much more wise, he preserves the melody entire, and suits his harmony as he best can to the case. Much has been said and written upon this very point, both for and against, in regard to the Canto Fermo. Great was the outcry against some singers who first dared to innovate upon the old practice, and use the *major* seventh and other novelties.[a] But with regard to the manner of performing these and other passages in the Scotish songs, we are to be guided by the traditional way of singing them, as preserved among the great body of the people of the country: by the *modus populi*, and not by a *modus chori*. And it is fortunate that we have been able to prove by the Skene MS. that this *modus populi*—this national way of singing—tallies exactly, in its great leading features, with the music as it is there written. The melody is there represented in the *simplest* (and, as we believe, the true) form; a form congenial at once to the nature of the music, and to the principles of the ancient tonality. Let any one, whose ears are not sentinelled by prejudice, try the effect of changing the G natural into G sharp in the third bar before the end of No. II.; or in the second before the end of No. XX., Skene MS.; or in the closing bar of "My luve's in Germany;" or of "Ca' the ewes to the knowes," and many other of our current airs of this mould, and he will find, not only in these, but in many other passages where the *minor* seventh of the scale is used, that, after the ear gets accustomed to such use of the natural diatonic modulation, he will give his verdict in favour of it, in preference to the other. And the reason is plain, because it is more consonant with the nature and style of the music. To alter such passages to modern forms is at once to deprive them of their peculiar expression, and to blot out one of the distinguishing marks of the ancient tonality. And (as we said before) if there are two different tonalities, they certainly *ought* to be kept distinct.[b] While we would insist upon the preservation of the ancient tonality in those tunes which seem evidently formed upon it, we by no means overlook the fact, which must be

[a] Examples of the harmonic treatment of the *minor* seventh of the scale may be seen in the works of Vogler, Choron, Reicha, &c. See also Marpurg's "Traité de la Fugue et du Contrepoint," chap. 3. *Sur les modes des anciens*, et *les tons d'église;* where he shows the difference of treatment to be observed in regard to these *tones*, and music composed in the modern tonality.

[b] Dr Burney, after speaking of Palestrina's *Studj*, which contain chants by himself and some of his great contemporaries, says: "Ears not accustomed to ancient modulation would at *first* be surprised, and perhaps offended, with some of the transitions in these fragments; but they must be differently organized from mine, if, *after the prejudice of habitude* is a little subdued, they should continue insensible to the solemnity and grandeur of such harmonical combinations." *History of Music*, vol. iii. p. 201.

obvious to every body, that there are many tunes formed also upon the modern tonality. Some of these are as beautiful as those of the other class, although the style is necessarily different: And if the style of melody be different, so also should the style of harmony be different.

We have enlarged upon this point rather too fully perhaps, but it appeared to us right to say so much, in order to establish sure grounds for preserving the purity and integrity of one of the most essential elements of our national music. Besides, we have preferred noticing these peculiarities more fully here, that they might be brought into closer contact with what we had to say regarding their harmonic treatment. There are, however, other important points to be taken into account, in this respect, as the intelligent reader will naturally infer from what we have already said regarding the structure of Scotish music. We shall now merely add some general remarks on accompaniment.[a] The nature and style of a melody influences, or ought to influence, the kind of accompaniment applied to that melody. This, however, is not always kept in view. We often see melodies of all ages, and of all countries, and of all styles, treated, as to accompaniment, precisely in the same way. But surely this is not right. What should we say of a poet who makes shepherds and heroes speak in the same style; or of the painter who would deck out a Turk in the garb of a Highland chieftain? Would we not characterize such proceeding as a piece of absurdity and incongruity? Equally absurd and incongruous appears to us the dressing up of our Scotish melodies in German, or Italian, or even in English costume—and modern costume too! They require little accompaniment, and that of the simplest kind. And it should be borne in mind, that, in them, the *melody* is the principal point of attraction; and that, therefore, the accompaniment is only appropriate and judicious in proportion as it reflects, as it were, that melody in its true and native colours. And when it does not do this, be the contexture of the whole even of the most exquisite workmanship, it fails to exhibit faithfully the marked features of the national music, which are thus wrought, it may be, into a beautifully contrived piece of art, which every body must admire as music, but which, in this state, is *not Scotish* music.[b]

As to the harmonic accompaniment employed in the tunes of the Skene MS. it is of a very simple kind. It consists of octaves, thirds, fifths, and sometimes of

[a] By accompaniment we mean, the adding of other parts, whether vocal or instrumental, to a melody: in other words, the clothing a melody with harmony.

[b] On the subject of *accompaniment*, as regards melody in the ancient as well as the modern tonality, we refer the reader to Mr G. F. Graham's book already quoted. He will there find, at pp. 68, 69, 70, many sound and valuable remarks well worthy the serious attention of the musician.

the common chord. These are thinly sown, and put down only here and there. But it is the *melody* that is the valuable part of this MS. to us of the present day, as it most probably also was to the original possessor, who looked upon the book merely as a depository of favourite *melodies*.

We now close these remarks on Scotish music. It is a curious and interesting subject, not merely on account of the intrinsic beauty of the music, but as connected with the early history of the art.[a] It deserves to be more thoroughly investigated than our space has permitted us to do in this brief sketch. We intend, however, to take it up again ourselves, at some future time; but shall be glad if any thing we have said here may prove useful to others labouring in the same field.

[a] That Scotish music is considered in this light by accomplished musicians, there are many instances to show. We remember, some years ago, having accompanied the Chevalier Neukomm and Felix Mendelssohn Bartholdy to the Competition of Pipers held in this city, and there witnessing the lively interest with which they listened to the music. We know, also, that, during their visit here, these gentlemen took every opportunity of hearing our national music in private.

No. II.

MUSIC.

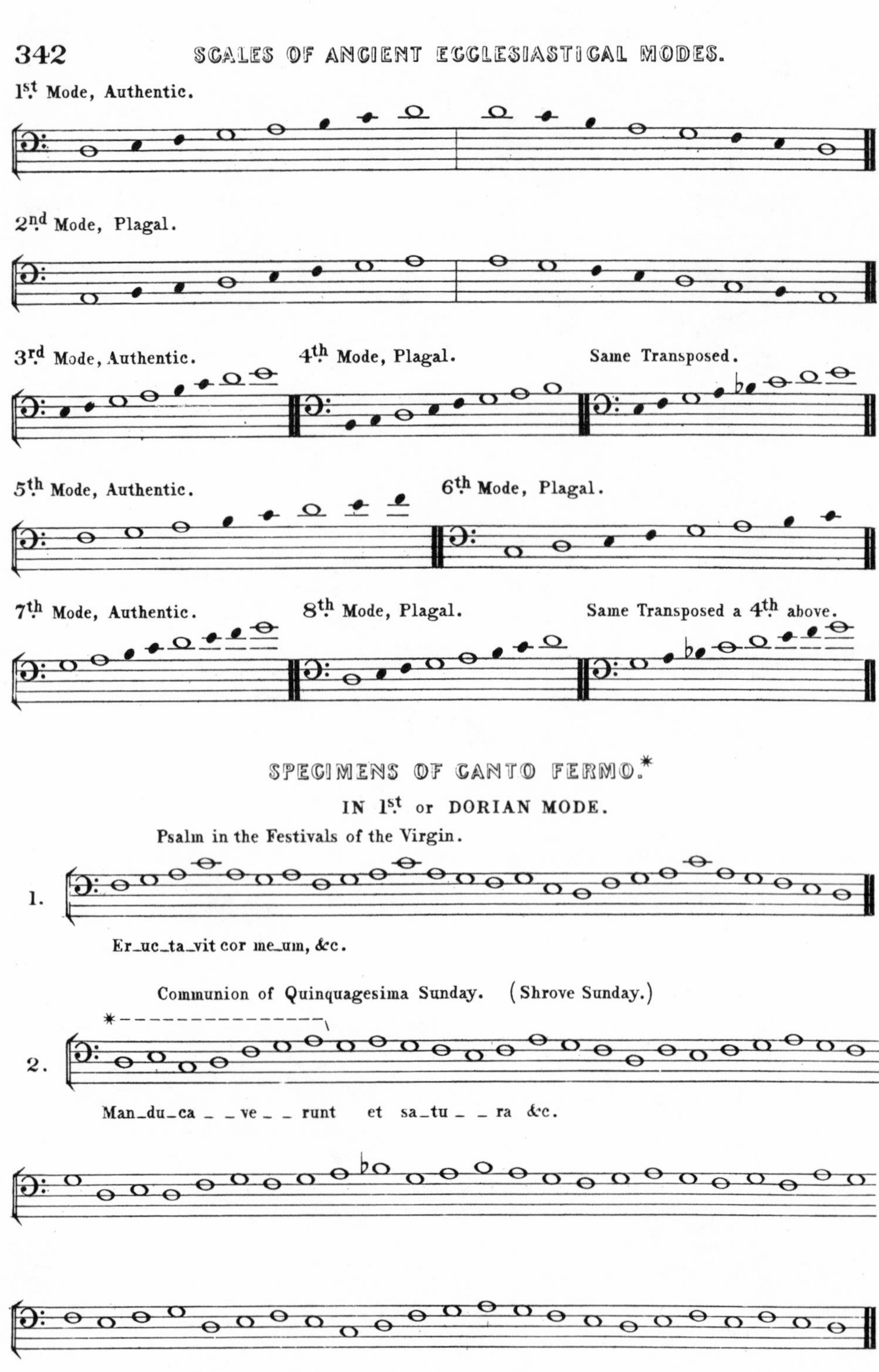

*See Choron, 'Principes de Composition', Vol. 1.

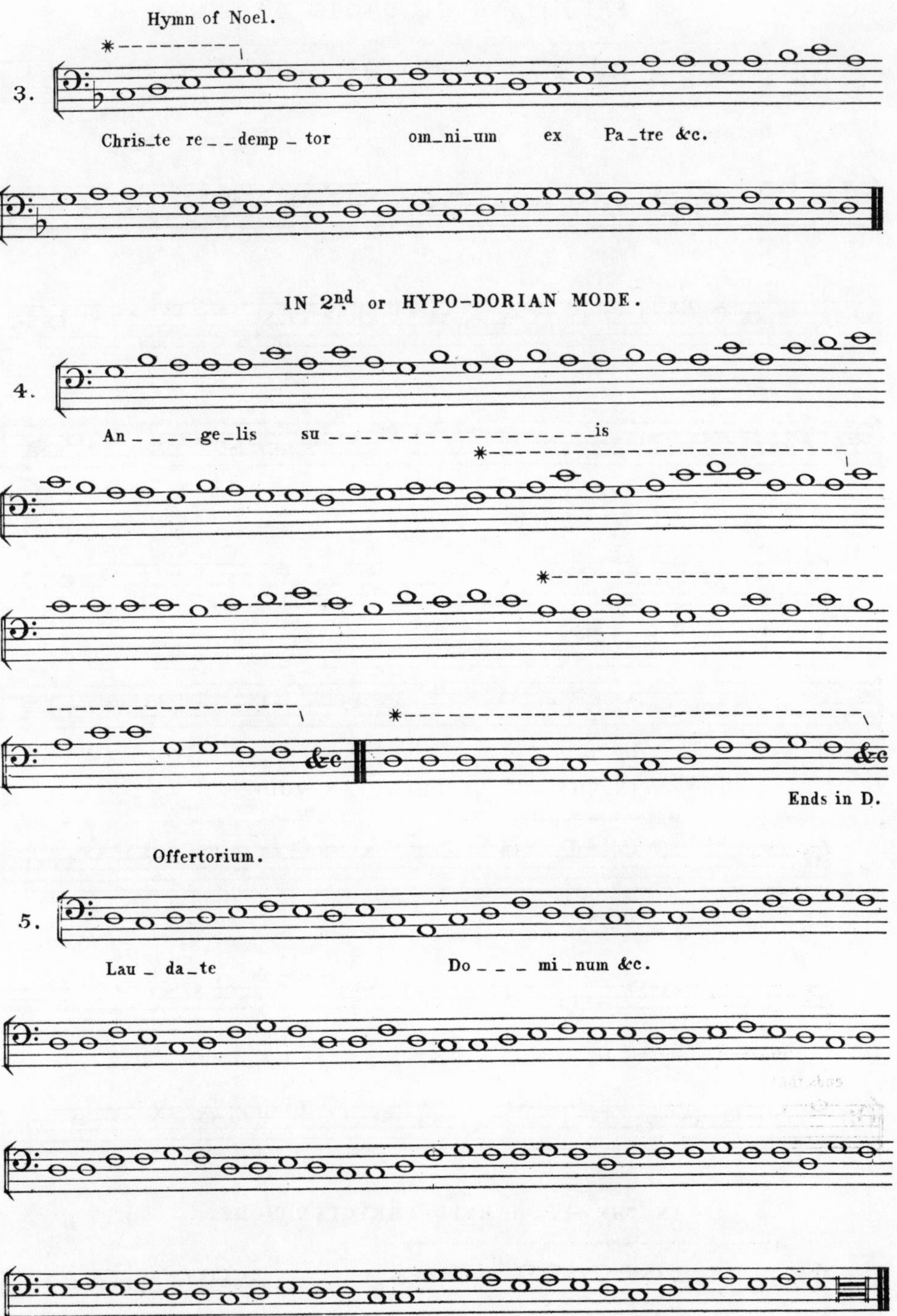
Hymn of Noel.
3.
Chris_te re_ _demp _ tor om_ni_um ex Pa_tre &c.
IN 2nd or HYPO-DORIAN MODE.
4.
An_ _ _ge_lis su_ _ _ _ _ _ _ _ _ _ _ _ _ _ _ _ _is
&c
&c
Ends in D.
Offertorium.
5.
Lau _ da_te Do_ _ _ mi_num &c.

SPECIMENS OF CANTO FERMO.

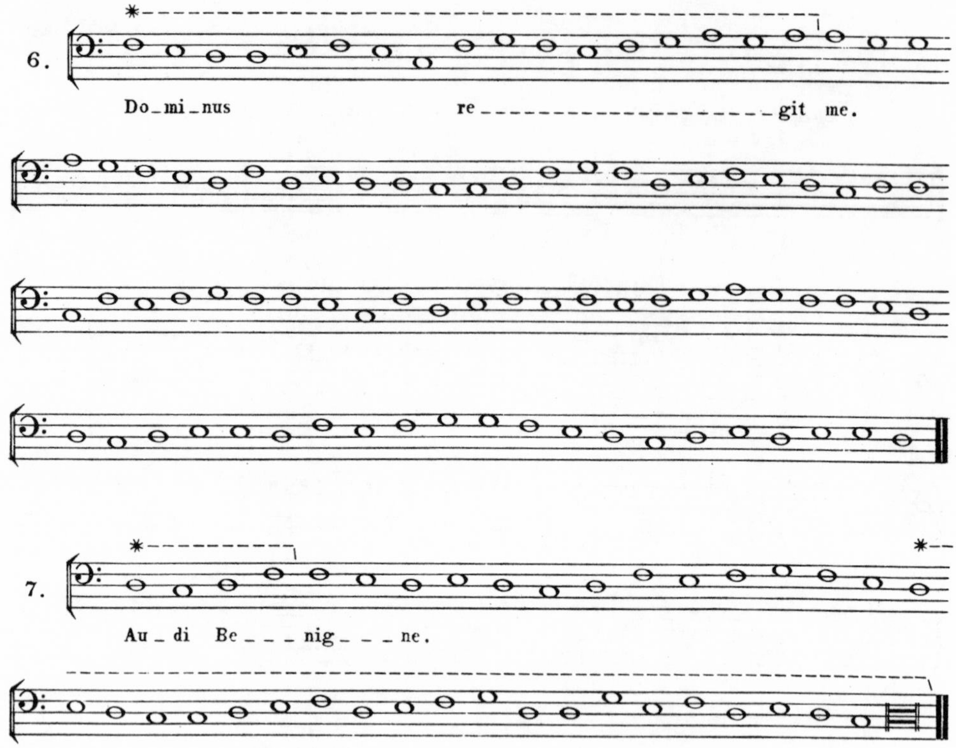

6. Do_mi_nus re_ _ _ _ _ _ _ _ _ _ _ _ _ _ _ _ _ _ _git me.

7. Au_di Be_ _ _nig_ _ _ne.

IN THE 3rd or PHRYGIAN MODE.

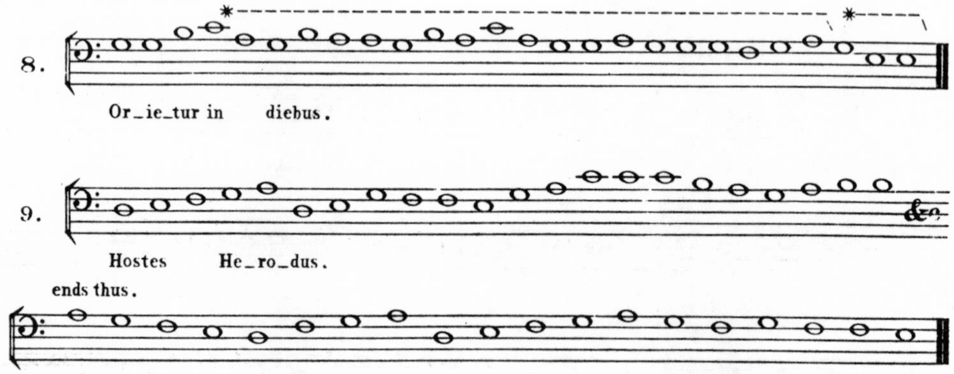

8. Or_ie_tur in diebus.

9. Hostes He_ro_dus. &c

ends thus.

IN THE 4th or HYPO-PHRYGIAN MODE.

10.

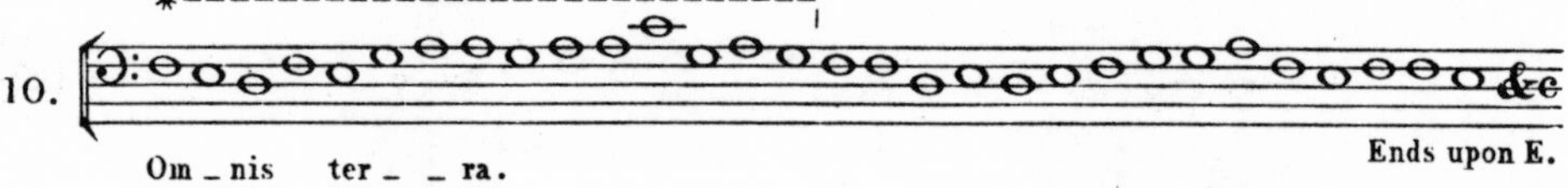

Om_nis ter_ _ra.

Ends upon E.

SPECIMENS OF CANTO FERMO.

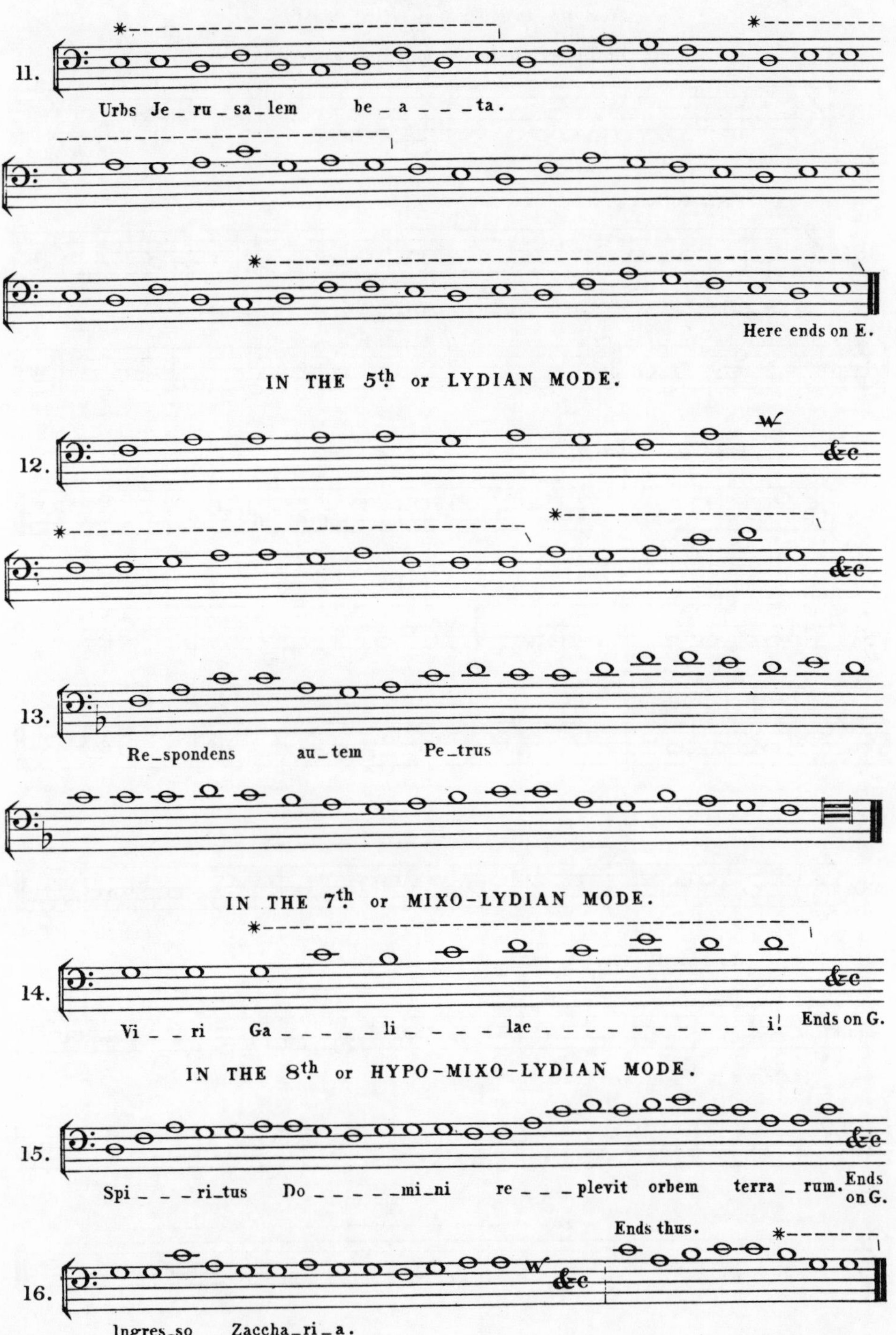

SPECIMENS OF CANTO FERMO
OF THE YEAR 400,
From MS. in Monastery of St. Blasius.*

In the lectio libri Apocalipsis the following passage occurs.

*See Gerbert 'De Cantu et Musica Sacra', vol. I. p. 392.

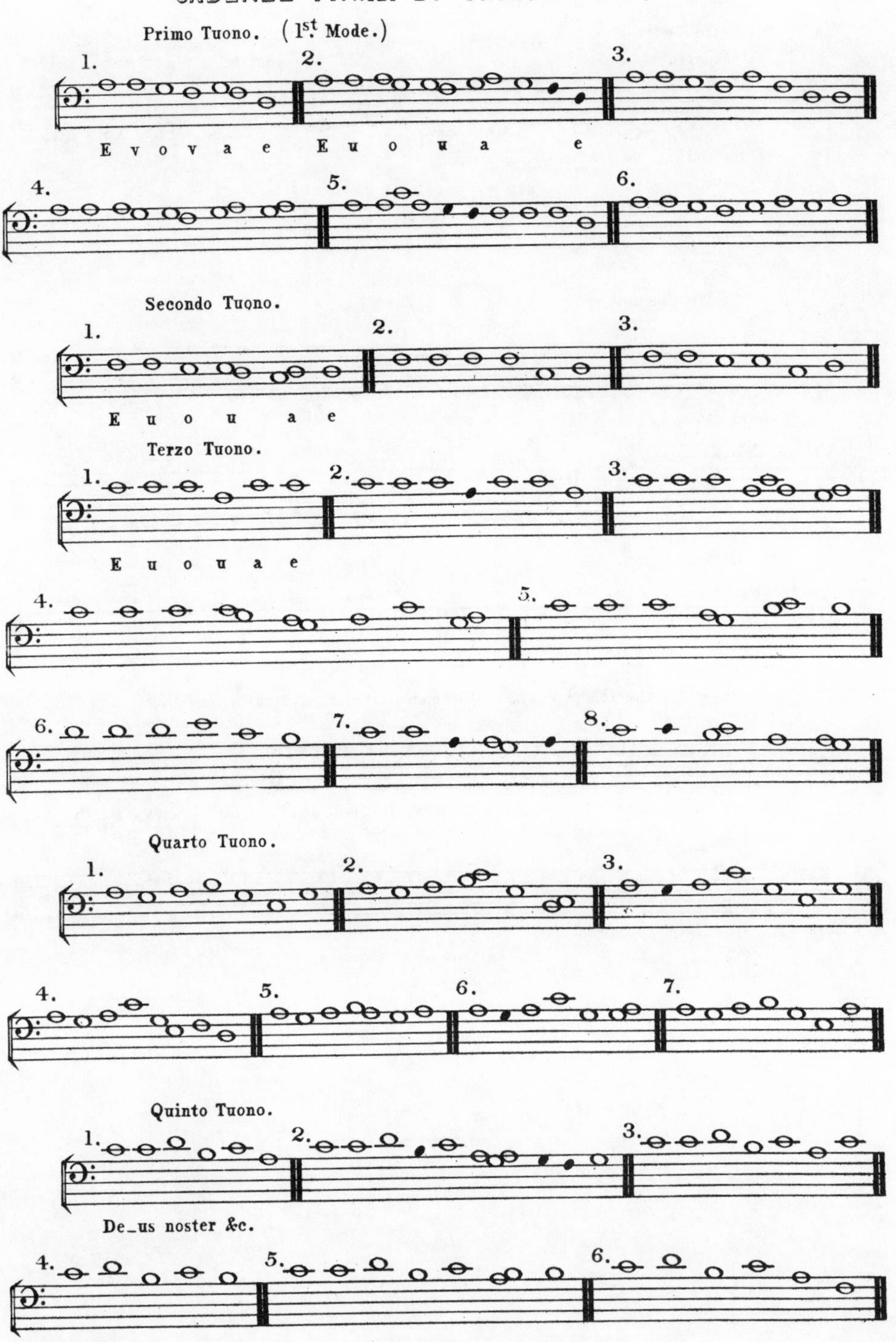

*See Padre Martini.

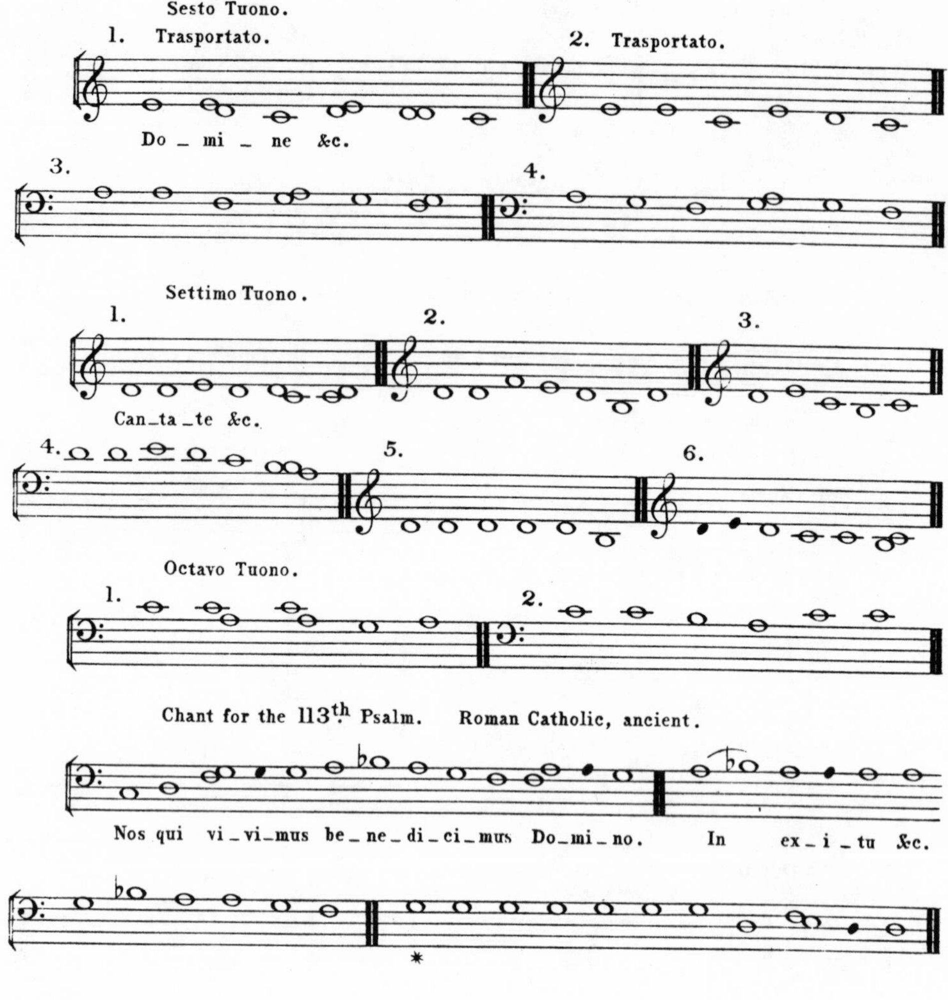
Sesto Tuono.
1. Trasportato.
2. Trasportato.
Do _ mi _ ne &c.
3.
4.
Settimo Tuono.
1.
2.
3.
Can_ta_te &c.
4.
5.
6.
Octavo Tuono.
1.
2.
Chant for the 113th. Psalm. Roman Catholic, ancient.
Nos qui vi_vi_mus be_ne_di_ci_mus Do_mi_no. In ex_i_tu &c.

* From the Rowallan MS. 1620. See Dissertation, pp. 120, 138.
† From Mr. Blaikie's MS. 1692. See Dissertation, p. 144.
‡ From Mr. Blaikie's MS. 1692, also MS. Advocates Library. 1704. See Dissertation, p. 145.
‖ From Mr. Blaikie's MS. 1692.

THE LAST TIME I CAME OE'R THE MUIR. Common Version.

THE FLOWERS OF THE FOREST. Common Version.

JENNY DRINKS NAE WATER. Common Version.

*See Dissertation, p. 204, and Nº 7 Notes and Illustrations.

THE FLOWERS OF THE FOREST.

From the Skene MS. with Symphonies and Accompaniments, by G. F. Graham, Esquire.

2

At bughts in the morning, nae blithe lads are scorning,
Lasses are lanely and dowie and wae;
Nae daffin, nae gabbin, but sighing and sabbing
Ilk ane lifts her leglin and hies her away.

3

In har'st at the shearing, nae youths now are jeering,
Bandsters are runkled and lyart or grey;
At fair or at preaching, nae wooing nae fleeching,
The Flowers of the Forest are a' wede away.

4

At e'en in the gloaming, nae younkers are roaming
'Bout stacks with the lasses at bogle to play;
But ilk maid sits dreary, lamenting her dearie,
The Flowers of the Forest are weded away.

5

Dool for the order sent our lads to the Border,
The English for ance by guile wan the day;
The Flowers of the Forest that fought aye the foremost
The prime of our land lie cauld in the clay.

6

We'll hae nae mair lilting at the Ewe milking,
Women and bairns are heartless and wae;
Sighing and moaning on ilka green loaning,
The Flowers of the Forest are a' wede away.

Robert Horne. Engraver. Edin.r

No. III.

EXTRACTS FROM DOCUMENTS PRESERVED IN THE GENERAL REGISTER HOUSE AT EDINBURGH.

I.—EXTRACTS FROM THE ACCOUNTS OF THE LORDS HIGH TREASURERS OF SCOTLAND RELATIVE TO MUSIC.

1474.

Item, gevin at the kingis command iij° Septembris, to John Broun, lutare, at his passage our sey to leue his craft, ... v. ti.

Item, to the trumpates, vj. eln of blew for their gownes, price of the elne xvj. s̃.

Item, iv. elne of blak for their hose, xiij. s̃. the elne.

Item, x. elnes of blak holmefs fustian to the trumpatis doublats, iij. s̃. the eln.

Item, fra Will of Rind, to the kingis lutare, the boye, ij. eln of fustiane.

Item, gevin to Ando. Balfour xi. Junij, to by lyning and smale grath to the kingis litle lutare, ... vj. s̃. viij. đ.

1489.

Jun.—Item, to Cunnynghame the singar, at the kingis commande, a demy, xiij. s̃.

July 1.—Item, to Wilzeam, sangster, of Lithgow, for a sang bwke he brocht to the king be a precept, ... x. ti.

Jul. 10.—Item, to Inglis pyparis that com to the castel yet and playit to the king, viij. ti. viij. s̃.

1490.

Apr. 13.—Item, to the trumpatts, ... v. ti. viij. s̃.

Item, to Blind Hary, ... xviij. s̃.

Item, to Benat, ... xviij. s̃.

Item, to ane oder fydlar, ... v. s̃.

Apr. 19.—To Martin Clareschaw, and ye toder ersche clareschaw, at ye kingis command, xviij. s̃.

May.—Till ane ersche harper, at ye kingis command, . . xviij. s̃.

1491.

Apr. 5.—Item, to the trumpets, ... vj. unicorns.
Item, to Blind Hary, ... xviij. s̃.
Item, to Benat, ... xviij. s̃.
Item, til a harper, ... xviij. s̃.
Aug. 21.—Item, to iiij. Inglis pyparis, viij. unicorns, . . vij. ti. iiij. s̃.

1496.

April.—Giffin to James Mytson the harpar, at the kingis command, xiij. s̃. iiij. đ.
June.—To tua wemen that sang to the king, ... xiij. s̃.
July.—To lundoris the lutare, at the kingis command, . . . xiij. s̃.
——.—To Jacob the lutar, at the K. command, . . . xiij. s̃.
July 17.—To John of Wardlaw, the lutar, ... xviij. s̃.
Aug. 1.—Item, that same day, giffin to the harpar with the a hand, . ix. s̃.
Mar. 14.—Item, that samyn day, to a man that playit on the clarscha to the king, vij. s̃.

1497.

Apr. 10.—Item, to John Hert, for bering a pare of monicordis of the kingis fra Abirdene to Strivelin, ... ix. s̃.
Apr. 19.—Item, to the tua fithelaris that sang Graysteil to ȝe king, . ix. s̃.
July 21.—To the pyonouris to gang to the castill to help with Mons doun,* x. s̃.
Item, to the menstrallis that playit before Mons doun the gate, . xiiij. s̃.

1500.

Mar. 1.—Item, to Jacob, lutar, to lowse his lute that lay in wed, . xxxij. s̃.

1502.

Aug. 30.—Item, for xx. elnis franch tanne to the foure Italien menstrales,
xiij. ti. vj. s̃. viij. đ.

1503.

Aug. 13.—Item, to viij. Inglis menstrales, be the kingis command, xl. french crownis,
xxviij. t.
Item, to the trumpetis of Ingland, ... xxviij. t.
Item, to the Quenis four menstralis that remanit with hir, . . vij. t.
Item, to the Erle of Oxfurdis tua menstrales, . . . v. t. xij. s̃.
Item, to the five lowd menstrales, ... xxviij. t.

* The famous piece of ordnance called "Mons Meg."

Aug. 21.—Item, that nycht to the cartis to the king, and syne giffin to the Inglis harparis, iij. li. x. s.

Sept. 10.—Item, to the four Italien menstrales to fe thaim hors to Linlithqw, and to red thaim of the toun, ... lvj. s.

Sept. 29.—Item, to Bountas, that playit on the cornut in the Quenis chamer, xxviij. s.

Item, to four Italien menstralis, . . . lvj. s.

Sept. 30.—Item, to ane of the menstrales, to pas to Edinburgh, to by him ane schalme, be the Kingis command, ... xxviij. s.

Oct 2.—Item, to the cornut, to by him quhissillis, be the kingis command, xlij. s.

Oct. 6.—Item, to the commoun piparis of Abirdene, . . xxviij. s.

Oct. 25.—Item, to Bountas that play,it on the cornut, . . xxviij. s.

Item, to Pate Harper, clarscha, ... xiiij. s.

Oct. 31.—Item, to the four lowd menstrales, . . . xxviij. s.

Item, the first day of Januar giffin to thir menstralis vndervrittin, that is to say, Thomas Hopringill, John Hopringill, Alex[r]. Caslaw, Pete, Johne, and Johne, trumpet, ilk ane, xiiij. s. . . . . iij. li. x. s.

Item, to Alex[r]. Harper, Pate Harper, Pate Harper clarscha, Hew Brabanar, and the blind harper, harperis, ilk ane, xiiij. s. . . . . . iij. li. x s.

Item, to Robert Rudman, Cuddy the Inglis boy, Sowtar lutar, Adam Dikesoun, and Craik, lutaris, ilk ane, xiiij. s. . . . . . iij. li. x. s.

Item, to Ansle Guilliam Portuous and Quhynbore, taubroneris, . lvi. s.

Item, to Adam Boyd, Bennet, and Jame Widderspune, fithelaris, . xlij. s.

Item, to the commoun piparis of Edinburgh, . . . xxviij. s.

Item, to the Quenis lutar, ... lvj. s.

Item, to Bountas, the cornut, ... lvj. s.

Item, to the four Italien menstralis, ... vij. li.

Item, to Hog, the tale tellar, ... xiiij. s.

Feb. 24.—Item, that samyn nycht in Bigar to ane pipar and ane fithelar, be the Kingis command, ... xiiij. s.

Item, to the Countes of Craufurdis harper, ... xiiij. s.

1504.

Aug. 21.—Item, to tua Inglise wemen that sang in the Kingis pailzeoune, xxiij. s.

Item, that samyn nycht (15 Oct.) in Dunnottir to the cheild playit on the monocordis, be the Kingis command, ... xviij. s.

1505.

Item, the xiiij. day of Aprile pasch tis day to thir menstralis underwrittin. In the first, to Thomas Hopringill, &c., trumpetis, ... liiij. s.

Item, to the four Schawmeris and ther iiij. childer, . . iij. ti. xij. s̃.
Item, to the More taubroner, guilliam taubroner, &c., ilk man, ix. s̃. . liiij. s̃.
Item, to Adam Dikeson, lutair, the Countes of Craufurdis lutair, Robert Rudman, the sowtar lutar, &c., ilk man, ix. s̃. . . . . . . liiij. s̃.
Item, to Alexander harper, Pate Harper clarscha, his son, the ersch clarscha, &c., &c., ilk man, ix. s̃. . . . . . iij. ti. xii. s̃.
Item, to Sir George Lawederis fithelar, ane fithelar of Strivelin, &c., ilk man, ix. s̃. xlv. s̃.
Item, to the tua piparis of Edinburgh, the franch quhissalar, the Inglis pipar with the drone, ilk man, ix. s̃. . . . . . xxxvj. s̃.

1507.

Jan. 1.—Item, that day giffin to divers menstrales, schawmeris, trumpetis, taubroneris, fithelaris, lutaris, harparis, clarscharis, piparis, extending to lxix. persons, x. ti. xj. s̃.
Jan. 12.—Item, to the chanoun of Halyrudhous that mendit the organis in Strivelin and Edinburgh, ... vij. ti.
Sep. 17.—Item, to the crukit vicar of Dumfreise that sang to the king in Lochmabane, be the kingis command, ... xiiij. s̃.
Dec. 31.—Item, to xxx dosane of bellis for dansaris delyverit to Thomas Boswell, iiij. ti. xij. s̃.

1508.

Jan. 22.—Item, to Gray Steill, lutar, ... v. s̃.
Feb. 16.—Item, to Wantonnes that the king fechit and gert hir sing in the quenis chamer, xiij. s̃.
Mar. 6.—Item, to Wantones and her tua marrowes that sang with hir, . xiij. s̃.

1511.

Item, to Gilleam, organist, makar of the Kingis organis, for expensis maid be him on the said organis in gait skynnis, and parchment for the belles, in naillis and sprentis of irne, in glew, papir, candill, coill, &c., ... viij. ti. iiij. s̃.
Sept. 20.—Item, in the new havyne to Gilleam taberner, and to the Scottis and Italiane trumpatis in drinksilver, ... xiiij. s̃.

1512.

Mar. 27.—Item, to foure scolaris, menstralis, be the Kingis command, to by thame instrumentis in Flandris, vij. ti. gret, answerand in Scottis money to xxi. ti.; and help thair expensis and fraucht, lvj. s̃. And therefter, becaus thai plenyeit thai gat our litill expens and fraucht, deliveret uther lvj., . . . xxxvj. l̃i. xij. s̃.

Jan. 1.—Item, gevin to the menstralis, that is to say, Italianis, Franche men, Scottis trumpettis, lutaris, harparis, and uther Scottis menstralis, to the nowmer of xxv. personis, to euerilk ane of thame xiiij. s̃., ... xvij. l̃. x s̃.

Item, the third day of Januar. gevin till ane barde wife callit Agnes Carkill, at the Kingis command, ... xlij. s̃.

Mar. 17.—Item, the said day to the curat of the Canongait for the tyrement of ane Italiane trumpet, ... xiiij. s̃.

Jul. 11.—Item, to Odonelis, (Ireland man,) harpar, quhilk past away with him, at the kingis command, ... vij. l̃i.

Item, to xiiij. menstralis, Italianis, Franchemen, trumpettis, schawmeris, ꝛ tawbrouneris, to thair clathis, ilk man for his goune, doublattis, and hois, vj. l̃. x. s̃., . lxxxxj. l̃i.

Item, ye x. day of November, to Juliane Drummond and his vij. complicis, Italiane menstrallis and trumpettis, for the monethis of December instant and Januar to cum, to ilk ane of thame iiij. l̃. vij. s̃. vj. d̃. be the said tyme.

Item, the said day to James davencourt, boncruss, and thair complicis, menstrallis, Franchemen, quhilk ar vj. personis in the haile, for thair wagis of the saidis monethis of November, December, and Januar, to ilkane of thame, . iiij. l̃i. vij. s̃. vj. d̃.

1513.

Aug. 6.—Item, to the Italiane menstralis, for thame and the franche taberneris, fidlaris, organeris, trumpettis, extending to the nowmer of xj. personis, to every ane of thame iiij. l̃i. vij. s̃. vj. d̃., for thair termis wagis of lamis last bypast, xlviij. l̃i. ij. s̃. vj. d̃.

1515.

Dec. 30.—Item, to Bountans franche menstrall, at my Lord governouris command, in part of payment of his wagis, ... xl. s̃.

Item, to v. Italiane menstrallis, viz. Vincent Auld, Juliane Younger, Juliane, Anthone, and Bestiane Drummonth, and George Forest, Scottisman, with them makand vj. personis, ... lxxviij. l̃i. xv. s̃.

Item, the samyn day, be my Lord Governours command, to Bestiane Drummonth, ane of the said menstrallis, becaus he past with licence to vesy his frendis in Itale, to help his expens, by his wagis abuff written, ... x. l̃i.

1516.

Aug. 8.—Item, to James Cabban, now the Kingis menstrale in Striveling, at the Lordis deliverans, for his goun, dowblat, and hois, . . . iiij. l̃i. xviiij. s̃.

Sept. 12.—Item, to Nicholas Abernethy, the sangistar, at my Lord Governors command, ... xx. li.

1530.

Item, to Cabroch fidlar, be the Kingis command, . . . vj. li. vj. s.
Item, to Anthoun, talburnar, ... xij. li. xj. s.

1533.

Oct. 19.—Item, for ane dozen luyt stringis send to the Kingis grace in Glasgow, vj. s.
Nov. 2.—Item, for iiij. dosane luyt stringis send to the Kingis grace in Falkland, xxiiij. s.

LEUERAIS.

Item, to Anton, talbonar, for his liveray, ... xij. li. xj. s.
Item, to Thomsoun, quhissillar, ... v. li. xij. s.
Item, to Wille Thomsoun, quhissillar, his bruthir, ... xl. s.
Item, to Cabroch, fiddillar, ... v. li. xij. s.

1537.

In primis, to iiij. trumpetouris, iiij. tabernaris, and iij. quhislaris, quhilkis passit in the schippis to France the vij. day of Maij, xxxiij. elnis reid birge satyne and yallow, equaly to be thame dowblatis, ... xvj. li. xij. s. vj. d.
Item, gevin to the King of Francis trumpettis for their new ȝeir giftis.
Item, gevin to his howboyis, ... xxij. cronis.
Item, gevin to his siflers, ... vj. cronis.
Item, gevin to the cornatis, ... xvj. cronis.
Item, gevin to the Quene of Navernis howboyis, . . . x. cronis.
Item, gevin to the Quene of Scotlandis tabirnar, . . . xij. cronis.

1538.

Ordinare Feis and yeirlie Pensionis, &c.

Item, gevin to the five Etalianis for thair twa leverais in the yeir, . lxv. li.
Item, to the foure menstralis that playis upon the veolis for thair yeirlie pensioun, payit to thame quarterlie, ... ij^c. li.
Item, gevin to twa menstralis that playis upon the Swesch talburn, . l. li.
Item, to foure mynstralis that playis upoun the trumpettis of weir, . j^c. li.
Dec. 16.—Item, gevin to Jakkis Collumbell, player upon the veolis, becaus his leveray is

reid, v. elnis dimmegrave, to be his cote and hois, and to his uther thre collegis, playeris on the veolis, &c. . . . . . . xxiij. li. xvij. s.

Item, deliverit to the uther thre that playis upoun the veolis, iij. reid bonettis,* price of the pece, xvij. s. . . . . li. s.

Item, for ane lute and twa dosane of stringis to Johne Barbour, . lvj. s.

1542.

In the first deliverit to be x. coittis and x. pair of hois to the four playaris on the veolis, four trumpettis of war, and twa taburnerris, xxxij. elnis of dummegrave, price of the elne, xxviij. s. and xviij. elnis Frenche ȝallow, price of the elne, xx. s. &c. &c. lxij. li. xvj. s.

Item, gevin to the v. Italianis for thair liverais usit and wount, lxv. li.

1548.

Item, viij. Aprilis, ane to play throw the toun with the swesche, to raise certane men of weir to pas to Yaister, ... iij. s.

Item, to the vyolaris that playit to my Lorde Governour the tyme of pasche, xliiij. s.

Item, to Stewyn, tabronar,† and ane other harpar with him.

Item, to Cunynghame, lwtar, quhay playit the haill holy dayis of pasche to my Lorde Governour.

1550.

Item, to certane Franchemen that playit on the cornettis, vj. li. xviij. s.

EXTRACTS FROM THE HOUSEHOLD BOOK OF LADY MARIE STEWART, COUNTESS OF MAR.

Edinburgh. (*No date.*)

1638.

May 16.—To ane blind singer, who sang the time of disner, . . xij. s.

Sept. 8.—To twa hieland singing women, at my Laidies command, . vj. s.

Sept. 23.—To ane lame man callit Rosse, who playes the plaisant, . iij. s.

* In the time of Chaucer it was customary for all minstrels to wear red hats.

" He was no cardynall
With a redde hatte as usen minstrals."—*The Plowman's Tale.*

† In Dissertation, p. 74, an anecdote is related from Knox's History respecting " Sandy Stevin, Menstrall." The reader will also find some notice of " Steven, Taburner," in Pitscottie's History, p. 230. (Edition 1778.)

1641.

March 4.—To blind Watt ye piper that day, as my Laidy went to the exercise, iiij. s̃.
Aug. 18.—To the drummers and piffarers ye second time, . . xij. s̃.

1642.

To ane woman clarshochar who usit ye house in my Lord his tyme, . xij. s̃.
June 20.—Item, that day given to three English piffereris, . . xviij. s̃.

II.—EXTRACTS FROM ACCOUNTS OF THE COMMON GOOD OF VARIOUS BURGHS IN SCOTLAND, PRESERVED IN THE GENERAL REGISTER HOUSE, RELATIVE TO MUSIC SCHOOLS, &c.

Aberdeen, 1594—1595.

Item, to the maister of the grammer schoil for his fee of the twa termis, xxxiij. li. vj. s̃.
Item, to the maister of the sang schoill, &c., . . xiiij. li. xiij. s̃. iiij. d̃.

Air, 1627—1628.

Item, to the Mr of the grãmer scule his stipend, . . . j^c. li.
Item, to the Mr of musik scule, for teaching of the musik scule and taking up the psalmes in the kirk, . . x. bolls victuall, and xlji. li. vj. s̃. viij. d̃. of silver.

(The same repeated for 1633 and 1634.)

Couper, 1581.

Item, to the maister of the sing scole fe, . . . vj. li. xiij. s̃. iiij. d̃.
Item, to Mr Alexander Tyllideaphe, Mr of the musick scõl, . . j^c. li.

Dumbarton, 1621.

Item, to Mr Alexr. Home, scholemaster, for his feall and hous maill, 1621, iiij^c. lxvj. li. xiij. s̃. iiij. d̃.
Item, to the teicher of the Inglische schoole and musick, . . j^c. li.

Dundee, 1602.

Item, to the maister of the grammer scole, . . . ij^c. merkes.
Item, to the master of the sang scule, ... lxxx. li.

EXTRACTS.

1603.

Item, the masters of gramer and sang schol, . . lxx. li. xiij. s. iiij. d.

1621—1622.

Item, to Mr John Mow, Mr of the music schoole, for his fee and hous maill, ccl. li.

1628.

Item, to Mr John Mow, maister of the music scule, . ij^{c}lxvj. li. xiij. s. iiij. d.

Elgin, 1633—1634.

Maister of the grammer and musick schuillis, . . . ij^{c}xxx. li.

1622.

First, to the master of the gramer scole, . . lxvj. li. xiij. s. viij. d.
To the master of the music scole, ... j^{c}. li.

Inverness, 1634.

Item, giffen to the Mr of the grammer scoil, . . . iiij^{xx}. li.
Item, giffen to Mr of the musick scoil, ... xxxvj. li.

Irving, 1633.

Our schoolmaister, ... lxxx. merkis.
Our doctour and musicianer, ... j^{c}. li.

Lanark, 1627—1628.

Item, to the scholemaister of the said bruche that teiches the grāmer for the saidis tua termes, (Mertimes and Witsonday,) . . . . . . j^{c}. li.
Item, to ane wther scholemaister that teichis the musick, iij^{xx}vj. li. xiij. s. iiij. d.

St Andrews, 1626—1627.

Item, to the publict reader, ... j^{c}. li.
Item, to the maister of the musik scholl, and for taking up of the psalme at preaching and prayeris of fie, ... ij^{c}. li.

(The same repeated for 1632 and 1633.)

2 R

Tayne, 1628.

Item, to Mr Thomas Ross, master of the gramour schooll, . . j$_c$. li.
Item, to Mr Johne Tullidef, reider and master of the musick schooll, . j$_c$. li.

(The same repeated for 1634.)

Wigton, 1633.

Imprimis gevin to ane schoolmaister for teiching the grammer schoole, reiding and raising the psalmeis in the kirk yeirlie, ... iij^c. merkis.

In a Minute of the Town Council of Glasgow, dated 24th December 1588, "the scuile, sumtyme callit the sang scuile," is mentioned as a part of the common good which it was resolved to sell in order to liquidate the heavy charges which the town had incurred in consequence of the pest, &c. And in the Treasurer's accounts for the same burgh, in 1609, we find the following item—"Gifin upon the third day of Marche 1608, (erroneously printed 1808,) to Jon Buchan, Mr of the sang scole, for Witsonday and Martymes termes, maill of his hours, (apparently a misprint for *house*,) 1608, L.xx." See a volume printed for private distribution, entitled "Memorabilia of the city of Glasgow, selected from the Minute Books of the Burgh, 1588—1750." Glasgow, 1835, pp. 27 and 70.

No. IV.

"INFORMATION TOUCHING THE CHAPPELL-ROYALL OF SCOTLAND."

"To the King's most excellent Majestie, the Information and Petition of your Majestie's humble Servant, Edward Kellie, touching your Majestie's Chapell-Royall of Scotland.

"When first your Majestie intended to goe into your kingdome of Scotland, I was employed by your Majestie, and such of your Councill of that kingdom as were then at courte; To provide psalmes, services, and anthymnes for your Majestie's said chappell-royall there, as in your chappell here. Thereupon I caused make twelve great books, gilded, and twelve small ones, with an organe-book wherein I caused write the said psalmes, services, and anthymnes, and attended the writing thereof fyve monethes here in London. At that tyme, alsoe, I provided the same musick that was at your Majestie's coronation here, with one Bible for your Majestie, and two great Bibles for the Deane and for the Readers of the said chappell. Thereafter, I procured your Majestie's warrante for deposeing all insufficient persons that had places in your said chappell-royall, and for placing others more qualified, upon examination, in their roomes. Herevpon, I carryed home an organist and two men for playing on cornets and sakbuts,[a] and two boyes for singing division in the *versus*, all which are most exquisite in their severall faculties. I caused the said organist examine all the aforesaid musick-books and organ-books; and

[a] Hawkins (Hist. vol. ii. p. 267) says, that "in the Statutes of Canterbury Cathedral, provision is made for players on sakbuts and cornets, which, on solemn occasions, might probably be joined to, and used in aid of the organ." The sakbut, or *tuba tractilis*, was a bass wind instrument of the trumpet kind, contrived so as to be drawn out to different lengths, according to the acuteness or gravity of the sound, similar to the trombone of modern times.

finding them right, convened all the musicians of your Majestie's said chappell, some whereof (being after triall found insufficient for such service) I deposed, and choosed some others in their roomes, whereby I made vpp the number of sixteen men beside the organist and six boyes; who all of them sung there psalmes, services, and anthymnes, sufficiently, at first sight, to the organe, *versus*, and chorus, soe being confident of their abilitie to discharge the service, I desired the lordes of your Majestie's honourable councell, and others of authoritie, skillfull in that facultie, to heare them; which lords, after their hearing, in token of their approbation, gave me a testificate under their hands, witnessing that I had fully performed my former vndertakings, and showing that the like service was never done there before by any soe well, or in soe good order. This testificate I have here to showe your Majestie. Then for my assurance in tyme comeing, I took bond of the said musicians, that they should be ready at all tymes to vndertake and discharge the seruice. This bond I have here alsoe to showe. Herafter your Majestie was gratiously pleased, by your letters vnder your highnes privie seall, with consent of the Deane of your said chappell-royall, to constitute mee collector and distributer of the rents pertayning to your said chappell, and to see such good orders established in the same, as the service therein might be well and faithfully done, and that none but persons sufficiently qualified should have any place there, and that they should be all keept at daily practise; and for that effect, your Majestie appointed mee ane chamber within your pallace of Halyrudehouse, wherein I have provided and sett vpp an organe, two flutes, two pandores with violls, and other instruments, with all sorts of English, French, Dutch, Spaynish, Latin, Italian, and old Scotch musick, vocall and instrumentall. In the said chamber, the said organist and the boyes doe remain, and the remanent musicians and vnder officers doe meet therein twice a-week to practise and to receive directions for the next service. For observance of these meetings, and many other good orders, I have likewise taken bond of the said musicians, which bond I have also here to showe. In tyme of service within the chappell, the organist and all the singingmen are in black gownes, the boyes are in sadd coloured coats, and the vsher and the sexten and vestrie-keeper are in browne gownes. The singingmen doe sit in seats, lately made, before the noblemen, and the boyes before them, with their books lay'd, as in your Majestie's chappell here. One of the great Bibles is placed in the midle of the chappell, for the reader, the other before the Deane. There is sung before sermon ane full anthymne, and after sermon ane anthymne alone in versus with the organe. And thus every one attendeth the charge in his place in a very grave and decent forme.

"At this tyme, for your Majestie's now intended journey into your said native kingdome, and for your highnes coronation there, I have not as yet had any commandment. Nevertheless, I am alwayes in readinesse in manner aforesaide, with the said musick for your Majestie's coronation, and all other musick necessary, with cornets, sakbuts, and other instruments, with men to play thereon, ready vpon advertisement.

"If, therefore, it shall please your most sacred Majestie to ratifie these my former powers and warrantes, for ingathering of the rents and ordering your said chappell, as I have begunne, your Majestie's exchequer by that meanes will be disburdened: And I, your Majestie's servant, shall vndertake either to give your Majestie good assurance by a new testificate from your councell of my present abilitie for performance of the service with greater credite to your Majestie's native kingdome, then it can be done by strangearis, and with no greater charge vnto your Majestie then is allready due: Or else I shall give tymouse advertisement vnto your highnes that your musicians here may be carryed thither for the service; which, vndoubtedly, will be a great and needless charge, if your Majestie's servants at home can doe the same, all things being provided and ready for the purpose. These premisses I most humbly referr vnto your Majestie's princely consideration, and desire your Majestie's speedy resolution and answer herein. And because this information hath no man else to [be] answerable for what is in it but my selfe, whoe have formerly given good proofe of my care and affection to your highnes service; Therefore, that your Majestie may be assured that I attempt nothing but what is faire, and what I am confident to performe, as I shall be answerable for, according to my vndertaking, I have subscrived these presents with my hand, at Whitehall, 24th Januarii 1631, after the English account.

"E. Kellie."

POSTSCRIPT.

SINCE closing the Preliminary Dissertation and Notes, we are enabled to present our readers with some additional information which augurs favourably for the farther success of the enquiries in which we have been engaged.

It appears that the MS. volume, mentioned pp. 84 and 147, Dissertation, is in the possession of Mr Chalmers of London. It is written in Lute Tablature, on a stave of six lines, and was presented to Dr Burney, in June 1781, by Dr George Skene, Professor of Humanity and Philosophy in Marischal College, Aberdeen. The title of the work is, " An Playing Booke for the Lute. Where in ar contained many cvrrents and other mvsical things. *Musica mentis medicina mœstæ*. At Aberdein. Notted and collected by Robert Gordon, (the well-known Sir Robert Gordon of Straloch.) In the year of our Lord 1627. In Februarie ;" and on the back of the title there is a drawing of a person playing on the lute. Its contents were inserted in the Gentleman's Magazine for February 1823 ; and, as we have not seen the original volume itself, we here transcribe the list of the tunes as given in that work, although we have neither time nor space to accompany them with any remarks. It should be premised, that, besides those here mentioned, there are others which are simply distinguished as " Ballets," or " Currants :"—

" The Buffens.—Sleepe wayward thoughts.—Sannicola.—Sheepheard saw thou not.—What if a day.—Give caire does cause men cry.—Canaries.—Finis, quod Ostend, (no title.)—Finis ballat, or Almon.—Hurries Current.—Queen's Current. —Frogge's Galzeart.—Lyke as the Dumbe.—When Daphne did.—The Prince Almon.—The day dawes.—Cum sueit Love lett sorow ceasse.—Finis, Haddington's mask.—Thir Gawens.—Finis, Queene's Almone, as it is played on a fourteen cord lute.—A Saraband.—Ther wer three Ravns.—In a gardeen so green.—Haddington's maske.—The barg of maske.—Begon sueit night.—Tell me Daphne.—Lachrymy.—A stryng of the Spanish Pavin.—Finis, Darges Current.—Fantasie. —A passing sour.—Ballart's Current.—The quadro pavin.—The galziart of the pavin.—In till a mirthful May Morning.—Orlio's Current.—Hebrun's Current.—A Port.—Port Priest.—Before the Greekes.—Brangle, simple.—The Old Man. —I long for the Wedding.—Gray steel.—Put on the Sark on Munday.—Brail de

Poyctu.—Ostende.—God be with the Geordie.—A Pasmissour.—A Brangle with the braking of it.—A Braill: second, third, fourt, fift, sext braill.—Thoes rare and good in all.—Finis, Lilt Ladie: An. Gordone.—A daunce.—Green greus þ[e] rashes. —Com Love lets walk.—Finis. Cum lett us walk into yon springe.—Hunter's carrerre.—Vpon a Sommer's time.—Its a wonder to see how þ[e] world doos goe.— An thou wer myn oun thing.—Finis port Jean Kinsay.—Cock-stouns hoggie.— Wo betyke thy waerie bodie.—Ladie Laudion's Lilt.—Have over the water.— . . . . From the fair Lavinian shore.—Keath keares not for thy kyndnes.—Earlie in the Mornning.—Galua Tom.—The tript of Diram.— Kist her while she blusht.—God be with my bonnie love.—Whip my toudie.— Bon acord.—My beelful breest.—Hench me malie Gray.—Thir gawens ar gey.— A preludium.—Finis huic libro impositus. Anno D. 1629. Ad finem. Decem. 6. In Stra-Loth."

The Editor has also seen a copy of the collection referred to in the Dissertation,[a] called "Flores Musicæ," and announced in the advertisement to have been "collected from a variety of *old MSS.* wherein the errors that have crept into the former editions of the Scots tunes are traced," &c.; but the expectations which such an announcement was calculated to raise have been greatly disappointed. The work had most probably been confined to the *first* number, and contains the following airs:—The Birks of Invermay—The Broom of Cowdenknows—The Blatherie o't—The Yellow-haired Laddie—The Braes of Ballendine—My Nanie, O—The Lass of Patie's Mill—Logan Water—Killicrankie—The Mill, O—Bush aboon Traquair—Hey Jenny come down to Jock—Roslin Castle—Robin Cushie—The last time I came o'er the moor—To danton me—Tweedside—I'll never leave thee—I wish my love were in a mire—Woes my heart that we should sunder—My mother's ay glowering o'er me—Bonny Dundee.

Several of these airs are not ancient. "Roslin Castle," and "The Braes of Ballenden," are said to have been composed by Oswald, and "The Yellow-haired Laddie" is probably of an age little anterior to his. Neither does the music bear the least semblance of its having been taken from collections older, at all events, than the beginning of last century; and yet the Editor, in his preface, says that he has examined a variety of old manuscripts, and "endeavoured, with the utmost accuracy, to trace out the errors of former editions." The following passage of that preface, however, is worth quoting, as it contains some truth, though blended with a good deal of that random assertion so common at the time when the work was published.

[a] P. 3. This Collection was published in 1773; not in 1775, as there mentioned.

"David Rizzio is now generally fixed upon as the composer of the best of these delicate songs; but how so gross a falsehood comes to be so universally believed, is not easy to determine. That the Scots music is of no older a date than two centuries ago, no one, we hope, will venture to assert, who is, in the least, acquainted with the history of this kingdom; yet, some writers have, of late, so confidently affirmed them to be his compositions, that they are now generally termed *the Songs of Rizzio;* although it will plainly appear to any person who will take the trouble to look into the transactions of those times, that the finest of these songs were very currently known in Scotland some centuries before that unhappy man first landed on its coast.

"That they have received some improvements from Rizzio, by being more regularly set, we pretend not to dispute; but to prove that they were not originally composed by him, many instances might be brought from private as well as public records; as we find many of these tunes mentioned prior to the reign of James I."

The reader is by this time aware that of the two facts assumed in the last sentence—that Rizzio had improved the Scotish music, and that Scotish airs now known to us existed anterior to the reign of James I. of Scotland, the monarch here alluded to—we have no historical evidence whatever.

It may be proper also to mention, that, since this work was printed, a volume has been put into our hands, entitled "A Collection of National English Airs, consisting of Ancient Song, Ballad, and Dance Tunes, interspersed with remarks and anecdote, and preceded by an Essay on English Minstrelsy." This work has been very recently published in London, and we believe that farther researches of the same kind are in the course of being actively carried on in the southern part of the kingdom, from which much interesting information of a literary and historical nature may be derived. We should think, however, that it would be of more consequence to the musical world if public attention were directed to Ireland and Wales, from both of which countries music of a distinctive national character might be obtained: whereas, with respect to the national music of England, little can be expected. And notwithstanding the laudable industry which Mr Chappell has here evinced, nothing has as yet transpired of a nature to affect the opinions which we have had occasion to express, or the conclusions to which we have come on this subject.[a] We confess that we have never yet been able to comprehend in what the alleged nationality of the English music consists, and this collection has left us as much in the dark on that point

[a] See Dissertation, pp. 197, 198, 199, 200.

as ever. We see a great many songs and tunes with English words and verses attached to them; but we cannot perceive in what respect the *melodies* differ from those of other nations. There is nothing marked, striking, or uncommon in the succession of their intervals, their cadences, time, rhythm, or accent; and even the most ancient of them, some of which might have been composed before the modern tonality or system of keys and scales was fully established, possess none of the antique characteristics which might have been looked for. We only speak, however, of what we have seen, which has not extended to more than sixty airs. The work, we believe, is to be continued, and we are still open to conviction.

Two collections are spoken of in the preface to the work last mentioned, one published at Haerlem in 1626, another at Amsterdam in 1634, and both are said to contain English airs. It is observed that "the existence of two such collections, a century before any published collection of Irish or Scotch tunes, is a proof of the high estimation of English airs" at this time. But it should be remembered that, although some of the English airs might have been found congenial to the taste of the phlegmatic Hollanders in 1626, the tunes of Scotland had, as early as 1564, found their way into at least one of the musical publications of the more lively and accomplished natives of France.

From what the Editor states, (p. 44,) we find that the air of the Spanish Lady, the original of which we have given in the Skene MS., was not lost in England, as Mr Ritson supposed, but had appeared in "The Quaker's Opera," in 1728, "The Jovial Crew," in 1731, &c. Our copy is certainly the more perfect of the two in a melodic point of view, and tallies more precisely with the words; which is not surprising, considering the changes to which popular tunes are liable in the course of time, and that our version has been drawn off so much nearer the fountainhead than that contained in the English collection.

In p. 54, the Editor has a remark upon the dance-tune called in England "Roger de Coverly," and in Scotland, "The Maltman comes on Monday"—a coincidence which we happen to have incidentally pointed out in a note to p. 260. He says, "From Allan Ramsay's having written a song, called 'The Mautman comes o' Monday,' to this tune, it has been *erroneously* put under that name in modern collections." Whether this tune be English, Scotish, or Irish, (and it is perhaps more like the latter than either of the other two,) we shall not positively assert: but if there has been any error in classing it among the airs of Scotland, Allan Ramsay, at all events, must be exculpated, as the MS. to which we have referred, and in which we find it along with other popular Scotish tunes, under the name of "The Maltman comes on Monday," is dated 1706, at a time when Ramsay was pursuing the humble vocation of a wig-maker, and several years before he had ventured into the regions of rhyme.

Having laboured so assiduously to correct the errors of others, it is right that before taking leave of the public we should say a few words in regard to our own. In a remark which we have made, p. 78, we find that we had overlooked an obsolete Scotish statute, 1621, c. 25, § 10, "anent banqueting and apparel," in which honourable mention is again made of minstrels by their being exempted from certain sumptuary restrictions, although this class of persons had been passed over in a preceding statute during the same reign. We fear, also, that notwithstanding the care which we have bestowed on the preparation of this work, and our anxious wish to ensure accuracy, it may have happened that amidst the extensive range of matter, the circumstantial nature of the details, and the obscurity which overhangs a great part of the subject—other errors of more importance may, very probably, have escaped us. Whether these relate to the views or to the facts which we have brought forward, we shall only say that it will afford us equal pleasure to see them corrected. Mistakes and fallacies are common to all historical enquiries, and the example of the wisest of those who have gone before us has sufficiently shown that they are peculiarly incident to the topics which we have here brought under the notice of the reader. It is only by a careful examination of our statements along with those of others, that the public can ultimately be disabused of error, and clear, distinct, and satisfactory information obtained. What we have endeavoured to do has been merely, as we professed at the outset, to collect materials for a history of Scotish music; and these have not yet been fully amassed. More research must be applied, more manuscripts recovered, and much more information, historical and traditional, be brought to bear upon them. We should rejoice if the Skene MS. should, in the end, be the precursor of such a work; but until all the requisite facts are brought to light, its execution need not be attempted.

EDINBURGH, *November* 1, 1838.

INDICES.

GENERAL INDEX.

A

B

C

D

E

F

G

H

I

J

K

L

M

N

O

P

Q

R

S

T

V

W

Z

INDEX OF AIRS.

A

B

C

D

G

H

I

J

K

L

M

N

O

P

R

S

T

U

V

W

ERRATA.

Page 7, line 18, insert "Let not crueltie dishonour bewtie."
—— 40, — 29, for "seems," read "seem."
—— 75, — 6, for "Edward I.," read "Edward II."
—— 87, — 15, for "Fordun," read "Bower, the continuator of Fordun."
—— 111, — 28, for "four," read "five."
—— 152, — 16, for "Mrs," read "Miss."
—— 185, — 9, insert "remote" between "the" and "antiquity."
—— 268, — 19 and 20, for "mordendo," read "morendo."
—— 270, — 9, for "thirty-seven," read "thirty-six."

EDINBURGH PRINTING COMPANY, 12, SOUTH ST DAVID STREET.